Customer Reviews on Amazon.com (5 St

(GRE Analytical Writing: Solutions to the Real Essay To

C000039294

This new edition of GRE Analytical Writing by Vibrant Publishers has 60 solved AWA essays. Most of the solutions are bang on! All these topics are from the official GRE essay list, so the probability of one of these essays coming in your actual GRE is very high. In fact, in my GRE, I was asked one of the issue topics that was already solved in this book. Having already read the solution had two advantages, 1) I had a good idea of how to go about writing the essay and 2) I felt a lot more confident, and all my exam stress went away. I will give this book 5 stars!

Great book to help prepare for the GRE essays!! Very helpful strategies, and the essays are also detailed. I have read through only a few topics as yet but will definitely read through all of them. If I get the time to read all the 60 Issues and Arguments, there'll be no looking back. I am glad I made this purchase.

Good book. Each topic is followed by multiple pointers to help you construct the essay. A sample essay is also provided for reference. But what I liked the most about the book is they covered over sixty writing topics. Great for practice.

The book starts with an introduction to the analytical writing section, then explains an Analyze an Issue task and Analyze an Argument task, including scoring patterns for both. It gives strategies for writing Issue and Argument tasks. It then takes 30 Issue topics and guides us to write an essay on each of those topics. Strategies include how to interpret the topic, different positions that can be taken for the topic in question, ways to support the position you take, examples, and more. At the end, a sample essay is also given which can be used as a benchmark. After the Issue topics, 30 Argument topics are covered. Again, each topic is followed by strategies and a sample essay. The author has addressed many possible positions of an Issue, assumptions in an argument, the evidence required and questions to be answered, making the writing task look easy as pie.

Customer Reviews on Amazon.com (5 Star Ratings)

(GRE Analytical Writing: Solutions to the Real Essay Topics - Book 2)

This is an excellent book for GRE Analytical Writing exams. I found this book to be very comprehensive about all aspects of Analytical Writing.

In terms of example essays: there are some very good and well written essays, but at the same time I felt there were some first-person essays that I could have improved upon. Overall, it gives you a good idea about different types of writing styles and essays that are needed for passing the GRE Analytical Writing.

This book was a great buy and a must-read for all GRE test takers. The content in the book was useful, thought provoking, and I have several ideas to work with now. In addition, the content is presented well too.

I found very few books that focus on the GRE writing section; and of those, I prefer this book.

I bought this for myself and I had no problem with the Quant section of the GRE and the verbal prep was not bad either. I didn't know anything about the Analytical writing section as I had kept the prep for this section towards the end. Glad I made this purchase now I feel much more confident than I was a week ago. One more week for my real test hope to see a 5 at least in the GRE.

The author has done a fantastic job. The elaborate explanation of each topic helped me immensely, I could gather my thoughts, streamline them and put them into appropriate words. Highly recommended .

VIBRANT
PUBLISHERS

TEST PREP SERIES

GRE®

ANALYTICAL WRITING SUPREME:
SOLUTIONS TO THE REAL ESSAY TOPICS

2022

Sample solutions to 145 official Issue and Argument topics

Expert strategies to be used as benchmark

Simplified methods to produce focused responses

Online access to printable Answer sheets

Second Edition

GRE® Analytical Writing Supreme:
Solutions to the Real Essay Topics
Second Edition

Paperback ISBN-10: 1-63651-053-1
Paperback ISBN-13: 978-1-63651-053-8
E-book ISBN-10: 1-63651-054-X
E-book ISBN-13: 978-1-63651-054-5
Hardback ISBN-10: 1-63651-089-2
Hardback ISBN-13: 978-1-63651-089-7

Library of Congress Control Number: 2020939579

This publication is designed to provide accurate and authoritative information in regard to the subject matter covered. The Author has made every effort in the preparation of this book to ensure the accuracy of the information. However, information in this book is sold without warranty either expressed or implied. The Author or the Publisher will not be liable for any damages caused or alleged to be caused either directly or indirectly by this book.

Vibrant Publishers books are available at special quantity discount for sales promotions, or for use in corporate training programs. For more information please write to bulkorders@vibrantpublishers.com

Please email feedback / corrections (technical, grammatical or spelling) to spellerrors@vibrantpublishers.com

To access the complete catalogue of Vibrant Publishers, visit www.vibrantpublishers.com

GRE is the registered trademark of the Educational Testing Service (ETS) which neither sponsors nor endorses this product.

Table of Contents

5   Government and Politics   79

6   Philosophy   135

7   Science and Technology   201

8   Society   223

12 Government and Politics   371

13 Science and Technology   399

14 Society   447

Dear Student,

Thank you for purchasing **GRE Analytical Writing Supreme: Solutions to the Real Essay Topics**. We are committed to publishing books that are content-rich, concise and approachable enabling more students to read and make the fullest use of them. We hope this book provides the most enriching learning experience as you prepare for your GRE exam.

Should you have any questions or suggestions, feel free to email us at reachus@vibrantpublishers.com

Thanks again for your purchase. Good luck for your GRE!

– Vibrant Publishers Team

//////////// GRE Books in Test Prep Series ////////////

TITLE	PAPERBACK ISBN
6 Practice Tests for the GRE	978-1-63651-090-3
GRE Analytical Writing Supreme: Solutions to the Real Essay Topics	978-1-63651-053-8
GRE Analytical Writing: Solutions to the Real Essay Topics - Book 1	978-1-63651-067-5
GRE Analytical Writing: Solutions to the Real Essay Topics - Book 2	978-1-63651-069-9
GRE Master Wordlist: 1535 Words for Verbal Mastery	978-1-63651-083-5
GRE Quantitative Reasoning Supreme: Study Guide with Practice Questions	978-1-63651-091-0
GRE Reading Comprehension: Detailed Solutions to 325 Questions	978-1-63651-063-7
GRE Text Completion and Sentence Equivalence Practice Questions	978-1-63651-064-4
GRE Verbal Reasoning Supreme: Study Guide with Practice Questions	978-1-63651-057-6
GRE Words In Context: The Complete List	978-1-63651-051-4

For the most updated list of books visit
www.vibrantpublishers.com

Introduction to the Analytical Writing Measure

The Analytical Writing Measure is intended to assess your ability to think critically and write effectively about a topic while following specific directions. You will not need any specific content knowledge to complete either task in this portion of the test. The purpose of both writing pieces is to determine your readiness to perform appropriately at the graduate level.

During this portion of the test, you will complete two writing tasks that are complementary in nature: Analyze an Issue and Analyze an Argument. For each task, you will have 30 minutes to read the prompt and directions and to plan and execute your response.

During the Analyze an Issue task, you will write persuasively as you express your point of view on the selected topic, which may be in the form of an opinion, a recommendation, a claim and reason, or the presentation of two points of view. It is important to read the directions carefully to ensure that your response is addressing the prompt correctly and to enable you to receive the highest score.

During the Analyze an Argument task, you will evaluate an argument to determine the strength of the facts and assumptions that it presents. You may be asked to evaluate the evidence to determine if the assumptions are correct, formulate questions that will need to be answered before determining if the assumptions are correct, what further evidence is necessary before the argument can be declared correct, or what steps should be completed before accepting a recommended course of action. As in the Analyze an Issue task, in the Analyze an Argument task, reading and following the directions carefully is the best way to ensure that you receive a high score for your efforts.

Strategies for Completing Analytical Writing Measure

Each portion of the writing measure is 30 minutes long. In that period of time, you must read the statement or brief passage and the directions for creating your response, plan how you want to respond, and write your essay. If you spend too much time taking notes and organizing your thoughts, you may not have enough time to finish writing your essay. On the other hand, completing a prewriting activity sufficiently will help you write your essay more quickly. Budgeting your time is crucial and responding to some of the prompts published on the ETS site, ets.org will help you to do that. Although the GRE readers are aware of the time limit and that your essay is essentially a draft, they will expect you to perform at a high level. Leave a few minutes at the end of each writing section to review your essay for errors in spelling, grammar, usage, and sentence structure.

This page is intentionally left blank

Chapter **1**
Overview of the GRE General Test

The Graduate Record Examinations (GRE) General Test is required for admission to most graduate programs. The most competitive programs tend to require comparatively higher scores. This book is designed to prepare students for the GRE General Test. The GRE revised General Test was renamed in 2016 and is now known as the GRE General Test, but the content and scoring of the test remain the same. Note that some graduate programs require applicants to take specialized GRE Subject Tests which will not be covered in this book. Before preparing to take the GRE, please review the admissions criteria for the programs you are interested in applying to so that you know whether you need to take subject tests in addition to the GRE General Test. To learn more about subject tests, visit the Subject Tests section at ets.org.

The GRE General Test is not designed to measure your knowledge of specific fields. It does not measure your ability to be successful in your career or even in school. It does, however, give a reasonably accurate indication of your capabilities in certain key areas for graduate level work, such as your ability to understand complex written material, your understanding of basic mathematics, your ability to interpret data, and your capacity for reasoning and critical thinking. By using this book to prepare for the GRE General Test, you will not only improve your chances of scoring well on the test, but you will also help to prepare yourself for graduate level study.

Format of the GRE General Test

The GRE General Test is offered as a computer-delivered test throughout the year. Post Covid, ETS provides test-takers with the option to take the test from home.

Whether you are taking the GRE General Test at the testing centre or at home, the format of the test will essentially be the same. The GRE General Test At Home follows the same format as the computer-delivered version of the GRE General Test. The test consists of three main components: Analytical Writing, Verbal Reasoning and Quantitative Reasoning. The total time for the test will be about 3 hours 45 minutes.

The first section of the test is always the Analytical Writing component which is broken down into two sections. In the first section, you will be asked to write an argumentative essay that takes a position on an issue of general interest. In the second section, you will be asked to analyze an argument for logical validity and soundness. You will be given 30 minutes for each section.

The remainder of the test will be split between sections devoted to Verbal Reasoning and Quantitative Reasoning. There will be two sections devoted to Verbal Reasoning and another two devoted to Quantitative Reasoning. You will be given 30 minutes to complete each section of Verbal Reasoning and 35 minutes to complete each section of Quantitative Reasoning. Each section will contain 20 questions. At any point during the test, you may be given an unscored section on either Verbal or Quantitative Reasoning; since this section will not be identified, it is important that you try your best at all times. Also, it is possible you will be asked to complete a research section that will allow ETS to test the efficacy of new questions. If you are given a research section, it will appear at the end of your General Test. Unscored and research sections may vary in number of questions and time allotted.

Outline of the GRE General Test

The Verbal Reasoning and Quantitative Reasoning sections of the GRE General Test are section-level adaptive. This means that the computer will adapt the test to your performance. Since there are two sections each of Verbal Reasoning and Quantitative Reasoning, the difficulty of the second section will depend upon how well you did on the first section. The overall format of the GRE General Test will be as follows:

Component	Number of Questions	Time Allowed
Analytical Writing (2 sections)	1 Analyze an Issue 1 Analyze an Argument	30 minutes 30 minutes
Verbal Reasoning (2 sections)	20 questions per section	30 minutes per section
Quantitative Reasoning (2 sections)	20 questions per section	5 minutes per section
Unscored Section	Variable	Variable
Research Section	Variable	Variable
		Total Time: 3 hours 45 minutes

Note that the GRE General Test At Home follows the same format as the computer-delivered version of the GRE General Test.

While taking the GRE General Test, here are some things to remember:

❏ You can review and preview questions within a section, allowing you to budget your time to deal with the questions you find most difficult.

❏ You will be able to mark questions within a section and return to them later. This means that if you find a question especially difficult, you will be able to move on to other questions and return to the one you had trouble with, provided you stay within the time limit for the section.

❏ You will be able to change or edit your answers within a section. This means that if you realize you made a mistake, you can go back and correct yourself provided you stay within the time limit for the section.

❏ You will have an onscreen calculator during the Quantitative Reasoning portions of the test, allowing you to quickly complete any necessary computations.

The following will briefly introduce the three main components of the GRE General Test.

Analytical Writing Assessment

The first section of the GRE General Test is the Analytical Writing assessment. This component of the GRE is designed to test your ability to use basic logic and critical reasoning to make and assess arguments. The Analytical Writing assessment is broken into two assignments, each of which must be completed within 30 minutes. In the first assignment, you will be asked to develop a position on an issue of general interest. You will be given an issue and a prompt with some specific instructions on how to approach the assigned issue. You will be expected to take a position on the issue and then write a clear, persuasive and logically sound essay defending your position in correct English. You will be assessed based on your ability to effectively defend your position with supporting evidence and valid reasoning, your skill in organizing your thoughts, and your command of English. In the second assignment, you will be presented with a passage in which the author sketches an argument for their position on an issue. Here, you will be expected to write an essay that critically evaluates their argument in terms of the evidence used and the logical validity of their reasoning. You will be assessed based on your ability to parse the author's argument and effectively point out the strengths and weaknesses of their reasoning, using good organization and correct English.

Task	Time Allowed	Answer Format
Analyze an Issue	30 minutes	Short essay on an issue of general interest that clearly and carefully addresses the prompt
Analyze an Argument	30 minutes	Short essay that analyzes another person's argument for validity, soundness and supporting evidence

The Analytical Writing assessment tests your ability to:

- ❑ coherently develop complex ideas

- ❑ write in a focused, organized manner

- ❑ identify relevant evidence and use it to support your claims

- ❑ critically evaluate another person's argument for clarity and effectiveness

- ❑ command the elements of standard written English

Verbal Reasoning

The Verbal Reasoning portion of the GRE assesses your reading comprehension, your ability to draw inferences to fill in missing information, and your vocabulary. You will be given two sections on Verbal Reasoning, each consisting of 20 questions and lasting 30 minutes. Verbal Reasoning questions on the GRE General Test are mostly multiple-choice and will be drawn from the following three types: Reading Comprehension, Text Completion, and Sentence Equivalence. Reading Comprehension questions will ask you to read a short passage several paragraphs long and then answer questions about the passage. Text Completion questions will have a short passage with 1-3 blanks which you will need to fill in by choosing the best of several multiple-choice options. The Sentence Equivalence section will ask you to fill in the blank in a passage, using the two words that will complete the sentence in such a way that the meaning will be as similar as possible.

Time	Question Type	Answer Format
You will have 30 minutes to complete the entire section, which will include a mixture of different question types	Reading Comprehension	Multiple choice: select one answer choice Multiple choice: select one or more answer choices Highlight a section of text
	Text Completion	Multiple choice: fill in one or more blanks to complete the text
	Sentence Equivalence	Multiple choice: select the two options that produce two sentences with the most similar meanings

The Verbal Reasoning section measures your ability to:

❑ comprehend, interpret and analyze complex passages in standard written English

❑ apply sophisticated vocabulary in context

❑ draw inferences about meaning and authorial intent based on written material

Quantitative Reasoning

The Quantitative Reasoning section of the GRE evaluates your ability to use basic mathematics, read and interpret graphs and figures and engage in basic reasoning involving math and numbers. You will be given two sections on Quantitative Reasoning with 20 questions in each section. You will have 35 minutes to complete each section. There are two basic question types: multiple-choice and numerical entry. For multiple-choice questions, you will be asked to choose the best answer or answers from several possibilities; for numerical entry questions, you will be asked to enter a numerical answer from your own calculations. Some questions will be designed to test your knowledge of basic algebra and geometry while others will be designed to test your ability to read and interpret different presentations of data.

Time	Question Type	Answer Format
You will have 35 minutes to complete the entire section, which will include a mixture of different question types	Multiple Choice	• Select one answer choice • Select one or more answer choices
	Numeric Entry	• Solve the problem through calculation and enter a numeric value
	Quantitative Comparison	• Evaluate two quantities to decide whether one is greater than the other, whether they are equal, or whether a relationship cannot be determined
	Data Interpretation	• Multiple choice: choose the best answer or answers • Numeric entry: enter a value

The Quantitative Reasoning section tests your ability to:

❑ use mathematical tools such as basic arithmetic, geometry, algebra and statistics

❑ understand, interpret and analyze quantitative information

❑ apply basic mathematical and data interpretation skills to real-world information and problems

Registering for the GRE

Before you register to take the GRE, be sure to consider your schedule and any special accommodations you may need. Be aware that the availability of testing dates may vary according to your location. Be sure to give yourself plenty of time to prepare for the GRE and be sure you know the deadlines for score reporting and application deadlines for all the schools you are applying to. For general information about deadlines and the GRE, visit GRE section at ets.org. For more information on how to register for the GRE, visit the Register for GRE section at ets.org. For information on special accommodations for disabled students, visit the Disabilities or Health-related Needs section on ets.org.

If you are taking the GRE General Test At Home, there are certain equipment, environment, and testing space requirements you need to fulfill before you can start the registration process. For more information on these requirements, read the At Home Testing section on ets.org.

How the GRE General Test is Scored

Scoring for the Analytical Writing Section

In the Analytical Writing section, you will be scored on a scale of 0-6 in increments of 0.5. The Analytical Writing measure emphasizes your ability to engage in reasoning and critical thinking over your facility with the finer points of grammar. The highest scores of 5.5-6.0 are given to work generally superior in every respect - sustained analysis of complex issues, coherent argumentation and excellent command of the English language. The lowest scores of 0.0-0.5 are given to work that is completely off topic or so poorly composed as to be incoherent.

Scoring for the Verbal and Quantitative Reasoning Sections

The Verbal and Quantitative Reasoning sections are now scored on a scale of 130-170 in 1-point increments.

General Strategies for Taking the GRE

There are strategies you can apply that will greatly increase your odds of performing well on the GRE. The following is a list of strategies that will help to improve your chances of performing well on the GRE:

❑ Review basic concepts in math, logic and writing.

❑ Work through the test-taking strategies offered in this book.

❏ Work through mock GRE tests until you feel thoroughly comfortable with the types of questions you will see.

❏ As you are studying for the GRE, focus your energy on the types of questions that give you the most difficulty.

❏ Learn to guess wisely. For many of the questions on the Verbal and Quantitative Reasoning Sections, the correct answer is in front of you - you only need to correctly identify it. Especially for questions that you find difficult, you should hone your ability to dismiss the options that are clearly wrong and make an educated guess about which one is right.

❏ Answer every question. You won't lose any points for choosing the wrong answer, so even a wild guess that might or might not be right is better than no answer at all.

Preparing for Test Day and Taking the GRE

How you prepare for the test is completely up to you and will depend upon your own test-taking preferences and the amount of time you can devote to studying for the test. At the very least, before you take the test, you should know the basics of what is covered on the test along with the general guidelines for taking the GRE. This book is designed to provide you with the basic information you need and give you the opportunity to prepare thoroughly for the GRE General Test.

Although there is no set way to prepare for the GRE, as a general rule you will want to:

❏ Learn the basics about the test - what is being tested, the format, and how the test is administered.

❏ Familiarize yourself with the specific types of questions that you will see on the GRE General Test.

❏ Review skills such as basic math, reading comprehension, and writing.

❏ Learn about test-taking strategies.

❏ Take a mock GRE test to practice applying your test-taking skills to an actual test.

Remember, you don't need to spend an equal amount of time on each of these areas to do well on the GRE so allot your study time to your own needs and preferences. Following are some suggestions to help you make the final preparations for your test, and help you through the test itself.

Preparing for Test Day

❏ In the time leading up to your test, practice, then practice some more. Practice until you are confident with the material.

❏ Know when your test is and when you need to be at the testing center or in front of your computer at home.

❑ Make a "practice run" to your testing center so that you can anticipate how much time you will need to allow to get there. For the At Home test, make sure to sign in at least 15 minutes before the test.

❑ Understand the timing and guidelines for the test and plan accordingly. Remember that you are not allowed to eat or drink while taking the GRE, although you will be allowed to snack or drink during some of the short breaks during testing. Plan accordingly.

❑ Know exactly what documentation you will need to bring with you to the testing center. If you are testing at home, you will have to provide a valid government-issued identification document as well.

❑ Relax, especially in the day or night before your test. If you have studied and practiced wisely, you will be well prepared for the test. You may want to briefly glance over some test preparation materials, but cramming the night before will not be productive.

❑ Eat well and get a good night's sleep. You will want to be well rested for the test.

The Test Day

❑ Wake up early to give yourself plenty of time to eat a healthy breakfast, gather the necessary documentation, pack a snack and a water bottle, and make it to the testing center well before your test is scheduled to start.

❑ Have confidence: You've prepared well for the test, and there won't be any big surprises. You may not know the answers to some questions, but the format will be exactly like what you've been practicing.

❑ While you are taking the test, don't panic. The test is timed, and students often worry that they will run out of time and miss too many questions. The sections of the test are designed so that many students will not finish them, so don't worry if you don't think you can finish a section on time. Just try to answer as many questions as you can as accurately as possible.

❑ Remember the strategies and techniques that you learn from this book and apply them wherever possible.

Frequently Asked Questions

General Questions

What changes have been made to the GRE General Test post Covid-19?

Due to Covid-19 restrictions, test-takers are now able to take the GRE General Test at home. Content and scoring have remained the same. Study materials that reference the GRE General Test are still valid and may be used for test preparation.

Can I take the GRE test at home?

Yes. ETS now provides students with the option to take the test from home. If your local test centres are closed or you prefer a familiar testing environment, you can take the GRE from home. You will have to check the equipment, environment, and testing-space requirements for the at-home test and whether it's an option for you. For detailed information on the requirements for the home test, check the At Home Testing section at ets.org.

Are there any changes in the format and content of the GRE test due to COVID-19?

No. The format and content of the GRE General Test remains the same.

How do I get ready to take the GRE General Test?

To take the GRE General Test, there are several steps you'll need to take:

❑ Find out what prospective graduate/professional programs require: Does the program you're interested in requiring additional testing beyond the GRE General Test? What is the deadline for receipt of scores?

❑ Sign up for a test date. You need to sign up for any GRE testing. Act in a timely manner so that you have plenty of time to prepare and are guaranteed that your scores will be sent and received on time. For the in-center test, testing dates are much more restricted, so if you know that you will need to take the GRE General Test at the center, make arrangements well in advance of the application deadline for your program. There are additional requirements if you're taking the test at home, check the requirements well in advance.

❑ Use resources provided by ETS and Vibrant Publishers to familiarize yourself with the format of the GRE and the types of questions you will face. Even if you are confident about taking the test, it is essential to prepare for the test.

Does the GRE General Test measure my proficiency in specific subject areas?

No. The GRE General Test is designed to measure general proficiency in reading, critical reasoning, and working with data, all abilities critical to graduate work. However, you won't be tested on your knowledge of any specific field.

Where can I get additional information on the GRE General Test?

Educational Testing Service (ETS), the organization that administers the GRE, has an informative website entirely devoted to information about the test at the GRE section at ets.org. There, you can find links that further explain how to sign up for testing, fees, score reporting, and much more.

Preparing for the Test

How should I prepare for the test?

The first thing you should do is thoroughly familiarize yourself with the format of the GRE General Test. Read about each section of the test, how many questions are there per section, and the required format for answers. You can find general information about the structure of the test earlier in this chapter.

How do I prepare for the questions I will be asked on the GRE General Test?

There are plenty of resources by Vibrant Publishers, including this book to help you prepare for the questions you will face on the GRE General Test. A list of books is provided at the beginning of this book. For the most updated list, you may visit the Test Prep Series section on vibrantpublishers.com.

How much should I study/practice for the GRE?

Study and practice until you feel comfortable with the test. Practice, practice and practice some more until you feel confident about test day!

Are there additional materials I can use to get even more practice?

Yes. ETS offers a free full-length practice test that can be downloaded from the GRE section at ets.org. Also, after you have signed up for testing through ETS, you are eligible for some further test preparation materials free of additional charge.

Test Content

How long is the GRE General Test ?

The overall testing time is about 3 hours and 45 minutes.

What skills does the GRE test?

In general, the GRE is designed to test your proficiency in certain key skills you will need for graduate level study. More specifically:

❏ The Analytical Writing section tests your ability to write about complex ideas in a coherent, focused fashion as well as your ability to command the conventions of standard written English, provide and evaluate relevant evidence, and critique other points of view.

❏ The Verbal Reasoning section is an assessment of your ability to understand, interpret and analyze complex passages, use reasoning to draw inferences about written material and use sophisticated vocabulary in context.

❏ The Quantitative Reasoning section is an assessment of basic, high school-level mathematical skills and knowledge, as well as your ability to analyze and interpret data.

What level of math is required for the Quantitative Reasoning section?

You will be expected to know high school level math - arithmetic, and basic concepts in algebra and geometry. You will also be expected to be able to analyze and interpret data presented in tables and graphs.

Scoring and Score Reporting

How are the sections of the GRE General Test scored?

The GRE General Test is scored as follows:

❑ The scores of the Verbal Reasoning section are done in 1-point increments on a scale of 130-170.

❑ The scores of the Quantitative Reasoning section are done in 1-point increments on a scale of 130-170.

❑ The scores of the Analytical Writing section are done in increments of 0.5 on a scale of 0-6.

When will my score be reported?

It depends on when you decide to take the GRE General Test. In general, scores for the test are reported in 10-15 days. You can find your scores in your official ETS account. An email notification from ETS is sent when the test scores are made available. ETS will also send an official Institution Score Report to the institutions you've chosen to send the test scores to.

Check the GRE section at ets.org for updates on score reporting and deadlines.

How long will my scores be valid?

Your score for the GRE General Test will remain valid for five years.

Other Questions

Do business schools accept the GRE instead of the GMAT?

An increasing number of business schools accept the GRE as a substitute for the more standard test for admission to an MBA program, the GMAT. Before you decide to take the GRE instead of the GMAT, make sure that the programs you are interested in applying to will accept the GRE. You can find a list of business schools that currently accept the GRE in the GRE section at ets.org.

How is the GRE administered?

The GRE is administered continuously year-round at designated testing centers, where you can take the test free from distraction in a secure environment that discourages cheating. The GRE Test At Home is also available for those who are more comfortable in a familiar environment. For information on testing centers in your area and important dates, visit the GRE section at ets.org.

I have a disability that requires me to ask for special accommodation while taking the test - what sort of accommodation is offered?

ETS does accommodate test-takers with disabilities. For information on procedures, visit the GRE Disabilities and Health-related Needs section at ets.org.

Will there be breaks during testing?

Yes. You will be given an optional 10-minute break after the third section of the test and one-minute breaks between the remaining sections.

Will I be given scratch paper?

Yes. The test administrator will provide you with scratch paper to use during the test, which has to be returned to the testing center staff without any pages missing.

For the At Home test, you cannot use regular note paper. You may use either of the following materials:

❑ One small desktop white board with an erasable marker.

❑ A sheet of paper placed inside a transparent sheet protector. You can write on this with an erasable marker.

At the end of the test, you will need to show the proctor that all notes you took during the test have been erased.

Should I bring a calculator to the test?

No. There will be an onscreen calculator for you to use.

Chapter **2**
Analyze an Issue Task

As you complete this task, you will have an opportunity to express your point of view on an issue. Because it is essentially your opinion, there is no "correct" answer. You must, however, support your point of view with sufficient evidence to show the strength of your argument. You may agree completely with the statement about the issue, partially agree with it, or completely disagree with it. Be certain you stay on topic and follow the directions carefully.

For example, you might be presented with a statement similar to the following:
It is always best to look before you leap.

One interpretation of this statement is that one should consider potential consequences before taking any action. The directions may instruct you to write a response in which you discuss the extent to which you agree or disagree with the statement and explain your reasoning for the position you take. If you agree with the statement, you should recall examples from your reading, your studies, or your own experience that support your position. Think about Holden Caulfield's actions in The Catcher in the Rye. His impulsive decision to spend some time alone in New York City before going home after his expulsion from Pencey Prep had unsatisfactory consequences. You may have taken some action in your own life that you regretted afterwards. On the other hand, you may disagree with the statement. Early explorers like Christopher Columbus had little idea about what they would find as they set out in their relatively small sailing vessels. If they had thought only about the dangers of their ventures, the new world would have been discovered much later. You can also take a qualified approach by agreeing with the statement to some extent. Remember, the best approach to a given prompt is the one you can argue the best. The GRE essay readers are trained to evaluate a wide variety of approaches to the issue and evaluate them on their strengths and weaknesses and not on the opinion expressed.

The following is a comprehensive list of the instructions that can accompany the statements in the Analyze an Issue task.

- ❑ Write a response in which you discuss the extent to which you agree or disagree with the statement and explain your reasoning for the position you take. In developing and supporting your position, you should consider ways in which the statement might or might not hold true and explain how these considerations shape your position.

- ❑ Write a response in which you discuss the extent to which you agree or disagree with the recommendation and explain your reasoning for the position you take. In developing and supporting your position, describe specific circumstances in which adopting the recommendation would or would not be advantageous and explain how these examples shape your position.

- ❑ Write a response in which you discuss the extent to which you agree or disagree with the claim. In developing and supporting your position, be sure to address the most compelling reasons and/or examples that could be used to challenge your position.

- ❑ Write a response in which you discuss which view more closely aligns with your own position and explain your reasoning for the position you take. In developing and supporting your position, you should address both of the views presented.

❑ Write a response in which you discuss the extent to which you agree or disagree with the claim and the reasons upon which that claim is based.

❑ Write a response in which you discuss your views on the policy and explain your reasoning for the position you take. In developing and supporting your position, you should consider the possible consequences of implementing the policy and explain how these consequences shape your position.

You may have had some experience with writing persuasively in high school or college, but you do not need to worry about employing specific rhetorical devices to receive a high score. It is important to stay on topic, present your argument in a coherent and cohesive manner, and to acknowledge counterarguments to strengthen your own. You should also make every attempt to use correct grammar, mechanics, and a variety of sentence structures to improve the fluency of your essay. The scoring guide that follows is reprinted from the Practice Book for the GRE Revised General Test, developed by Educational Testing Service.

Scoring Guide

Score 6

In addressing the specific task directions, a 6 response presents a cogent, well-articulated analysis of the issue and conveys meaning skillfully.

A typical response in this category:

❑ articulates a clear and insightful position on the issue in accordance with the assigned task

❑ develops the position fully with compelling reasons and/or persuasive examples

❑ sustains a well-focused, well-organized analysis, connecting ideas logically

❑ conveys ideas fluently and precisely, using effective vocabulary and sentence variety

❑ demonstrates facility with the conventions of standard written English (i.e., grammar, usage and mechanics), but may have minor errors

Score 5

In addressing the specific task directions, a 5 response presents a generally thoughtful, well-developed analysis of the issue and conveys meaning clearly.

A typical response in this category:

❑ presents a clear and well-considered position on the issue in accordance with the assigned task

❑ develops the position with logically sound reasons and/or well-chosen examples

❑ is focused and generally well organized, connecting ideas appropriately

❑ conveys ideas clearly and well, using appropriate vocabulary and sentence variety

❑ demonstrates facility with the conventions of standard written English but may have minor errors

Score 4

In addressing the specific task directions, a 4 response presents a competent analysis of the issue and conveys meaning with acceptable clarity.

A typical response in this category:

❑ presents a clear position on the issue in accordance with the assigned task

❑ develops the position with relevant reasons and/or examples

❑ is adequately focused and organized

❑ demonstrates sufficient control of language to express ideas with reasonable clarity

❑ generally, demonstrates control of the conventions of standard written English but may have some errors

Score 3

A three response demonstrates some competence in addressing the specific task directions, in analyzing the issue and in conveying meaning, but is obviously flawed.

A typical response in this category exhibits ONE OR MORE of the following characteristics:

❑ is vague or limited in addressing the specific task directions and/or in presenting or developing a position on the issue

❑ is weak in the use of relevant reasons or examples or relies largely on unsupported claims

❑ is poorly focused and/or poorly organized

❑ has problems in language and sentence structure that result in a lack of clarity

❑ contains occasional major errors or frequent minor errors in grammar, usage or mechanics that can interfere with meaning

Score 2

A two response largely disregards the specific task directions and/or demonstrates serious weaknesses in analytical writing.

A typical response in this category exhibits ONE OR MORE of the following characteristics:

❏ is unclear or seriously limited in addressing the specific task directions and/or in presenting or developing a position on the issue

❏ provides few, if any, relevant reasons or examples in support of its claims

❏ is unfocused and/or disorganized

❏ has serious problems in language and sentence structure that frequently interfere with meaning

❏ contains serious errors in grammar, usage or mechanics that frequently obscure meaning

Score 1

A one response demonstrates fundamental deficiencies in analytical writing.

A typical response in this category exhibits ONE OR MORE of the following characteristics:

❏ provides little or no evidence of understanding the issue

❏ provides little evidence of the ability to develop an organized response (i.e., is extremely disorganized and/or extremely brief)

❏ has severe problems in language and sentence structure that persistently interfere with meaning

❏ contains pervasive errors in grammar, usage or mechanics that result in incoherence

Score 0

A typical response in this category is off topic (i.e., provides no evidence of an attempt to respond to the assigned topic), is in a foreign language, merely copies the topic, consists of only keystroke characters, or is illegible or non-verbal.

The Analyze an Issue task presents you with a statement that expresses a point of view about a topic of general interest. The statement is followed by a set of specific instructions that will determine the manner in which you respond. You may find yourself agreeing or disagreeing with the statement almost immediately. How you feel about the statement is not important, but you will be expected to present a strongly developed case for your own point of view. As you think about your own point of view, consider other perspectives as well. Before you begin to write, read the instructions carefully. Take some brief notes, list some questions that the issue generates, and organize your ideas in a logical manner. This task will assess your ability to think critically and write clearly, using varied and accurate vocabulary, a meaningful variety of sentence structures, and correct grammar, spelling, and usage.

General Strategies

❑ Restate the issue in a way that makes sense to you.

❑ You could also determine what question is being answered by the statement Creating a question may help you determine your position on the issue. If someone were to ask you this question, would you say yes, no, or maybe?

❑ Next, create a statement that expresses the opposing viewpoint, using language similar to that of the original statement.

❑ Think about alternative viewpoints. Is there another way to look at this issue? Can you qualify the original recommendation in some way? How can you answer all or some of the questions that you generated earlier?

❑ From here, you must decide which point of view to address in your essay. Before you decide, carefully consider the following questions. You will have addressed several of them in the exercises you will perform below.

    i.   What, precisely, is the central issue?

    ii.   What precisely are the instructions asking me to do?

    iii.   Do I agree with all or any part of the claim? Why or why not?

    iv.   Does the claim make certain assumptions? If so, are they reasonable?

    v.   Is the claim valid only under certain conditions? If so, what are they?

    vi.   Do I need to explain how I interpret certain terms or concepts used in the claim?

    vii. If I take a certain position on the issue, what reasons support my position?

    viii. What examples - either real or hypothetical - could I use to illustrate those reasons and advance my point of view? Which examples are the most compelling?

❑ Once you have decided on a position to defend, consider the perspectives of others who might not agree with your position. Ask yourself:

    i.   What reasons might someone use to refute or undermine my position?

    ii.   How should I acknowledge or defend against those views in my essay?

The next step should be listing the main reasons that support your position. Keep in mind that the GRE readers scoring your response are not looking for a "right" answer—in fact, as far as they are concerned, there is no correct position to take. Instead, the readers are evaluating the skill with which you address the specific instructions and articulate and develop an argument to support your evaluation of the issue.

This page is intentionally left blank

Chapter 3
Arts

1

Issue Task 1

The most effective way to understand contemporary culture is to analyze the trends of its youth.

Write a response in which you discuss the extent to which you agree or disagree with the statement and explain your reasoning for the position you take. In developing and supporting your position, you should consider ways in which the statement might or might not hold true and explain how these considerations shape your position.

 Strategies

Restate the Issue:

How can you change the statement without changing its meaning?

In other words:

The least effective way to understand contemporary culture is to ignore the trends of its youth.

Or: The surest way to misunderstand contemporary culture is to ignore the trends of its youth.

Determine what question is being answered by the issue statement.

How can one understand contemporary culture?

Creating a question will help you to think about how you would respond. Your answer to the question can help you develop your response to the statement.

Now think about the parts of the statement that provide evidence that you can affirm or refute.

◆ **most effective** – Most is the superlative form of many; nothing is more effective.

◆ **understand** – This statement assumes that one can understand contemporary culture.

◆ **analyze** – Analysis is the process of breaking something down into its components. What are the

   components of the trends?

◆ **youth** – What age group specifically? Does the term, youth, extend to those in college?

Opposing statement:

The most effective way to understand contemporary culture is not to analyze the trends of its youth.

Identify the parts of the opposing statement that provide evidence you can refute or affirm.

not – In this case, the implication is that one should ignore the trends of a culture's youth. Including those trends might give a false impression of the culture.

Alternatives:

Is there another way to look at this issue? Can you qualify the original issue statement in some way?

New viewpoint:

Analyzing the trends of its youth is one component in understanding contemporary culture.

Identify the parts of the new statement that provide evidence to affirm or refute.

◆ **one** – This implies that there are others.

◆ **contemporary** – The culture of this time.

 ## Sample Essay

The culture of any era is defined by a variety of elements and may be the result of past influences. Analyzing the trends of today's youth is only one of those elements. One also needs to analyze the kinds of work that adults are pursuing or the activities its senior citizens are participating in. To rely solely on analysis of youth trends is short-sighted. The youth of a culture are heavily influenced by the latest, hottest fad. Their greatest need is to fit in and to be cool. They change their clothes, their hair, and their phones as soon as the newest fashion is featured in print or on television. Their permanence is ephemeral, and their influence may be longer lasting. A big chunk of their time would be spent just keeping up. Anyone attempting to analyze the trends of youth will barely finish before the trends change.

1

The most widely-exposed youth culture of the last half century is that of the 1960's and 70's. The youth of that era advised others to tune in, turn on, and drop out. Drugs, sex and rock and roll permeated the culture of youth in those decades. Because burning draft cards and bras was so widely publicized, it would be tempting to believe that all youth behaved in such a manner. That would be a mistake. Despite the presence of SDS chapters, peace rallies and sit-ins on college campuses across the country, most students quietly went about attending classes, graduating and getting traditional jobs. The counterculture of the 60's and 70's had its greatest influence on later decades. Those days of rebellion and revolution led to increased opportunities for minorities and women. The young people of that era are now nearing retirement and are living very different lives from the senior citizens of previous generations. They have tuned in, but they have not dropped out. They are healthier, better educated, and leading more active lives than their parents or grandparents did.

An analysis of youthful trends reveals what effect advertising has had on a culture's young people. To fully understand contemporary culture, one must analyze the hopes, fears, and actions of all the groups that comprise it. A culture's youth is blissfully ignorant of a culture's realities. The struggle of adults to find satisfying work, to pay the bills, to provide security for themselves and their children define the attitudes and behaviors of contemporary culture.

Issue Task 2

When old buildings stand on ground that modern planners feel could be better used for modern purposes, modern development should be given precedence over the preservation of historic buildings.

Write a response in which you discuss the extent to which you agree or disagree with the statement and explain your reasoning for the position you take. In developing and supporting your position, you should consider ways in which the statement might or might not hold true and explain how these considerations shape your position.

 Strategies

Restate the Issue:

In this case, you might reverse the order in which the parts of the issue appear and use a negative phrase. In other words:

In other words:

The preservation of historic buildings should not be given precedence over using the ground they stand on for modern purposes that have a better use. Determine what question is being answered by the issue statement.

You could also determine what question is being answered by the statement.

Should the preservation of historic buildings be given precedence over modern development?

Asking a question may help you to formulate your response to the issue.

Now think about the parts of the statement that provide evidence that you can affirm or refute.

- ◆ **old** – This implies outdated or rundown. New is better.

- ◆ **better used** – better is a comparative word. It is more than good but less than best.

- ◆ **modern purposes** – Modern implies improved. It is the opposite of old-fashioned.

- ◆ **development** – This word also has a positive connotation. It implies improvement, evolution.

◆ **precedence** – Whatever is being proposed is more important than other ideas. It should come ahead of other plans or ideas.

◆ **preservation** – Again, the connotation is positive. To preserve is to save.

◆ **historic** – Something historic is a representation of history. One generally thinks favorably of something that is described as being historic.

Opposing viewpoint:

Modern development should not be given precedence over the preservation of historic buildings that stand on ground, which modern planners feel could be better used for modern purposes.

The only new evidence in the opposing statement is the word not, which simply reverses the original position.

Alternatives:

Is there any other way to look at this issue? Can you qualify either of the statements? Are there any cases where one or the other of the statements might be true or not true?

New viewpoint:

When the preservation of historic buildings becomes a financial struggle or the land on which they stand could be used for community betterment, modern development should be given precedence over that preservation.

Identify parts of the new viewpoint that provide evidence for you to refute or affirm.

◆ **financial struggle** – Surely communities and special interest groups cannot afford to preserve every building of an historic value.

◆ **community betterment**– This is subjective. What one feels is betterment, another might feel is a detriment to the community. Who decides?

Examples:

a) Auschwitz is crumbling. There is strong debate over preserving what remains of the infamous Nazi concentration camp or the suitability of letting the buildings crumble. Is there a better use for this land?

b) Urban renewal generally involves tearing down existing structures to make way for improved buildings to house new business or offices or to improve traffic flow.

 ## Sample Essay

The value of any object is subjective. Nostalgia for the simpler life of bygone days causes us to attach more value than appropriate to objects from the past. Historic buildings let us envision the people who lived in them and the daily activities they pursued. However, the needs of communities have changed, and sentiment may need to be discarded to meet those needs. Due to this fact, historic buildings may need to be taken down or otherwise changed to accommodate the needs of the current population.

Some cities have found ways to preserve historic buildings by erecting the new ones over them. Their front walls become part of the new façade. The cities' needs for more office space or apartments have been met and a record of the past has been saved for present and future generations. Many communities in the United States have historical societies who raise money for historic preservation; and, in some cases, old buildings can be listed in the Register of Historic Places and are supported by public funds. The future of projects like these depends on continued interest, and emerging generations may have different priorities.

How essential are old buildings in maintaining the character of a place? When one looks at several cities in Europe, he sees a cityscape very different from the one that existed prior to WWII when both Allies and Axis bombs destroyed ancient structures. The citizens of those towns and cities had no choice but to rebuild. Life went on. Currently, there is debate about the future of Auschwitz. What remains of the notorious Nazi concentration camp is in disrepair. Buildings that were not built to last in the first place are crumbling. Maintaining them is costly. Although many countries around the world have donated millions to the preservation of the site, some wonder if allowing the site to return to its pre-WWII state is a more fitting memorial to what happened there. Could the money needed to restore the barracks, the crematoria and to maintain the museum be used in a more appropriate way to teach future generations about the dangers of hatred and prejudice?

Modern technology has made the preservation of old buildings and landmarks possible through photographs and video recordings. In fact, it is possible, with the click of a computer mouse, to take virtual tours of places one has never physically visited. These photos and videos live on the World Wide Web forever, and maintenance costs will be minimal. Access to these historic buildings is no longer restricted to those who can make the trip to their physical sites but is available to anyone with an Internet connection.

Change for the sake of change is frivolous and usually unnecessary, but towns and cities are challenged to make the best use of the spaces they have. Their needs have changed. A small city may need assisted living quarters for its senior citizens or recreational facilities for its young people. To accomplish this, city planners may have to make difficult choices, some of which could include the razing of old buildings.

Issue Task 3

Some people believe that government funding of the arts is necessary to ensure that the arts can flourish and be available to all people. Others believe that government funding of the arts threatens the integrity of the arts.

Write a response in which you discuss which view more closely aligns with your own position and explain your reasoning for the position you take. In developing and supporting your position, you should address both of the views presented.

 ## Strategies

Restate the Issue:

Consider each view separately before deciding which of them you most closely agree with.

Point of view 1:

Restate the view by saying what cannot, rather than what can.

In other words:

The arts cannot flourish and be available to all people without government funding of the arts.

You might also determine what question is being answered by the statement.

How can we ensure that the arts can flourish and be available to all people?

Or: *What role should the government play to ensure that the arts can flourish and be available to all people?*

Think about the way that you would answer one or both of these questions to help you determine your position.

Now identify elements in the statement that provide evidence for you to affirm or refute.

◆ **Some people** – This indicates that the opinion is not unanimous.

◆ **necessary** – This implies a requirement. Without government funding the arts would not flourish.

◆ **flourish** – This means to thrive, a stronger action than survival.

◆ **available** – Another way to say this might be accessible. Art would be accessible or open to all people.

Point of view 2:

Restate the view by making it a negative statement.

In other words:

The integrity of the arts cannot survive with government funding.

You should formulate the question that requires this statement as an answer.

What effect would government funding have on the integrity of the arts?

Or*: How does government funding threaten the arts?*

Now identify elements in the statement that can provide evidence for you to affirm or refute.

◆ **others** – The implication is that there are two points of view.

◆ **threatens** – This word always has a negative connotation. The response to a threat is defense.

◆ **integrity** – One thinks of strength, honesty and wholeness.

The directions do not allow for alternative positions. Even though you may not be in complete agreement with either of the positions, you must decide which one most closely matches the way you think about the issue. Make certain to acknowledge the opposite viewpoint as you develop your response.

 Sample Essay

Some may say, "I don't care about painters or sculptors", but the creative arts encompass so much more. It is not strictly high-brow. The artists include writers of fiction, drama, poetry, and journalism. They include composers of country music, Broadway scores, and classical pieces. Many people don't realize the number of ways that they are exposed to art in their everyday lives. The National Endowment for the Arts supports programs all around the United States that promote exposure to all of the creative arts. The NEA also funds grants for various artists and projects through an application and award process. There is little doubt that, without this organization, children in otherwise culturally-deprived areas of the country would have no introduction to the creative arts. The struggling artist may be a popular stereotype in film and fiction, but the fact of the matter is that new artists in nearly every field do struggle, at least for a time. The NEA allows these artists to apply for grants to help them get a start.

However, since it is funded by the government, the NEA budget depends on the whims of Congress. Senators and congressmen also feel entitled to attempt to place restrictions on the type of artwork or artist supported by NEA grants. There arises the paternalistic attitude that says," If I'm paying for it, I'll decide how it gets used." Congress has attempted to censor some forms of artistic expression by claiming that it is pornographic or demeaning to one group or another, even that it is unpatriotic. It is difficult, if not impossible, for an artist to express his vision if that vision is clouded by requirements placed upon it by otherwise well-meaning public servants.

What are the alternatives to public funding of the arts? It used to be that gifted artists would have wealthy patrons who were individuals or even the Vatican itself in the case of the sculptor/architect, Bernini. Of course, the Catholic Church placed restrictions on the kinds of work completed. Other patrons generally made demands of the artists they supported as well. The artists, however, did stave off starvation and homelessness. Patrons of the arts still exist and invest in Broadway productions, pay for visiting musicians at local concert halls, and donate paintings to museums. This still limits accessibility to the arts for those who live in rural or otherwise remote areas.

Does one require live experiences to say that he/she has been exposed to the arts? The World Wide Web allows anyone with an Internet connection to view works of the masters and hear recorded performances or see video of live performances. Nearly everyone with a cellular phone carries around a camera and a video recorder, and they upload their recordings to YouTube by the thousands every day. Those second-hand viewings and audio may not replace a visit to the Louvre or La Scala, but they do make the arts accessible. Local libraries have a service for their card holders that enables the patrons to download best sellers to their electronic readers or tablets, making a trip to the library, itself, unnecessary.

Men and women of ideas and artistic talent can create followings on the Internet by daily writing and uploading to their own blogs. There is a better opportunity for artists in every medium to retain their integrity and freedom of expression if they let the public decide who shall succeed and who shall not rather than relying on funds that may have strings attached.

Chapter 4
Education

Issue Task 4

4

Governments should offer a free university education to any student who has been admitted to a university but who cannot afford the tuition.

Write a response in which you discuss your views on the policy and explain your reasoning for the position you take. In developing and supporting your position, you should consider the possible consequences of implementing the policy and explain how these consequences shape your position.

 Strategies

To get started, break down the statement and identify the assumptions made.

Statement Breakdown

- ◆ Governments – The proposed policymakers

- ◆ University Education – The subject of the policy

- ◆ Low-Income Students – The proposed policy targets

Assumptions

- ◆ Governments have an obligation to help low-income students.

- ◆ The number of students who fall into the category postulated by this claim is reasonable enough that the government can afford to offer a free education.

- ◆ Students who cannot afford tuition will be able to afford to apply to a university.

After breaking down the statement and identifying assumptions, come up with pros and cons (or statements for and against) the topic given. You do not need to pick a side yet, but knowing potential counterarguments will help you to develop a stronger essay once you do.

Pros and Cons

Pros

👍 Students who would be able to attend university with this government-sponsored program would have better career/income outcomes.

👍 European countries currently offer this, with seemingly high success rates.

👍 Governments have an obligation to support their people.

Cons

👎 It is unclear what would happen if a student was admitted to multiple universities and could afford some but not others.

👎 The number of students that this would pertain to likely would not be financially feasible for the government.

👎 Attending university for free is not the only indicator of success in low-income college students.

Examples

Include examples in order to make your essay as strong as possible. These are some potential routes you may take when choosing examples:

a) History contains many examples of arguments that support either side of this policy.

b) European countries that have "free tuition" models may have examples that support or oppose this policy.

c) Recent legislation in the US that aims to develop this policy may have examples that support or oppose this policy.

Finally, come up with an outline of your essay. This may feel like it slows you down, but your essay will benefit from having an underlying structure.

 Sample Essay

Education has been strongly linked to increased income and better career prospects across the board. However, there are some groups within the United States who are unable to attain higher education by attending a university because they are unable to afford the tuition. The policy proposed here asks that the government offer free tuition for any student who has been admitted to a university but who cannot afford the tuition. While this may seem to be a good policy proposal initially, this proposal could stand to benefit from increased specificity in implementation. It is currently unclear whether this program would cover tuition fees for a program that a student has been admitted to and cannot afford if the student has also been admitted to a program that they can afford. In addition, the number of students to which this would likely pertain may not be financially feasible for the government.

The vast majority of universities offer financial aid programs for students who cannot afford full tuition, and at most universities less than half of the student body pays full tuition at any given time. Given this fact, it is not uncommon for low-income students to be offered financial aid packages from schools that they have been admitted to in order to give them the financial opportunity to attend. However, not all financial aid packages can be afforded by the student, even with the reduction in cost. In the event that a student was admitted to two universities, one that provided enough aid for the student to be able to afford to attend and one that did not, this policy implies that the student would receive free tuition for the program that he or she cannot afford, in spite of the fact that they have been admitted to a program that they can afford. This policy should be amended to state that free tuition is only offered if the student is admitted to a program that he or she cannot afford and has not been admitted to any other programs the student can afford. Otherwise, this may lead to wasteful spending for students who wish to attend universities with higher tuition but cannot afford to do so.

Along this line, a significant portion of the US population qualifies as "low-income" to the point where it is unlikely that they would be able to afford to attend a university. While the US is a relatively wealthy country, it is unlikely that the federal government could afford to cover that amount of tuition fees without having to make sacrifices within other areas of the discretionary budget. This program would then quickly be disbanded, leaving matriculating students who were previously supported by government funding with no financial ability to remain a student at that university. Some limitations would have to be put in place on this policy to restrict the number of people that the federal government would sponsor (similar to standard scholarships) to ensure that the government would be able to fund the selected students throughout their college careers.

Giving a low-income student the opportunity to attend a university has the potential to permanently change their life for the better. However, the implementation of policy to reach this end must be mindful of the financial limitations of the federal government and focus on students who cannot afford to attend any university without external support instead of students who cannot afford to attend a particular university. With these changes, this policy has the potential to result in positive consequences for low-income students.

Issue Task 5

Formal education tends to restrain our minds and spirits rather than set them free.

Write a response in which you discuss the extent to which you agree or disagree with the statement and explain your reasoning for the position you take. In developing and supporting your position, you should consider ways in which the statement might or might not hold true and explain how these considerations shape your position.

 ## Strategies

Restate the issue. In this case, the issue is stated in the positive. It tells what formal education does. What does formal education not do?

In other words:

Formal does not set our minds and spirits free.

You could also determine what question is being answered by the issue statement.

What effect does formal education have on our minds and spirits?

Making the statement an interrogatory may clarify the issue. The original issue statement is only one of several possible answers to the question.

Now think about the parts of the statement that provide evidence that you can affirm or refute.

◆ **formal** – Formal simply means that it has a form. Would students, even outside the formal educational setting, develop or create a form for studying what they choose? Is some form necessary or inevitable?

◆ **restrain** – Does formal education hold back our minds and spirits?

◆ **tends** – Tends is not a strong word. Does this weaken the issue statement?

Next, create a statement that expresses the opposing viewpoint, using language similar to that of the original issue statement.

Opposing viewpoint:

Formal education tends to unleash our minds and spirits.

Identify the parts of the opposing statement that provide evidence to affirm or refute.

◆ **unleashes** – removes restraints or sets free

Alternatives:

Is there any other way to look at this issue? Can you qualify the original issue statement in some way? Perhaps a combination of structure and freedom is the best way to educate our citizens.

New viewpoint:

A formal structure combined with the choice to select areas of study is the most effective way to set our minds and spirits free.

Identify the parts of the new statement that provide evidence to affirm or refute.

◆ **combination** – Does a combination dilute the effectiveness of one or both of the components?

◆ **choice** – At what level of formal education are students competent to choose their course of study?

Now you must decide which point of view to address in your essay. Completing the prewriting activities has given you several choices and ideas for defending any of those choices. Even the viewpoints that are opposite of yours will have points that you can use in writing your response. As you review your notes, decide which of your ideas offer the strongest support for your position; you do not have to use all of them. Keep in mind that others may disagree with your position, so address their concerns in your response. Before you decide, carefully consider the following checklist. You will have addressed several of them in the exercises you have completed above.

◆ I have identified the central issue.

◆ I understand the instructions.

◆ I have decided that I agree/disagree/partially agree with the issue and why.

◆ I have identified the assumptions in the claim and determined whether or not they are reasonable.

◆ If necessary, I can explain how I interpret any or all of the concepts and terms used in the claim.

◆ I have identified my reasons for the position I have taken.

◆ I have compelling examples to support my position.

The next step should be listing the main reasons and support for your position. You may use any of the above prewriting activities as you prepare evidence for supporting your point of view. Remember that the GRE readers scoring your response are not looking for a "right" answer. The readers are evaluating your ability to address the specific instructions and articulate and develop an argument to support your understanding and evaluation of the issue.

Position:

Formal education is the most effective means for introducing students to a wide variety of subjects in order for them to discover what sets their minds and spirits free.

Examples and reasons:

a) variety – formal education in America is comprised of content from various disciplines. Students will be exposed to grammar, writing, literature, science, math, foreign language, art, music

b) discover – exposure to a variety of disciplines provides opportunities to be inspired by a topic that students might never have found on their own

c) most effective – most is a qualifier – not saying it's the only means, just the best – as other types of education may work better for some students

d) introducing – from primary grades through the first two years of most colleges, students are introduced to a variety of subjects – no major focus is determined, generally, until the end of the second year in college

Your notes do not have to be exhaustive. As you begin to write your essay, your brain will generate new ideas. Make certain that you keep the directions in mind as you develop your ideas. Use as many or as few paragraphs as you consider appropriate for your argument, but create a new paragraph when you move on to a new idea or example of support for your position. The GRE readers are not looking for a specific number of ideas or paragraphs. Instead, they are reading to determine the level of understanding of the topic and the complexity with which you respond.

In this task, you are asked to discuss the extent to which you agree or disagree with the statement. You may completely agree or disagree with the statement, or you may agree under certain conditions. You are also instructed to explain your reasoning and consider ways in which the statement might or might not hold true and explain how these considerations shape your position.

You may use any organizational strategy or form of reasoning to present your position as clearly and succinctly as possible. You may recall writing strategies that you learned in high school or a writing–intensive course you took in college, but it is not necessary to employ any of those strategies. It is important that your ideas follow a logical progression and display strong critical thinking.

 ## Sample Essay

In the book of Genesis in the bible, the story of creation reveals that God saw the world as void and having no form, so he took it upon Himself to give it form. He divided the land from the sea, populated his new world with animals and plants of every kind, separated the night from the day, and, finally, created man. Even God recognized the need for form. Without form there is void. Formal education is, at its most basic level, education with some structure applied to it. Without structure in education, there is a void.

Some might argue that formal education is too restrictive; the prescribed curriculum in most schools inhibits creativity and free thinking; and pedagogy confines the imaginations of students. Some find a syllabus to be onerous, an anthology to be limiting, and a bell schedule to be jarring. Within this structured environment, however, is the opportunity to sample courses in Shakespeare, poetry, philosophy, geography, American history, sociology, French, Spanish, biology, physics, algebra, statistics, art, music, and physical education. This smorgasbord of academic offerings will surely contain something to tempt the palate of even the fussiest scholar.

Others may point to the structure or formality that exists outside of the world of education as a justification to similarly define academia. Upon leaving one's education behind, the former student will need to follow the structure imposed upon the world of work. The discipline to do so will have been developed during the years of formal education.

Left to his own devices, a child can indulge his whims by studying whatever interests him. Rarely does a child have the discipline to sustain that interest. He will move on to the next fleeting attraction. A variety of factors may influence his exposure to the world: his parents' educational level, family income, geographical location, and availability of arts and cultural performances. Through a formal education, these differences need not matter. Every child will get the same opportunities to read absorbing books, construct and perform scientific experiments, attend school assemblies, and connect to the Internet. Without public education, there will likely be a void in this child's experience of the world.

Issue Task 6

The best way to teach is to praise positive actions and ignore negative ones.

Write a response in which you discuss the extent to which you agree or disagree with the statement and explain your reasoning for the position you take. In developing and supporting your position, you should consider ways in which the statement might or might not hold true and explain how these considerations shape your position.

 Strategies

Restate the Issue:

This statement tells what one should do. What shouldn't one do?

In other words:

The best way to teach is not to ignore positive actions or draw attention to negative ones.

Determine what question is being answered by the statement.

What is the best approach to teaching?

The question may help you develop alternative points of view. The original statement is only one of several answers to the question.

Now, think about the parts of the original statement that provide evidence that you can affirm or refute.

- ◆ **best** – This is the superlative form of good. Nothing can surpass it.

- ◆ **praise** – Does the praise have to be verbal? It might be a gold star on a chart or a special privilege.

- ◆ **positive actions** – Positive may be subjective and unclear in the mind of the child. Do the actions have to be physical, or can they include doing well on a test or handing homework in when it is due? It might be volunteering to help another student or cleaning the blackboard.

- ◆ **ignore** – To ignore something is to pretend it doesn't exist.

◆ **negative [actions]** – What is negative depends on the teacher's values. Again, are these overt behavioral issues or do they include failing a test or not turning in work?

Opposing viewpoint:

The best way to teach is to expect positive actions and correct negative ones.

Now think about the parts of the opposing statement that provide evidence that you can affirm or refute.

◆ **expect** – It is sometimes true that, if you expect children to be well behaved, they will be. The opposite can be true as well; expect bad behavior and you will probably get it.

◆ **correct** – Some children have not been taught or modeled good behavior. They need to have their bad actions corrected. This does not necessarily imply punishment.

Alternatives:

Is there another way to look at this issue? Can the original statement be qualified in some way?

New viewpoint:

Modeling good behavior is the best way to obtain it from others.

Identify the parts of the alternative statement that can provide evidence for you to refute or affirm.

◆ **modeling** –This implies setting an example. If a teacher is polite, her students are likely to imitate that behavior. If she is inconsistent, children will be confused and not know how to behave.

 ## Sample Essay

Every child's first school is his home, and his parents are his first teachers. Whether a child is raised by one or both parents, step parents, grandparents, or foster parents, the child observes and, in most cases, imitates the behaviors of those adults. This imitation is so important that parents often say to their children, "Do as I say, not what I do" when they fear that they may be setting a bad example. A young child's undeveloped brain cannot rely on observation alone to understand how to behave; he or she will make mistakes and act inappropriately from time to time. Occasionally, children need to be corrected.

Children will move on to more formal education around the age of five. Teachers will act in loco parentis, in the place of their parents. Some children enter school with an innate understanding of how to act in this new environment; others will struggle. Teachers have the best interests of their young charges in mind at all times but understand that some children need more direction than others. Ignoring negative actions can actually be dangerous. Running around a classroom, a child can trip and fall or run into a desk, a chair, or another student. Should the teacher be expected to wait until the child tires of running and praise him or her for stopping?

These children will eventually enter the halls of high school, where the potential for danger increases tremendously. Chemistry class, alone, has equipment and materials that have the potential to seriously injure those who handle them incorrectly. The teacher who ignores dangerous actions performed by students in this situation should probably be fired. Additionally, there are classes where children may use stoves, irons, pneumatic wrenches, or table saws. For their safety, students must be told when they are using those tools improperly.

Even in classes that are seemingly danger free, accidents can happen. In an otherwise tame English class, students throw pens across the room. These projectiles can end up in another student's eye. Let's not overlook the compasses that students use in math class. Any number of injuries can result from the sharp tip on that instrument.

Teaching continues after children have finished their education. Employers are not likely to overlook negative actions in the workplace. The bottom line depends on everyone performing his or her job correctly. Children whose negative actions have been ignored throughout their lives will be in for a rude awakening after they leave the safe haven of home and school. Ignoring negative actions may, in the end, be setting children up for future failure.

Issue Task 7

7

Teachers' salaries should be based on their students' academic performance.

Write a response in which you discuss the extent to which you agree or disagree with the claim. In developing and supporting your position, be sure to address the most compelling reasons and/or examples that could be used to challenge your position.

 Strategies

Assumptions:

What are the assumptions in the claim? These are statements that you can either affirm or refute.

Assumption 1: Teachers will become better teachers if their salaries are based on student performance.

Assumption 2: Student performance will improve if teacher salaries are based on that performance.

Assumption 3: Teachers will feel more valued if they are rewarded for being successful.

Assumption 4: Student academic performance – good or bad- depends on teacher pay.

Opposing viewpoint:

Teachers' salaries should not depend on a student's academic performance.

What are the assumptions in the opposing claim?

Assumption 1: Teachers' salaries should be determined in the way they have been previously.

Assumption 2: Student performance does not depend on teacher pay.

Assumption 3: Teacher pay should be determined by some criteria other than student performance.

Alternative claim:

Student academic performance should be one of several criteria used to determine a teacher's salary.

Support for alternative claim:

Example: Teachers may lower their standards to allow students to earn better grades. It should not be the only criterion for determining salaries

Example: Incentives are used in the business world to encourage increased productivity.

Example: Treating student academic performance as a commodity does not take into consideration their individual natures.

 # Sample Essay

Teacher salaries traditionally depend on a step or seniority system. First-year teachers all make the same salary, as do second-year teachers, and so on. The only way to increase one's salary on any step of the pay scale is to get an advanced degree. Some teachers supplement their salaries by serving as coaches or advisers to school clubs and organizations. All school systems have an evaluation system which does not have an impact on the amount of money an individual teacher makes. Although this system protects teachers from becoming victims of a popularity contest, it also enables incompetent teachers to continue to adversely affect the quality of education delivered to students.

Reform is long overdue, and the criteria for evaluating a teacher's worth must be carefully considered and include more than one critical element. Local school systems, states, and countries are continuously compared with each other based on standardized test scores and other measures of student achievement. Teachers and administrators feel pressured to raise test scores. The unfortunate result can be the cheating scandal that occurred in Georgia earlier this year, when teachers and principals in some districts changed student answers on a standardized test. The temptation to take this action could increase if teacher pay were based on student achievement.

In addition to standardized test scores, student grades are an indication of student achievement. Most school systems still use numerical averages and letter grades to demonstrate student success. These grades place students on honor rolls that are generally published in local newspapers which parents can point to with pride, and they determine class standing as a piece of information requested on college applications. If higher grades are a sign of teacher effectiveness and affect teacher pay, teachers may be tempted to lower their standards to make it easier for their students to earn those higher grades. Student achievement can be used to determine teacher effectiveness and, perhaps, pay, but there first needs to be a better means of measuring and reporting student success.

In the world of business, employees are often rewarded monetarily for their success in meeting or exceeding goals. In most of those cases, workers are producing or selling items that are easily made identical. Quality control is a matter of ensuring that each item will perform in the way it was designed to. This is a process impossible to replicate when the product is a human being. Teachers can present the same lessons in the same way year after year and have different results in terms of student success every year. The characteristics of each year's cohort are different. Therefore, achievement will be different.

Teachers do need to be held accountable for student learning. They also need to be evaluated in a manner that fosters and encourages professional growth. When teachers are given a clear direction in which to proceed, they will take their students along. Educational leaders would serve their schools, their states, and their countries well if they ceased comparing their achievements with others. Teacher pay cannot be based on achievement that is loosely defined or compared to test scores in other parts of the state, country, or world.

Issue Task 8

College students should base their choice of a field of study on the availability of jobs in that field.

Write a response in which you discuss the extent to which you agree or disagree with the claim. In developing and supporting your position, be sure to address the most compelling reasons and/or examples that could be used to challenge your position.

Strategies

Assumptions:

What are the assumptions in the claim?

Assumption 1: Some courses of study are more valuable than others.

Assumption 2: Students should not pursue what they love if it does not lead to ready employment.

Assumption 3: Some careers are more highly valued than others.

Assumption 4: These careers will always be in high demand.

Opposing viewpoint:

College students should not base their choice of field on the availability of jobs in that field.

What are the assumptions in this claim?

Assumption 1: College students should study what they love.

Assumption 2: College students should base their choice of a field of study on their strengths.

Assumption 3: All jobs are valuable.

Is there another way of looking at the claim? What reason would someone have for making this claim?

Reason 1: Students will need immediate employment to pay off accumulated college debt.

Reason 2: Jobs are more plentiful and readily available in some fields.

Alternative claim

College students must be encouraged to choose a field of study that interests them and addresses their personal and academic strengths.

Support for alternative claim:

8

Example: Nurses and nurse practitioners are in great demand today. If a student has great difficulty with the sciences, he or she will find it virtually impossible to complete a nursing program successfully. What happens to the job market if colleges and universities produce a surplus of nurses?

 ## Sample Essay

The ranks of the unemployed are filled with people of all ages at all levels of education who believe that, if you work hard, you will be successful. They never could have envisioned the day when their skills would become obsolete or their jobs would be sent to another country where the overhead is lower. They may very well have listened to the advice presented in the original claim when they were going off to college. With visions of dollar signs filling their heads, they enrolled in programs that guaranteed employment post-graduation. They were simply being practical. Therefore, students should not pick their undergraduate majors based on the careers available at that moment because there is no guarantee that those careers will still be available once they graduate.

One can imagine parents today telling their children to follow the words of the claim. In the second decade of the twenty-first century, practicality seems more important than ever. The cost of college discourages students from always following their dreams. Left with college debt that may range from $20,000 to more than $100,000, students must consider how they will repay the loans. The unemployment rate, as well, drives students into careers that promise an immediate and steady paycheck. Dreams and passions are put on hold.

All prospective college students should know that the demand for employees in specific careers ebbs and wanes. For the past few years, officials have been predicting shortage of teachers as many current teachers will reach retirement age shortly. High-school graduates took this as a call to major in education in college, believing that their skills would be in high demand after graduation. Then the recession hit, and states and local school systems had to make budget cuts, accomplished, in part, by eliminating teaching positions. In Texas, alone, the state eliminated 49,000 teaching positions. Not only are those positions unavailable to new college graduates, the teachers who once filled them are now looking for work. Because baby boomers are nearing old age, jobs in the medical field are plentiful. The classifieds are filled daily with ads for nurses, nurse practitioners, and pharmacists. If new college students focus on those careers in great numbers, they will soon create a glut of medical professionals, and many of them will not find work in their fields.

No matter what students choose to study, they should be made aware that they may have to change careers at some point in their lives. They might as well choose a career they are passionate about. The most important skill they might learn in college is how to learn. In today's changing job market, employees must be prepared to update their skill sets. Advancing technology, by itself, has changed the way that traditional jobs are done today. If college students choose a career with the skills and environment that suit them, they will be good at what they do. Eventually, if not immediately, they will be rewarded financially. Do what you love, and the money will follow. It is said that if you choose a job you love, you will never work a day in your life. The true reward of a career choice may reside in the feeling of satisfaction at the end of the day and leaving work with eagerness to return the next day.

8

Issue Task 9

Universities should require every student to take a variety of courses outside the student's field of study.

Write a response in which you discuss the extent to which you agree or disagree with the recommendation and explain your reasoning for the position you take. In developing and supporting your position, describe specific circumstances in which adopting the recommendation would or would not be advantageous and explain how these examples shape your position.

9

 Strategies

Restate the Position:

You may create a version that negates the original in more than one way.

In other words:

Universities should not allow students to take only courses in their fields of study.

You could also determine the question that is being answered by the recommendation.

What kinds of courses should colleges require their students to take?

Or: *How can universities ensure that they are turning out well educated graduates?*

Creating a question can help you think about the way that you would answer it. Consider what you would deem to be the composition of a good college education.

Now think about the parts of the original recommendation that provide evidence that you can affirm or refute.

- ◆ **require** – This allows for no alternative. One must fulfill a requirement. How many and what types of courses should universities require? Should they require any courses?

- ◆ **every** – Again, there is no option.

- ◆ **variety** – Variety implies more than one type. How many types of courses should universities require outside a student's field of study?

◆ **outside** – How far outside? If one is studying literature, should he or she be required to take chemistry?

Opposing viewpoint:

Universities should not require every student to take a variety of courses outside the student's field of study.

Identify the parts of the opposing statement that provide evidence to affirm or refute. In this case, the only new word is not, and it simply serves to negate the original statement.

Alternatives:

Is there any other way to look at this statement? Should colleges require students to take a variety of courses before they declare a major? Should requirements exist only within a course of study?

New viewpoint:

Colleges and universities should require enough courses to complete a field of study to ensure that a student is sufficiently educated in that field.

Identify the parts of the opposing statement that provide evidence to affirm or refute.

◆ **enough** – What is enough? Are there options for gaining a degree in a field of study?

◆ **ensure** – This means to make certain. Is it a college's responsibility to make sure that a student takes the courses he or she will need to satisfy a degree in a field of study?

◆ **sufficiently** – This is similar to the word, enough. What does it mean to be sufficiently educated? Should it be enough to gain employment in the field?

Position:

Universities should require every student to take a variety of courses outside the student's field of study.

Examples and reasons:

a) At the beginning of a student's college career, he may not know the field in which to major. The student may discover an area of interest in the variety of courses required during the first two years of college.

b) A student may discover an avocation while taking a variety of courses. A required course in art history may lead to a lifelong passion for collecting fine art or visiting museums around the world.

c) The workplace is always changing. One may find himself out of work at some point, and a required course outside of his field may lead him to a new career.

 ## Sample Essay

Universities are large educational institutions that offer courses in a wide variety of disciplines. At some point, generally by the end of the second year, students are required to declare a major. In some cases, students begin classes in a program of study from the minute they enter the university. Some college freshmen seem to have been called to a particular profession at an early age, and their determination to become a teacher, doctor, or engineer has never wavered. On the other hand, most freshmen are waiting for the fires of inspiration to be lit. The surest way to accomplish this is to take a variety of courses in a range of disciplines. It is a fact that, in the United States, only 1 in 4 college students graduates in four years. The greatest number finishes after five years of college, usually because they changed their majors along the way. It is unrealistic to expect today's seventeen or eighteen–year–olds, whose life expectancies are around eighty five years, to decide what they want to do for the rest of their lives. Gone are the days when an individual would obtain a job in a company and remain there for his or her entire working life. Surveys reveal that the average working person today changes careers every ten years. What career selection he or she makes may derive from a course taken in college. Limiting what courses a student takes in college may limit his or her career choices later in life

On the other hand, the job market today is a minefield. If some college student missteps, his or her chances for a career may blow up. Some students may be frustrated by a requirement to take courses outside their fields of study. Their focus on taking as many courses as possible in the field they wish to pursue may be impressive in the job application process. College students may feel that their exposure to a variety of courses in high school is sufficient, so repeating them in college is redundant.

At a traditional university, a student will enroll in five courses per semester; that's a total of forty classes in four years. Narrowing one's choices could have disadvantages. It is realistic to assume that a student could burn out from the lack of variety. The courses may be taught by professors who fail to expire, and those professors may teach all of the courses in the field. After a couple of years, the student may decide that he or she made a mistake in choosing it and now has no option but to continue to the bitter end or start from scratch.

Universities should require students to take a variety of courses in several disciplines. Courses that teach the nuts and bolts in any field generally are offered to college juniors and seniors in any case. At the end of the college career, a student will have the skills and knowledge he or she needs to pursue a career beyond college, as well as exposure to areas of knowledge that might spark a lifelong interest in some hobby or other avocation.

Issue Task 10

In order to become well-rounded individuals, all college students should be required to take courses in which they read poetry, novels, mythology, and other types of imaginative literature.

Write a response in which you discuss the extent to which you agree or disagree with the recommendation and explain your reasoning for the position you take. In developing and supporting your position, describe specific circumstances in which adopting the recommendation would or would not be advantageous and explain how these examples shape your position.

 ## Strategies

Restate the Issue:

The original statement tells what students should do. Rephrase it by telling what students should not do without changing the meaning of the original statement.

In other words:

In order to become well-rounded individuals, all college students should not finish college without first taking courses in which they read poetry, novels, mythology, and other types of imaginative literature.

Or: *College students will fail to become well-rounded individuals if they are not required to take courses in which they read poetry, novels, mythology, and other types of imaginative literature.*

You could determine what question is being answered by the original issue statement.

What required courses should all college students take in order to become well-rounded individuals?

Thinking about your answer to the question can help you as you develop your response to the original statement.

Now think about the parts of the statement that provide evidence that you can affirm or refute.

◆ **well-rounded** – This is both subjective and vague. What does it mean to be well-rounded, and who decides if one is well-rounded? Should the goal of college be to create well-rounded individuals?

◆ **all students** – This leaves no room for doubt and no exceptions. The statement assumes that these courses have the power to make all students well-rounded.

◆ **required** – A requirement is a need. This is like saying that all college students need these courses to become well-rounded.

◆ **other types of imaginative literature** – Isn't most literature imaginative?

Opposing viewpoint:

In order to become well-rounded individuals, all college students should be required to take a variety of courses in several disciplines.

Identify the parts of the opposing statement that provide evidence that you can refute or affirm.

◆ **variety of courses** – Well-rounded individuals may be those that have exposed themselves to a variety of courses in several disciplines.

Alternatives:

Is there any other way of looking at this issue? Can you qualify the original statement in some way? Why wouldn't taking a variety of courses in the social sciences make one a well-rounded individual?

New viewpoint:

In order to become well-rounded individuals, college students shouldn't restrict their selection of academic classes to those within one discipline.

Identify the parts of the new statement that provide evidence to affirm or refute.

◆ **restrict** – This means to limit oneself. A restriction is something one cannot do.

◆ **selection** – Choice and selection are synonymous.

◆ **within one discipline** – This is a narrow perspective. Narrow is contradictory to well-rounded.

Position:

It should not be the goal of colleges and universities to turn out well-rounded individuals.

Support:

- ◆ **cost** – Education is too costly today for students to focus on courses that have no practical value.

- ◆ **interest** – By the time a student is in college, he or she should be allowed to choose courses that they have an interest in.

 # Sample Essay

It is impossible to identify well-rounded individuals on the street, in the workplace, or at the gym. It is unlikely that anyone is choosing his or her friends based on their being well-rounded. It is probably impossible to define well-rounded; everyone would have a point of view. It is true that in the early days of higher education, one aimed to become a "man of letters", knowledgeable to some degree in a variety of subjects. That luxury is no longer desirable or practical. University students are entering a different world.

I like to think of myself as well-rounded. I am interested in a variety of topics, and I participate in a variety of activities. I carry on conversations easily with my friends and family as well as people I meet in the grocery store or at an airport. My seatmates on trains and planes find me engaging. I answer most of the questions on Jeopardy! correctly, and I can complete the New York Times crossword puzzle. I like and can cook food from a variety of cuisines. I can order correctly from a menu written in French. I like HGTV, the Food Network, and action movies. My friends think I'm funny, and I cry over sappy commercials on TV. None of my self-perceived well-roundedness is a result of courses that I either did or did not take in college.

These interests can also stem from outside influences. My mother taught me to knit and sew. I got my love of gardening from my father. I taught myself to read. My sister taught me how to see different perspectives of an issue. I learned to swim during lessons on cold mornings at the local pool. I learned to play the piano from an older lady who tapped out the measures with a plastic knitting needle on the top of the piano. I learned to drive from a kind and patient man who did not use deodorant and wouldn't let his students roll down the car windows in the heat of the summer. My friends taught me about friendship. I obtained all of these skills before I went to college.

So, what did college teach me? College taught me how to live in close quarters with hundreds of other girls from different states and backgrounds. College taught me to understand football, to party on the weekends, and how to join the best sorority on campus. College taught me to sign up for classes that ended by 1:00 pm and met on Mondays, Wednesdays, and Fridays, so I'd have two full days off from classes. College eventually taught me how to manage my time. It taught me the classes I would need to get a degree in my major.

High school seniors plan to enter colleges and universities with the goal of getting a job after graduation, and that is what college should do. When today's high-school seniors graduate from college, they will have enormous debt. While in college, they must focus on courses that serve practical purposes. They will need immediate employment in order to meet their financial obligations. They will become well-rounded by living their lives after college, not by taking a variety of courses in the humanities.

Issue Task 11

Colleges and universities should require their students to spend at least one semester studying in a foreign country.

Write a response in which you discuss the extent to which you agree or disagree with the recommendation and explain your reasoning for the position you take. In developing and supporting your position, describe specific circumstances in which adopting the recommendation would or would not be advantageous and explain how these examples shape your position.

11

Strategies

Restate the Recommendation:

Restate the recommendation by telling what students should not do while retaining the original meaning.In other words:

In other words:

Students should not complete college without being required to spend at least one semester studying in a foreign country.

You could also determine what question is being answered by the recommendation.

What should colleges recommend that all of their students do before completing their education?

Or: *Should colleges recommend that all of their students spend at least one semester studying in a foreign country?*

Creating a question will allow you to think about the way you would answer it and why you would answer it in that way.

Now identify the parts of the recommendation that provide evidence that you can affirm or refute.

- ◆ **require** – This word leaves no room for choice. By the time students are in college, they should be able to make some choices about where they study.

- ◆ **all** – Again, there is no room for compromise. Will all college students benefit from studying abroad? Some fields of study may be enriched by a semester abroad.

Opposing viewpoint:

Colleges and universities should not require all of their students to spend at least one semester studying in a foreign country.

Now identify the parts of the recommendation that provide evidence that you can affirm or refute.

◆ **require** – As in the original recommendation, this word leaves no room for equivocation. In this case, it is followed by the word not, so the requirement is negated.

◆ **all** – This word allows no exceptions. When a statement includes not before all, one may interpret it to mean some. Should some students be required to study abroad?

Alternatives:

Is there another way to look at this issue? Many colleges and universities do have required classes for students seeking degrees in particular majors. Should candidates in some majors be required to study abroad? Would it be a financial hardship for some? Should study abroad simply be an available option for college students? Many colleges and universities make study abroad available for the third year.

New viewpoint:

Colleges and universities should make study in a foreign country available to all of its students.

Examples and Reasons:

a) the global economy – A country's economy relies on those of countries around the world. Students in business or economy could benefit from studying those aspects of a foreign country in that country itself.

b) foreign language students – These students would most obviously benefit from studying the language immersed in the culture of the country and living with native speakers of the language.

c) requiring a semester abroad could be a financial hardship for students. Many students have to work their way through college. The likelihood of being able to work in a foreign country is slim.

d) non-traditional students. Most colleges today have a number of non-traditional students. They are older and may be married with children. They may have jobs, and forcing them to study abroad is shortsighted.

e) online colleges

Sample Essay

The chance to earn college credit while studying abroad is an attractive option, and that is what it should remain. The world's shrinking size makes it seem practical to require students to spend at least one semester studying in a foreign country. Most of those students would develop a better understanding of the global perspective, but it simply isn't a practical option for many young people. Colleges and universities must look at the issue from several sides before adopting this requirement.

Students in some programs of study would benefit from study abroad, while for students in other programs, the requirement would be a burden. Those who are studying a foreign language are the most obvious beneficiaries of studying in another country. What better way to learn French, for example, than to immerse oneself in the culture of France. Rubbing shoulders on a daily basis with people whose native tongue is French is the best way to grasp the nuances of the language that are virtually impossible to impart in a classroom setting. Familiarity with the landscape, the food, and the arts of a country impart a depth of understanding that would be difficult to obtain in any other manner. Earning credit while strolling on the Champs Elysees or reading a textbook while lounging on the Rive Gauche is similar to earning a bonus at work. As idyllic as this seems, it is a hardship for some students, even those studying foreign languages. College is an enormous financial commitment, and many can't do it without holding down at least one job while attending school. For those who would have to forfeit a job for even a semester, this requirement would be onerous.

Another segment of the college population that might derive a benefit from studying in another country are those who plan to enter the world of finance or economics. No country stands alone in the global economy. Goods are produced and sold across borders every day. Gone are the days of a country producing all of the consumables for its citizens. The American stock and commodities markets fluctuate hourly based on what is happening in markets around the world. For students entering this arena, studying other markets first hand would be more enlightening than reading a textbook about it. These students, however, may get that opportunity after obtaining a job in a multinational organization and visit other countries on someone else's dime. In addition, such opportunities are limited, so some students would likely be placed with a company that has no relation to their preferred career path.

Colleges and universities must consider the non-traditional students on their campuses. No longer are campuses populated only by 18 to 22-year-olds. Women are entering college after raising their children; displaced adult workers are returning to learn new skills; and veterans are taking advantage of college tuition earned while serving their country. Should schools require these students, who have other responsibilities, to leave everything behind and spend a semester in a foreign country?

Finally, one must ask if the emerging online universities should embrace this requirement. Online students are enrolled for the convenience of being able to complete coursework from the comfort of their own homes. Requiring them to study abroad for a semester seems contradictory to the philosophies of these schools. Finishing the traditional course of study is enough of a challenge for most students without the additional burden of living and studying in a foreign country. Universities should, nonetheless, make available the option to spend at least a semester abroad, but this should not be a mandatory requirement.

Issue Task 12

A nation should require all of its students to study the same national curriculum until they enter college.

Write a response in which you discuss the extent to which you agree or disagree with the recommendation and explain your reasoning for the position you take. In developing and supporting your position, describe specific circumstances in which adopting the recommendation would or would not be advantageous and explain how these examples shape your position.

 Strategies

Restate the Position:

This statement says what the situation should be. How can you retain the meaning of the statement by telling what should not be? In other words:

In other words:

A nation should not allow its students to study a curriculum that is not a national curriculum.

You could also determine what question is being answered by the statement.

Should a nation require all of its students to study the same curriculum until they enter college?

Or: *How can a nation ensure that all of its students are ready for college?*

Or: *How can a nation ensure that all of its students develop the same skills?*

Now identify elements in the statement that can provide evidence for you to affirm or refute.

- ◆ **require -** A requirement is something one must do. There is no equivocation. Maybe a national curriculum should be an option. National decision makers could create a recommended curriculum.

- ◆ **curriculum -** A curriculum is a course of study. It is possible that all of a nation's students should know how to do the same things, but should all of them be required to study the same materials and take the same tests? Would this curriculum include physical education and the arts, or would it include only the core courses?

◆ **all -** This leaves no room for exceptions. What about students in special education programs, or students with physical disabilities?

◆ **until they enter college -** Does this mean that vocational courses should be eliminated from high school offerings? Should students, at some point, have an opportunity to explore courses that might **determine** what kind of post-secondary education they will seek?

◆ **national-** Should state and local school systems have some input regarding curriculum creation?

Opposing viewpoint:

A nation should allow states and local school systems to create curriculum based on national guidelines.

12 Identify parts of the opposing statement that provide evidence to affirm or refute.

◆ **states -** In the case of the United States, there would be 50 different plans for curriculum.

◆ **local -** Allowing local control would create even more variety in curricular plans.

◆ **guidelines -** National decision makers might create an outline for states and localities to use.

Alternatives:

Is there another way to look at this issue? Can you qualify the original recommendation in some way? How can you answer all or some of the questions that you generated earlier?New viewpoint:

New viewpoint:

A nation should require all of its students to study the same national curriculum until they enter high school.

Or: A nation should have a comprehensive list of skills and knowledge in which its students must show proficiency before graduating from high school.

Position:

A nation should develop a list of common skills and knowledge in which all graduating seniors in high school must demonstrate proficiency.

Examples and reasons:

a) learning styles - children of all ages are hard wired to learn in a variety of ways. They are visual, auditory, kinesthetic learners.

b) AP or Advanced Placement course - many high schools have AP classes in a variety of disciplines, and these courses have an outline around which teachers must develop curriculum. Even in those classes there is room for variation.

c) vocational programs- a national curriculum could have a negative effect on vocational programs offered in most regions in every state in the US. Do students interested in the trades need the same curriculum as students bound for four-year colleges?

d) expense - not all schools are prepared to adopt a national curriculum. If a curriculum prescribes materials as well as objectives, local school districts will face an onerous financial burden.

Sample Essay

A national curriculum would be ideal if every student in a country had the same body of knowledge and set of skills upon graduation from high school. However, this is only possible if every student were the same as every other student. Some may argue that a ready-to-use curriculum would save individual school districts and teachers the time it takes to develop curriculum of their own. Others may point out the expense of purchasing textbooks and other materials needed to follow a national curriculum. In the case of the United States, there is a continuous comparison between what American students achieve and what students in other industrial nations achieve. On the surface, the US does not compare favorably with many of those countries. A national curriculum may be the solution to that problem. However, each of the fifty states must be convinced to give up control over its own educational philosophy.

The logistics of creating a national curriculum in the United States is daunting. The US has the third largest population in the world, divided among fifty separately governed states. It was and continues to be a nation of immigrants. Those immigrants come from all over the world, bringing their languages and customs with them. Immigrants have a greater impact on some states than on others. Schools are challenged to educate children who can't even speak English. A national curriculum may be the straw that breaks the camel's back, educationally. Under ideal conditions, school districts would need considerable financial and technical support to adopt a national curriculum; added to other obstacles that already tax the abilities of some districts, a national curriculum could cause a mutiny.

A national curriculum would be likely to focus on the core areas of education: math, science, language arts, and social studies. One would be hard put to find someone who disagrees with the idea that all children of a country should have the same math skills, the same understanding of science, the same abilities to read and communicate effectively, and the same knowledge of history, geography, and government. However, many would also argue that there is great benefit in participating in the arts, knowing how to cook a meal or sew on a button, and being physically active. Others may hope their children learn the basics of a vocational trade such as carpentry, auto mechanics, or welding. The implementation of a national curriculum necessitates that some subjects fall to the wayside, preventing students from encountering fields that they may need, either to develop necessary career skills for the future or for their own personal interests. interests.

Two compromises come to mind. The first entails requiring a national curriculum through grade eight. From kindergarten through middle school, all teachers would adhere to a national curriculum. These are the grades in which students learn the fundamentals of reading, writing, math, and social studies. Every student would be well-prepared for high school, where teachers develop a curriculum that encourages students to further develop the skills they learned in the lower grades. The four years of high school would focus on the core areas but allow students the time to explore other areas of interest. The second compromise consists of a set of guidelines or standards that enumerate the skills and knowledge that every student must be able to demonstrate with proficiency before graduating from high school. Every teacher would know what his or her students must be able to do or understand and use instructional strategies and materials to make that possible.

A nation's desire to promote the educational wellbeing of its children is laudable and, perhaps, necessary. However, it does not necessitate the implementation of a national curriculum and doing so would be a disservice to its people. To foster creativity and individuality, the means to accomplish this should be left to the practitioners who also have the best interests of children at heart.

12

Issue Task 13

Claim: *When planning courses, educators should take into account the interests and suggestions of their students.*

Reason: *Students are more motivated to learn when they are interested in what they are studying.*

Write a response in which you discuss the extent to which you agree or disagree with the claim and the reason on which that claim is based.

 Strategies

Restate the Issue:

Combine the claim and reason into one statement using a subordinate clause. In other words:

In other words:

Because students are more motivated to learn when they are interested in what they are studying, educators should take into account the interests and suggestions of their students when planning courses.

What are the assumptions present in the claim and reason? These will provide evidence that you can either affirm or refute.

◆ Students are more motivated to learn material in which they are interested.

◆ Students will be more successful when studying material in which they are interested.

◆ Educators will be more effective when they teach material in which their students have some interest.

◆ Students will be less successful when forced to study material in which they have little or no interest.

◆ Educators will be less effective when teaching material in which their students have little or no interest.

◆ Student motivation is extrinsic.

Next, create a statement that expresses the opposing view, using language similar to that in the original issue.

Opposing viewpoint:

Claim - *When planning courses, educators should ignore the suggestions and interests of their students.*

Reason - *Students do not understand what they need to learn for success as adults.*

What are the assumptions present in the claim and reason? These will provide evidence that you can either affirm or refute.

- ◆ *Educators have a better understanding of what students should study.*

- ◆ *Student opinions and suggestions are not important.*

- ◆ *Students lack the maturity to choose what they need to study.*

Alternative viewpoint:

Claim - *In some cases, educators should consider the suggestions and interests of their students when they plan their courses.*

Reason - *Students may have special needs or learning styles.*

Examples:

a) **Core Courses in college** - students are required to take specified courses before selecting a major

b) **Exploration** - most students don't know what they want to study in college. Required courses in a variety of disciplines allow them to explore their options.

 Sample Essay

When I was considering my choice of colleges to attend and the course of study to pursue, I was overwhelmed. Many of my classmates even said they were going to postpone going to college because they didn't know what they wanted to do, and it would be a waste of money to attend in that case. One of my teachers finally asked, "How will you discover what you want to do if you don't go to college?" I realized that I would have the opportunity to broaden my horizons by taking classes in subjects that heretofore I had not been exposed to. The world of higher education would become my oyster, and I was eager to partake. I was eighteen years old and hardly experienced enough to advise college professors about their courses. It was hardly my place to demand that college professors consider my interests or ask for my suggestions for planning their courses.

Like any aspect of life, an education should be balanced. A child, lacking knowledge and a sophisticated palate, would choose to eat hot dogs or macaroni and cheese every day. Such a diet, over a long period of time, would leave the child without vital nutrients to ensure his optimum physical health. Eventually he must add fruits and vegetables to his daily regimen. His mother must eventually override his interests and suggestions and consider his well-being. Although the child may protest initially and leave his veggies on the plate, his hunger will eventually compel him to give them a try. As he grows, he may become involved with athletics. His desire to compete successfully may even lead him to research the best diet for his level of activity.

This same child will begin school around the age of five and decide that recess or coloring is his favorite daily activity. Should his teacher allow him to pursue his favorite activity all day every day, his first year of education will poorly prepare him for his second year. He may become proficient on the monkey bars and always color inside the lines, but he will not know his numbers or letters, leading to lack of success at the next grade level. In this case, his teacher must intervene, perhaps by making recess or coloring a reward for completing an academic activity. In the same way that veggies in his diet will improve his physical health, academic rigor in his classroom will improve his intellectual health. Working with numbers may lead him to discover a natural ability in math or learning his first words may inspire him to become a voracious reader or prolific writer.

While most of us need parents or teachers to help us balance our physical and intellectual diets, some are capable of making those choices independent of their older and wiser parents or counselors. One of my friends attended a private women's college with no core requirements. She could have taken four years of courses in just Italian, or just math, or just psychology if she so chose. In fact, she took courses in horseback riding and kayaking, which probably caused her parents to question their decision to let her attend this prestigious college. Eventually, my friend took a class, The Deaf Child, that met at a school for the deaf located just behind the campus. She uncovered an interest in speech and hearing science and, after two years at the college, she transferred to a large state university and earned an undergraduate degree in that field of study. She found her way by taking courses whose content had been proscribed by educators and developed a strong, healthy intellect.

It might be nice to have educators, employers and even parents take our interests and suggestions into account before making decisions that affect us. A number of problems arise from these considerations. In a classroom or workplace or family home, several disparate interests reside. Whose interests or suggestions are more worthy of consideration? Imagine the time lost by those in authority while attempting to accommodate everyone. Some students, employees, and children will be left as dissatisfied as if no one's interests had never been considered. A college course catalog provides opportunities for students to explore and develop new interests. Deciding upon which courses to offer should be left up to the professors who must use their areas of expertise to develop the content of those courses.

13

Issue Task 14

Educational institutions should actively encourage their students to choose fields of study that will prepare them for lucrative careers.

Write a response in which you discuss your views on the policy and explain your reasoning for the position you take. In developing and supporting your position, you should consider the possible consequences of implementing the policy and explain how these consequences shape your position.

 Strategies

Restate the Issue:

Restate the issue, perhaps by reversing the order of the sentence components.In other words:

In other words:

To prepare their students for lucrative careers, educational institutions should actively encourage their students

Determine what question is being answered by the statement. This will help you begin to think how you would answer it and whether or not you agree with the original statement.

Which fields of study should educational institutions actively encourage their students to choose?

Parts of the original statement that provide evidence that you can affirm or refute.

◆ **Educational institutions -** Does this include technical schools, education one may receive in the military, etc.?

◆ **actively encourage - i**mplies promoting through direct contact with students, advertising, etc.

Next, create a statement that expresses the opposing viewpoint, using language similar to that of the original statement."

Opposing statement:

Educational institutions should actively encourage their students to choose fields of study that will prepare them for careers that are in high demand.

Educational institutions should not actively encourage their students to choose fields of study that prepare them for only lucrative careers.

Parts of the opposing statement that provide evidence that you can affirm or refute

◆ **high demand** – more jobs available increases the likelihood of finding work

Is there any other way to look at this issue? Can you qualify the original statement in some way? Is it possible to partially agree with the statement?

Alternative viewpoint:

Overlooking less lucrative careers will create a lack of practitioners in other vital areas.

Parts of the alternative statement that provide evidence that you can affirm or refute.

◆ **create a lack** – there will not be people seeking jobs that are not lucrative

◆ **vital** – jobs that are necessary to provide safety

 ## Sample Essay

The job market is highly competitive. Many college graduates have failed to find work in their chosen careers, and many have even returned home to live with their parents. The demand for practitioners in some careers has risen while the demand for others has fallen. Presuming that students who study for jobs in lucrative careers will have more luck finding employment may be shortsighted. Considering the vagaries of today's workplace, students should pursue courses of study for careers they will find rewarding in ways other than just financially.

Literature is replete with tales that warn us of the dire consequences attached to the pursuit of money. Charles Dickens gave us the character, Ebenezer Scrooge, as a morality lesson to demonstrate how focusing on the acquisition of wealth leads to loneliness and bitterness. In Greek mythology, one finds King Midas who was able to turn everything he touched to gold. His downfall came when he touched his beloved daughter, also turning her to a lifeless statue made of gold. Readers of such tales are meant to infer that relationships are more important than any amount of money.

It has been said, "Do what you love, and the money will follow." Choosing a career one loves will make it easy to go to work each day. A small business owner who sells a product he loves will convey that affection to his customers. They will enjoy shopping with him and recommend his store to their friends and family. As his customer base expands, he will sell more products and make more money. In contrast, the shop owner who works only for the money may resent spending his days doing something he doesn't enjoy, and his attitude may be reflected in his treatment of customers. His pursuit of money alone may lead to the opposite result as his customers desert him for more pleasant experiences elsewhere.

Over time, demand for practitioners in various careers ebbs and wanes. At one time, teachers were in short supply, so high school graduates went to college to become teachers. In a short span of time, there was a surplus of newly-minted educators, many of whom could not find jobs in their chosen careers. The practice of law promises great financial rewards. More people have trained for that route to riches than there are positions to be filled, and many lawyers now occupy places in graduate schools to learn a new skill.

Adopting this policy not only leads to a glut of people trained for lucrative careers but leads to a shortage of people trained to fill lower-paying but, nonetheless, important positions. If people seek only lucrative jobs, institutions will lack custodians to clean and maintain their facilities. Small-town police and fire departments will lack sufficient personnel to ensure the safety of their communities.

Following a career path for any reason other than love of the work involved with it will certainly lead to dissatisfaction and unhappiness. The young woman who wants nothing more than to dance all day long will be happier working at union scale in a dance troupe than seeking a management position in a bank.

Just yesterday, Pope Francis repeated the biblical warning; the love of money is the root of all evil. Encouraging students to seek only money rather than intangible rewards leads to the downfall of individuals or large groups of people. The Ponzi scheme created by Bernie Madoff is a prime example. He convinced people to invest their life savings in his company which was nothing but a house of cards. When it collapsed, ordinary people lost everything; Madoff, himself, went to prison, and his son committed suicide.

In order to function, the world needs people to fill a wide variety of jobs. Not all are lucrative, but they ensure the safety of the world's citizens by protecting them from crime, disease, and disasters. These occupations produce rewards that cannot be purchased with any amount of money.

Issue Task 15

Claim: *Colleges and universities should specify all required courses and eliminate elective courses in order to provide clear guidance for students.*

Reason: *College students - like people in general - prefer to follow directions rather than make their own decisions.*

Write a response in which you discuss the extent to which you agree or disagree with the claim and the reason on which that claim is based.

 Strategies

Restate the Recommendation:

Combine the claim and the reason into one statement using a subordinate clause.

In other words:

Because college students prefer to follow directions rather than make their own decisions, colleges and universities should specify all required courses and eliminate elective courses in order to provide clear guidance for students.

What are the assumptions stated or implied in the claim and reason? These will provide evidence that you can refute or affirm in your argument.

◆ Elective courses are not necessary to a good education.

◆ People dislike making decisions.

◆ Providing guidance means making decisions for others

Opposing viewpoint:

Claim: *Colleges and universities should not specify all required courses and eliminate elective courses.*

Reason: *College students - like people in general-prefer to make their own choices rather than follow directions.*

Assumptions:

◆ College students are capable of choosing their own courses.

 Sample Essay

If people only and always followed directions, little new would ever be discovered. To presume that college students can succeed only when their courses are carefully proscribed diminishes the ability of young adults to make wise choices. Students may willingly accept some direction in their choice of courses but don't necessarily want to follow directions. Those who choose their own path may be more satisfied. Those who provide guidance usually make suggestions and allow those whom they are guiding to make their own choices.

Most high-school students, especially in small towns, have little choice in selecting courses. State departments of education and local administrators establish guidelines for graduation requirements which generally include a specific number of credits in English, social studies, science, and math. Electives are rare. Students are apt to relish the opportunity to take some elective courses in college. In doing so they may discover areas of interest in disciplines they didn't even know existed or discover strengths and talents they didn't know they had.

I have two sisters who exemplify the opposite extremes of choice. In the fall of each of our senior years in high school, we traveled for several days with our mother to visit colleges we were interested in attending. Despite being raised in the same house by the same parents, each of us had different interests and personalities, so each of our trips included a variety of colleges. My mother and my older sister embarked on their journey, schedule of visits and interviews in hand. They went to the campuses of large universities, business schools, and small private colleges. Each had something to recommend it until they visited a small school in western Massachusetts. My sister rejected it out-of-hand because it had too little structure. There were no required courses: students were free to enroll in any class they desired. She eventually selected an all-women's college that was fairly liberal but did have required core courses for the first two years. A few years later, my younger sister took the trip with Mom. Eventually, she, too, settled on an all-women's college, but one that had only one requirement, a single semester of a writing-intensive course. She explored a variety of courses and took some unorthodox electives. She discovered a discipline that she wanted to pursue and, after two years, transferred to a large state university in the Midwest. If all colleges set rigid course guidelines and eliminated electives, my older sister may have been just fine, but my younger sister would likely have felt stifled and may have quit college altogether.

Limiting choices stifles creativity. A college student majoring in art, for example, may want to focus on one medium, but the college has created required courses in each medium. The art student's lack of ability to focus on sculpture as his means of expression may frustrate him to the extent that he will pack his bags and leave. In contrast, the art student may want to dabble in each medium, but he is forced by the college to choose only one and must spend the years in college painting when he would have liked to explore sculpture or mixed media. This student, too, may leave the school. In these cases, the rigid structure of required courses may result in the college's losing population and tuition dollars

Humans want some guidance and structure in their lives. It is helpful to know when to show up for work and how long the workday will be. They like knowing what their responsibilities at work include and how to complete their tasks. However, they want to choose the type of employment and employer. Communist Russia forced people into specific occupations based on the country's need to accomplish certain tasks. There was virtually no unemployment. However, lack of choice led to less productivity, and communism ultimately failed. Forcing people to work at jobs they haven't chosen or college students to take courses they don't want can only lead to discontent and poor performance.

Issue Task 16

Educational institutions should dissuade students from pursuing fields of study in which they are unlikely to succeed.

Write a response in which you discuss the extent to which you agree or disagree with the statement and explain your reasoning for the position you take. In developing and supporting your position, you should consider ways in which the statement might or might not hold true and explain how these considerations shape your position.

 Strategies

Restate the Recommendation:

A good starting point is to break down the statement and identify the assumptions it makes. Look for ambiguous phrasing and consider all possible exceptions – they represent weak points that you can defend or attack depending upon your chosen position.

Statement breakdown:

◆ **Educational institutions** – Do they have the right/responsibility to make this judgment? Is this compulsory or optional for each institution? What level is the institution: middle school, high school, university?

◆ **Dissuade** – How forceful would the dissuasion be? What methods will be employed?

◆ **Fields of study** – General fields of study or specific programs? How broad do they consider the field?

◆ **Unlikely to succeed** – How do they measure success? How accurate are they when measuring success? How is success measured across universities?

Assumptions:

◆ Educational institutions have the right to dissuade students from following certain programs

◆ Educational institutions know better whether a student is likely to succeed

◆ Course enrolment should be judged on likelihood of success

◆ Students are not reliable self-evaluators

Pros and Cons:

Pros

👍 Schools would have higher graduation rates.

👍 People will be happier with and more confident in their choices.

👍 Experts can better evaluate what skills and talents are necessary for success in a specific field.

👍 Experts can identify problem areas and suggest professional support

Cons

👎 Schools already have guidance counselors, partially for this reason.

👎 Strong methods of dissuasion would be a breach of freedom for students.

👎 This dissuasion can lead to feelings of inadequacy.

👎 Assessments of the likelihood of success may be biased.

👎 There is no standardized measure of success – different universities will have different measures of success.

👎 Students with learning disorders would score lower than other applicants.

👎 There already are entrance exams, such as the SAT/ACT.

👎 How would success be determined – based on an interview? School records?

👎 Young students may not have yet developed their aptitudes at the time of this determination.

16

Examples:

a) Graduation rates and levels of interest in a topic

b) Studies about the accuracy of predicting success

c) Admission procedures

 Sample Essay

Education is a cornerstone of civilization. It is one of the most important investments a country can make in its people and its future; it is critical to reducing poverty and inequality. As John Dewey said, "Education is not preparation for life; education is life itself." Given this, it is important to ensure that students get the proper education so that their talents can flourish. However, having institutions decide which talents a student excels in based on arbitrary criteria of measuring success is a big restriction on their freedom of choice.

First and foremost, most educational institutions already have guidance counselors and admission policies in place to help students discover and decide on potential career paths. Their job is to ensure that students can apply to schools that put their talents to the best use, that they are happy with the choice they made, and that their choices reflect not only their abilities but also their personalities. If schools were to use abilities and prior performance as an indicator of success, it's important to note that people often have abilities that clash with their personalities. In this case, examining a person based solely on their abilities would not be an accurate indicator of success – they would be able to perform the required task, but they would hate it or be too nervous to do it to the extent that perhaps a lesser skilled but passionate person would. In this vein, work ethic should also be taken into consideration, as, for instance, many clever children feel unchallenged and slack off since they notice that they can get by with little effort. Meanwhile, some children have to work to maintain the same level of grades – they develop a strong work ethic that should be an indicator of success.

Furthermore, there is no standardized measure of success. Different schools will have different standards, so a student rejected for applied mathematics at one school can get enrolled at a different one. Some schools might consider previous academic achievements as accurate predictors of success, whereas others might consider interviews or additional testing. Assessments of success are subjective; and, as numerous studies have shown, not accurate indicators. The main reason why people are not able to accurately assess success is that they evaluate based on their ideas of how the world works and end up having prejudiced insights. In the example of interviews, psychologists have shown that people are highly influenced by physical appearances, nonverbal communication, and other factors such as social background and speech patterns. The issue with this type of assessment is that people with anxiety disorders, while otherwise competent, will score lower than less capable people that happen to project an air of confidence.

Evaluating potential for success is problematic not just with interviews but when it comes to school records as well. Some people can develop their abilities later in life. For instance, a student can discover a new passion for mathematics at the end of middle school, but based on his prior performance records, he could end up being dissuaded from attending a math–oriented profile in high school. This also begs the question of when this process of steering should start – from what age? Considering that education systems are geared towards providing more general education for the earlier stages of learning, such measures would at the very least have to be aimed at higher education.

Lastly, it is a question of whether or not educational institutions have the right to interfere to such an extent in a student's choice. This is a decision that is best left to the students themselves. Schools should offer advice but not limit a student's options, given that they cannot always have the whole picture or make accurate assessments about a person's likelihood of success. Thomas Edison was judged as 'addle minded' and had to drop out of school because his teachers could not accurately assess his potential. Some of the world's greatest inventors and artists have been wrongly assessed by their teachers because their yardstick for measuring success did not apply to them.

16

Issue Task 17

Competition for high grades seriously limits the quality of learning at all levels of education.

Write a response in which you discuss the extent to which you agree or disagree with the statement and explain your reasoning for the position you take. In developing and supporting your position, you should consider ways in which the statement might or might not hold true and explain how these considerations shape your position.

 Strategies:

Begin by restating the issue. The original issue statement tells what competition for high grades does to the quality of education. Try changing the order of the statement.

17

In other words:

The quality of learning at all levels is seriously limited by the competition for high grades.

Determine what question is being answered by the original issue statement.

What effect does the competition for high grades have on the quality of learning at all levels?

The question should help develop alternative points of view. The original issue statement is only one of several possible answers to the question.

Now think about the parts of the original issue statement that provide evidence that you can affirm or refute.

◆ **competition** - Competition exists in other areas of school life. Competition exists in areas of life outside of school.

◆ **seriously limits** - Could the effect be somewhat limiting?

◆ **quality of learning** - Is competition for grades the greatest influence on the quality of learning? What about instructional methods? Curriculum materials?

Next, create a statement that expresses the opposing viewpoint, using language similar to that of the original issue statement.

Opposing viewpoint:

Competition for high grades enhances the quality of learning at all levels.

Or: *Competition for high grades has no effect on the quality of learning at any level.*

Identify the parts of the opposing statement that provide evidence to refute or affirm.

◆ **enhances -** improves or adds to the quality

◆ **no effect -** competition may be a non-factor in the quality of learning – it is neutral

Now you must decide which point of view to address in your essay. Completing the prewriting activities has given you several choices and ideas for defending any of those choices. Even viewpoints opposite of yours will have points that you can use in writing your response. As you review your notes, decide which of your ideas offer the strongest support for your position; you do not have to use all of them. Keep in mind that others may disagree with your position, so address their concerns in your response. Before you decide, carefully consider the following checklist. You will have addressed several of them in the exercises you have completed above.

◆ I have identified the central issue.

◆ I understand the instructions.

◆ I have decided that I agree/disagree/partially agree with the issue and why.

◆ I have identified the assumptions in the claim and determined whether or not they are reasonable.

◆ If necessary, I can explain how I interpret any or all of the concepts and terms used in the claim.

◆ I have identified my reasons for the position I have taken.

◆ I have compelling examples to support my position.

The next step should be listing the main reasons and support for your position. You may use any of the above prewriting activities as you prepare evidence for supporting your point of view. Remember that the GRE readers scoring your response are not looking for a "right" answer. The readers are evaluating your ability to address the specific instructions and articulate and develop an argument to support your understanding and evaluation of the issue.

Position:

Competition for high grades enhances the quality of learning at all levels.

Your notes do not have to be exhaustive. As you begin to write your essay, your brain will generate new ideas. Make certain that you keep the directions in mind as you develop your ideas. Use as many or as few paragraphs as you consider appropriate for your argument, but create a new paragraph when you move on to a new idea or example of support for your position. The GRE readers are not looking for a specific number of ideas or paragraphs. Instead, they are reading to determine the level of understanding of the topic and the complexity with which you respond.

In this task, you are asked to discuss *the extent* to which you agree or disagree with the statement. You may completely agree or disagree with the statement, or you may agree under certain conditions. You are also instructed to explain your reasoning and consider ways in which the statement might or might not hold true and explain how these considerations shape your position.

You may use any organizational strategy or form of reasoning to present your position as clearly and succinctly as possible. You may recall writing strategies you learned in high school or a writing-intensive course that you took in college, but it is not necessary to employ any of those strategies. It is important that your ideas follow a logical progression and display strong critical thinking.

Sample Essay

17

That competition for high grades exists is not debatable. As colleges become more selective and the cost of higher education soars, students are compelled to achieve at the highest level to gain entry to the best schools and to receive scholarships to offset the cost of those schools. In schools where grades are weighted, students also take honors or

Advanced Placement courses to elevate their GPAs. Whether or not this competition diminishes learning is debatable. Consider the benefits of competition in the private sector. Before competition existed, monopolies dominated the business world in America. Moguls like John D. Rockefeller and Andrew Carnegie cut prices on their products and forced their competitors out of business. With no alternatives, the buying public was forced to pay whatever prices those titans of commerce chose to charge them. To relieve the financial burden that the citizens of the country had to bear, antitrust laws were enacted. As a result, goods and services became available at fair prices that enabled everyone to live in some degree of comfort. Today, the American consumer can elect to buy discount goods at Walmart and other big-box retail outlets or opt to purchase luxury goods at designer boutiques like Coach or Louis Vuitton. Competition keeps businesses on their toes as they strive to produce goods of a quality and price that their customers demand. Competition is good for the consumer as they are presented with a wide array of goods and services from which to choose.

Now consider how learning benefits from the competition for grades. Before it became virtually mandatory for every American child to attend some post-high-school educational institution, many students were content to learn the minimum required to pass a course. After all, they were entering the world of work after high school, and their grades in algebra or chemistry wouldn't matter a bit to their employers. Teachers, recognizing this, taught the minimum required to satisfy that demographic. The world has changed, and no longer is it possible to obtain employment in most places without additional training or education beyond high school. Teachers have been charged with the responsibility to prepare their students for this eventuality. Students must do more in high school to get more out of life. In addition, many careers now require job seekers to have advanced degrees, extending the competition for grades into college and beyond.

The final product of competition for grades must be increased learning. When students are working harder to earn better grades, teachers are working harder to meet the demand. They are designing more advanced curriculum units and applying standards more rigorously. Teachers are creating a product that consumers – in this case, colleges and employers – are demanding. Colleges and businesses will have more choices when they shop for students and employees.

17

This page is intentionally left blank

Chapter 5
Government & Politics

Issue Task 18

Scandals are useful because they focus our attention on problems in ways that no speaker or reformer ever could.

Write a response in which you discuss the extent to which you agree or disagree with the claim. In developing and supporting your position, be sure to address the most compelling reasons and/or examples that could be used to challenge your position.

 Strategies:

To get started, break down the statement and identify the assumptions made.

Statement Breakdown

◆ Scandals – can be leveraged to focus attention on problems, the claim argues that this is the superior approach

◆ Speaker/Reformer – an alternative approach to focusing attention on problems

◆ Problems – the focus of the ability to draw a person's attention

Assumptions

◆ Scandals focus attention.

◆ Speakers and reformers do not always focus attention.

◆ Scandals, speakers, and reformers always relate to problems.

After breaking down the statement and identifying assumptions, come up with pros and cons (or statements for and against) the topic given. You do not need to pick a side yet, but knowing potential counterarguments will help you to develop a stronger essay once you do.

Pros and Cons

Pros

👍 Scandals tend to be published by more news sources.

👍 Scandals tend to evoke more emotional responses from audiences.

👍 Speakers and reformers do not consistently evoke emotional responses.

Cons

👎 Scandals are typically short-lived.

👎 Speakers and reformers can engage their audiences more effectively.

👎 Repeated scandals result in people not paying as much attention.

👎 Scandals and speakers are not mutually exclusive.

Examples

Include examples in order to make your essay as strong as possible. These are some potential routes you may take when choosing examples:

a) History contains many examples for both sides of this argument.

b) Current U.S. politics contains many examples of how scandals and speakers can grab focus in different ways.

c) Think about examples where a scandal was a speaker or reformer.

Finally, come up with an outline of your essay. This may feel like it slows you down, but your essay will benefit from having an underlying structure.

 ## Sample Essay

There are a variety of ways to focus the attention of a group of people towards a specific topic. Some of these approaches are ideal if the goal is to hold the group's attention in the long term, whereas some may be better if the goal is to effect short term change. Two approaches to maintaining a hold over the attention of a group of people are scandals and the use of a speaker or reformer. The former approach tends to focus attention using shock, by presenting a surprising event for the audience that they likely want to know more about. On the other hand, the use of a speaker or reformer generally assumes that the audience will seek out an event where the speaker is present because of their personal interest in the topic. However, these two approaches are not mutually exclusive, and the claim that scandals focus our attention in ways that no speaker or reformer ever could is false because it is entirely possible for a speaker to also be a scandal.

During the Civil Rights Era, Martin Luther King Jr. gave a well-known speech entitled "I Have a Dream" at the March on Washington in Washington D.C. This is clearly an example of a speaker/reformer being used to focus the attention of both the attendees of the march, as well as the nation as a whole, but it was also a scandal because of the resultant shock of his speech and the march as a whole. Thousands of people did seek out King's speech by attending the March on Washington, but millions more had it presented to them through television broadcasting of the event. In addition, although this was a scandal, it was far from short-lived.

Approaching this issue from the other side, the Clinton Administration found itself immersed in a scandal when Former President Bill Clinton was accused of cheating on his wife by having sexual relations with a White House Intern named Monica Lewinsky. However, this is also an example of a speaker focusing the attention of the nation during his public declaration that he "did not have sexual relations with that woman," a statement that would later be revealed to be false. Similarly, to King's speech at the March on Washington, this scandal was not short-lived, and Clinton's speech was broadcasted across the country, further fueling the scandal.

In summary, while it is true that the manner in which traditional scandals focus our attention is different from the way that traditional speeches do, one cannot say that scandals focus our attention on problems in ways that no speaker or reformer ever could.

18

Issue Task 19

The surest indicator of a great nation is represented not by the achievements of its rulers, artists, or scientists, but by the general welfare of its people.

Write a response in which you discuss the extent to which you agree or disagree with the statement and explain your reasoning for the position you take. In developing and supporting your position, you should consider ways in which the statement might or might not hold true and explain how these considerations shape your position.

NOTE: The above topic has wording similar to Issue Task 26 and 29 in this book. However, if you read carefully you will notice that the task instructions are different. Hence, it is very important to read the topic as well as its instructions completely before you start to write your response.

 Strategies:

Statement breakdown:

- ◆ **Surest indicator** – Welfare is not the only indicator of greatness; it is not a causality relationship – welfare doesn't cause greatness, but can be used to measure it

- ◆ **Great nation** – what constitutes a great nation? How do you define it? In terms of power, size, economy etc.?

- ◆ **Rulers, artists or scientists** – categories of people whose contributions can be significant – are they the only ones with memorable achievements? What about athletes, spiritual leaders, military heroes, brilliant businessmen and other people that brought significant advancements in their fields?

- ◆ **General welfare** – what is the degree of welfare? Meeting the basic needs of the people? What indicators do you use to measure it – safety, buying power etc.?

Assumptions:

- ◆ Great nations have a high level of welfare

- ◆ The welfare of the people is more important than the achievements of rulers, artists and scientists

◆ Rulers, artists and scientists are the only ones with notable contributions

Pros and Cons:

Pros

👍 High living standards are a hallmark of civilized society

👍 Rulers, artists and scientists are not the only ones whose achievements contribute to a country's greatness

👍 Welfare is an indicator – something that when measured can tell the state of a country – it's economical and cultural prosperity

👍 Welfare encourages scientific development in the sense that if people's basic needs are met, that gives them the freedom to pursue their vocations/ideals

👍 More programs and support systems for artists and scientists (scholarships, research funding etc.)

👍 Happiness studies are directly linked with productivity/ creativity

👍 People centered modern day philosophy; human resources are the most valuable

👍 Great thinkers (scientists) and artists are great in themselves, regardless of the nation they came from – their contributions transcend boundaries

Cons

👎 Historically speaking, countries are memorable due to the achievements of their rulers, artists and scientists

👎 Great rulers make welfare possible; hey promote policies that support good living conditions for the citizens of the state

👎 Scientific advancements make life easier, increase the living standards

👎 Greatness is measured in contributions to world benefit – ruling principles like democracy, freedom of speech etc.

👎 Good rulers and scientific advancements drive the economy. Strong economies are indicative of great nations.

👎 A country's power is an indicative of greatness, and a major contributing factor in scientific advancements

👎 Cultural ideals help shape not only a nation, but the entire world

Examples:

a) Civilizations of the past, to showcase what history considers being great nations

b) Current great nations

c) Economical theories on welfare

d) Great achievements in the fields of science, great artists and commanders

 ## Sample Essay

Current society, as a whole, has become highly invested in people centric policies – from governments that ensure the welfare of the citizens to companies that place customer and employee values at their core. This transformation is in the spirit of Mahatma Gandhi's teachings that "man becomes great exactly in the degree in which he works for the welfare of his fellow men."

Throughout the ages, welfare has been an indicator of a nations' economic and cultural prosperity. High living standards point to economic stability, growth, abundance of resources – all of which are necessary to ensure that the populations' necessities are met. Moreover, the presence of welfare signals the existence of a cultural system capable of fostering the ideas necessary to support it. High living standards and civilization have always been linked. Take for instance the great nations of the past, like Ancient Greece or Rome, hallmarks of civilization that have left a deep imprint on the world. In both of these cases, the quality of life of the average citizen was well above that of the people living in the neighboring countries – they had the buying power and the possibility to enjoy a wider variety of products and leisurely activities, while being less concerned with day to day survival.

In this sense, it can be said that welfare encourages creativity, by meeting people's basic needs which in turn gives them the freedom to pursue their vocations/ideals. Maslow's hierarchy of needs supports this idea. Maslow's theory states that an individuals' fundamental needs have to be fulfilled before he can focus on the higher-level needs. What this means is that, for instance, metabolic requirements will tend to supersede self-actualizing actions, namely, artistic or creative activities will have to take a backseat to hunger or thirst. Countries where people's basic needs are being taken care of can afford to dedicate more time and resources to higher pursuits.

Moreover, countries with a high standard of living have the means to create programs and support systems for artists and scientists. Countries in northern Europe famous for the quality of life of the average citizen have significant government support when it comes to education. Their tuition fees are much lower than in the USA, and they invest a greater deal of resources into scholarships and research funding than countries like India. More than that, the northern European countries strive to ensure not just the physical welfare of their citizens, but also their mental and ideological wellbeing by providing an open–minded climate where diversity can thrive. As Plato postulated in the Republic, the stability and success of a political community depends upon the moral character of the people who make up that community

From these arguments, it becomes apparent that rulers, artists and scientists are not the only ones whose achievements contribute to a country's greatness. But rather, economical power, one of the main characteristics of a strong nation, is dependent upon the consumers and their buying power.

Ultimately, when assessing a nation's greatness, it all comes down to what traits best represent it. From what we have seen so far, the welfare of a nation's citizens, closely tied to their economic power, provides a nurturing environment for talents that will end up shaping the rest of the world and contributing to the benefit of mankind. As such, it can be said that general welfare is one of the surest indicators of a country's greatness.

19

Issue Task 20

Claim: *Governments must ensure that their major cities receive the financial support they need in order to thrive.*

Reason: *It is primarily in cities that a nation's cultural traditions are preserved and generated.*

Write a response in which you discuss the extent to which you agree or disagree with the claim and the reason on which that claim is based.

 ## Strategies:

Combine the claim and reason into one statement using a subordinate clause

In other words:

Because it is in cities that a nation's cultural traditions are preserved and generated, governments must ensure that their major cities receive the financial support they need in order to thrive.

What are the assumptions in the claim and reason? These will provide evidence that you can either affirm or refute in your argument.

◆ Cities generate and preserve most of a nation's cultural traditions.

◆ Small towns and rural areas do not generate or preserve a nation's cultural traditions.

◆ Cities are unable to thrive without financial support from the government.

◆ Cultural traditions should be preserved.

◆ Funding cities in order to preserve cultural traditions is a valuable use of government money.

Next, create a statement that expresses an opposing point of view, using language similar to that in the original statement.

Opposing viewpoint:

Claim: *Governments must ensure that communities of all sizes receive the financial support they need to thrive.*

Reason: *All communities help to generate and preserve a nation's cultural traditions.*

What are the assumptions in the claim and reason? These will provide evidence that you can either affirm or refute in your argument.

◆ No type of community should be ignored as a preserver of cultural traditions.

◆ Cities and small towns should receive equal financial support as preservers of cultural traditions.

◆ Some cultural traditions may disappear if certain types of communities are allowed to flounder financially.

Is there any other way to look at this issue? Can you qualify the original statement in some way? Is it possible to partially agree with the statement?

Alternative viewpoint:

Claim: *Governments should not fund their major cities in order to preserve cultural traditions.*

Reason: *Cultural groups should be responsible for preserving their own traditions.*

What are the assumptions in the alternative claim and reason?

◆ Governments should not fund the preservation of cultural traditions.

◆ Government should fund projects that benefit the greatest number of people rather than small groups of people.

◆ Each cultural group should do what it takes to preserve its own traditions.

 ## Sample Essay

America is a country of immigrants. Over the course of this country's brief history, groups or individuals have made their way to our shores to escape persecution, starvation, or any number of disasters. Language, religious, or other barriers led them to seek those from similar backgrounds, creating communities and neighborhoods where many cultural traditions have been preserved through several generations. These are traditions that they carried with them from their countries of origin. As a nation, America has very few original cultural traditions. The most notable of these is Thanksgiving. We also celebrate our own Independence Day on July fourth and Columbus Day in October. They were neither generated in major cities, nor are they preserved exclusively in major cities. Americans generate and preserve cultural traditions in communities both large and small. Whether these traditions help major cities to thrive is questionable, and whether government funding of their preservation is warranted is subject to debate.

20

I grew up in a part of Maine that had a significant number of people whose ancestors came from Sweden during the last half of the nineteenth century. In fact, my own ancestors made that journey and settled in Stockholm, obviously named for the capital of their homeland. These Swedes were principally farmers, and they cleared the heavily-forested land and grew crops amenable to a short growing season. They established Lutheran churches, married other Swedish immigrants, and prepared meals in the Swedish culinary tradition. Eventually mills designed to manufacture products from the abundant timber were built along the stream that ran through town, and Acadian-French people moved to Stockholm to work in the mills.

The schools, once populated by children whose surnames were Anderson, Johnson, and Soderberg now included Plourdes, Rossignols, and Doucettes. The inevitable occurred: French people fell in love with and married Swedish people. Today, there may not be more than a handful of residents who can claim unadulterated Swedish blood. Despite the decline in population and the dilution of the bloodlines, the Swedish community celebrates Midsummer every year. To mark the longest day of the year, residents and visitors alike dress in quaint Swedish costumes, decorate and raise a Maypole, perform Swedish folk dances and eat Swedish food. This is accomplished without the infusion of state or federal funds; volunteers from the community do it all. I'm sure it's all lovely. I wouldn't know because I've never attended the festivities. Even though half of my ancestors are of Swedish descent, I have never lived anywhere but America. I am an American, not a Swedish-American, nor, more correctly, a Swedish-Irish-English-Dutch-American. Because cultural traditions are unique to specific religions, races, or ethnicities, they tend to separate people rather than pull them together. These traditions help individual cultures, rather than entire communities, to thrive.

The vitality of America's major cities relies on factors other than the preservation of cultural traditions. Major cities or any community requires a sound infrastructure to ensure its survival. Without sufficient streets in good repair residents cannot go to work during the day or to places of entertainment in the evening. Without an efficient means of delivering water and eliminating waste, cities would become breeding grounds for disease. A lack of electricity would cripple all forms of industry. Major cities must provide access to health care and education to its residents. Any level of financial support on the part of the government should be allocated to projects that make living in major cities more comfortable. When residents are comfortable, they can pursue activities that help their communities to thrive.

Over recent decades, uniquely American cultural traditions have lost their significance. Thanksgiving has been reduced to a day to prepare for Black Friday, the kickoff to the Christmas shopping season. Stores open earlier than normal and offer desirable merchandise at drastically reduced prices. Entire families spend time on Thanksgiving plotting their shopping strategies. They camp out at stores or get up extra early to be first through the doors when they open, often pushing other bargain hunters out of the way. In 2012, some major chain stores actually opened in the evening on Thanksgiving Day. When America's citizens have so little regard for the country's traditions, the government would be unwise to provide funds to major cities in an attempt to preserve them.

20

Issue Task 21

Some people believe that in order to be effective, political leaders must yield to public opinion and abandon principle for the sake of compromise. Others believe that the most essential quality of an effective leader is the ability to remain consistently committed to particular principles and objectives.

Write a response in which you discuss which view more closely aligns with your own position and explain your reasoning for the position you take. In developing and supporting your position, you should address both of the views presented.

 Strategies:

Combine the claim and reason into one statement using a subordinate clause

Restate the Issue:

Consider each view separately before deciding which of them you most closely agree with.

Point of view 1: Restate the position using negative terminology.

In other words:

Some people believe that political leaders who do not yield to public opinion and fail to compromise cannot be effective.

Think about the question that is being answered by the statement.

What should political leaders do to be effective?

Now identify elements in the statement that can provide evidence for you to affirm or refute.

◆ **Some people** – This implies that there are two sides to the issue. Not all people agree with position 1.

◆ **effective** – To be effective is to have an effect on something or to effect or create a change.

◆ **yield** – To yield is to give up something. Yielding to an opponent is generally to surrender your own ideas.

21

◆ **public opinion** – One generally thinks of majority opinion in this case. The entire public never seems to share the same opinion.

◆ **abandon** – This is a strong word. Abandoning an object, person, or idea is likely permanent.

◆ **principle** – A principle is akin to an ideal. Principles develop over a period of years and determine what individuals find acceptable or unacceptable.

◆ **sake** – Sake is a synonym for interest or benefit.

◆ **compromise** – In compromise, all parties give up something. The phrase, a strong compromise, is oxymoronic.

Point of view 2: Restate the position using negative terminology.

In other words:

Others believe that the most essential quality of an effective leader is the refusal to abandon principles and objectives to which they are committed.

This statement answers the same question as the first statement does.

Now, identify the elements in this statement that can provide evidence for you to affirm or refute.

◆ **others** – Like some people in the first point of view, others are not inclusive. It could just as easily be some.

◆ **most essential** – This phrase contains redundancies. Essential is the most; nothing is more needed than the essential part.

◆ **consistently committed** – A foolish consistency is the hobgoblin of little minds. Consistently means that circumstances cannot affect one's commitment to an idea, person, etc.

◆ **objectives** – Objectives must be accomplished on the way to reaching a goal.

The directions do not allow for alternative positions. Even though you may not be in complete agreement with either of the positions, you must decide which one most closely matches the way that you think about the issue. Make certain to acknowledge the opposite viewpoint as you develop your response.

 ## Sample Essay

More than a century ago, Ralph Waldo Emerson said that a foolish consistency is the hobgoblin of little minds. When one becomes enamored of an idea or principle, he or she becomes blind to alternatives. It is as though a hobgoblin or little monster has entered the imagination and blocked off new ideas or the ability to see a different perspective. When opposing parties in a debate refuse to acknowledge any value in their opponents' ideas, nothing is accomplished. We certainly see this today in the United States Congress. Poll numbers are on the decline for the president and most senators and representatives because of their inability to get anything done. Compromise may seem like giving in or giving up, but the alternative is to leave problems unsolved

The United States may have been governed very differently than it is today if it were not for the Great Compromise. In the early days of America, there was heated debate about the way states would be represented in the national government. One plan called for a unicameral congress where the number of representatives from each state would be based on the state's population. This plan favored states with larger populations. The other plan stated that each state should have the same number of representatives, again in a unicameral legislature. This would leave the people in states with larger populations underserved. The Great Compromise created the bicameral system we have today in America. One body, the Senate, is composed of two senators from each state, creating a body in which each state, regardless of population, is represented equally. The lower house, the House of Representatives, is comprised of representatives from each state based on population. In this manner, most citizens of the United States are served equally by their elected officials.

The world has become increasingly complex since those early days of America and debate still rages in the halls of government in Washington, DC. A flagging economy, rising unemployment, greater numbers of housing foreclosures, threats to entitlement programs, and bank failures have sparked contrasting ideas about fixes for these problems. Citizens watch while their president or senator or congressmen declare to the media that there will be no bill if their own ideas are not included. Those whose terms in congress next year are already making campaign promises with no sufficient plan to pay for those promises.

21

Therefore, there must be compromise. After all, promise is part of compromise. Those who are retired or near retirement worry about proposed cuts to Social Security and/or Medicare, and the young workers worry about rising taxes to pay for those entitlements and wonder what will be left for them when they reach retirement age. Current and prospective workers worry about the exportation of jobs to other countries while they are trying to pay for their homes or save money to send their children to college. Students in college worry about the debt they will be saddled with after graduation and if there will be jobs for them once they have their sheepskin in hand. The president and Congress should look to the past and see that compromise was the vehicle that placed them in the positions they now have. They must combine their promises for the good of every citizen.

Issue Task 22

Politicians should pursue common ground and reasonable consensus rather than elusive ideals.

Write a response in which you discuss the extent to which you agree or disagree with the recommendation and explain your reasoning for the position you take. In developing and supporting your position, describe specific circumstances in which adopting the recommendation would or would not be advantageous and explain how these examples shape your position.

 ## Strategies:

Combine the claim and reason into one statement using a subordinate clause

Restate the Issue:

The original statement tells what politicians should do. Create a statement that tells what politicians should not do without changing the meaning of the statement.

In other words:

22

Politicians should not pursue elusive ideals instead of pursuing common ground and reasonable consensus.

You could also determine what question is being answered by the recommendation.

What is the best way for politicians to serve the electorate?

Now think about the parts of the recommendation that provide evidence that you can affirm or refute.

- ◆ **common ground** – This implies agreement or standing together.

- ◆ **reasonable** – This is something that is arrived at by using reason or logic.

- ◆ **consensus** – The implication is agreement, coming together.

- ◆ **elusive** – Something elusive is not easily caught or understood. It is slippery.

◆ **ideals** – An ideal is the perfect form of something.

◆ **pursue** – To pursue is to chase or follow.

Opposing viewpoint:

Politicians should avoid common ground and reasonable consensus in the pursuit of elusive ideals.

Identify the parts of the opposing statement that provide evidence that you can refute or affirm.

◆ **avoid** – When avoiding something, you stay away from it.

Alternatives:

Is there any other way to look at the recommendation? Can parts of it be qualified in any way? Should politicians retain some of their ideals while pursuing common ground and reasonable consensus?

New viewpoint:

Politicians should not abandon their ideals as they pursue common ground and reasonable consensus.

22

Sample Essay

Men and women enter the political arena ready to do battle against special interest groups and pork barrel spending. They've promised their constituents that they're going to clean up that mess in Washington or the capital in the state they serve. The voters are confident they've elected someone who will stick to his or her guns. Without dreams of making a change for the better, politicians would not exist. But as poet Robert Burns said, "The best laid plans of mice and men often go awry." It doesn't take long for politicians to realize that their individual voices aren't very loud, or that they may not have a full understanding of the policy that they are attempting to argue.

Everyone who chooses politics as a career must possess at least a modicum of naiveté. If the candidate didn't think he or she could make a difference, there would be no reason to run for office. Changing the world is a lofty goal, but it is generally accomplished at a snail's pace and one compromise at a time. We learn to compromise as young children. Our parents tell us if we clean our rooms, we can have a treat. If compromise means that both sides give up something to get something, then the deal we made with Mom is compromise. We give up some free time to clean our rooms and get in return more TV time or a candy bar. Mom gives up some peace and quiet but gets a clean room.

Political compromise is more difficult to achieve, and the stakes are higher. The principle, however, is the same. Reaching a consensus takes a little sleight of hand and a gift for rhetoric. The idealistic politician may have to temper his or her enthusiasm when choosing from the list of persuasive techniques at hand to lead his fellow politicians to common ground. This politician must keep the constituents in mind as he seeks the consensus that will allow him to retain his ideals. Today, in the halls of Congress and in the White House, there is great debate about the budget. Senators and congressmen on both sides of the debate are finding it difficult to find common ground. The ideals of some make them refuse to consider raising taxes for any citizens in America, while others believe that the wealthy should pay more taxes. Some feel so protective towards the poor and the elderly that they refuse to make cuts in any of the tax-funded programs that serve those groups, while others say that those programs must be reduced in scope to protect everyone. It is sometimes difficult for citizens watching this debate to determine if their representatives in Washington are holding steadfast to the ideals they took with them to Congress, or if they are spouting the rhetoric, they believe will get them re-elected.

All politicians, whether on the local, state, or national level would do well to revisit the Preamble to the Constitution, whose first line includes the words, "in order to form a more perfect union". Perfect means ideal and union means agreement. Whatever the issue may be, politicians should strive for perfect agreement. In the end, the agreement may not seem perfect to every politician, but it should serve the needs of the people they represent.

Issue Task 23

People should undertake risky action only after they have carefully considered its consequences.

Write a response in which you discuss the extent to which you agree or disagree with the recommendation and explain your reasoning for the position you take. In developing and supporting your position, describe specific circumstances in which adopting the recommendation would or would not be advantageous and explain how these examples shape your position.

NOTE: The above topic has wording similar to Issue Task 40 in this book. However, if you read carefully you will notice that the task instructions are different. Hence, it is very important to read the topic as well as its instructions completely before you start to write your response.

 Strategies

Restate the Position:

The original recommendation suggests how people should behave regarding risks. How would the recommendation read if it were couched in negative terms?

In other words:

People should not take risks until they have considered the consequences.

The meaning of both recommendations is essentially the same.

You could also determine what question is being answered by the recommendation.

Should individuals take risks?

Or: *Under what conditions should people take risks?*

Now think about the parts of the recommendation that provide evidence that you can affirm or refute.

◆ **only** – This leaves no other option. It is akin to saying always. Are there no exceptions?

◆ **risky** – This can be relative. What may appear risky to one may be commonplace for another.

◆ **carefully** – The meaning of carefully can vary, as well. How much consideration is considered careful?

◆ **considered** – To consider something is to think about it. it does not require taking any action. Does one only need to think about the consequences of one's actions? Does understanding the consequences prevent everyone from engaging in risky behavior? Does consideration necessarily lead to understanding?

Opposing viewpoint:

People should undertake risky action regardless of the consequences.

Think about the parts of the opposing statement that provide evidence to affirm or refute.

◆ **regardless** – This means without regard. To regard something is to look at it. One should take risks without looking at the consequences.

◆ **should** – This is not a command. Should implies choice.

Alternatives:

Is there another way to look at this recommendation? Can it be qualified? Are some risks worth taking despite the possible consequences? Can risks be minimized?

New viewpoint:

Even with the possibility of negative consequences, some risks are worth taking.

23

Examples and reasons:

a) Marie and Pierre Curie – When they began experimenting with radiation, the risks were unknown. Marie Curie died from radiation sickness, but her contribution to the advancement of medicine is immeasurable.

b) early explorers– When the Vikings set out in their boats and headed west, they could not imagine what they would find. They found rich fishing grounds. Columbus, Cook, Drake, Magellan all risked their lives to set out across seas that no man had navigated before.

c) space exploration

d) Bill Gates and Steve Jobs – Both are pioneers in computing technology, Gates with software and Jobs with McIntosh computers

Sample Essay

Some people are born risk takers. Psychologists will tell you that it is a component of one's personality, and those who take risks sometimes exhibit negative behavior while others take risks that ultimately benefit themselves and others. The names of risk takers can be found in various halls of fame as well as on Wanted Posters. Famous risk takers range from the infamous like Al Capone and Bernie Madoff to the innovators like Bill Gates, Mark Zuckerberg, and Frank Lloyd Wright. Even though these and others knew the possible consequences of their actions, they were not deterred from reaching their goals. Those who do not take risks will not suffer the possible negative consequences, but neither will they experience the rewards.

Where would we be without those who took great risks with general disregard for the consequences? Marie and Pierre Curie literally risked their lives to experiment with radioactivity. The medical progress that resulted from their work not only earned the Curies the Nobel Prize but made possible the early treatment of some cancers. Other scientists followed in their footsteps, and the benefits to mankind have been enormous. Other medical pioneers include Jonas Salk who saved countless children from death or paralysis when he tested his new polio vaccine on himself, his wife and his own children. Risking his and his family's lives led to the mass administration of the vaccine to school children all over America, and virtually made the iron lung obsolete.

Early explorers risked traveling to areas marked on maps with the foreboding phrase, "Here there are dragons", and expanded the known world. In efforts to find a shorter route to India, sailors like Christopher Columbus set off with his crew in three small boats and bumped into the Western Hemisphere. Charles Lindbergh flew solo across the Atlantic in a small plane in hopes of reaching the European continent. Since that time, man has used flight to reach the moon and establish space stations. If these adventurers had spent too much time thinking about the consequences, they may very well have just stayed home.

In the later years of the twentieth century, pioneers in technology arose. Bill Gates, founder of Microsoft and one of the richest men in the world, dropped out of prestigious Harvard University to pursue computing. Steve Jobs, the brains behind Apple computers, also dropped out of college. These men defied the popular wisdom that one needs a college education to get anywhere in this world and created a universe of communication on a level never before seen.

Great political leaders have taken great risks for the sake of reform or revolution. Martin Luther King, Jr and Mohandas Gandhi (after whom King modeled his protests), risked everything and, ultimately, lost their lives for the sake of equality and independence. Both men certainly considered the consequences of their actions but deemed that the potential rewards made the risks acceptable. All minorities and repressed populations in the United States lead lives of greater opportunity thanks to the leadership of Martin Luther King, Jr, and India exists as an independent country as a result of Gandhi's actions.

Just as there are consequences for taking risks, there are consequences for failing to take risks. Those who fear the unknown are doomed to live meager lives. It may be trite but nonetheless true to say that if you do what you've always done, you'll get what you've always had.

Issue Task 24

Leaders are created by the demands that are placed on them.

Write a response in which you discuss the extent to which you agree or disagree with the statement and explain your reasoning for the position you take. In developing and supporting your position, you should consider ways in which the statement might or might not hold true and explain how these considerations shape your position.

 Strategies

Restate the Issue:

This statement tells how leaders are created. How are they not created?

In other words:

Leaders do not arise until demands have been placed on them.

Determine what question is being answered by the issue statement.

How are leaders created?

Or: *Under what conditions do leaders emerge?*

How would you answer the questions? Your answer will help you develop your response to the statement.

Now think about the parts of the statement that provide evidence that you can affirm or refute.

◆ **created** – This assumes that leaders are made and not born. There must be some process by which leaders come to be.

◆ **demands** – These are like orders. One cannot avoid or ignore a demand.

◆ **placed upon them** – This implies a lack of choice.

24

Opposing viewpoint:

Leaders arise through some preparation to lead.

Identify the parts of the opposing statement that provide evidence that you can refute or affirm.

◆ **Arise** – This implies that those that are prone to leadership will assume it when the situation requires.

◆ **preparation** – Leaders don't appear spontaneously. Through some desire or proclivity for leadership, they have prepared to assume it when called upon.

Is there another way to look at this issue? Are some leaders reluctant to lead? Are they leading by default? Did they assume a leadership role out of a sense of responsibility rather than the desire to lead? Do some seek leadership? Can the two stated viewpoints be combined?

New viewpoint:

Some leaders are forced into that position by circumstances, while others develop leadership skills over a lifetime.

Identify the parts of the new viewpoint that provide evidence for you to refute or affirm.

◆ **Some** – This leaves room for exceptions. It is not all.

◆ **forced** – This suggests a lack of willingness to lead. There may be no options.

◆ **circumstances** – This is the same as a situation. The implication is the situation is unexpected.

◆ **develop** – Development implies growth. Some leaders have grown into more sophisticated leadership abilities.

◆ **lifetime** – Real leadership isn't something that happens overnight. As situations change, leaders learn to adapt.

Position:

Some leaders are forced into that position by circumstances, while others develop leadership skills over a lifetime.

Examples and Reasons:

a) **The lost battalion** – Major Whittlesey's sudden elevation to military leadership

b) **Flight 93** – Regular citizens taking over in a crisis.

c) **Military generals –** They are career leaders.

Sample Essay

Leadership positions are best filled by people whose nature enables them to endure both the successes and failures that accompany the challenges a leader will face. Some leaders are made by their circumstances, which push them to acquire traits that they may not have otherwise. This leadership can be transient – that is, leaders can be made by a particular situation and then return to their non-leadership position once the situation has been handled. History contains many examples of all such leaders.

When the United States entered WWI, Charles Whittlesey, a mild-mannered, Harvard-educated lawyer was commissioned an officer in the US Army. He led a battalion of young infantrymen out of the trenches and into the Argonne Forest in France in an attempt to retake land that was occupied by the Germans. Having been given incorrect information, Major Whittlesey and his men became trapped behind enemy lines where they endured artillery attacks by the Germans who outnumbered them. They even came under friendly fire when the Allies used incorrect coordinates in an effort to attack the Germans with cannon fire. After 5 days, the battalion was rescued. Of the more than 500 men who entered the forest with Whittlesey, fewer than 200 walked out of the forest with him. The remainder had been killed, captured by the enemy, or wounded. After the war ended, Whittlesey, who received the Congressional Medal of Honor for his heroic deeds, returned to the practice of law. Three years later, Charles Whittlesey booked a cruise, and while on that cruise, jumped overboard. Major Whittlesey became a leader through the demands placed upon him. Even though he acted with honor and effectively saved the lives of hundreds of the men in his charge, the loss of so many more weighed so heavily on him that he took his own life.

Renowned leaders have arisen from the ranks of the US armed forces. American history texts recount the exploits of brave men like General Douglas McArthur who promised the people of the Philippines that he would return. General Dwight Eisenhower was the supreme Allied Commander during the invasion of Normandy on D-Day in 1944 and went on to serve two terms as President of the United States. The difference between these men and Charles Whittlesey was their choice of a military career. They embraced the challenges, celebrated the victories, and accepted the loss of life.

On rare occasions, situations do arise that force ordinary citizens to assume leadership and perform extraordinary acts of bravery. Ten years ago, passengers on United Airlines flight 93, after learning what had happened at the World Trade Center in New York City, decided to take action that would prevent their own hijacked plane from causing a similar disaster and stormed the cockpit where terrorists had assumed control of the plane. As a result, the plane that was on a course that would have taken it to the nation's capital, crashed in a field in Pennsylvania, averting disaster while killing everyone on board.

While events occasionally conspire to force individuals into leadership roles, effective, long-term leadership is best left to those whose proclivities cause them to desire the responsibilities of leadership. Reluctant or ineffectual leaders may cause more harm than good, either to themselves or those they are leading.

24

Issue Task 25

To be an effective leader, a public official must maintain the highest ethical and moral standards.

Write a response in which you discuss the extent to which you agree or disagree with the claim. In developing and supporting your position, be sure to address the most compelling reasons and/or examples that could be used to challenge your position.

 Strategies

Assumptions:

What are the assumptions in the claim?

Assumption 1: Ethics and morals determine effectiveness.

Assumption 2: Ethical and moral standards of leaders must be higher than those of average people.

Assumption 3: Leaders are held to a higher standard than the average person.

Assumption 4: Ethical and moral standards are easily defined and constant everywhere.

Assumption 5: Leaders outside of the public arena do not need to meet the same standards as those who are in the public arena.

Assumption 6: Ethics and morals are essentially the same part of someone's character. Can one be ethical while being immoral?

Opposing viewpoint:

A public figure does not have to maintain the highest ethical and moral standards to be an effective leader.

Assumption 1: A leader's effectiveness depends on elements other than high ethical and moral standards.

Alternative claim:

As long as it doesn't affect his service to the people, a public official should be held to standards no higher than those of the rest of society.

Assumption 1: A public official's private behavior should not necessarily be used to judge his effectiveness as a leader.

Assumption 2: Public officials can separate their private lives from their public ones.

Support for alternative claim:

Example: President Franklin Delano Roosevelt kept a mistress. Did this detract from his ability to lead America out of the Great Depression?

Example: Adolph Hitler was supremely successful as a leader despite his lack of ethics and morals.

Example: J. Edgar Hoover, director of the FBI, was a cross dresser.

 # Sample Essay

Are morals and ethics the same thing? Can one behave ethically in business, medicine, or politics while exhibiting immoral behavior in private? Numerous examples throughout history portray the effectiveness of leaders who displayed, either publicly or privately, behaviors or beliefs that would be considered unethical or immoral. If the constituencies of a public official are being well served, do they care about the private behavior of those officials? When the public good is being served, the public is likely to be satisfied and willing to disregard other parts of an official's life.

History has declared Franklin Delano Roosevelt to have been a supremely effective leader of the United States of America through some of its darkest days despite the fact that he had a long–time mistress. Unprecedented in the history of the US is Roosevelt's election to four consecutive terms in the White House. He must have been doing something right. Taking office at the height of the Great Depression, FDR, himself a child of privilege, began to demand of Congress that they institute programs that would lead to the nation's recovery. The New Deal was born and spawned such programs as the Civilian Conservation Corps, the Tennessee Valley Authority, and the Works Progress Administration. All of these provided jobs for Americans who otherwise would have spent their days standing in bread lines or sleeping on the streets.

On Sunday, December 7, 1941, the Japanese attacked the American military fleet at Pearl Harbor, and FDR had to make the painful decision to declare war against Japan. Although FDR did not live to see the atomic bombs dropped on Hiroshima or Nagasaki, the US was the eventual victor in the war he had declared. The fact that he

25

was with his mistress when he died in Warm Springs, Georgia did not stop Americans from lining up by the thousands to watch the train carrying his body back to Washington, D.C. The citizens' interests had been served and preserved by this great man, and that was what mattered to them.

Despite his obvious lack of morals, Adolph Hitler is recognized as an effective leader. A contemporary of FDR's, he rose to power when Germany was suffering economically because of the reparations laid on the country after WWI, as well as the Great Depression. Hitler's promise to lift Germany out of the economic quagmire attracted the votes of the German people, and Hitler became Chancellor of Germany. His efforts to recoup Germany's losses included invading nearby countries. He also sought to punish those he felt responsible for Germany's downfall, namely Jewish bankers and businessmen, who, in his mind, had far too much control of the finances of Europe. Because their welfare was secure, the citizens of Germany lived and worked in towns next to concentration camps in which Jews, Catholics, homosexuals and the mentally feeble were systematically being exterminated and claimed that they didn't know what was taking place. Using immoral and unethical means, Hitler served the interests of a subset of the German people, and that was what mattered to them.

It has been said that a group eventually gets the leadership it deserves. Whether the leader is upright and moral or unethical and immoral may depend on the character of the people who elect him/her. It just may be that if the standards are too high, men and women who, otherwise, would be effective leaders, will not seek to lead.

25

Issue Task 26

Claim: *The surest indicator of a great nation is not the achievements of its rulers, artists, or scientists.*

Reason: *The surest indicator of a great nation is actually the welfare of all its people.*

Write a response in which you discuss the extent to which you agree or disagree with the claim and the reason on which that claim is based.

NOTE: The above topic has wording similar to Issue Task 16 and 29 in this book. However, if you read carefully you will notice that the task instructions are different. Hence, it is very important to read the topic as well as its instructions completely before you start to write your response.

 Strategies

Restate the Claim:

Combine the claim and reason into a single statement.

In other words:

The surest indicator of a great nation is actually the welfare of all its people rather than the achievements of its rulers, artists, or scientists.

What are the assumptions in the claim and reason? These will be statements that you can either affirm or refute in your response.

Assumption 1: The achievements of rulers, artists, or scientists are not a nation's most important achievements.

Assumption 2: People judge a nation's success by the achievement of its rulers, artists, or scientists.

Assumption 3: The welfare of its people is the most important accomplishment of any nation.

Assumption 4: The achievements of a nation's rulers, artists, or scientists do not contribute to the welfare of its people.

26

Next, create a statement that expresses the opposing point of view, using language similar to that in the original claim. In this case, the reason could become the claim, and the claim becomes the reason.

Opposing viewpoint:

Claim – *The surest indicator of a great nation is not the welfare of all of its people.*

Reason – *The surest indicator of a great nation is the achievements of its rulers, artists or scientists.*

How does this new claim and reason affect the earlier assumptions?

Assumption 1: The accomplishments of a nation's rulers, artists, or scientists determine a nation's greatness.

Assumption 2: The welfare of a country's people does not determine the greatness of that nation.

Assumption 3: Outsiders judge a nation by the accomplishments of its rulers, artists, or scientists.

Alternative claim:

An important indicator of a nation's greatness is the achievements of its rulers, artists, or scientists.

Alternative reason:

The welfare of a nation's people depends on those achievements.

Assumption 1: A country is judged by the achievements of its rulers, artists, or scientists.

Assumption 2: The achievements of a nation's rulers, artists, or scientists affect the welfare of its people.

Support for alternative claim and reason:

Example 1: The achievements of Abraham Lincoln had a profound effect on the welfare of all Americans. The Civil War reunited the states. The Emancipation Proclamation freed the slaves.

Example 2: The Human Genome Project has enabled doctors and scientists to isolate genes responsible for deadly diseases.

Example 3: Adolph Hitler and Joseph Mengele performed atrocities upon specific populations in Europe during the 1930's and 1940's.

Sample Essay

It is nearly impossible to separate the welfare of a nation's population from the achievements of that nation's rulers, scientists, or artists. Whether the citizens' welfare is enhanced or diminished depends upon the type and scope of those achievements. History is replete with examples of rulers who made history-changing decisions, of scientists whose research and experiments altered the lives of millions, and of artists whose words or images affected the thinking of a nation's citizenry. As these two ideas are so thoroughly intertwined, the surest indicator of a great (or poor) nation is a combination of the welfare of the population and the achievements of its leaders.

The welfare of every American was affected by decisions that Abraham Lincoln made during his presidency in the nineteenth century. His belief that a nation divided cannot stand led to the decision to declare war on the Confederate states and an eventual reunification of the states of the United States. During the Civil War, Lincoln issued the Emancipation Proclamation intended to free the slaves. That proclamation had both immediate and long-range effects. Although discrimination still exists in America, the descendants of those freed slaves have more opportunities than their ancestors. Martin Luther King, Jr, in the middle of the twentieth century, led the struggle to validate the meaning of the Emancipation Proclamation and brought change for all disenfranchised groups in the country.

Perhaps the most reviled leader of the twentieth century is Adolph Hitler. Der Fuhrer's achievements led to the near eradication of an entire religious group in eastern Europe. His insidious actions forced millions of Jews to leave their homes and businesses to live in ghettos and, eventually in relocation or concentration camps where they were systematically killed through overwork, starvation, and disease. Dr. Joseph Mengele conducted medical experiments on that same group of people with the ostensible goal of serving humanity. No one, apart from Megele himself, derived any benefit from his actions. The only tangible artistic accomplishment during Hitler's reign was the theft of great works of art from the countries that Germany occupied.

In the world of the present, the actions of one nation's ruler, scientists, or artists can influence the welfare of people in many nations. The world has grown small. The butterfly effect can apply to any action. If a child in Africa dies from the AIDS virus, it is a signal to the entire world that effective treatment of the disease is still not widely available, and the cry goes out to governments and drug companies to act. If a terrorist in Japan releases deadly Sarin in a subway station, the rest of the world goes on alert. If Muslim extremists fly passenger planes into the tallest buildings in the United States, reprisals against people of Middle Eastern descent are carried out in small towns and cities around the world. Whether rulers make the decision to declare war on terrorism, or scientists develop better antidotes for deadly poisons, or artists create depictions of the horrors of violent death, the welfare of people in all countries is affected in ways that may not be demonstrated for years or decades.

The welfare of a nation's citizens is irrevocably tied to the achievements of its rulers, artists, and scientists. The standard of living, excellence of education, accessibility to quality health care, and feelings of security in any nation reflect decisions made by its rulers, advances accomplished by its scientists, and representations of the culture depicted in the words and images of its artists. History serves as the final judge of the eras in which those events occurred.

Government & Politics

Issue Task 27

Governments should not fund any scientific research whose consequences are unclear.

Write a response in which you discuss the extent to which you agree or disagree with the statement and explain your reasoning for the position you take. In developing and supporting your position, you should consider ways in which the statement might or might not hold true and explain how these considerations shape your position.

Strategies

A good starting point is to break down the statement and identify the assumptions it makes. Look for ambiguous phrasing and consider all possible exceptions. They represent weak points that you can defend or attack depending on your chosen position.

Statement breakdown:

◆ **Governments** – is it their responsibility?

◆ **Should not fund** – officially or unofficially? How big of a deterrent is it? What about company and private funding?

◆ **Any scientific research** – how about other fields that have dangerous consequences?

◆ **Consequences are unclear -** some research applications can't be foreseen; what if the consequences are bad, but clear? How about 'good research' put to bad use?

Assumptions:

◆ Governments are responsible for overseeing the consequences of scientific research

◆ Government funding should stay clear of controversial research

◆ Not having government funding would hinder scientific endeavors

◆ Scientific research should have foreseeable consequences

27

◆ Scientific research will always be used for intended purposes

◆ Scientific research without foreseeable consequences is bad

Pros and Cons:

Pros

👍 Government resources are not infinite, money should be spent wisely

👍 Scientists can produce dangerous things

👍 Research can fall into the wrong hands

👍 It is easier to weigh the benefits risk ratio if you know the consequences of research

👍 Will make researchers focus on clear and definable goals

Cons

👎 Does not stop potentially dangerous research before it stops (just does not fund it)

👎 Can be used as a publicity stunt (keep their name in the clear, while allowing the research to continue)

👎 Restricted to official, public channels

👎 Not all technological applications can be foreseen (they can be used for something other than the intended purpose)

👎 Some research can be used both for good and for bad – nuclear power, vaccines

👎 Some fields of inquiry don't start from hypothesis but from observations

👎 Some research can produce accidental inventions

27

Examples:

a) Past and present controversial research

b) Inventions that started out as something else

c) Movies and books about the dangers or benefits of research

d) Countries that have similar policies in place

e) Percentage of research funds obtained from government funding as opposed to corporate or private funding

 # Sample Essay

Cutting edge scientific research can often be controversial, especially when funded by entities that stand to gain from its success. The government is one such entity, in that it funds a plurality of US research for its own gain. To this effect, it is widely believed by some that governments should not support scientific research that does not have clear goals. However, not funding potentially dangerous research only serves to keep the government name in the clear so that the politicians in charge can continue to enjoy the population's support. In fact, most current research is sponsored through private or corporate donations. According to OECD (the Organization for Economic Co-operation and Development), two thirds of the funds for scientific research come from industry donations, 20 % comes from universities and only about 10% comes from the government. In this case, not funding a certain scientific inquiry is more of a statement – taking a position - than any deterrent for the research.

Then there is the question of whether or not the research endeavor in question receives government funding through unofficial channels. Just because the government claims to not be associated with some type of research does not necessarily make it true. In fact, the US government has a history of revealing previous involvement in human experimentation, which at the time was kept secret for fear of public reprisals. One example of this occurred during the Cold War, when the US was involved in testing out torture and interrogation techniques, or as in the case of the Holmesburg Prison, conducting chemical experiments with dioxin on the prisoners.

Furthermore, not all technological applications can be foreseen; as is often the case, inventions end up being used for something other than their intended purpose. The popular breath freshener, Listerine, started out as an antiseptic, to be used by doctors. Coca–Cola started as a cure for morphine addiction and Play–Doh as wallpaper cleaner. We live in a complex world that is difficult to predict; at the time it was created, nobody could have foreseen the world changing impact of DARPA that later became known as the internet. As such, history shows us that it is difficult to predict with any level of significant accuracy the potential uses and consequences of any given technology.

Even if the consequences of the research are known, that does not guarantee that they will be used for the intended purpose: the Russians stole the US research about the nuclear bomb (even when it was under strict security). In fact, matters are even further complicated by the fact that some scientific innovations occur by accident – like the discovery of penicillin, where not only the consequences, but the intended purpose and design of the research was focused on a completely different aspect. The same can be said for fields of study that start with observations and experiments, and through analysis after the fact construct working models or concepts of the world. Take astrophysics and the research into dark matter;it is hard to anticipate what would be found, let alone how that information would influence the rest of the world, especially since we are talking about something that is not likely to have any physical consequences.

27

Ultimately, if it is a question of scientific research being harmful, then wouldn't it be better to create regulations to stop the research from being performed, or at least set up regulations to make sure that safety procedures are in place?

Issue Task 28

Claim: *Nations should suspend government funding for the arts when significant numbers of their citizens are hungry or unemployed.*

Reason: *It is inappropriate - and, perhaps, even cruel - to use public resources to fund the arts when people's basic needs are not being met.*

Write a response in which you discuss the extent to which you agree or disagree with the claim and the reason on which that claim is based.

Strategies

Combine the claim and the reason into one statement using a subordinate clause.

In other words:

Because it is inappropriate to use public resources to fund the arts when people's basic needs are not being met, nations should suspend government funding for the arts when significant numbers of their citizens are hungry or unemployed.

What are the assumptions stated or implied in the claim and reason? These will provide evidence that you can refute or affirm in your argument.

◆ Supporting the arts is less important than feeding the hungry or creating jobs.

◆ The arts are not a basic need.

◆ The amount of money dedicated to funding the arts is equal to the amount needed to feed the hungry and create jobs.

◆ Eliminating funding for the arts will alleviate hunger and unemployment.

◆ Funding for the arts can be resumed when people's basic needs are being met.

Opposing viewpoint:

Claim: *Nations should provide funding for the arts even when significant numbers of their citizens at hungry or unemployed.*

28

Reason: *It is appropriate - and perhaps necessary - to fund the arts even when people's basic needs are not being met.*

What are the assumptions stated or implied in the claim and reason? These will provide evidence that you can refute or affirm in your argument.

◆ A nation's artistic accomplishments are as important as the welfare of its citizens.

Alternative viewpoint:

Claim: *Nations should reduce government funding for the arts when significant numbers of their citizens are hungry or unemployed.*

Reason: *Reducing the funding may help alleviate hunger and unemployment until they reach acceptable levels.*

What are the assumptions stated or implied in the claim and reason? These will provide evidence that you can refute or affirm in your argument.

◆ A temporary reduction in funding is the best course.

◆ Eliminating funding for the arts altogether is unnecessary.

 # Sample Essay

Some may believe that art is a luxury and has little to do with people's basic needs. When a country is facing economic challenges, it seems easy and logical to eliminate or reduce funding for the arts. Even on a local level, school boards often recommend cutting art classes and music programs when budgets are strained. Others contend that the arts are an essential part of life and education. Evidence exists in both history and science that supports sustaining the arts even when funding them seems inappropriate.

During the Great Depression, President Roosevelt and Congress created numerous projects that put unemployed Americans to work. Among them was the Federal Writers Project which paid both professional and amateur writers to produce pieces that reflected the culture of the country. Despite criticism, the project continued for four years, eventually employing teachers, librarians, and college graduates. The result was a collection of oral histories, state informational guides, children's books, ethnographies, and other works. National funding for the arts during America's greatest financial crisis actually alleviated unemployment and preserved our cultural identity.

It is difficult to imagine what other countries would know about America or what Americans would know or understand about other countries without the arts. Before the advent of photography, painters provided depictions of the great cities of Europe as well as scenes of daily life. Writers like Charles Dickens illuminated the turmoil in Paris during the French Revolution in A Tale of Two Cities. The Russian composer, Tchaikovsky, composed

28

the 1812 Overture to commemorate the Russian army's defense of the motherland against Napoleon's invading army. Fireworks displays in America would lack drama without the accompaniment of that piece of music. Lack of government funding for the arts in school or for public performances diminishes the ability to identify with the struggles that all humans have faced.

Funding the arts during challenging economic times today can help people meet their basic needs. A theater production requires many people to fill all jobs necessary to bring the project to fruition. In addition to actors, a play requires people to construct sets, provide lighting, sew costumes, and apply makeup. Someone must sell tickets, and others need to clean the theater each evening. Funding an orchestra provides work for dozens of musicians. When all of these individuals earn paychecks, they can provide food, shelter, and clothing for themselves.

Knowledge of the human brain informs us of the connection between music and learning. Students who have had music lessons consistently perform better on standardized tests and get higher grades in math courses. Music also has health benefits. Music and dance therapy are used in combination to help stroke victims regain or improve movement. People with autism also receive benefits from music therapy. Failure to fund the arts on an institutional level can reduce the ability of individuals to achieve their full potential.

I recently visited the Detroit Institute of Art which is home to an impressive Diego Rivera mural which covers four walls of a large room and depicts scenes from the auto industry, the foundation of the greatness Detroit once experienced. Since then, Detroit has declared bankruptcy, and one suggestion to ameliorate its financial burden is to sell the great works of art housed at the DIA. In the short term, the idea may seem to have merit, but removing access to symbols of the city's culture along with representations from other cultures and periods of history may only further impoverish this once-great city.

Monetary considerations cannot stand alone when considering the value of a country's artistic tradition. Making the connection between funding the arts and unemployment and hunger may be a stretch. To assume that cancelling the funding will alleviate or eliminate unemployment and hunger in a country arises from a misunderstanding of abstract benefits versus concrete ones. A country's aesthetic health is as important as its physical wellbeing.

Suspending government funding for any program is fraught with risk and may put the existence of the program in limbo for an extended period of time or eliminate it altogether. The funding that was once earmarked for the arts may be impossible to retrieve from other programs to which it has been diverted.

28

Issue Task 29

Claim: *The surest indicator of a great nation must be the achievements of its rulers, artists, or scientists.*

Reason: *Great achievements by a nation's rulers, artists, or scientists will ensure a good life for the majority of that nation's people.*

Write a response in which you discuss the extent to which you agree or disagree with the claim and the reason on which that claim is based.

NOTE: The above topic has wording similar to Issue Task 16 and 26 in this book. However, if you read carefully you will notice that the task instructions are different. Hence, it is very important to read the topic as well as its instructions completely before you start to write your response.

 Strategies

Combine the claim and the reason into one statement using a subordinate clause

In other words:

Because they will ensure a good life for the majority of a nation's people, the achievements of its rulers, artists, or rulers must be the surest indicator of a great nation.

What are the assumptions stated or implied in the claim and reason? These will provide evidence that you can refute or affirm in your argument.

◆ A nation's greatness is predicated on achievements in leadership, art, and science.

◆ When a country's leaders, artists, and scientists are successful, the rest of the people in the country benefit.

◆ The accomplishments of other groups - educators, business leaders, engineers - have little effect on the wellbeing of society.

Opposing viewpoint:

Claim: *The achievements of its rulers, artists, and scientists are not the surest indicators of a nation's greatness.*

29

Reason: *Great achievements by a nation's leaders, artists and scientists do not ensure a good life for the majority of its citizens.*

What are the assumptions stated or implied in the claim and reason? These will provide evidence that you can refute or affirm in your argument.

◆ Things other than the achievements of a nation's rulers, artists, and scientists determine the greatness of that nation.

 ## Sample Essay

Rulers of a country can create conditions that make it possible for citizens to enjoy a good life. Artists can create masterpieces that generate admiration for the society that provides a home for them. Scientists can improve the lives of the citizens in the country where they live. What motivates rulers, artists and scientists determines the results of their efforts, and they can elevate their citizens or create undesirable conditions for them.

When President Johnson declared a war on poverty in the 1960's, he created the Job Corps and the Head Start program. Nearly fifty years later, both institutions continue to provide opportunities for success to underprivileged young people in America. The Job Corps creates a pathway to high school graduation and vocational training for youth who have failed in traditional settings. Head Start prepares very young children to enter kindergarten with the necessary skills to succeed socially and academically. The longevity of these programs is a result of their proven ability to create better lives for at–risk young people in our society.

Scientists in many fields have improved the lives of humans around the world. Medical advances have not only delivered cures for many cancers and other deadly diseases but made the treatment of them less debilitating. Some former killers, like smallpox and polio, have been virtually eliminated. Other scientists have developed cleaner fuels for the motors that make us mobile and keep us warm or cool in our homes. A majority of citizens benefit from breathing cleaner air and suffering fewer respiratory ailments.

The achievements of a country's artists may be an indication of its greatness but may have little to do with creating a good life for a majority of its citizens. One can see the great works of the Renaissance in Italy and conclude that the atmosphere of the fifteenth century supported the efforts of artistic giants like Leonardo Vinci and Michelangelo. Without wealthy patrons or the support of the Vatican however, many Italian greats might have labored in obscurity, struggling to obtain materials or even feed and clothe themselves. The artistic achievements do not reflect the conditions under which most Italians at the time lived. Ordinary citizens accrued no benefit from the accomplishments of great painters, sculptors or composers.

Likewise, the achievements of the leaders and scientists in Nazi Germany during the 1930's and 40's did not indicate the greatness of that nation. It did not take long for the other countries of Europe to uncover Hitler's motivation for assuming power and invading neighboring countries. Attempting to eradicate entire groups of people does not speak to a leader's ability to engender loyalty and trust in his countrymen. Additionally, Hitler encouraged the perverted medical experiments conducted by Dr. Mengele on inmates of the concentration camps. Hitler's monomaniacal behavior eventually led to Germany's defeat in WWII.

Areas of achievement omitted in the claim include business and education. Without great achievements in education, prospective leaders, artists, and scientists may never have gained the opportunity to reach their potential. The access to free, public education for all of its citizens has had the greatest impact on their ability to ensure a good life for themselves and their families. Many leaders, artists, and scientists would likely acknowledge the fact that they discovered their love of politics, painting, or biology in a classroom.

Achievements in the business arena also contribute to the well-being of a nation's citizens. The ability of the United States to ensure the safety of its citizens during wartime arose in large part from manufacturing concerns that procured raw materials and fashioned warships, fighter planes, and munitions. Giant retailers hire tens of thousands of sales associates to help them provide all manner of goods to the general public. Their paychecks help these workers provide for their families' welfare.

The achievements of leaders, artists, scientists, educators and others cannot contribute to a country's greatness unless those achievements ensure better lives for the citizens of that country. When their achievements ignore the basic tenets of humanity, the citizens of their societies will suffer.

Issue Task 30

Claim: *Major policy decisions should always be left to politicians and other government experts.*

Reason: *Politicians and other government experts are more informed and thus have better judgment and perspective than do members of the general public.*

Write a response in which you discuss the extent to which you agree or disagree with the claim and the reason on which that claim is based.

 Strategies

Combine the claim and the reason into one statement using a subordinate clause.

In other words:

Because politicians and other government experts are more informed and thus have better judgment and perspective than do members of the general public, they alone should make major policy decisions.

What are the assumptions stated or implied in the claim and reason? These will provide evidence that you can refute or affirm in your argument.

◆ Major policy decisions occur only at the government level.

◆ People other than politicians and government experts are not well informed enough to make major policy decisions.

◆ No groups other than government experts or the general public are likely to make policy decisions.

Opposing viewpoint:

Claim: *Major policy decisions should not always be left to politicians and other government experts.*

Reason: *Politicians and other government experts are no better informed or have better judgment and perspective than do members of the general public.*

What are the assumptions stated or implied in the claim and reason? These will provide evidence that you can refute or affirm in your argument.

30

◆ People other than politicians and government experts are capable of making major policy decisions.

 Sample Essay

Major policy decisions guide the actions of people in virtually all walks of life. The Federal Reserve determines policy regarding interest rates that banks charge their biggest customers and, consequently, the interest rates that the average consumer pays for mortgages and auto loans. Although the Fed chairman is appointed by the President, he or she must have autonomy to make monetary decisions independently of politicians. Certainly, the average citizen lacks the specific knowledge necessary to create fiscal policy for the entire country. However, many policies that guide the lives of Americans today would not exist were it not for activism on the parts of ordinary citizens. When policy decisions affect the basic rights of humans, the contributions of the general public cannot be overlooked.

Politicians do not always display better judgment than the general public when they make or uphold policy. For generations, states in the South enforced laws arising from the policy of segregation. Black Americans were banned from eating in white restaurants, using white restrooms, or attending white schools. In 1892, Homer Plessy, in an act that foreshadowed Rosa Parks' behavior on a Montgomery bus in 1951, sat in a designated "white" car of the East Louisiana Railroad. After Plessy identified himself as a black man, authorities arrested him. Plessy's case went all the way to the Supreme Court, where, in 1896, all but one justice declared that the policy of separate but equal facilities for white and black people was acceptable and did not violate the Fourteenth Amendment. The facilities for black people never reached the equal level of those for white people. Their schools were inferior; the buildings were run down, and the books had been discarded by white schools. For decades, black children were banned from riding school buses and often had to walk long distances to attend schools designated for them. Nearly half a decade after the Plessy case, the NAACP sponsored a case in Topeka, Kansas, that represented several parents who wanted their children to be allowed to attend schools in their neighborhoods rather than the "separate but equal" schools. In a unanimous decision in 1954, the Supreme Court in Brown v the Board of Education of Topeka, Kansas, ruled that the separate but equal policy was unconstitutional, thereby integrating public schools throughout the country. Left to their own devices, politicians and other government experts would have continued to allow de facto segregation in the United States. Without the impetus from those suffering under the policy, little change would have occurred or would have come much later.

When a policy has been in effect for a long time, it becomes difficult to change. Even though the Supreme Court decision of 1954 prohibited segregation, people in the South were reluctant to grant civil rights to their black neighbors. They held onto their belief in the superiority of the white man, a remnant of the days of slavery on southern plantations. Their leaders devised requirements for voting that made it virtually impossible for black men and women to exercise their right of suffrage. When any group of citizens cannot vote to change policy or elect legislators who represent their interests, repressive laws and regulations persist. Without the efforts of the NAACP, the Freedom Riders, student activists from northern universities and the leadership of Martin Luther King, Jr., President Lyndon B. Johnson may not have been convinced to sign into law the Civil Rights Act of 1964.

30

One should not assume that politicians and government experts are better informed than the general public and, therefore, the only ones capable of making or changing major policy decisions. Senators, representatives, and the president all select advisers from the general public. They look for the best and brightest in a variety of fields to fill positions in their offices and the cabinet. The expertise they gained while plying their trades in the public sector makes them valuable assets at the national level. Although average citizens do not have the power to create policy, their voices contribute to the choices those politicians and government experts make to change the manner in which the business of everyday life is carried out.

30

Issue Task 31

The effectiveness of a country's leaders is best measured by examining the well-being of that country's citizens.

Write a response in which you discuss the extent to which you agree or disagree with the statement and explain your reasoning for the position you take. In developing and supporting your position, you should consider ways in which the statement might or might not hold true and explain how these considerations shape your position.

 Strategies

Restate the issue, perhaps by reversing the order of the sentence components.

In other words:

The well-being of a country's citizens is the best measure of its leaders' effectiveness.

Determine what question is being answered by the statement. This will help you begin to think how you would answer it and whether or not you agree with the original statement.

What are the best means of measuring the effectiveness of a country's leaders?

Parts of the original statement that provide evidence that you can affirm or refute.

 ◆ Effective leaders ensure the wellbeing of a country's citizens.

 ◆ Other measures of a leader's effectiveness are less important than the wellbeing of the country's citizens.

Next, create a statement that expresses the opposing viewpoint, using language similar to that of the original statement.

Opposing viewpoint:

The effectiveness of a country's leaders is not best measured by the well-being of that country's citizens.

Is there any other way to look at this issue? Can you qualify the original statement in some way? Is it possible to partially agree with the statement?

31

Alternative viewpoint:

The well-being of a country's citizens is one measure of its leaders' effectiveness.

 ## Sample Essay

When history judges the effectiveness of a country's leader, it considers the decisions he or she made that led to a good life for the citizens of the country. High employment rates, accessibility to affordable health care, a good school system, a reasonable inflation rate, and security from invasion by enemies are some of those important measures. When those conditions exist for an extended period of time, the leader can be called effective, perhaps even great.

America has elected presidents who displayed great leadership in areas other than government, believing that their skills would create a sense of well-being for its citizens. General Dwight D. Eisenhower, Supreme Commander of the allied troops in Europe during WWII, created the strategy for the D-Day invasion of Normandy that eventually decided the war in favor of the Allies. "I Like Ike" became the campaign slogan that helped to elect him president in 1952 and again in 1956. Eisenhower's demonstrated ability to secure victory over communism and fascism in Europe made him the popular choice to lead post-war America. The prosperity of Americans during the '50s would make it reasonable to conclude that Eisenhower was an effective leader.

Perhaps no other president in the twentieth century faced more challenges during his term of leadership than Franklin Delano Roosevelt. First elected in 1932, he faced the Herculean task of lifting the country out of the Great Depression. Large numbers of Americans were unemployed, hungry, and homeless. With the blessings of Congress, FDR established the New Deal which contained programs like the CCC (Civil Conservation Corps) that provided both paying jobs for Americans and a necessary service in America's woodlands. During the first year of FDR's third term, on December 7, 1941, the Japanese attacked American ships at Pearl Harbor. As a result, American would become engaged in WWII, fighting both in Europe and the Pacific. FDR's ability to lead during wartime was exemplified by his ability to forge an alliance with the USSR, a former adversary. Americans were so convinced of this president's ability to improve the wellbeing of all citizens that they reelected FDR for an unprecedented fourth term.

Some might argue that leaders in the twenty-first century have made some decisions that were designed to secure the wellbeing of Americans but have infringed on citizens' rights or have not had the intended consequences. After the terrorist attacks on the World Trade Center in 2001, the leaders of America declared war on Al Qaeda and vowed to hunt down those responsible for the attacks and prevent further threats to America's safety. Patriotic fever swept the nation, and most citizens heartily approved of President Bush's decision. Twelve years later, American troops were still fighting in Iraq and Afghanistan, and the American people grew weary of the protracted war. The Patriot Act was created to enable the tracking of suspected terrorists in the United States, but many citizens protested the invasion of privacy inherent in that act. Travel by air throughout the country became a more laborious undertaking with security measures implemented at every airport. Even though Americans feel safer when they travel, they feel that some freedoms have been lost. The well–being of the majority may occur at the price of individual freedom.

Just recently, the government of Syria used chemical weapons in the form of poisonous gas on its own citizens. President Obama immediately declared that the US should take military action against Syria to eliminate these chemical weapons. Should Syria continue to use chemical weapons, American troops and civilians in the Middle East may be in danger. A military strike might ensure their wellbeing. On the other hand, Syria and its allies could retaliate, putting even more Americans in danger. Decisions about protecting the wellbeing of Americans are often fraught with conflicting consequences; the right choice is not always obvious or easy, and leaders are subject to harsh criticism if their choices are unpopular.

Leaders of the free world do attempt to secure the wellbeing of their citizens by maintaining a vibrant economy, protecting individual rights, and ensuring their safety by eliminating threats both foreign and domestic. Many of those leaders also try to improve the lives of people who are oppressed or murdered by their own leaders in other countries. The effectiveness of any leader to secure the well-being of the citizens may not become apparent until his or her actions are viewed from a historical perspective.

Issue Task 32

Governments should place few, if any, restrictions on scientific research and development.

Write a response in which you discuss the extent to which you agree or disagree with the recommendation and explain your reasoning for the position you take. In developing and supporting your position, describe specific circumstances in which adopting the recommendation would or would not be advantageous and explain how these examples shape your position.

 Strategies

The best place to start your analysis is by breaking down the statement and identifying the inherent assumptions.

Statement breakdown:

◆ Governments – places the restrictions in the realm of the law

◆ Restriction –the nature and extent of the restrictions is unknown - this gives you a lot of room to explore – are the restrictions about scientific conduct? Do they include testing? How about work safety or waste management?

◆ Scientific research and development – give you the scope of the restriction

Assumptions:

◆ Governments have the responsibility of placing/lifting restrictions

◆ Scientific research is bound by law

◆ Restrictions on scientific research hinder progress

Once you have completed these steps, you need to write down the pro and con arguments, regardless of which position you take. Knowing the counterarguments (ideas in opposition to your own position) allows you to present a more rounded view of the subject and gives you the opportunity of identifying contradicting evidence.

32

Pros and Cons:

Pros

👍 More creativity

👍 More daring

👍 Reaching previously unexplored fields

👍 Faster research-development-production rate

👍 Less bound by current societal practices/notions of morality

Cons

👎 Ethics/crossing moral boundaries

👎 End justifies the means

👎 Untested products can find their way on the market

👎 Problems with work-safety

👎 Handling waste products and the environment

👎 Cruelty to animals/human experimentation

👎 Risk of science turning into business (profit over safety)

👎 Division of country based on beliefs (stem cell)

Examples:

For a truly well-rounded essay, examples are crucial. Here are some avenues that are potentially worth pursuing:

a) History is rife with examples – both the unethical human experimentation, and the great accidental discoveries (like penicillin) that greatly benefited mankind.

b) The same goes for the news – scientific research that is testing the boundaries is always bound to attract controversy – think of stem cell research, cloning.

c) In this case, Science Fiction books and movies love showing the consequences of pushing the boundaries of science.

32

Lastly, spend a few minutes coming up with a roadmap. While at first it will slow you down, once you become adept at outlining, your writing speed will increase, and your essay will benefit from having a logical structure.

 Sample Essay

Scientific research has always been tangled with the ethical dilemma of whether the end justifies the means. There is even an entire philosophical field called 'normative ethical theories' dedicated to examining standards for the rightness and wrongness of action and determining how an individual should act. In this case, while giving researchers a carte blanche allows science to explore uncharted territory and enables a faster research-development-production rate, it also opens the door to the horrors of unethical experimentation.

Even though studies have shown that animal research is neither necessary nor is it predictive for humans, animals still continue to be the most common subject of scientific experimentation. The existing Animal Welfare Act offers reduced protection, removing all the restrictions on scientific research and giving scientists a free pass to conduct experiments that would otherwise have been seen as animal cruelty, on the basis of inducing unnecessary pain. Furthermore, having no regulations when it comes to the species that can be used in experimentation can lead to an increase in poaching when it comes to animals with rare properties or genetic similarities to humans. As Thomas Edison said, "Until we stop harming all other living beings, we are still savages."

Unrestricted scientific research would not only impact the treatment of animals but also how human experimentation is conducted. The history books are fraught with examples of experiments that were often performed illegally, without the knowledge, consent, or informed consent of the test subjects. In the US for instance, the Cold War era brought about numerous psychological experiments for testing effective torture and interrogation techniques. There is even the famous case of the Holmesburg prison in Pennsylvania, where in the 60's and 70's, chemical experiments were performed on the prisoners who were injected with dioxin, a highly toxic compound. Perhaps the most telling and horrific example is that of the Nazi human experiments, from genetics to vivisections and poison studies and transplantation without anesthesia. What particularly draws attention to this case is not just the extent of human suffering, but also the justification used for the experiments: at the trial, several of the doctors argued in their defense that there was no international law regarding medical experimentation. This raises the question of how to judge abuses in regard to scientific experimentation without a body of law that governs the scientific practices.

Another issue also presents itself; no research restrictions mean no regulation when it comes to testing. Take the example of the pharmaceutical industry. On the one hand, experimental treatments can find their way on the market much faster – on the other, pharmaceutical companies run the risk of becoming a business where profit supersedes safety. Current regulations require years of trials before drugs can be released for production; without them, companies can cut corners and push products on the market that can have serious untested side effects. Without government regulations, taking punitive action against companies that promote dangerous drugs to the market becomes difficult if not impossible, especially since, according to the law, they would not be committing any crimes

32

Then there is the question of how to handle dangerous scientific research (viruses, chemical weapons etc.). Having no restrictions means people who are insufficiently prepared or have destructive agendas can get involved in potentially dangerous experiments. Researching subjects that would be better left alone and dealing with the consequences of pushing the boundaries of science are prominent themes of science fiction. Most post-apocalyptic scenarios of both books and movies come about from scientific experimentation – creating dangerous viruses that escape containment, like in The Stand, or opening up inter-dimensional portals to worlds of horror in Stephen Kings' The Mist.

Ultimately, no matter how seductive the promise of freedom of research, rules and regulations have to be set in place to ensure that in the quest for knowledge we don't end up sacrificing our own humanity. Existing restrictions have evolved based on our previous experiences with the potential horrors of unsanctioned experimentation, and they have been set in place to protect us – from ourselves.

Issue Task 33

Governments should offer college and university education free of charge to all students.

Write a response in which you discuss the extent to which you agree or disagree with the statement and explain your reasoning for the position you take. In developing and supporting your position, you should consider ways in which the statement might or might not hold true and explain how these considerations shape your position.

 Strategies

A good starting point is to break down the statement and identify the assumptions it makes. Look for ambiguous phrasing and consider all possible exceptions – they represent weak points that you can defend or attack depending on your chosen position.

Statement breakdown:

◆ **Governments** – state funded education

◆ **College and university** – does it include masters, PhDs?

◆ **Free of charge** – what expenses are paid (tuition, board etc.)? How about following multiple studies simultaneously? What about existing scholarships and welfare packages?

◆ **All students** – including exchange students?

All statements are based on a set of assumptions about the world and the way it works – many of these social norms are implicit due to subconscious associations. The basis of outlining assumptions is asking 'why': why should the government provide free education? Why should education be free for all?

Assumptions:

◆ College and university education is desirable

◆ Having more educated people is good for the state

◆ The government has the resources to provide free university education

33

◆ All students should benefit – including exchange students

Pros and Cons:

Pros

👍 No more crippling debt (like seen in the US)

👍 An educated workforce is an economic imperative

👍 It is an investment in the country's own future (more students mean more contributions)

👍 Bridges the gap between 'haves' and 'have-nots' – high tuitions can be a deterrent for brilliant students without financial means

👍 Compulsory education is already state funded

👍 Free education does not mean having lower standards – students still have to pass admission tests

👍 Stimulates the economy around universities based on the expected influx of students

👍 Educational excellence attracts talents from around the world

👍 Loyalty effect – talented people will not desert the country in search for better options

👍 Higher education is related to culture and civilization

Cons

👎 Existing programs already cover students that have financial issues (grants, scholarships, welfare etc.)

👎 It would be expensive – it would incur increased taxes or other trade-offs

👎 System abuse – lingering or unsure students that waste taxpayer's money on studies they won't complete

👎 No pressure to finish – a lowering of study quality (people can stretch out the education for as long as it takes, or put less effort into it)

👎 Exchange students will use the program and then return to their own countries (and contribute to society there)

👎 More graduates would dilute the value of a degree (a degree would become the norm, instead of a differentiating criteria)

33

👎 Oversaturation of the job market (many graduates would be unemployed or underemployed)

👎 College degrees do not guarantee learning ability or job preparation

Examples:

a) Look at nations across the globe, some have free university education (Denmark, Norway, Sweden etc.), while others don't (USA, Romania, Germany etc.)

b) Percentages of employed university graduates

c) Economical contribution (pay grade and its relationship with graduation)

d) The relationship between literacy rate and economical power

e) Scientific and technological advancements

f) Tuition fees and debt

 ## Sample Essay

Education plays an important part in everyone's life, it helps people overcome superstitions, keep in touch with the advancements of the world and gain a deeper understanding of how things function, instills respect, teaches people how to function and contribute to society while maintaining their own independence. As Nelson Mandela said, "education is the most powerful weapon you can use to change the world."

Governments from across the globe have understood this crucial fact and acted in accordance by making education up to a certain level compulsory and free. Why should this government funding not extend to higher education as well? There is no doubt that promoting education is an investment in the future, as many studies have demonstrated by linking the literacy of a country with its economic growth. An educated workforce is an economic imperative: more students means more contributions, both in terms of finances and when it comes to scientific, technological and cultural advancements. Given the potential of a highly skilled workforce, some nations have already implemented policies that ensure free access to higher education for all students. In Sweden, attending university is free for all EU students. Denmark and Norway have similar policies. It is interesting to note that these countries have some of the highest living standards in the world and that their policies have been in place for several years with no major drawbacks to speak of.

On another note, state funded university education can also help bridge the gap between the haves' and 'have–nots'. High tuition can be a deterrent for brilliant students without financial means: valuable talent can be lost to menial labor or even other countries, as students can leave in search of better opportunities. While most countries already have some scholarship programs set in place, they only cater to the extremely brilliant and

33

promote a highly competitive environment. The students that fall just shy of the requirements have to contend with paying tuition, and in some countries, like the US, that lands them into crippling debt. Student loan debt in the US has made the front page of international newspapers with stories of ruined lives and people that have to dedicate a good portion of their life just to paying off the tuition fees. Having no debt means graduates have more buying power and can invest more in the economy.

Free university education can even have a direct effect on the micro–economy surrounding the campus based on the expected increase in the number of attending students. As in the cases of Cambridge and Harvard, universities encourage the growth of towns next to campus sites – small businesses that cater to the students' needs tend to flourish. An increase in the number of attending students can even have an effect on the construction market as dormitories get expanded to accumulate the intake of students.

Additionally, funding the student's education can have a loyalty effect: Talented people will not desert the country in search for better options. It should also be noted that free education does not mean that there will be a drop–in standards as students still have to pass admission tests and pass their classes. This way, the system ensures that only the people that possess the necessary skills and determination to graduate can enroll. The Dutch system provides a good application of this principle. Dutch students get a loan from the government for their university tuition and upon graduation, the loan is given as a gift. In essence, in the Netherlands, higher education is free – as long as the student graduates, which serves as a good motivation for people not to slack off or take on more studies than they can handle.

This goes to show that there are viable solutions for implementing free university education policies. Moreover, numerous countries have applied these policies with success for a considerable number of years. Given these practical examples and the potential benefits of a highly educated workforce, it would be a shame not to invest in our future.

33

Issue Task 34

Nations should pass laws to preserve any remaining wilderness areas in their natural state, even if these areas could be developed for economic gain.

Write a response in which you discuss your views on the policy and explain your reasoning for the position you take. In developing and supporting your position, you should consider the possible consequences of implementing the policy and explain how these consequences shape your position.

 Strategies

When developing a response to an Analyze an Issue question, you are required to present both sides of the argument and choose one to support. A 5- or 6-paragraph structure is recommended for this style of essay. Make sure to have an Introduction, Body (2 or 3 supporting points and 1 counter-point), and Conclusion.

It is highly recommended that regardless of the position you choose, the first 5 minutes should be devoted to brainstorming a few points that agree with the policy issue at hand and a few that disagree with it. Here is a sample brainstorm for this question:

Agree:

◆ Wilderness forms the basis of our world's ecosystems, and millions of species of animals depend on access to the wild. By enacting laws to protect the wilderness, we are ensuring the long-term survival of the earth.

◆ Humans occupy a large area of the available land in the world. However, as the population grows, we should commit to building up and not out. Single families do not need private tennis courts, swimming pools, and gardens at the expense of nature. Left to their own devices, humans are greedy – so it is up to the nations to be altruistic.

◆ Humans are in favor of natural wilderness areas, as they allow for hiking, traveling, and exploring. People can enjoy the wilderness as a form of entertainment, nourishment, and spiritual fulfillment, and preserving these areas would increase the well-being of humans as well as other species.

◆ In the United States, for example, National Parks and National Forests are a source of pride and an attraction in and of themselves. Such locations do not need to be developed in order to attract tourism, and economic systems are built around the parks themselves.

◆ There are many examples of countries that developed areas for economic gain that ended up a disaster. China's overdevelopment and stripping of natural resources left the country with serious health problems resulting from severe pollution.

Disagree:

◆ There are still plenty of areas that humans will likely never develop, so laws are not required to ensure this. For example, Canada is sparsely populated, and it does not require formal laws to remain as such.

◆ Managed growth is as good as or better than leaving the wilderness untouched. For example, planned fires and the weeding out of invasive species that arrived there through other human activities or accidentally (e.g., the invasion of Japanese species after the 2011 tsunami). By both exploiting and regulating the wilderness, a win–win situation is created.

Now, you are ready to get started on the essay.

 ## Sample Essay

The human population continues to grow. With this growth, we demand an ever-increasing amount of natural resources, such as land, oil, and agricultural products. Yet, we must also balance this requirement with the knowledge that we must maintain sustainability to ensure the survival of our species and of Earth itself. Overexploitation of resources will deplete the available stock and affect fragile ecologies worldwide. To ensure that we (and the earth) continue to flourish for generations to come, nations have the responsibility to enact laws protecting existing wilderness areas regardless of whether they can be exploited for economic gain.

Proponents in favor of using wilderness for economic gain suggest that exploitation and preservation are not mutually exclusive. By controlling and regulating forest fires, conducting managed growth, and farming sustainably, proponents suggest that we can benefit from natural resources and preserve as large of a wilderness area as possible. They claim that instead of laws to preserve the wilderness in its natural state, we should create a wilderness development program that ensures the survival of all species through adequate managed growth.

However, managed growth does not target the root of the problem of exploiting natural resources: the negative externalities generated by developing wilderness areas. More specifically, the advantage of wilderness areas is that they have well-established ecosystems, including old trees with deep roots. Logging and clearing these trees and replacing them with new saplings reduces the amount of photosynthesis that occurs in the area; in turn, increasing amounts of human-generated carbon dioxide does not convert fast enough to oxygen, leading to high pollution. For example, China both logged their forests and exploited other resources (e.g., coal) while developing industries on the land. They are suffering the consequences of these decisions as their population is exposed to increased pollution and widespread health problems. The only feasible way to slow or reverse these would be to stop exploiting the natural wilderness and let nature do the healing.

34

In addition, wilderness areas can be used as a resource without being exploited specifically for economic gain. For example, many people view the wilderness as a form of spiritual retreat away from their busy lives. It is the final frontier where they can go hiking, mountain biking, and camping in nature. On another note, many animals such as fish rely on an untouched wilderness to thrive. The effects of interfering with the natural habitat of these fish (e.g. the rivers that salmon spawn in) or attempting to manage their growth have backfired as fish in the hundreds of thousands have disappeared or died because of human interference, which is opposite to our goals of creating a sustainable fishing population in the oceans and seas. To ensure that we are able to continue to enjoy these fish, we must see the wilderness as a resource that we cannot interfere with and preserve it under law.

Therefore, we do not understand the wilderness well enough to manage it effectively at this point and although we might believe that we are capable of using our wilderness resources in a sustainable fashion, our performance shows otherwise. For nations looking to continue to grow and thrive and build successful industries, the benefits of protecting the wilderness in its natural state in the long run far outweigh those of developing wilderness areas for economic gain in the short run.

34

Chapter **6**

Philosophy

Issue Task 35

In any field of endeavor, it is impossible to make a significant contribution without first being strongly influenced by past achievements in that field.

Write a response in which you discuss the extent to which you agree or disagree with the statement and explain your reasoning for the position you take. In developing and supporting your position, you should consider ways in which the statement might or might not hold true and explain how these considerations shape your position.

 Strategies

You might begin by restating the issue. In this case the issue is a negative statement that includes the word impossible. Consider how the statement would look if you replaced impossible with the word, possible.

In other words:

The only way that it is possible to make a significant contribution in any field of endeavor is to first be strongly influenced by past achievements in that field.

Or: *The only possible way to make a significant contribution in any field of endeavor is to first be strongly influenced by past achievements in that field.*

You could also determine what question is being answered by the issue statement.

By what means is it possible to make a significant contribution in a field of endeavor?

The interrogatory form of the statement may help some writers develop alternative viewpoints. The original issue statement is only one of several possible answers to the question.

Now think about the parts of the statement that provide evidence that you can affirm or refute.

◆ **the only possible way** – Is there no other way to make a significant contribution? Is nothing really original? Is everything derivative?

◆ **any field of endeavor** – Are there fields of endeavor that can be excluded from this statement? Can we even imagine fields of endeavor that might arise in the future?

◆ **strongly influenced** – Is it possible to be mildly influenced or tangentially influenced by past achievements?

35

◆ **contribution** – What kind of contribution? Is it a new invention? An idea? A procedure?

Next, create a statement that expresses the opposing viewpoint, using language similar to that of the original issue statement.

Opposing viewpoint:

In any field of endeavor, it is possible to make a significant contribution without being strongly influenced by past achievements in that field.

Or: *Being strongly influenced by past achievements in any field of endeavor is not the only way to make a significant contribution to that field.*

Identify the parts of the opposing statement that provide evidence to refute or affirm. Some of these may look very similar to those in the list generated above.

◆ **contribution** – How does one determine the significance of any contribution? Significance may be subjective.

◆ **any field of endeavor** – Are there fields of endeavor that can be excluded from this statement?

◆ **influence** – What form of influence? Is it a product? An idea? A procedure?

◆ **not the only way** – How might one contribute significantly without being influenced by past achievements?

Alternatives:

Is there any other way to look at this issue? By what means other than strong influence from past achievements can someone make a contribution to a field of endeavor? Begin by listing important fields of human endeavor: medicine, science, art, philosophy, literature, flight, etc. Think about experiences you have had, books you have read, courses you have taken and come up with some examples of contributions to that field.

◆ **Medicine** – Fleming and penicillin

◆ Native Americans and willow bark

◆ **Science** – Galileo and heliocentrism

◆ **Art** – Picasso and cubism

◆ **Literature** – Ezra Pound and imagism

◆ **Energy** – prehistoric man and fire

35

What statements can you make about the items in your list? Fleming's, Galileo's, and prehistoric man's contributions came in the form of discovery. Picasso's and Pound's contributions came in the form of rejecting the previous achievements in their fields of endeavor. Galileo's discovery occurred also as he rejected the church's theory of the Earth as the center of the universe. Now you have two specific means of contribution: discovery of something new and rejection of something old.

Create a statement that expresses a viewpoint using the new ideas that you have uncovered.

New Viewpoint:

It is possible to make a significant contribution in any field of endeavor by rejecting past achievements in that field.

Or: *All significant contributions in any field of endeavor occur as a result of an important discovery.*

What evidence exists in these statements that provide points to support or refute?

◆ **rejecting past achievements** – Is it possible to transform rather than reform an existing idea or product?

◆ **discovery comes before achievement** – Every field of endeavor arises from an important discovery.

Now you must decide which point of view to address in your essay. Completing the prewriting activities has given you several choices and ideas for defending any of those choices. Even viewpoints opposite of yours will have points that you can use in writing your response. As you review your notes, decide which of your ideas offer the strongest support for your position; you do not have to use all of them. Keep in mind that others may disagree with your position, so address their concerns in your response. Before you decide, carefully consider the following checklist. You will have addressed several of them in the exercises you have completed above.

◆ I have identified the central issue.

◆ I understand the instructions.

◆ I have decided that I agree/disagree/partially agree with the issue and why.

◆ I have identified the assumptions in the claim and determined whether or not they are reasonable.

◆ If necessary, I can explain how I interpret any or all of the concepts and terms used in the claim.

◆ I have identified my reasons for the position I have taken.

◆ I have compelling examples to support my position.

The next step should be listing the main reasons and support for your position. You may use any of the above prewriting activities as you prepare evidence for supporting your point of view. Remember that the GRE readers scoring your response are not looking for a "right" answer. The readers are evaluating your ability to address the specific instructions and articulate and develop an argument to support your understanding and evaluation of the issue.

Position:

All significant contributions in any field of endeavor occur as a result of an important discovery.

Examples:

a) Fire – Once man learned to control it, he developed uses for it and sources of fuel to feed it.

b) Medicine – Man discovered that leaves, roots, and bark of trees and plants ameliorated pain and relieved the symptoms of other maladies

c) Water power – Man could harness the power of flowing water to turn wheels to grind grains and seeds.

Your notes do not have to be exhaustive. As you begin to write your essay, your brain will generate new ideas. Make certain that you keep the directions in mind as you develop your ideas. Use as many or as few paragraphs as you consider appropriate for your argument, but create a new paragraph when you move on to a new idea or example in support of your position. The GRE readers are not looking for a specific number of ideas or paragraphs. Instead, they are reading to determine the level of understanding of the topic and the complexity with which you respond.

In this task, you are asked to discuss the extent to which you agree or disagree with the statement. You may completely agree or disagree with the statement, or you may agree under certain conditions. You are also instructed to explain your reasoning and consider ways in which the statement might or might not hold true and explain how these considerations shape your position.

You may use any organizational strategy or form of reasoning to present your position as clearly and succinctly as possible. You may recall writing strategies that you learned in high school or a writing-intensive course you took in college, but it is not necessary to employ any of those strategies. It is important that your ideas follow a logical progression and display strong critical thinking.

Sample Essay

The premise that significant contributions in any field can only be made through the influence from past achievements in that field holds true in the modern world. Modern appliances, advanced medicine, and improved fuel efficiency are founded on earlier models. The next big thing is simply a version of the last big thing. It may be thinner, smaller, faster, or more intuitive; but, fundamentally, it is the same thing. The ubiquitous television sets

35

in people's homes today are probably hanging on the wall and have plasma or LCD screens. These bigger, brighter versions essentially perform the same function as the older, bulkier vacuum tube models; they bring moving pictures into our homes. The Band-Aids found in every medicine chest come in a variety of sizes, colors, with or without an antibacterial cream embedded, and even in liquid form. These superior bandages also perform the same function as their predecessors; they cover cuts and scrapes. In actuality, everything new is not very original. They are adaptations.

One must turn to the ancient world to recognize that the greatest contributions in any field of endeavor have come through discovery rather than invention or advancement. Early man discovered fire and realized that he could use it to cook his food, warm his cave, and keep predators at bay. Eventually, he learned how to create it, preserve it, and carry it with him as he migrated to better hunting grounds or more temperate climates. Modern man has witnessed the harnessing of fire to create steam that powered ships and locomotives. It still heats our homes and cooks our food, but it also takes us into outer space.

At some point, ancient man realized that round objects move more effectively over the ground than do square or rectangular objects, that the power of water could help man to accomplish tasks more easily, and that the leaves, roots, and bark of plants and trees provided relief from pain and other maladies. Thus, we have the wheel, grist mills on local streams, and aspirin in tablet form. Were it not for Franklin's flying a kite during a thunderstorm or Fleming's discovery of penicillin, we would live in the dark and die from bacterial infections. When bold seafarers from Scandinavia and Western Europe sailed east and failed to fall off the edge of the earth, they discovered the fishing banks off the coast of Newfoundland and treasures in Mexico and opened the doors to modern-day travel.

In the final analysis, it is appropriate to assert that no one can contribute significantly in any field of endeavor without first being influenced by past achievements in that field. While those contributions generally improve the quality of our lives, it is likely that the next important discovery will have a profound effect.

35

Issue Task 36

In any field of inquiry, the beginner is more likely than the expert to make important contributions.

Write a response in which you discuss the extent to which you agree or disagree with the statement and explain your reasoning for the position you take. In developing and supporting your position, you should consider ways in which the statement might or might not hold true and explain how these considerations shape your position.

Strategies

A good starting point is to break down the statement and identify the assumptions it makes. Look for ambiguous phrasing and consider all possible exceptions – they represent weak points that you can defend or attack depending on your chosen position.

Statement breakdown:

◆ **Any field** – is it applicable to all fields? How about highly complex ones that require specialized knowledge?

◆ **Beginner** – how do you classify the beginner? Based on age? Experience? Knowledge?

◆ **More likely** – does it refer to statistical probability (numbers game)? Does it refer to inherent qualities of the beginner?

◆ **Important contributions** – what constitutes an important contribution? What is the classification criterion: applicability, usefulness, impact?

Assumptions:

◆ Beginners are more likely to contribute, since there are more beginners than experts

◆ Important contributions are not based on experience

◆ Beginners have more creative minds, while experts are set in their ways

Pros and Cons:

Pros

👍 Thinking outside the box (integrating and reorganizing existing understandings – a process essential to beginners

👍 With age, cognitive abilities deteriorate, it becomes harder to process new information (experts are often older)

👍 Beginners are determined – they have something to prove

👍 Beginners are freer to experiment – experts are set in their ways

👍 There are greater numbers of beginners, so a larger chance to bring accidental contributions

👍 Beginners have more willingness to try or evaluate new paths

👍 Beginners have more time (experts are committed to multiple projects and often have to perform supervisory roles)

👍 Beginners have less to lose by pursuing risky avenues

Cons

👎 Beginners that make important contributions are considered experts

👎 The ageing brain is similar to the creative brain (based on neural imaging) – low inhibitions, high scores on crystallized IQ

👎 Experts are more productive, have a better work ethic

👎 Some fields are very complex (entry level knowledge is insufficient to provide deep insight)

👎 For beginners, lack of practical application can lead to correct but irrelevant insight (researching avenues that lead to nowhere

👎 Focused research (knowing the field allows you to conduct a targeted research)

👎 Historically, most of the great inventions come from experts between the ages of 30 to 50

👎 Experts have more freedom of choice when it comes to the research topic (beginners are limited by supervisors

👎 Experts can get more funding, or obtain it easier than beginners can (reputation)

👎 Experts enjoy more credibility

36

Examples:

a) Inventors and scientific contributors from the past

b) Studies linking age and creativity

c) Problem solving skills and methods (you can pair them up with the group that fits best)

d) Current research practices

Sample Essay

Humans have conquered their surroundings and overcome their limits in leaps and bounds marked by great innovations. Our ability to integrate and reorganize existing understandings, to bring new order to chaos, has been the driving force of our progress. It is no wonder that people seek to understand the process of innovation and encourage those that are most likely to succeed in revolutionizing the world.

So far, invention has been considered the patrimony of experts, and one of the reasons is the fact that in order to be able to combine fragments of knowledge in new ways, one needs to have sufficient knowledge in the first place. It is not difficult to understand why such perceptions abound, especially if we consider highly complex fields that require specialized, in depth, knowledge. Take for instance astrophysics or microbiology: a beginner in these fields would only possess summary knowledge of the forces at play and the processes involved. They wouldn't be able to revolutionize theories on dark matter without a basic understanding of quantum theories; and by the time they would have acquired this knowledge, they would be considered experts. This is also the case of Albert Einstein, whose major contributions in the field came as a steady progression after getting his PhD. Most important of all, Einstein's theory of relativity only started taking shape after years of teaching theoretical physics at universities in Zurich and Prague, and two years spent studying continuum mechanics, the molecular theory of heat, and the problem of gravitation.

When it comes to establishing whether beginners or experts are more likely to revolutionize a new field, it is important to note that a lot of the past inventions have come from people who had to constantly struggle with a specific problem. A lot of the people who have contributed to the advancement of society were experts in a field (in the proper circumstances to encounter the problem and possessing sufficient knowledge to recognize and solve the issue at hand). This is the case of prominent physician, John Snow, whose field work in tracing the 1854 cholera outbreak in London is regarded as the founding event of epidemiology. He encountered many cases of viral diseases as a physician, which, alongside his skepticism of the then dominant miasma theory of infection, spurred him on to research the Soho epidemic and discover the source of the outbreak.

Moreover, one should always keep in mind that it's not sufficient to have a good idea; a researcher should also be able to support it and make it known. This holds especially true when considering the basic conditions for any form of research to be considered a major contribution in a field. Namely, said research should revolutionize its

36

Philosophy

field of study; it should be known by other experts in the discipline and obtain external validation (even if at a later point in time). In this sense, experts enjoy more credibility than beginners, and are likely to be taken more seriously. Furthermore, experts already have networks in place and get quicker access to information like interesting research proposals and latest advancements. Companies and other researchers will choose to go to the person with a better reputation. The same can be said in terms of funding, experts can attract more funds for promising research– simply because they have more experience and an established reputation.

Studies have shown that experts are more productive and have better work ethic and time management skills. In addition, being an expert doesn't signify the death of creativity, like the statement implies, blindly sticking to one method has more to do with personality. The same goes for linking expertise with age, as neuroimaging studies have shown that the ageing brain is more creative, uninhibited and shows better crystallized IQ. Benjamin Jones has also found that over the past 100 years, the major scientific discoveries have come from people with ages between 30 and 50.

Overall, when it comes to having major contributions in a field, experts possess the advantage. They have more knowledge, an increased ability to organize the information they possess, more resources to fund research and a better work ethic than beginners.

Issue Task 37

As we acquire more knowledge, things do not become more comprehensible, but more complex and mysterious.

Write a response in which you discuss the extent to which you agree or disagree with the statement and explain your reasoning for the position you take. In developing and supporting your position, you should consider ways in which the statement might or might not hold true and explain how these considerations shape your position.

 Strategies:

A good starting point is to break down the statement and identify the assumptions it makes. What is interesting to note in this particular case is the fact that the statement is counter intuitive: it seems to contradict common sense. The nature of the statement makes it suitable for philosophical and psychological arguments

Statement breakdown:

◆ **We** – general we of humanity

◆ **Acquire more knowledge** – knowledge is cumulative – how to quantify it? Is it "true" knowledge? Is it "useful"?

◆ **Things – an** all-encompassing term for the subject of knowledge; vague term specific things that become less understandable?

◆ **Comprehensible** – understandable; how do you gauge a person's understanding? Based on how 'true' it is, or how much it conforms to a current scientific trend.

◆ **Complex and mysterious** – suggest awe in the face of the vastness of the universe; is it a feeling rather than fact–based speculation?

Assumptions:

◆ The universe cannot be fully known – the sum of all knowledge cannot be attained

◆ Discovering something always opens up new avenues of research

◆ Knowledge is measurable – walking in the direction of "true knowledge"

◆ We are not "equipped" to be able to grasp all knowledge

Pros and Cons:

Pros

👍 Knowledge is not linear – we also take steps back in our quest for truth

👍 What is 'true' now will end up being proved wrong in the future, as our understanding grows

👍 Knowledge is influenced by society/dominating paradigms

👍 Each new question answered raises other questions

👍 More knowledge gained shows us just how complex things are (scientific models always grow in complexity)

👍 Our minds are not suitable for understanding the level of complexity of the universe

👍 We can only perceive what our senses tell us

Cons

👎 Knowledge is quantifiable

👎 knowledge is attainable, step by step (knowledge building)

👎 Not 'understanding" is a feeling – psychological effect

👎 Should not compare current knowledge with sum of all knowledge – but with how little we knew in the past (progress measured by how far we have come, not how far we still have to go)

👎 People feel overwhelmed by how much there is still to discover/ the vastness of the universe – it is a psychological effect (fallacy of insignificance)

👎 A fully known universe is boring – and that is frightening

👎 Average human intelligence has grown significantly

👎 High level, complex knowledge is attained by the brilliant and then parsed down

👎 We don't only accumulate information but also know how to process and understand it – we don't gather information for information's' sake

37

Examples:

a) Scientific discoveries can prove how much we know or do not know about the universe

b) Psychology can show how our mind reacts to the universe, its vastness, and how human minds are able to process knowledge and complex issues

c) Philosophy – the study of epistemology (understanding knowledge and how it is acquired)

d) Researchers – what do the foremost minds involved in the knowledge gathering process think about it

e) Biochemistry – abilities or limitations of the human mind

f) Books and movies that have explored the theme before

Lastly, spend a few minutes coming up with a roadmap. While at first it will slow you down, once you become adept at outlining, your writing speed will increase, and your essay will benefit from having a logical structure.

 ## Sample Essay

The universe has always fascinated us from the very dawn of civilization, when everything seemed shrouded in mystery and the unexplainable was the realms of the gods. The curiosity inherent inhuman nature is the driving force of our accelerated evolution and the reason why we have developed methods of systematic study so that we are better able to understand and control our surroundings. As Sir Francis Bacon said, "knowledge is power".

At the heart of knowledge is the search for truth. Of the many ways people try to unravel the mysteries of the universe, scientific research is deemed to yield an accurate understanding of the world. That is because, in essence, scientific research is based on gathering observable and measurable evidence by formulating and testing hypotheses in reproducible experiments. Epistemology, the study of knowledge and how it is acquired, shows us that knowledge gathering is a cumulative process: new theories, no matter how revolutionary, have a basis in previous theories.

Saying that things become more complex and mysterious as we acquire more knowledge means operating under the false assumption that progress is measured by how much we have yet to discover. When humanity is at the start of the line, in terms of understanding the universe and its secrets, progress should be measured by how far we have come, not how far we still have to go. We should not compare our current knowledge with the sum of all knowledge, but rather with how little we knew in the past.

Take, for instance, biology and how much we have progressed beyond believing that human sickness is the result of an imbalance of humors to the current day advanced understanding of organs, tissues, cells – right down to the DNA level. The same can be said for the rudimentary notions of geography of the past, namely the idea that

37

the earth was flat and the sun was orbiting around it. Comparing these notions to the current understanding of tectonics, landscape formation and astrophysics theories like the existence of dark matter, we can see how far our understanding of the universe has progressed, one step at a time. And while we can in no way say that we know everything there is to know, we can certainly say that we are able to accomplish so much more than in the past, all thanks to a better understanding of our environment.

As such, the amount of knowledge the average individual possesses has been steadily growing over the ages, and the same can be said for our comprehension. What children learn and are able to grasp in schools today would have been part of the mystery of the universe in the past. This increase in knowledge was observed by Buckminster Fuller and named, "the Knowledge Doubling Curve". He noticed that until 1900 human knowledge had doubled approximately every century; and by the end of World War II, knowledge was doubling every 25 years. If one were able to travel through time to a period like the Middle Ages, our knowledge, technology, behaviors and speech would be seen as witchcraft. As Arthur C. Clarke said, "Magic's just science that we don't understand yet."

Part of thinking that the universe becomes progressively incomprehensible is our wonder at the universe, which, while understandable, also inspires the idea that true knowledge is somehow unattainable. People feel overwhelmed by the vastness and complexity of the universe and hold the belief that our simple minds cannot comprehend it – this is a psychological phenomenon called the fallacy of insignificance. Colin Wilson in The Stature of Man claims that this fallacy is an effect of modern–day society that conditions individuals to lack self–worth, as a mechanism of ensuring compliance; people want to become part of the system to escape their feelings of unimportance. People end up operating on the idea that as an individual, they do not matter much in the grand scheme of things, which is why they should belong to something greater that gives their existence meaning.

Last, but not least, people want to believe that the universe maintains its shroud of mystery because the idea of attaining full, complete knowledge is frightening – a fully known universe is predictable and boring, like professor Farnsworth from Futurama stipulates, "And, now that I've found all the answers, I realize that what I was living for were the questions!"

Issue Task 38

The increasingly rapid pace of life today causes more problems than it solves.

Write a response in which you discuss the extent to which you agree or disagree with the statement and explain your reasoning for the position you take. In developing and supporting your position, you should consider ways in which the statement might or might not hold true and explain how these considerations shape your position.

 Strategies

Restate the Issue:

In this case, the position is stated in the positive. It tells what the rapid pace of life does. Create a statement that expresses the issue in the negative.

In other words:

The increasingly rapid pace of life does not solve more problems than it causes.

You could also determine what question the statement answers.

What are the results of the increasingly rapid pace of life?

Creating a question may help you formulate alternative answers.

Now think about the parts of the original statement that provide evidence that you can refute or affirm.

◆ **increasingly** – This implies that the pace of life is more rapid than it used to be, and that the rate is still increasing.

◆ **today** – This may lead to the assumption that the pace of life did not increase before now and that it is a current phenomenon.

◆ **more**– This is a comparative word and is almost always followed by 'than'. In this case, there are more problems than solutions.

Opposing viewpoint:

The increasingly rapid pace of life does not cause more problems than it solves.

Or: *The increasingly rapid pace of life today solves more problems than it causes.*

Identify the parts of the opposing statement that provide evidence to affirm or refute.

In this case, they would be the same as in the original statement.

Alternatives

Is there any other way to look at this statement? What would life today be like if the pace were slower? Is this a new phenomenon?

New viewpoint:

The increasingly rapid pace of life today is exciting for those who embrace it but overwhelming for those who do not adapt.

Identify parts of the new statement that can create evidence for you to refute or affirm.

◆ **exciting** – This can also mean stimulating. The rapid pace of life may stimulate one's creativity or sense of adventure.

◆ **embrace** – To embrace something is to accept it willingly. Embrace has a positive connotation.

◆ **overwhelm** – Being overwhelmed means that one's abilities or emotions are unable to handle an event.

◆ **adapt**– Adaptation is essential to the theory of evolution. Those who fail to adapt do not thrive.

Position:

The increasingly rapid pace of life today creates both obstacles and opportunities.

Examples of obstacles:

a) Some people feel compelled to try to keep up with everything. They stretch themselves too thin.

b) Cultures are losing their unique qualities thanks to rapid travel and communication.

c) The rapid pace tries people's ability to adapt.

Examples of opportunities:

a) Medical research is closing in on cures for deadly and debilitating diseases.

b) The world has become a global village thanks to rapid travel and communication.

 Sample Essay

Since the onset of the Industrial Revolution, people have complained about the pace of change and bemoaned the "good old days". In the beginning, man and horsepower were replaced in the fields and on the roads by machines that could perform tasks more quickly and efficiently. Men who were no longer needed in the fields found work in the factories building the machines that had taken their places. Communication kept pace with automation. The telegraph gave way to the telephone, and when the Atlantic cable was laid, communication with other continents became possible. Man discovered the ability to travel above the earth and, eventually, people could cross the oceans in a matter of hours rather than weeks. Men and women around the world seized the opportunity to take advantage of these changes and believed that if they built a better mousetrap, the world would beat a path to their doors.

Some retreated from this progress, seeing all this technology as a distraction from the true meaning of life. Some, like Thoreau, did it for philosophical reasons, while others, like the Amish, did it for religious reasons. Others could not afford to participate in this revolution and continued to survive by their wits. Pockets of resistance exist to this day, populated by survivalists who see the advances of the late twentieth and early twenty-first century as signs of impending doom. These groups are heavily armed and supplied with sufficient provisions to fight off and hold out against those who they are convinced will someday attack them. Others have taken a gentler approach and simply desire to live by the sweat of their own brows.

The conundrum remains. Does one accept and attempt to keep pace with change, or does one retreat from change and adhere to a simpler philosophy? The downside of the rapid pace is reflected in the busy lives that family members lead, leaving little time to spend "quality" time together. Couples with children frequently maintain a giant calendar in the kitchen on which they keep track of each person's daily activities to schedule who must be where and when. Mothers and fathers separately take their children to before–school practices and after–school or weekend games, recitals, or other competitions. Children play at least one sport per season, take dance or karate classes, belong to the Boy Scouts or Girl Scouts, and work at a part–time job. Amid these activities, they must complete school work. Rarely are all family members at home at the same time except to sleep. It's a rat race.

On the upside are the advances that benefit humans. The rapid pace of medical research has led to successful treatments for a variety of deadly and/or debilitating diseases. It was not long ago that a cancer diagnosis was a death sentence. Today, many cancers are curable, and lives have been extended. Smallpox has been eradicated, and vaccines exist that promise the same end for diseases that used to scar or kill those who contracted them. A future free of cervical cancer can only be promising for the women of the world. Advances in communication have made knowledge of new discoveries readily available around the world. Ultimately, individuals must discriminate between activities and advances that enhance their lives. The problems created by the increasingly rapid pace of life today are likely created by the choices individuals make for themselves.

Issue Task 39

If a goal is worthy, then any means taken to attain it are justifiable.

Write a response in which you discuss the extent to which you agree or disagree with the statement and explain your reasoning for the position you take. In developing and supporting your position, you should consider ways in which the statement might or might not hold true and explain how these considerations shape your position.

 Strategies

Restate the Issue:

Restate the issue by making the phrasing of it in the negative.

In other words:

No means of attaining a goal should be overlooked if the goal is worthy.

You could also determine what question is being answered by the issue statement.

Should any and all means possible be used to obtain a worthy goal?

Or: *Is any goal worth achieving at any cost?*

These questions may help you think about how you would answer them. Your answers can help you develop your response to the issue.

Now think about the parts of the statement that provide evidence that you can refute or affirm.

◆ **worthy** – Worth of anything, including a goal, is subjective. If everyone believed all goals are worthy, there would be no need to take any extraordinary or unjustifiable action to reach the goal.

◆ **any means** – This is expansive. In this case, any can mean all.

◆ **justifiable** – To justify something is to explain or excuse it. Should we do anything that needs an explanation or excuse?

Opposing viewpoint:

39

No goal is worth enough to justify taking any means to attain it.

Identify the parts of the opposing statement that provide evidence to affirm or refute.

◆ **no** – In this case, it means none. This is pretty definitive.

Alternatives:

Is there any other way to look at this issue? In this case, it may be difficult. The original statement already qualifies the statement by using the word, if. The original statement is essentially saying that some goals are worth any means of achieving, and the opposing viewpoint says that no goals are worth that risk.

Position:

No goal is worth enough to justify taking any means to attain it.

Examples and reasons:

a) Guantanamo – Suspected terrorists are imprisoned at Guantanamo Bay, a military institution owned by the United States in Cuba. These prisoners have been subjected to water boarding, a particularly inhumane form of torture. Is information about terrorist activities important enough to justify torture?

 Sample Essay

To justify an action is to make it seem just or fair. It implies that the action is done to right a wrong. It is akin to the biblical philosophy, an eye for an eye. On the other hand, two wrongs don't make a right. Are any goals so lofty that one can justify taking any action to reach them? Is it okay to take these actions in the name of God or in the spirit of patriotism? Events of the past decade may make one believe that reprisals are justifiable.

Atrocities of such magnitude have been committed by groups or individuals around the world throughout history; one might agree that any means used to eliminate these perpetrators is justified. In 2001, extremists Muslims used the piloting skills they had learned in a flight school in the United States to fly two passenger planes into the towers of the World Trade Center in New York City: one into the Pentagon, and another aimed at the White House that went crashing into a field in Pennsylvania. These events caused the war on terrorism to become a focal point of US foreign policy. It became the goal of the United States military to hunt down and kill or capture the leaders of terrorist cells around the world. Chief among those targets was Osama bin Laden. In May 2011, an elite group of Seals burst into his home and killed him. The US government presented this as an incredible accomplishment – which it was – and worth the efforts needed to reach it. However, this is not necessarily true.

To reach this end, the United States invaded Iraq, believing that Saddam Hussein's regime had caches of WMDs, Weapons of Mass Destruction. That turned out to be false, but, nonetheless, the military hunted down and captured Hussein, after which he was tried and executed. During this span of time, other suspected terrorists were rounded up and detained at Guantanamo Bay, a US military institution in Cuba. There, these terrorists were systematically tortured to make them reveal information about the whereabouts of terrorist cells and, likely, bin Laden himself. Among the techniques used to extract information was waterboarding, a particularly inhumane process that causes the victims to feel like they are drowning.

Then, there's Abu Ghraib, a prison in Iraq, where US military personnel tortured and degraded the inmates held there. Considering the acts perpetrated by these terrorists on American soil, the actions taken by the United States appear justifiable. The flame of patriotism burned brightly and was reflected in the eyes of ordinary citizens and those called to battle. Across the country, acts of terrorism were perpetrated by those ordinary citizens against other citizens of Middle Eastern origin. Young men whose ancestors came here from countries like Syria and Lebanon generations ago were detained and strip searched at border crossings between the US and Canada. People in airports across the country looked askance at fellow passengers who looked or dressed differently. Members of the military who have served in Iraq and Afghanistan are experiencing post-traumatic stress disorder in numbers greater than seen before in our military history.

If the goal is to eradicate terrorism, isn't any action for the cause justifiable? Whenever humans are reduced to treating other human beings inhumanely, we must pause and consider the consequences of attaining this supposedly lofty goal. We must question whether any goal is worth the ultimate price one pays, especially when the actions taken are degrading or debasing to other groups of people, and the price is a loss of human dignity for the perpetrators and the victims.

Issue Task 40

40 *People should undertake risky action only after they have carefully considered its consequences.*

Write a response in which you discuss the extent to which you agree or disagree with the recommendation and explain your reasoning for the position you take. In developing and supporting your position, describe specific circumstances in which adopting the recommendation would or would not be advantageous and explain how these examples shape your position.

NOTE: The above topic has wording similar to Issue Task 23 in this book. However, if you read carefully you will notice that the task instructions are different. Hence, it is very important to read the topic as well as its instructions completely before you start to write your response.

 Strategies

Restate the Position:

The original recommendation suggests how people should behave regarding risks. How would the recommendation read if it were couched in negative terms?

In other words:

People should not take risks until they have considered the consequences.

The meaning of both recommendations is essentially the same.

You could also determine what question is being answered by the recommendation.

Should individuals take risks?

Or: *Under what conditions should people take risks?*

Now think about the parts of the recommendation that provide evidence you can affirm or refute.

◆ **only** – This leaves no other option. It is akin to saying always. Are there no exceptions?

◆ **risky** – This can be relative. What may appear risky to one may be commonplace for another.

◆ **carefully** – The meaning of carefully can vary, as well. How much consideration is considered careful?

◆ **considered** – To consider something is to think about it. it does not require taking any action. Does one only need to think about the consequences of one's actions? Does understanding the consequences prevent everyone from engaging in risky behavior? Does consideration necessarily lead to understanding?

Opposing viewpoint:

People should undertake risky action regardless of the consequences.

Think about the parts of the opposing statement that provide evidence to affirm or refute.

◆ **regardless** – This means without regard. To regard something is to look at it. One should take risks without looking at the consequences.

◆ **should** – This is not a command. Should implies choice.

Alternatives:

Is there another way to look at this recommendation? Can it be qualified? Are some risks worth taking despite the possible consequences? Can risks be minimized?

New viewpoint:

Even with the possibility of negative consequences, some risks are worth taking.

Examples and reasons:

a) Marie and Pierre Curie – When they began experimenting with radiation, the risks were unknown. Marie Curie died from radiation sickness, but her contribution to the advancement of medicine is immeasurable.

b) early explorers– When the Vikings set out in their boats and headed west, they could not imagine what they would find. They found rich fishing grounds. Columbus, Cook, Drake, Magellan all risked their lives to set out across seas that no man had navigated before.

c) space exploration

d) Bill Gates and Steve Jobs – Both are pioneers in computing technology, Gates with software and Jobs with McIntosh computers

Sample Essay

40   Some people are born risk takers. Psychologists will tell you that it is a component of one's personality: those who take risks sometimes exhibit negative behavior while others take risks that ultimately benefit themselves and others. The names of risk takers can be found in various halls of fame as well as on Wanted Posters. Famous risk takers range from the infamous like Al Capone and Bernie Madoff to innovators like Bill Gates, Mark Zuckerberg, and Frank Lloyd Wright. Even though these and others knew the possible consequences of their actions, they were not deterred from reaching their goals. Those who do not take risks will not suffer the possible negative consequences, but neither will they experience the rewards.

Where would we be without those who took great risks with general disregard for the consequences? Marie and Pierre Curie literally risked their lives to experiment with radioactivity. The medical progress that resulted from their work not only earned the Curies the Nobel Prize but made possible early treatment of some cancers. Other scientists followed in their footsteps, and the benefits to mankind have been enormous. Other medical pioneers include Jonas Salk who saved countless children from death or paralysis when he tested his new polio vaccine on himself, his wife and his own children. Risking his and his family's lives led to mass administration of the vaccine to school children all over America, and virtually made the iron lung obsolete.

Early explorers risked traveling to areas marked on maps with the foreboding phrase, "Here there are dragons", and expanded the known world. In efforts to find a shorter route to India, sailors like Christopher Columbus set off with his crew in three small boats and bumped into the Western Hemisphere. Charles Lindbergh flew solo across the Atlantic in a small plane in hopes of reaching the European continent. Since that time, man has used flight to reach the moon and establish space stations. If these adventurers had spent too much time thinking about the consequences, they may very well have just stayed home.

In the later years of the twentieth century pioneers in technology arose. Bill Gates, founder of Microsoft and one of the richest men in the world, dropped out of prestigious Harvard University to pursue computing. Steve Jobs, the brains behind Apple computers, also dropped out of college. These men defied the popular wisdom that one needs a college education to get anywhere in this world and created a universe of communication on a level never before seen.

Great political leaders have taken great risks for the sake of reform or revolution. Martin Luther King, Jr and Mohandas Gandhi (after whom King modeled his protests) risked everything and, ultimately, lost their lives for the sake of equality and independence. Both men certainly considered the consequences of their actions but deemed that the potential rewards made the risks acceptable. All minorities and repressed populations in the United States lead lives of greater opportunity thanks to the leadership of Martin Luther King, Jr, and India exists as an independent country as a result of Gandhi's actions.

Just as there are consequences for taking risks, there are consequences for failing to take risks. Those who fear the unknown are doomed to live meager lives. It may be trite but nonetheless true to say that if you do what you've always done, you'll get what you've always had.

Issue Task 41

People's behavior is largely determined by forces not of their own making.

Write a response in which you discuss the extent to which you agree or disagree with the claim. In developing and supporting your position, be sure to address the most compelling reasons and/or examples that could be used to challenge your position.

Strategies

Assumptions:

What are the assumptions in the claim? These will be statements that you can either affirm or refute.

Assumption 1: Behavior is influenced by outside forces.

Assumption 2: People can rationalize their behavior.

Assumption 3: There are forces beyond one's control.

Assumption 4: People don't have to take responsibility for their own actions.

Assumption 5: Both good and bad behavior is accidental.

Assumption 6: One's behavior is not deliberate.

Opposing viewpoint:

People's behavior is not determined by outside forces.

What are the assumptions in this claim? As before, they will be statements that you can either affirm or refute.

Assumption 1: People are responsible for their own behavior.

Assumption 2: People can ignore outside forces.

Assumption 3: People's behavior is influenced by something other than outside forces

Alternative claim:

In some cases, people's behavior is determined by outside forces.

Assumption 1: People's behavior may be influenced by outside forces.

Assumption 2: People's behavior is sometimes beyond their control.

 # Sample Essay

In the mid-1970's, San Francisco supervisor, Dan White, killed Mayor Moscone and supervisor Harvey Milk. White had become despondent over the actions of the mayor and the homosexual activist, Milk, to change the laws pertaining to homosexual rights in the city. White's lawyer claimed that White's deepening depression led him to eat foods high in sugar, which affected his behavior. One of the reporters during White's trial coined the term, "the Twinkie defense", named for the well–known snack cake. That phrase is resurrected every time a defendant in a particularly heinous crime claims that some circumstance beyond his control made him behave badly. History provides shining examples of when circumstances did not reduce humans to using excuses to behave badly.

In 1944, a teenage Elie Wiesel, his parents and sisters were forced from their home in Hungary and transported to the infamous concentration camp, Auschwitz. At the entrance to the camp, this Jewish boy and his father were separated from his mother and sisters. Elie was just fourteen years old at the time, but another man in line told him to lie and say that he was sixteen; otherwise, he would be considered too young to work and would be sent to extermination along with women and children. During the ensuing months, Elie and his father endured harsh living and working conditions and ultimately to starvation. When his father became ill, he tried to convince Elie to eat his ration of food, but Elie refused to sacrifice his father to ensure his own survival. Even when the prisoners were ordered to abandon the camp ahead of the Allies imminent arrival, Elie did everything he could to see that his father would survive. He watched as other fathers or sons abandoned those who could no longer endure the enforced race throughout the cold and snowy landscape but declined to forsake his own humanity.

History has recorded the deeds of others who, during the Holocaust, chose the high road rather than take the easy way out. Miep Gies, at great risk to herself, hid and supplied provisions to the family of Anne Frank while they hid in an attic in Amsterdam. Oskar Schindler made it possible for Jewish workers in his factory to escape the horrors of the Nazi regime. These heroes could have succumbed to circumstances, and history would likely have excused them. People can be the masters of their own destinies. Neither Twinkies nor "the devils made me do it" are acceptable excuses for relinquishing that mastery.

Issue Task 42

The best ideas arise from a passionate interest in commonplace things.

Write a response in which you discuss the extent to which you agree or disagree with the statement and explain your reasoning for the position you take. In developing and supporting your position, you should consider ways in which the statement might or might not hold true and explain how these considerations shape your position.

 Strategies

Restate the Issue:

In this case, you might invert the order of the ideas.

In other words:

A passionate interest in commonplace things gives rise to the best ideas.

Or: *It is not an interest in the uncommon that gives rise to the best ideas.*

You might determine what question is being answered by the issue statement.

From what do the best ideas arise?

Or: *Where do the best ideas come from?*

Creating a question may help you to formulate your own position on the issue and help you decide how strongly you agree or disagree with it.

Now think about the parts of the statement that provide evidence that you can affirm or refute.

◆ **best** – This is the superlative form of good. It doesn't get any better.

◆ **ideas** – Why not products or inventions? Are ideas themselves worth much unless they are the basis of a useful product or invention?

◆ **passionate** – This is a strong word. It carries more weight than a passing interest would.

◆ **commonplace** – A synonym is every day. Is it likely that most people take notice of everyday or commonplace things?

Opposing viewpoint:

The best ideas arise from a passionate interest in unusual things.

Identify the parts of the opposing statement that provide evidence for you to refute or affirm.

◆ **unusual** – This is the opposite of commonplace. Unusual means not usual or common or every day.

Alternatives:

Is there any other way to look at this issue? Perhaps it is not the things themselves that inspire, but the actions of the things in consideration.

New viewpoint:

The best ideas arise from a passionate interest in the behavior of commonplace things.

◆ **behavior** – The way things act may be the inspiration for new ideas.

Examples and reasons:

a) Observing the changes of the stars in the night sky being used for navigation.

b) Man's desire to fly like a bird.

 Sample Essay

One tends to think of visionaries as men and women who see things that the minds of mere mortals cannot even imagine. Modern conveniences like the telephone and the television seem like miracles. How can a camera take a moving picture on the other side of the world and send it to the television in my little corner of the world? How is it possible that my voice can travel into space and be retrieved by my friend on her phone in the middle of the country? These inventions are ultimately based on commonplace ideas and actions, such as looking up at a full moon as a child and wondering what it would be like to be there. Many wonders of the modern world do have their roots in objects that we observe every day.

Man has always envied birds. The desire to fly has given rise to myths as old as the ability of man to speak. The most familiar of these myths is populated by the master craftsman, Daedalus, and his son, Icarus. Icarus' desire to fly led his father to craft wings made of feather and wax. Daedalus copied what he could observe of the wings of birds. His only warning to his son was not to fly too close to the sun lest the wax melt and cause the wings to be destroyed. Icarus, enthralled by the freedom of flight, ignored his father's warning and soared higher and higher until he did indeed fly too close to the sun. The wax melted, the wings fell apart, and Icarus plummeted to his death in the sea. In the fifteenth century, Leonardo da Vinci drew plans for a flying device that became the inspiration for the modern helicopter. Some of the earliest planes attempted to imitate the motion of birds' wings. Now that man can actually fly not only around the world but out of it, one must wonder, "Do the birds envy man?"

As the birds move in the sky above us, so do the sun, the stars, and the moon. For much of the history of man, the stars and planets were sources of myth and inspired poets, artists and musicians. The earliest ideas about the sun and the stars made the earth the center of the universe. Later astronomers created the heliocentric theory of our solar system. The first practical use of the stars was for navigation. The longer the scientists observed the heavenly bodies, the greater the desire grew to reach them. When it became possible to measure the distances to the sun, the moon, and other planets, the idea of reaching them became a possibility. Now man has been to the moon and has set his sights on Mars. The Hubble telescope continues to send back crystal-clear pictures of deep space, and man's fascination continues to grow.

When man looks up, he cannot avoid seeing the birds and the heavenly bodies. They are ubiquitous, and man's envy, fascination, and eventual understanding of them have made incredible journeys possible. The best ideas of the future are likely to come from man's continued passion for commonplace things.

Issue Task 43

Critical judgment of work in any given field has little value unless it comes from someone who is an expert in that field.

Write a response in which you discuss the extent to which you agree or disagree with the claim. In developing and supporting your position, be sure to address the most compelling reasons and/or examples that could be used to challenge your position.

 Strategies

Assumptions:

Identify the assumptions in the claim. These will be statements that you can either affirm or refute.

Assumption 1: Only experts in a field are competent to critique or judge work in that field.

Assumption 2: Every field has an expert.

Opposing viewpoint:

It is possible to provide critical judgment of work in a given field even if one is not an expert in the field.

What are the assumptions in this claim?

Assumption 1: All critical judgment is valuable.

Assumption 2: One need not be an expert to judge the value of work in a given field.

Is there another way of looking at this claim? Why might someone make this claim? What is the claim trying to prove or disprove? Begin a dependent clause with the word, although, and follow it with the claim.

Although consumers of technology express opinions about the products, critical judgment…

There are a variety of choices, but whatever you choose can help you formulate your position and develop your response.

Sample Essay

To claim that the only valid judgment of a product that is the result of work in some field can arise from an expert in that field neglects the users or consumers of that product. The purpose of developing a new theory or designing a new object is, at its core, to be used by others. All work requires feedback to be either validated or improved, and this feedback should come from both experts in the field and people whose lives will be impacted by it.

At the most esoteric level, the claim can refer to scientific or mathematical theory. Perhaps the only qualified critics are other scientists or mathematicians. However, the practical application of the theories may include products intended for use by laymen. The first product that comes to mind is the personal computer. That the computing devices we use today evolved from ENIAC, a computer that filled two large rooms and could only complete mathematical computations, is almost beyond belief. It seemed for a while that the computer would remain the province of science and mathematics, and any improvements or advances in computing would be self-serving.

Once computers became small enough and reasonably priced, they became available to the average person. Consumers were enthralled. Once they mastered the functions possible on those early machines, they wanted - even demanded - more. The industry responded. The average consumer may not know how a computer works, but they know what they want it to do. As brilliant as computer scientists may be, they might not be able to imagine what the average Joe wants or needs. Even without computer science expertise, a consumer who uses their computer to shop online or search for recipes has had an impact on the industry.

At a more approachable level are contemporary writers. When a new novel is published, the phrase, critically acclaimed, should signal soaring success for the author. Some authors, in fact, are satisfied with critical approbation. It may not, however, herald financial rewards. If the purpose of writing is to be read, the inexpert public's opinion may be more valuable than the critics. If Stephen King, probably the best-selling author in the last forty years, had listened to the experts in his field, he would have stopped writing after Carrie was published. Instead, he listened to his own muse and turned out thrillers that have his readers clamoring for more.

On an even more mundane level are the household appliances intended to make life easier. Without the input of consumers, the wringer washer might still be the latest technology in laundry help. Customers would still be hanging rugs outside and using a paddle to beat the dirt out of them. The average person may not understand the technology involved in designing time-saving appliances, but they are experts in their use.

To say that critical judgment has little value unless the judgment comes from experts depends upon the purpose of the work and the intended audience. If something is accomplished for purely scientific reasons, the only critical judgment of value may be that of experts in the field. If one produces something for public consumption, he or she should not only expect, but welcome the public's opinion.

Issue Task 44

44

Claim: *Knowing about the past cannot help people to make important decisions today.*

Reason: *The world today is significantly more complex than it was even in the relatively recent past.*

Write a response in which you discuss the extent to which you agree or disagree with the claim and the reason on which that claim is based.

NOTE: The above topic has wording similar to Issue Task 48 of this book. However, if you read carefully you will notice that the task instructions are different. Hence, it is very important to read the topic as well as its instructions completely before you start to write your response.

 Strategies

Combine the claim and the reason into one statement using a subordinate clause.

In other words:

Because the world today is significantly more complex than it was even in the relatively recent past, knowing about the past cannot help people to make important decisions today.

What are the assumptions stated or implied in the claim and reason? These will provide evidence that you can refute or affirm in your argument.

◆ People cannot use their own or others' past experiences to help them make decisions today.

◆ The complexity of today's world makes past events and/or actions irrelevant in the decision-making process.

◆ The complexity of today's society contributes to the difficulty of making decisions.

Opposing viewpoint:

Claim: *Knowing about the past does help people make important decisions today.*

Reason: *The complexity of today's world is no more challenging than that of previous eras.*

Philosophy

What are the assumptions stated or implied in the claim and reason? These will provide evidence that you can refute or affirm in your argument.

Assumptions:

- ◆ The past can inform the present.

- ◆ Each time period is more complex than the one that preceded it.

- ◆ The degree of complexity is relative.

 # Sample Essay

The world today may be more complex than that of the past, but people's needs and motivations have not changed. People make decisions they think will benefit them in some way. According to Maslow's Hierarchy of Needs, all people desire the same things. They want their physiological needs met; they require food, water, sex, and sleep. They want to feel loved and safe. They desire self–esteem and the respect of others. Most humans make decisions to satisfy these needs, and they make use of their own or others' experiences to help them. This lack of change refutes the claim: it shows that the past is necessary to make new decisions even with the fast pace of our current world because history can be used to inform correct decisions based on similar past situations.

My grandparents are in their late eighties; they were born in the 1920's. In the eighty-plus years since their births, they have seen enormous and increasingly rapid changes occur in virtually every aspect of life. They have seen the advent of commercial flight, the construction of the interstate highway system, the invention of television, and the dominance of the computer in twenty-first century living. The first challenges they faced occurred when they were children during the Great Depression. They have used those experiences to inform most of the decisions they have made throughout their lives. Coming from childhoods of financial struggle, they don't waste anything. My grandmother saves used tinfoil and washes and reuses Ziploc bags. My grandfather holds onto even the smallest scrap of lumber from a construction project. He wears his clothes until they are entirely worn out. Whether the economy is good or bad, they manage because their past experiences have taught them the lessons that help them survive and thrive. The complexity of today's world has little effect on them. They make decisions based on their needs and habits.

President Obama faced some difficult choices concerning Syria's use of chemical weapons against its own citizens. He tempered his first instinct to initiate an air strike by considering how Americans feel about entering another conflict. When President George W. Bush reacted to the terrorist attack of 9/11/01 by sending troops into Iraq and Afghanistan, he had the support of most Americans. Twenty years later, Americans are weary of these wars and the great majority is not in favor of any more military action. Based on this twenty–year history of American troops in the Middle East, the President delayed an airstrike, awaiting the results of Russia's offer to help Syria dispose of its chemical weapons. Because the world is more complex, President Obama had to keep in mind America's recent past before making a decision that could have far–reaching effects. Failure to act against Syria may give other hostile countries the impetus to stockpile chemical weapons. Calling an air strike may cause retaliation against American troops abroad. His primary concern was the safety of Americans, and he used his knowledge of the past to inform his decisions.

A few years ago, the eastern seaboard was hit by superstorm Sandy. Lacking sufficient protection from the Atlantic Ocean, seaside resorts and amusement parks in New Jersey were destroyed, and downtown New York City was flooded. Both numerous lives and livelihoods were lost. The island of Manhattan was immobilized as subway tunnels filled with seawater and electricity was lost. Historically, this region does not experience such severe storms, so one could argue that looking to the past for guidance was unwise. However, based on this event, city planners were considering the construction of some sort of barrier that would prevent the ocean from entering New York Harbor in the event of another catastrophic storm. Ocean barriers have been used with success in the low countries of Europe, and New York City planners can use the historical success of these countries to help them make important decisions today.

The inherent complexity of living in today's world creates more complexity in the decision-making process. However, it does not preclude using the past as a reference for considering the consequences of those decisions. The world has changed, but its residents have the same needs as those in decades and centuries past, making the criteria for choosing a course of action similar to any in history.

Issue Task 45

The luxuries and conveniences of contemporary life prevent people from developing into truly strong and independent individuals.

Write a response in which you discuss the extent to which you agree or disagree with the statement and explain your reasoning for the position you take. In developing and supporting your position, you should consider ways in which the statement might or might not hold true and explain how these considerations shape your response.

45

 ## Strategies

Begin by restating the issue. In this case, try replacing prevent with the verb, create. What do the luxuries and conveniences of contemporary life cause?

In other words:

The luxuries and conveniences of contemporary life create individuals who are weak and dependent.

Or: Weak and dependent people are the product of the luxuries and conveniences of contemporary life.

You could also determine what question is being answered by the issue statement.

How are individuals affected by the luxuries and conveniences of contemporary life?

The question may help some writers develop alternative viewpoints. The original issue statement is only one of several possible responses to the question.

Now, think about the parts of the statement that provide evidence that you can affirm or refute.

◆ **luxuries and conveniences** - These are subjective labels. What may be a luxury for one may be a necessity or a convenience for another. Luxury is a value judgment.

◆ **contemporary life** - Have people in previous generations voiced the same complaint as better ways of completing tasks evolved? A generation ago, the bulky bag phone that plugged into a car's cigarette lighter was considered a luxury. Children often hear the lament, "In my day, I had to..." implying that each successive generation has it better than the one before.

Next, create a statement that expresses the opposing viewpoint, using language similar to that of the original issue.

Opposing viewpoint:

The luxuries and conveniences of contemporary life have made it possible for individuals to pursue their passions and develop their personal strengths.

Identify the parts of the opposing statement that provide evidence to refute or affirm.

- ◆ **pursue** - to follow in a direction that leads to obtaining a goal

- ◆ **passions** - the activities that excite one's desire for action or accomplishment

- ◆ **personal strengths** - may be physical but can be intellectual or artistic or altruistic

Alternatives:

Is there another way of looking at this issue? Who determines whether something is a luxury or a convenience? Are they subjective terms? An elevator in a two-story building may seem like a luxury, but, if you are in a wheelchair or use a cane to walk, it may be a necessity. If you use the elevator and you have no compelling physical reason to do so, are you less strong and independent? Have some conveniences become inconvenient or even dangerous? The cell phone is a convenience that is probably overused. If you are at the grocery store and someone calls you, do you feel obligated to answer, thus extending your time at the store? The news is rife with stories about automobile accidents that have been caused by texting and driving. Does your geographical location or economic situation help to define what items are luxuries and/or conveniences?

Alternative viewpoint:

Because the perception of what constitutes a luxury, or a convenience is subjective, a blanket statement about their ability to reduce one's level of strength and independence is bound to have exceptions.

Now you must decide which point of view to address in your essay. Completing the prewriting activities has given you several choices and ideas for defending any of those choices. Even viewpoints opposite of yours will have points that you can use in writing your response. As you review your notes, decide which of your ideas offer the strongest support for your position; you do not have to use all of them. Keep in mind that others may disagree with your position, so address their concerns in your response. Before you decide, carefully consider the following checklist. You will have addressed several of them in the exercises you have completed above.

◆ I have identified the central issue.

◆ I understand the instructions.

◆ I have decided that I agree/disagree/partially agree with the issue and why.

◆ I have identified the assumptions in the claim and determined whether or not they are reasonable.

◆ If necessary, I can explain how I interpret any or all of the concepts and terms used in the claim.

◆ I have identified my reasons for the position I have taken.

◆ I have compelling examples to support my position.

The next step should be listing the main reasons and support for your position. You may use any of the above prewriting activities as you prepare evidence for supporting your point of view. Remember that the GRE readers scoring your response are not looking for a "right" answer. The readers are evaluating your ability to address the specific instructions and articulate and develop an argument to support your understanding and evaluation of the issue.

Your notes do not have to be exhaustive. As you begin to write your essay, your brain will generate new ideas. Make certain that you keep the directions in mind as you develop your ideas. Use as many or as few paragraphs as you consider appropriate for your argument but create a new paragraph when you move on to a new idea or example of support for your position. The GRE readers are not looking for a specific number of ideas or paragraphs. Instead, they are reading to determine the level of understanding of the topic and the complexity with which you respond.

In this task, you are asked to discuss the extent to which you agree or disagree with the statement. You may completely agree or disagree with the statement, or you may agree under certain conditions. You are also instructed to explain your reasoning and consider ways in which the statement might or might not hold true and explain how these considerations shape your position.

You may use any organizational strategy or form of reasoning to present your position as clearly and succinctly as possible. You may recall writing strategies that you learned in high school or a writing-intensive course you took in college, but it is not necessary to employ any of those strategies. It is important that your ideas follow a logical progression and display strong critical thinking.

Sample Essay

I try to imagine myself carrying my dirty laundry down to the river and, after immersing the items in the cold water, beating them against a rock to get the really tough stains out. Without an enzyme detergent, I will find it difficult to remove the blood spatter on my skirt from the chicken I killed for last night's supper. Upon returning to my home, I will spread the wet clothes on the bushes in the yard and hope that they dry before the rain begins.

Otherwise, I will have to drape them on the furniture in front of the fire in the house and keep that fire going with wood that I will have to chop. Yes, I am a strong and independent individual, but I don't have time to think about what I can do for the advancement of mankind. Luxuries and conveniences free me to discover the strengths that I have in other areas of my life.

Time, after all, is the greatest luxury. All of the conveniences in my life simply enable me to have more time to devote to people or to pursue interests that might benefit me or members of my community in some way. Sure, I can get the dishes as clean washing them by hand as my dishwasher does, but while that machine is performing the task for me, I can be writing notes on the cards I want to send to friends who are either celebrating the birth of a new baby or mourning the loss of a grandparent. I can probably get as much water out of my freshly washed clothes using a wringer, but while my automatic washing machine is spinning the water away, I can finish the research for my paper that's due. I am able to buy a dishwasher and a washing machine and any number of other appliances, but I cannot buy time. If those conveniences help me preserve some of the time I have, they are well worth the price.

In reality, the definition of a luxury is subjective. An elevator in a two-story building may be considered a luxury, but, if I am injured or disabled, the elevator becomes a necessity. Owning an airplane may seem luxurious, but if I live in a remote area of Alaska where there are no roads, the plane becomes a necessary means of travel. One man's meat is another man's poison. There is always more than one way to look at an issue. In many ways, modern conveniences do become a burden. Everything one owns constitutes an obligation. It must be maintained, repaired, insured, and, above all, used. Conveniences can become inconvenient. If I am one of those who cannot leave home without my cell phone, I am obligated to answer it when it rings, whether I am walking down the street, shopping for groceries, or waiting at the dentist's office. I may feel the compunction to call someone while I'm standing in front of the meat counter and can't decide what to have for dinner. In this manner, the convenience does diminish my independence. At the end of the day, how my luxuries and conveniences contribute to my character is my choice.

45

Issue Task 46

Claim: *We can usually learn much more from people whose views we share than from those whose views contradict our own.*

Reason: *Disagreement can cause stress and inhibit learning.*

Write a response in which you discuss the extent to which you agree or disagree with the claim and the reason on which that claim is based.

Strategies

Combine the claim and reason into one statement using a subordinate clause.

In other words:

Because disagreement can cause stress and inhibit learning, we are more likely to learn from people whose views we share rather than those whose views contradict our own.

What are the assumptions in the claim and reason? These will provide evidence that you can either affirm or refute.

- ◆ We can only learn from those with whom we agree.

- ◆ We learn only when we are comfortable.

Opposing viewpoint:

Claim - *We can usually learn more from people whose views contradict our own than from those with whom we agree.*

Reason - *Agreement causes complacency and inhibits learning.*

What are the assumptions present in the claim and reason? These will provide evidence that you can either affirm or refute.

- ◆ Other points of view offer new information.

- ◆ Those with whom we agree echo what we already know or believe.

◆ Without disagreement there is no learning.

Is there any other way to look at this issue? Can you qualify the original statement in some way? Is it possible to partially agree with the statement?

Alternative viewpoint:

Claim - *We can learn from those whose views agree with our own as well as from those whose views contradict our own.*

Reason - *We don't have to agree with others to learn from them.*

What are the assumptions present in the alternative claim and reason?

◆ Every point of view has something to offer.

Examples:

a) Rumspringa - The year that Amish young people take off to live with the English. The Amish believe that exposure to the outside world makes those who return to the Amish life stronger members of the community.

b) High school debates - must know opposing viewpoint to strengthen support of one's own position

c) Politics - Decisions made by lawmakers do not always favor one party over another. Most laws result from considering both sides and reaching a compromise.

 ## Sample Essay

If you do what you've always done, you'll get what you've always had. Limiting yourself to eating only what you've always eaten prevents you from sampling cuisines from all over the world and, perhaps, discovering your new favorite food. Selecting your next novel from the same genre that you've always read limits your exposure to the talents of thousands of writers. Exposing yourself to new foods, new authors, or new ideas can be stressful, but it will either change your life in some way or reaffirm the choices that you've already made.

The Amish, who live apart from modern society and spurn any conveniences, encourage their young people to participate in the tradition known as Rumspringa. Generally, in their late teens, these young adults leave the comfort of their orderly communities and relocate to a city in order to live like the "English". At their own discretion, they make friends with those outside their faith, wear fashionable clothing, and attend parties where they may choose to drink alcoholic beverages. At the end of their year, they freely decide to return to the Amish lifestyle or remain in the secular world. The Amish elders understand that those who choose to return will become the strongest members of their society.

Freely spurning modern technology to live a life of hard physical labor accomplished only with the help of work horses displays a firm dedication to the religion and lifestyle practiced by generations of their ancestors. Certainly, there is some comfort in knowing what to expect of each day without the distractions of television, computers, and smartphones, or the stress of maintaining the fast pace of life in the English world. They take pleasure in contributing to their community through the work of their hands and their faith in God rather than in updating their Facebook statuses or incessant text messages. They have likely learned many life lessons from those with whom they have fundamental disagreements.

An exit-level assessment at the high school I attended is a team debate carried out in front of the entire senior class. We were given a list of topics from which to choose and were then randomly assigned to teams. The greatest challenge came when we were told whether we would be arguing in the affirmative or the negative. Several members of each team were compelled to support a point of view with which they disagreed. Imagine the groans of protest! My group had to debate comprehensive versus abstinence-only sex education in public schools. I was selected to debate the position with which I disagreed. It was frustrating and stressful to develop a cogent argument to support this contrary point of view, but it did not prevent my learning about the strengths of that position. Although I did not change my opinion on the topic, I learned a lot about the other side of the debate and understood its merit. In fact, one is likely to learn more by tackling new and sometimes disagreeable information.

During the Obama presidential election, I watched my friends and family debate the suitability of the candidates by posting supposed facts on Facebook. I'm sure they saw a posting by someone else, and they thought, "I agree. I'll repost this." Some of these postings, whether or not they aligned with my beliefs, seemed too pejorative to be true. On more than one occasion, I did some research and found, for example, that Michelle Obama did not have a greater number of personal assistants than former first ladies have had. Quotes ascribed to the president were taken out of context or said to be years before he became an elected official. Only by disagreeing with or, at the very least, questioning my Facebook friends did I come across information that was new to me.

Without change there is no progress. Without disagreement there is no change. Therefore, without disagreement, there is no progress. Had President Lincoln not disagreed with secessionists, America might still be a divided country. Had Galileo not disagreed with the Catholic Church, we might still think the Earth is the center of the Universe. Giants in the arts, literature, the humanities, and science have flouted the status quo, and we are better off as a result. This claim and reason are valid only for people who ignore history.

46

Issue Task 47

Young people should be encouraged to pursue long-term, realistic goals rather than seek immediate fame and recognition.

Write a response in which you discuss the extent to which you agree or disagree with the recommendation and explain your reasoning for the position you take. In developing and supporting your position, describe specific circumstances in which adopting the recommendation would or would not be advantageous and explain how these examples shape your position.

47

Strategies

Restate the issue perhaps by reversing the order of the sentence components.

In other words:

Rather than seek immediate fame and recognition, young people should be encouraged to pursue long-term realistic goals.

Determine what question is being answered by the statement. This will help you begin to think how you would answer it and whether or not you agree with the original statement.

Should young people pursue long-term goals or seek immediate fame and recognition?

Parts of the original statement that provide evidence that you can affirm or refute.

- ◆ **young people** - They are less likely to have the necessary maturity or skills to create goals

- ◆ **encouraged** - Provide reasons and information to help them rather than set the goals for them

- ◆ **long-term** - Goals that will not be achieved quickly

- ◆ **realistic** - Goals should be based on one's ability to achieve them

- ◆ **immediate** - Right now or in the near future; in the context of the statement, it has a negative connotation

- ◆ **fame** - Fame is a result of a variety of accomplishments, and, in this context, seems undesirable

- ◆ **recognition** - Recognition implies acknowledgement of good deeds or accomplishments

Next, create a statement that expresses the opposing viewpoint, using language similar to that of the original statement.

Opposing viewpoint:

Young people should be encouraged to seek immediate fame and recognition rather than pursue long-term, realistic goals.

The evidence in this viewpoint is essentially the same as in the original. Is there any other way to look at this issue? Can you qualify the original statement in some way? Is it possible to partially agree with the statement?

Alternative viewpoint:

Young people should be encouraged to pursue long-term, realistic goals as well as immediate fame and recognition.

◆ as well as - Both options should be available

List some circumstances under which each might be true.

Circumstances:

a) Advances in medicine occur as a result of long-range planning and study.

b) Business success derives from long-range planning.

c) A secure retirement requires planning and saving over many years.

d) Immediate fame is a suitable goal for professional athletes, whose careers are generally short-lived.

 ## Sample Essay

For most young people, setting long-term, realistic goals is the route to lifetime success. Those who choose this route are less likely to experience failure and become discouraged. However, setting long-term, realistic goals is not the best choice for some notable exceptions exist today and throughout history that demonstrate the wisdom of their choices. Those with special talents may be better served by seeking immediate fame and recognition.

The world of professional sports is populated by stellar athletes who made the decision to seek immediate fame and recognition. It used to be that those seeking careers as professional athletes would first complete a college degree and then enter the draft. In recent years, it has become more common for those with high–level skills to leave college early or never attend at all and be drafted right out of high school. Kobe Bryant and LeBron James went directly from high school into the NBA. At the ripe old age of eighteen, each was making millions of dollars per year. Would four years of college hoops have made them better players? Perhaps not. They may have run the risk of career–ending injuries, ultimately ending any chance of signing multi–year, multi–million dollar contracts. Seeking immediate fame and recognition was the right decision for these two superstars, both of whom have won multiple NBA championships with their teams.

Examples abound in the world of the arts of those whose talents may not have been recognized or rewarded had they been advised to set realistic goals. Every year, hundreds of thousands of hopefuls' audition for American Idol. Rather than testing their talents in small clubs or enduring rounds of auditions, these young singers take a single shot at the big time. Only one of them can win the prize, relegating the remainder to the ranks of also-rans. In the case of the winner and a select few of the top ten, great success ensues. In 2012, Phil Phillips won, and the song written for him to sing in the finale became the theme of the American gymnastics team at the London Olympics. Still a teenager, Phillips gained immediate fame and recognition. Had he not taken a chance on American Idol, he may have continued to sing in church and the school choir, and singing might have become a pleasant pastime in his adult life.

Situations do exist where long-term, realistic goals are more likely to ensure success. Medical research comes to mind. As scientists search for cures or treatments for serious, even deadly, diseases or genetic conditions, they must meticulously test and retest, create scientific trials, and seek FDA approval before releasing new drugs on the market. This process can take many years, and virtually none of those individual scientists gains fame or recognition.

A young woman from my hometown set a long-term goal for her life when she was a small child. She wanted to be an astronaut when she grew up. Toward that end, Jessica Meir worked hard in school and graduated as valedictorian of her class. She went on to Brown University and obtained her first degree. She completed research at the Scripps Oceanographic institute, becoming an aquanaut. Eventually, she attended the International Space University in Strasbourg, France. At the time of her selection as one of eight in the newest class of NASA astronauts she was an assistant professor of anesthesiology at Harvard. Now in her mid-thirties, Jessica has reached her lifelong goal by systematically setting a course that would lead her there. It is important to note that Jessica was not selected the first time she applied to become an astronaut, but she stayed the course and, eventually, reached her destination.

In reality, the vast majority of us benefit from setting long-term goals. The finish line is far in the future, and we will get there one step at a time. Making long-term, realistic goals will keep us from becoming discouraged or quitting altogether. Even very talented individuals sometimes spurn the chance for early fame and recognition in order to avoid the stress and public scrutiny that attend them. Young people should be encouraged to take the path that best suits their talents and circumstances.

Issue Task 48

Knowing about the past cannot help people to make important decisions today.

Write a response in which you discuss the extent to which you agree or disagree with the statement and explain your reasoning for the position you take. In developing and supporting your position, you should consider ways in which the statement might or might not hold true and explain how these considerations shape your position.

NOTE: The above topic has wording similar to Issue Task 44 of this book. However, if you read carefully you will notice that the task instructions are different. Hence, it is very important to read the topic as well as its instructions completely before you start to write your response.

48

 Strategies

Restate the issue, perhaps by reversing the order of the sentence components.

In other words:

Making important decisions today is not affected by knowledge about the past.

Determine what question is being answered by the statement. This will help you begin to think how you would answer it and whether or not you agree with the original statement.

Does knowing about the past help people to make important decisions today?

Parts of the original statement that provide evidence that you can affirm or refute.

- ◆ **Knowing** – does not imply understanding

- ◆ **past** – any time previous

- ◆ **cannot help** – inability

- ◆ **important** – some significance is attached

- ◆ **decisions** – Usually arrived at after considering facts and alternatives

Next, create a statement that expresses the opposing viewpoint, using language similar to that of the original statement.

Opposing viewpoint:

Knowing about the past can help people make important decisions today.

◆ **can** – expresses the opposite ability of the original position

Is there any other way to look at this issue? Can you qualify the original statement in some way? Is it possible to partially agree with the statement?

Alternative viewpoint:

Knowing about the past does not always help people make better decisions in the present.

◆ **not always** – Using the past to make decisions does not always lead to good decisions.

◆ **better** – People do make the same mistakes even when they know the poor results that occurred in the past.

Examples:

a) The Great Gatsby

b) Hangovers

c) Touching a hot stove

 ## Sample Essay

We have all been warned by the oft–repeated aphorism, "those who cannot remember the past are condemned to repeat it'. Past experiences on both a national and personal level should serve as lessons that inform decisions and choices in the present. At the very least, the past can serve as a point of reference. The conflict arises when people don't understand the past.

F. Scott Fitzgerald wrote what many claim to be the greatest American novel ever written, The Great Gatsby. The eponymous main character spent his early years attempting to escape his past. Ashamed of his working-class roots, James Gatz changed his name and created a semi-fictional curriculum vitae. While Gatsby served in WWI, the love of his life, Daisy Fay, married Tom Buchanan and proceeded to live in the lap of luxury in an upper-class community on Long Island. After the war, Gatsby amassed a fortune in some unspecified, illegal business venture and used his ill-gotten gains in an attempt to win Daisy back.

Philosophy   *www.vibrantpublishers.com*

48

When his neighbor, Nick Caraway, became complicit in Gatsby's scheme, he admonished Gatsby that one cannot repeat the past. Gatsby replied, "Not repeat the past? Of course you can." The sad fact is that Gatsby not only believed it but also was able to imagine that the intervening years never existed. As a result, Jay Gatsby was unable to use the knowledge of his past with Daisy to make considered decisions in the present. His gleaming mansion, his hand-tailored shirts, his extravagant parties, and his quest for Daisy ended in a preventable tragedy.

My mother's favorite movie of all time is Dr. Zhivago, a tale of forbidden love set in Russia during the Communist revolution. The audience is transported as the Zhivago's lose the privileges they enjoyed in czarist Russia and are reduced to living in a small apartment inhabited by the great unwashed of society. They watch the handsome, charismatic Yuri fall in love with the beautiful Lara and their escape to the frosty country home where the young doctor feverishly writes poetry. For her own sake and safety, Yuri relinquishes Lara and makes his way on foot across the frozen tundra, compromising his own health along the way. The movie ends as Dr. Zhivago suffers a fatal heart attack while trying to exit a bus after seeing Lara on the street. Despite having seen it many times, my mother never misses a chance to see it again when it airs on television. If you were to ask her why she has seen it so many times, she will tell you that "this time", it will end differently. Dr. Zhivago and Lara will reunite.

Both Jay Gatsby and my mother exemplify our inability to use the past to inform our decisions in the present. Man's weakness is his inability or unwillingness to intellectualize events that occurred in the past. We are either hopelessly optimistic or stubbornly arrogant. Humans believe that the same disaster couldn't possibly occur again or they will, by sheer dint of force, make events turn out differently despite approaching a problem in the same way. The Mississippi River, for example, floods on a regular basis, and many homes in its path are destroyed. The residents who have watched their homes and belongings float away vow to rebuild in the same place. This stubborn resolve, seen by some as courageous, is foolhardy and puts lives as well as property at risk.

Experience should be the best teacher, and in some cases, it is. The child who burns his hand on a hot stove will likely not touch it a second time. The tot bitten by a strange dog will shy away from the next one. On the other hand, a college student who suffers a hangover after a night of partying will not eschew the behavior that caused it when a party rolls around the next weekend. People choose what they want to remember. Humans are prone to remember what they want to and disregard the warnings that interfere with their own desires.

Issue Task 49

Claim: *The best test of an argument is its ability to convince someone with an opposing viewpoint.*

Reason: *Only by being forced to defend an idea against the doubts and contrasting views of others does one really discover the value of that idea.*

Write a response in which you discuss the extent to which you agree or disagree with the claim and the reason on which that claim is based.

 Strategies

49

Combine the claim and reason into one statement using a subordinate clause.

In other words:

Because one cannot discover the value of an idea without defending it, the best test of an argument is its ability to convince someone with an opposing viewpoint.

What are the assumptions stated or implied in the claim and reason? These will provide evidence that you can refute or affirm in your argument.

◆ Changing someone's mind is proof that you are right.

◆ Ideas have no value unless you are forced to defend them.

◆ One's ideas have no intrinsic value.

◆ The value of one's ideas is created by others.

Opposing viewpoint:

Claim - *The ability to convince someone with an opposing viewpoint is not the best test of an argument.*

Reason - *The argument may not be based on the best information.*

Is there any other way to look at this issue? Can you qualify the original statement in some way? Is it possible to partially agree with the statement?

Alternative viewpoint:

Claim - *One test of an argument is its ability to convince someone with an opposing viewpoint.*

Reason- *Defending an idea against the doubts and contrasting views of others is not more valid than other tests.*

Examples:

a) Debates

b) My own state governor

 ## Sample Essay

It is satisfying and self–affirming to be able to make someone accept our point of view. Nothing feels as good as being right and having others admit it. Problems can arise when trying to convince another that one's point of view is the correct one. The proponents of an argument may use facts selectively or manipulate conditions to strengthen the position. Those having an opposing point of view may concede simply to put an end to the ha-rangue of the other party. If one believes deeply in an idea, he or she should welcome the opportunity to examine the argument more closely.

I can appreciate an argument even when it fails to change my mind if I observe that its creator has researched his position and has used logic and verifiable facts and statistics to support it. When I was in high school, I partic-ipated in the debating club. The purpose of each debate was not to change anyone else's opinion but to create and deliver the most compelling argument. Topics, positions, and team roles were assigned in a random manner, and I found myself on more than one occasion having to defend a point of view with which I did not agree. This did not prevent me from winning more debates than I lost. I spent hours researching, compiling statistics and evidence that my opponents would find difficult to refute. While doing so, I came to appreciate others' views on controversial topics and understand why they would defend them.

The governor of my state appeared to believe that right is might. He has spent the two–and–a–half years of his tenure arguing that the state should allow more charter schools. His contention is that public education in the state is failing to meet the needs of its students, and the students should have more choice in selecting a high school. In order to prove the correctness of his argument, he took several steps to undermine public education. On the one hand, he proposed deep cuts in financing of public education, while, on the other hand, he advocated public funding of private and religious schools.

Many of his opponents claimed that he has used flawed evidence to promote his contention that private and religious schools provide a better education. In fact, those schools do not have to meet the same standards or administer the same tests as public schools must. Most recently, the Department of Education assigned letter grades from A–F to each public school in the state. Less than a month before releasing the grades, the Commissioner of Education revealed the criteria upon which the grades would be based, giving schools no time to address those criteria. A significant portion of the grade derived from standardized test scores in math and English from the previous year's administration of those tests. In addition, the grades were assigned on a bell curve, meaning that a specific number of schools would receive A's and roughly the same number would receive F's. When the grades revealed that only nine schools in the state had received a grade of A, the governor was able to say that he had been right all along about the poor quality of public education in the state. The governor's actions illuminate a weakness in attempting to defend an argument. One may be tempted to manipulate conditions to prove its veracity.

The best test of an argument may be the ability to both understand and appreciate the other point of view while remaining steadfastly convinced of one's own position. In matters of faith, for example, leaders of any religious denomination believe that the faithful should question the tenets of their belief system. Only by searching for answers can one become stronger in his or her beliefs.

49

Issue Task 50

Claim: *Any piece of information referred to as a fact should be mistrusted, since it may well be proven false in the future.*

Reason: *Much of the information that people assume is factual actually turns out to be inaccurate.*

Write a response in which you discuss the extent to which you agree or disagree with the claim and the reason on which that claim is based.

 Strategies

Combine the claim and the reason into one statement using a subordinate clause.

In other words:

Because much of the information that people assume is factual actually turns out to be inaccurate, any piece of information referred to as a fact should be mistrusted since it may well be proven false in the future.

What are the assumptions stated or implied in the claim and reason? These will provide evidence that you can refute or affirm in your argument.

◆ Most facts will eventually be proven false.

◆ One shouldn't trust what others claim to be true.

◆ People are generally willing to believe what others say is true.

Opposing viewpoint:

Claim – *No piece of information referred to as fact should be mistrusted, because it will hold true in the future.*

Reason – *Much of the information that people assume is factual actually is.*

Alternative viewpoint:

Claim – *Not every piece of information referred to as fact should be mistrusted, since some may well be proven false in the future.*

Reason – *A considerable amount of the information that people assume is factual actually is.*

Examples:

a) Gossip

b) Campaign Rhetoric

c) Advances in science

Sample Essay

A healthy dose of skepticism is recommended when digesting a meal of facts delivered by someone else. In most cases, however, one should trust that those who have expertise in a specific field have done due diligence before making claims they presume to be true. Over time and with improved technology, new discoveries may appear that alter or contradict the current facts, but that doesn't mean they weren't true for the time and conditions under which they were espoused.

Some facts are true in the context in which they appear, but the reporters of such facts have cherry-picked them to serve their own purposes. This is never more obvious than during a presidential election. Social media makes these "facts" spread like wildfire, and the uninformed willingly accept them as gospel, especially if they coincide with their own political leanings. One of the most pervasive claims during the last presidential election was based on a chart depicting the yearly salaries of the President and members of Congress. The chart intended to inflame readers by stating that those individuals get that salary for life. While the dollar amounts were correct, the duration of said salaries was not. The President, senators and representatives get a pension based on their salaries. Another fact intended to shame Michelle Obama for having 26 assistants. What a waste of taxpayer money! A little research reveals that Laura Bush and other First Ladies had similar numbers of assistants. Displaying a little mistrust concerning facts presented for political purposes is wise.

Gossip is, perhaps, the most egregious misuse of facts. Generally repeated sotto voce, gossip can easily be misheard or misinterpreted. The listener then hurries off to spread the facts as he or she understood them. By the time the inflammatory remarks return to the subject, there is little truth remaining. In the case of gossip, the issue's original claim and reason hold true, not just for the sake of accuracy but for the protection of those subjected to vicious gossip. Rumors have characteristics in common with gossip. However, while gossip is never intended to spread good news, rumors may be used to disseminate both good and bad information, and their effect can be just as harmful as gossip. I live in a small city that was devastated when a nearby Air Force base closed. It had been rumored that the base would close several times over the years. Each time that the rumors began, local citizens would become despondent with worry over their futures. A Save Loring Committee worked tirelessly to keep the base from closing and succeeded twice. When the rumors began the third time, the locals refused to believe them and instead believed the more positive rumors that, once again, the base would remain open. It was like the little boy who cried wolf. As in the fable, the wolf, in the form of BRAC, did finally make an appearance, and the citizens of my town were caught unawares.

Some facts that have been disproved have little or no effect, either positive or negative, on the course of human development. In recent history, Pluto has lost its status as a planet. It was always a little suspect, anyway. So, our solar system is reduced to eight planets. This fact reversal has no effect on the way the world proceeds or stands as an argument that one should mistrust factual information. A much earlier astronomical reversal, however, did have an impact on the world. The Catholic Church believed the earth to be the center of the universe. Since God had created the earth and all of the creatures in it, it must be the most important of His creations. Hence, the sun and other planets must be inferior and show obeisance to the earth by revolving around it. In the sixteenth century, Copernicus developed a model that disproved the geocentric theory and validated the heliocentric theory proposed centuries before. Even though the Church was wrong about the solar system, one should not necessarily mistrust everything the Church proclaims to be fact.

50

Every day begins with the immutable fact that the sun will rise in the east and ends when the sun sets in the west. Much of what happens in that span of time is open to interpretation, but the average human will not question the events that occur or the facts they hear. Those who do so relinquish the ability to simply enjoy the day that they have been given. The habit of mistrusting those in authority leads to a life filled with uncertainty.

Issue Task 51

It is more harmful to compromise one's own beliefs than to adhere to them.

Write a response in which you discuss the extent to which you agree or disagree with the statement and explain your reasoning for the position you take. In developing and supporting your position, you should consider ways in which the statement might or might not hold true and explain how these considerations shape your position.

 Strategies

Restate the issue, perhaps by reversing the order of the sentence components.

51

In other words:

Adhering to one's own beliefs is less harmful than compromising them.

Determine what question is being answered by the statement. This will help you begin to think how you would answer it and whether or not you agree with the original statement.

Is it more harmful to compromise one's own beliefs than to adhere to them?

Parts of the original statement that provide evidence that you can affirm or refute.

◆ **more harmful-** expresses a degree of harm

◆ **compromise-** give and take

◆ **one's own beliefs -** tenets or opinions

◆ **adhere -** stick to

Next, create a statement that expresses the opposing viewpoint, using language similar to that of the original statement.

Opposing viewpoint:

It is more harmful to adhere to one's own beliefs than to compromise them.

It is more harmful to adhere to one's beliefs than to compromise them.

Parts of the opposing statement that provide evidence that you can affirm or refute.

Evidence is the same as in the original statement.

Is there any other way to look at this issue? Can you qualify the original statement in some way? Is it possible to partially agree with the statement?

Alternative viewpoint:

Depending on the circumstances, it is as harmful to adhere to one's own beliefs as it is to compromise them.

Parts of the alternative statement that provide evidence that you can affirm or refute.

◆ **Depending on the circumstances** – allows both choices to be correct

Sample Essay

The nineteenth century transcendentalist writer, Ralph Waldo Emerson, wrote that a foolish consistency is the hobgoblin of little minds. Adhering to one's own beliefs can result in a stubborn refusal to consider other points of view. Ignoring or denigrating the beliefs of others can lead to persecuting individuals or entire groups of people. On the other hand, compromising can lead to a watered–down version of a plan or goal, leaving both sides in a conflict unsatisfied. Depending upon the situation, either steadfastness regarding one's beliefs or reaching a compromise may be the correct action.

In Germany during the 1930s, Adolph Hitler rose to power and began to invade neighboring countries in an effort to establish the supremacy of the Aryan race. His unshakable belief that those with Aryan blood were superior to all other races led to the systematic roundup and murder of other groups including Jews, gypsies, homosexuals, and the mentally defective in concentration camps. Hitler's beliefs were so entrenched and his rhetoric so impassioned that he created a legion of followers who carried out his orders. His refusal to compromise his beliefs led to his conquering many countries in central Europe and, ultimately, to his demise.

On a much smaller scale, the actions of the city council in my hometown have created an impasse between city management and local businesses. The council has devised a plan to alleviate a budget deficit for the coming year, reduce expenditures for years to come, and add properties to the tax rolls. It put up for sale by bid all of the municipally–owned parking lots in the downtown area. The building and business owners downtown did not know of the plan until the list of properties appeared in the local newspaper. In a special city council meeting, the mayor admitted that the council assumed that the building owners would purchase the lots abutting their buildings. At least two of the lots are protected by the urban renewal plan from the late 1960's, so they were removed from the list.

The building owners fronted by the other lots spoke about the inadvisability of selling them, citing the complexity of both buying and maintaining lots shared by multiple owners. Determined to reduce the city's responsibility for the lots, the mayor devised a new plan that requires people who park downtown for the entire workday to purchase annual parking permits. Again, building and business owners spoke to the council about the financial hardship that the new plan would put on workers downtown and the logistics of allocating spaces to preserve access to retail businesses. The issue has consumed way too much time and energy for the small savings that the city would see. In fact, the city's hiring someone to enforce parking regulations would offset the savings. Each side is more concerned about being right than understanding the other's point of view. Adhering to one's point of view, in this case, prevents further progress in solving the city's budget issues and creates resentment from business owners toward the council.

Adhering to one's beliefs is essential when attempting to redress wrongs committed against humanity. America today would be a very different place had Martin Luther King, Jr. compromised his belief that all men, regardless of color, were entitled to the same rights and freedoms. When he spoke on the steps of the Lincoln Memorial in Washington, DC fifty years ago, he did not proclaim that only some black men should be treated with equality or that only members of some religions should be treated with equality, but that black men and white men, Jews and Gentiles, Protestants and Catholics all should be granted the same freedoms guaranteed in the Constitution. In the same manner, Gandhi also adhered to his belief in freedom from oppression when he demonstrated against British rule in India. Despite their use of peaceful protest, both King and Gandhi were assassinated for their unwillingness to compromise their beliefs. Both men knew the inherent dangers of their actions but were not deterred from their objectives.

Although it may be painful to compromise one's beliefs, the most significant decisions in America's history are most often the result of the conflicting sides' willingness to concede at least a portion of their own plan. America's founding fathers compromised to find a balance between federal and state's rights, creating the legislature we still have today. The Missouri Compromise limited the expansion of slave states in America. When compromise limits the benefits of people affected by an idea or action, it should be abandoned in favor of adhering to one's beliefs.

Issue Task 52

True success can be measured primarily in terms of the goals one sets for oneself.

Write a response in which you discuss the extent to which you agree or disagree with the statement and explain your reasoning for the position you take. In developing and supporting your position, you should consider ways in which the statement might or might not hold true and explain how these considerations shape your position.

 Strategies

Restate the issue, perhaps by reversing the order of the sentence components.

In other words:

The goals one sets for oneself are the measures of true success.

Determine what question is being answered by the statement. This will help you begin to think how you would answer it and whether or not you agree with the original statement.

Is true success measured by the goals one sets for oneself?

Parts of the original statement that provide evidence that you can affirm or refute.

◆ **True success -** in this case, worthy of celebration or acknowledgment

◆ **measured -** quantified, valued

◆ **primarily -** most important

◆ **goals -** achievements, destinations

◆ **one sets for oneself -** as opposed to those set for one by others

Next, create a statement that expresses the opposing viewpoint, using language similar to that of the original statement.

Opposing viewpoint:

True success is not measured primarily by the goals one sets for oneself.

Parts of the opposing statement that provide evidence that you can affirm or refute.

◆ **not** - other measurements of success are equally or more important

Is there any other way to look at this issue? Can you qualify the original statement in some way? Is it possible to partially agree with the statement?

Alternative viewpoint:

True success is measured by the goals one achieves.

Parts of the alternative statement that provide evidence that you can affirm or refute.

◆ **achieves** - setting goals is not a sufficient measure of success

Sample Essay

People set goals that are sometimes simple and at other times complex. Rare is the individual who hasn't created a New Year's resolution to exercise more, lose weight, or quit smoking. Rarer still is the individual who has managed to keep that resolution. As important as individual goals are, so are those set by leaders in business, science and government. When the president of a country sets goals for his term of office, he considers the welfare of all citizens. When a CEO sets a goal for his company, he hopes that achieving it will benefit his workers and shareholders. Scientists hope to improve the lives of all humans when they set a goal to discover a treatment for a deadly disease. Small and personal or grand and universal, all goals are indications of people's seeking success.

Just yesterday morning, I watched as an IT specialist from North Carolina set off from a soccer field near my house to cross the Atlantic in a cluster balloon, a journey predicted to take from three to six days with the possibility of landing anywhere from Norway to Africa. It was like a scene from the movie Up as 365 colored, helium–filled balloons lifted Jonathan Trappe and his rubber boat silently into the air. The fantastic craft quickly disappeared into the morning mist. This same man has flown cluster balloons over the Alps and across the English Channel, but this was to be his most ambitious undertaking. It is unfortunate that this journey ended in Newfoundland just twelve hours after it began. However, if success were to be measured by the goals one sets for himself, Mr. Trappe would, indeed, be considered successful.

It could be argued that setting goals that are easily attainable is not real success. The poet Robert Browning said, "a man's reach should exceed his grasp." Man should strive for achievements beyond his current ability. It is

52

the only way to grow. When Christa McAuliffe was a young girl, she told a friend that she wanted to go into space someday. The opportunity arose when President Reagan made the decision to put a teacher on the space shuttle. Christa applied and saw her goal realized when she was selected to be the first teacher in space. where she planned to present lessons live from the Challenger. Less than a minute after takeoff, the shuttle broke apart and McAuliffe, along with the rest of the crew, was killed. Although her mission was cut short, she has been lauded for setting a lofty goal and undergoing the rigorous training to become an astronaut. Had the Wright Brothers not set a goal of achieving manned flight in the earliest decade of the twentieth century, space travel likely would have occurred much later. Orville and Wilbur Wright could have lived out the rest of their lives building and repairing bicycles, setting and achieving the goal of customer satisfaction with their excellent workmanship. However, setting loftier goals, the Wright brothers not only achieved success for themselves but inspired generations of fliers.

Ordinary individuals set their sights on reaching significant goals as well. They want to become more fit, so they join a gym. They want to lose a few or many pounds, so they join Weight Watchers. They want to quit smoking, so they join a cessation program at their local hospital. They all begin with great resolve and enthusiasm. After a few weeks, visits to the gym become less frequent, cake and ice cream become more appealing than pounds lost, and a cigarette after dinner becomes irresistible. Some of these individuals will fail to meet their goals, but others will try again and ultimately succeed. Without setting goals in the first place, they surely would have failed.

Many who have reached outstanding levels of achievement did not succeed in reaching their goals with their first attempt. The Wright brothers built many airplanes that failed to fly. Three NASA astronauts, including Gus Grissom, died in a pre launch test in 1967. Civil Rights workers were murdered in Mississippi. Setbacks did not stop the progress of flight, the space race, or the Civil Rights Movement. Failure is not measured by an individual's inability to meet his or her goals. Failure is the result of giving up or not trying at all. Setting a goal is the first step on the road to success.

52

Issue Task 53

In any field - business, politics, education, government - those in power should be required to step down after five years.

Write a response in which you discuss your views on the policy and explain your reasoning for the position you take. In developing and supporting your position, you should consider the possible consequences of implementing the policy and explain how these consequences shape your position.

Strategies

Restate the issue, perhaps by reversing the order of the sentence components.

In other words:

Those in power in any field - business, politics, education, government- should be required to step down after five years.

Determine what question is being answered by the statement. This will help you begin to think how you would answer it and whether or not you agree with the original statement.

When should those in power in any field be required to step down?

How long should those in power in any field be allowed to retain their positions?

Consequences of adopting this policy:

◆ Fresh ideas will be introduced every five years.

◆ Long- range planning becomes difficult.

◆ Ineffective leaders can be replaced quickly.

Next, create a statement that expresses the opposing viewpoint, using language similar to that of the original statement.

Opposing viewpoint:

In any field – business, politics, education, government – those in power should not be required to step down after five years.

Consequences of adopting this policy:

◆ More experience leads to better decisions.

◆ Those in power may become complacent.

◆ Long- range planning becomes possible.

Is there any other way to look at this issue? Can you qualify the original statement in some way? Is it possible to partially agree with the statement?

Alternative viewpoint:

In any field - business, politics, education, government - those in power should step down when they are no longer effective.

Consequences of adopting this policy:

◆ Effective leaders can remain in power.

 # Sample Essay

A five–year limit on tenure in any field appears arbitrary. Some in positions of power or leadership should leave office sooner, and some should be allowed to remain for as long as they want. Examples exist on the local, state, national, and international level that support either the original or the opposing point of view. It is impossible and impractical to establish hard–and–fast rules about the length of time anyone should serve in a position of power or leadership.

America's founding fathers, in order to eliminate the potential tyranny associated with sovereigns like kings, established a democracy in which the people would elect their leaders. They also established a four–year term as president. It was not until the middle of the twentieth century that the number of terms a president could serve was limited to two. US senators and representatives serve two–and six–year terms respectively, and they may

53

remain in office as long as the voters choose to keep them. The frequency with which they must seek reelection allows the voters to keep those who represent them well and eliminate those whose actions do not benefit them.

Many American presidents have served more than one term. President Franklin D. Roosevelt was elected for four consecutive terms during the most challenging period in our history. He led us out of the Great Depression by creating the New Deal replete with public works projects that provided honorable and necessary work for Americans who had lost everything. He was Commander in Chief during most of the WWII years. It would be difficult to imagine how America would have fared during those trying times if our nation's leader had been compelled to serve only 5 years. In contrast to the beneficial results of FDR's tenure, the Russians were suffering under the dictator, Stalin who did not have to run for reelection. Despite the Communist five–year plans for productivity, millions of Russians died from starvation and persecution. Whereas Americans were well–served by FDR's lengthy leadership, Russians would have been better off if Stalin had been forced out of office.

One negative consequence of limiting the tenure of those in positions of leadership is the inability to plan long–term. In virtually any field, the leader cannot effect change without first creating a cohort of like–minded individuals. Convincing those with the same point of view to work toward the leader's goals is difficult enough without also having to persuade those on the fence or diametrically opposed to his or her ideas. This can consume a great deal of time and energy. Once the cohort is established, the members are apt to want some concessions or compromises from each other before the final objective is clearly delineated. Additional steps in the process may include conducting polls, surveys, or research.

Several years can elapse during this process at the end of which, the leader may have little time remaining to fulfill his goals. If the leader is compelled to leave in the middle of the journey, the goal may never be achieved, and the new leader may have very different ideas about the needs of the institution he is directing and restart the entire complex process. In contrast, a leader who knows his time in office is limited may work more diligently to accomplish his objectives. When people have deadlines for completing tasks or assignments, they organize their time more efficiently. Imagine a student having a research project with no due date. He or she might procrastinate or never do the work at all.

Experience is the best teacher. A good leader in any field becomes more adept. He or she is apt to face similar situations over the course of his tenure and use what he has learned from past actions and consequences to inform his decision making. He will have learned what works, what doesn't, and how to negotiate for the best outcome. Longevity can also lead to stagnation, and some are inclined to do things the way they've always been done. They are resistant to change or even compromise. Because voters, company directors, and boards of education have the discretion and power to remove institutional leaders when no longer effective, an arbitrary term limit is not necessary. Term limits can truncate the careers of effective leaders or extend those of leaders who should have been removed soon after assuming their positions.

Issue Task 54

In any situation, progress requires discussion among people who have contrasting points of view.

Write a response in which you discuss the extent to which you agree or disagree with the statement and explain your reasoning for the position you take. In developing and supporting your position, you should consider ways in which the statement might or might not hold true and explain how these considerations shape your position.

 Strategies

A good starting point is to break down the statement and identify the assumptions it makes. Look for ambiguous phrasing and consider all possible exceptions – they represent weak points that you can defend or attack depending on your chosen position.

Statement breakdown:

54

- ◆ **Any situation** – this is a categorical statement; there are always exceptions

- ◆ **Progress** – this implies moving forward, solving an issue; can the issue be solved? What about time constraints?

- ◆ **Discussion** – another term for this is dialogue - are people willing to listen? Can they understand or is the point of view too remote from their own? What about communication errors?

- ◆ **Contrasting** – Radically opposing points of view? What about fringe viewpoints?

Assumptions:

- ◆ Any situation can be mediated through discussion

- ◆ People with contrasting views are willing to compromise

- ◆ People with contrasting views are willing to listen and understand each other

- ◆ Discussions will have positive results

Pros and Cons:

Pros

- 👍 Discussion leads to brainstorming, which may result in novel ideas or pathways.

- 👍 Discussion brings understanding between parties, which can lead to agreement

- 👍 Inclusion and equality – Both parties are happy to be included in making a decision; get to state their point of view

- 👍 Solving complex problems is typically easier with diverse backgrounds.

- 👍 Progress relies on opening new pathways

- 👍 No tyranny of the majority (one side does not get to impose their point of view)

- 👍 Perspectivism (Nietzsche) – the world is comprised of individual perspectives; reality is represented by the points where they overlap

Cons

- 👎 Not all discussions will be civilized or productive

- 👎 People with radically different values likely will not agree or compromise because the other person offends their core values.

- 👎 Some will treat the discussion like an opportunity for conversion, resulting in a lack of progress.

- 👎 Communication errors - Participants may interpret statements made by other members of the discussion differently from the intended meaning.

- 👎 Compromise with fringe ideas endangers ethical values.

- 👎 Compromising means that both sides get disappointed since neither gets what they want

- 👎 Time restricted situations require on the spot decision making (no time for discussions)

- 👎 Opposing debates can deteriorate a situation further

- 👎 Members of a society do not all need to agree to the societal terms in order for the society to function. (fragmentary nature of current society)

Examples:

a) Current and historical conflicts and their resolutions

b) Movies (especially about seeing the other person's point of view)

c) Controversial research

d) Conflict resolution methods

 ## Sample Essay

Human nature is often contradictory, which is evidenced by a history fraught with conflict. It is uncommon for people to be at peace with their own mindsets, let alone with others whose world views differ vastly from their own. While discussion is a very useful tool for expanding horizons and progressing societies, it is not always the right solution to a problem; as with any rule, there are exceptions.

Take, for instance, situations where the discussion of sensitive topics degenerates into conflict. Such situations are encountered not infrequently by the average person and are often characterized by participants squabbling over their differences, with no headways made on the issue at hand. This is something that any participant in a forum discussion knows very well. It is not just adolescents that engage in this behavior over the internet, but full–grown adults as well, such as in the famous Linux versus Minix debate. This type of squabbling can often de- lay, if not prevent progress altogether. A prime example of this fact is the Peary – Cook dispute over the discovery of the North Pole. All attempted discussions between the two explorers degenerated into arguments that often spilled over into the public realm (newspapers) and only served to drive the two friends to enmity. To this day, even long after their deaths, the dispute continues, backed by their respective supporters.

Another potential impedance to progress is the fact that people with completely opposite views are unlikely to end up agreeing on their points of dissent. Moreover, they see any interaction with the other as damaging to themselves, a form of personal attack because the other person offends their core values. Not to mention the fact that issues that touch upon a person's core values incite a person's passion, which in turn, has the propensity to move conversation away from the realm of reason. While emotional aspects should be considered during discus- sions when pertinent, purely emotional arguments often derail practical progress. A current example is a devout pro–life Christian and a freedom–of–choice atheist talking about abortion; both will see each other's viewpoints as personal attacks against their lifestyle. Similarly, one or more parties can end up treating the conversation like an opportunity for conversion via personal attacks. In this case, the devout Christian can try to 'shine the light' so that the other can see the error of their ways and repent. This type of behavior always ends up being perceived as combative, and as a result, at the end of the discussion, both parties will emerge even more fully convinced of the righteousness of their claims.

The previous examples do not take into account the fact that errors are pervasive in any form of commu- nication. Messages are not perceived directly by their intended target; they have to pass through communica- tion channels that can distort them (noise pollution, no visuals on the internet which means misunderstanding the tone of a statement etc.). Additional problems are created when then the messages need to be filtered through the person's perception and understanding of the world and are integrated with their idea of who the communicator is and what they are trying to achieve. Continuing the example from above, if an atheist thinks that a Christian is trying to convert him, he is likely to interpret all statements through that filter, and disregard even arguments that in the proper context would be reasonable based on the assumption that the other person is only trying to promote their own agenda.

All in all, discussion should not be seen as a universal cure or an absolute guarantee of progress, especially in instances where it all comes down to on the spot decision making due to limited time, or cases where participants hold radically opposing points of view and are likely to never see eye to eye.

54

Chapter **7**
Science & Technology

Issue Task 55

As people rely more and more on technology to solve problems, the ability of humans to think for themselves will surely deteriorate.

Write a response in which you discuss the extent to which you agree or disagree with the statement and explain your reasoning for the position you take. In developing and supporting your position, you should consider ways in which the statement might or might not hold true and explain how these considerations shape your position

 Strategies

To get started, break down the statement and identify the assumptions made.

Statement Breakdown

- Technology – is able to solve more and more problems, unclear as to whether those are problems that people typically encounter

- People – use technology to solve some problems, seem to be using it more than in the past

- The ability of humans to think – focus of the use of technology

Assumptions

- Technology solves problems that require human thought.

- People are actively using that technology to solve their problems instead of thinking.

- Lack of thinking causes the ability to think to deteriorate.

After breaking down the statement and identifying assumptions, come up with pros and cons (or statements for and against) the topic given. You do not need to pick a side yet, but knowing potential counterarguments will help you to develop a stronger essay once you do.

Pros and Cons

Pros

👍 People don't think about having to do certain tasks (i.e., balancing a checkbook vs. online banking) be cause of technology.

👍 Technology is developed to solve problems with increasing complexity.

👍 Not thinking about how to do a task makes it harder to do the same task in the future.

Cons

👎 Technology doesn't solve all problems, so thinking is still necessary.

👎 With more trivial problems solved by technology, people can think about more complex problems.

👎 Not everyone uses problem-solving technology, so changes in thinking are not universal.

Examples

Include examples in order to make your essay as strong as possible. These are some potential routes you may take when choosing examples:

a) History contains many examples from both sides of the argument.

b) Current technology trends/focuses highlight the types of problems that technology is solving.

c) Disparities between regional access to technology shows differences in how people rely on technology.

Finally, come up with an outline of your essay. This may feel like it slows you down, but your essay will benefit from having an underlying structure.

 ## Sample Essay

Technological advancements to solve any problem you can think of and more are being made at an accelerating rate. Moore's Law states that technology can advance at an exponential rate as the ability to fit data processing power on a single chip increases at similar speeds, so it is reasonable to think that the problems of humans today will not be the problems of the future. However, some are concerned that these developments in problem–solving technology will lead to a deterioration in the ability of humans to think. This deterioration would be caused by a lack of needing to think, as all of one's problems would be solved by technology. In reality, this is not the case, as historical trends in technological development, the focus of current technology development, and the disparities in global adoption of technology show.

If the development and usage of new problem–solving technology caused human thinking to deteriorate, humankind would have stopped innovating long before today. Early technology developed to solve problems of transportation; the invention of the wheel made resource movement more efficient, giving early humans more time to consider solutions to other problems. Similarly, in the present day, automobile technology allows people to move from one place to another quickly, leaving extra time to develop solutions for autonomous vehicles. New problems always arise once old ones are solved, requiring people to use their ability to think in order to tackle the next wave of issues.

Focusing on current technology, problem–solving technology often does not focus on problems that require people to expend significant energy in thinking. For example, an assistive device that perfectly cracks an egg into a frying pan can be used to replace the usage of one's hand to crack an egg into a pan; however this technological solution solves a problem that did not require significant thinking in the first place. Most consumer technology to-day is meant to be a gimmick – that is, it is meant to make the buyer believe that he or she has a problem when it is likely not the case. On the other hand, more advanced technology that is currently being developed is not used for problems encountered by the average person. The newest quantum computer being developed by Google in 2018 is designed to run hundreds or thousands of processes in parallel that would normally take years on a stan-dard computer. It is unlikely that there is a problem encountered by an average person that this would solve.

Finally, comparisons can be drawn between the usage of technology in developing versus in developed coun-tries. Developing countries typically have less new technology than developed countries do because of the lack of economic infrastructure present to allow for such developments. Based on the belief conveyed in the prompt, people living in developing countries would have greater ability to think for themselves than people who live in developed countries. This is clearly not the case; and, if anything, people from developing countries likely have a lower thinking ability due to their lack of education and the less complex types of problems, such as acquiring food for the week, that are prioritized in their lives.

Technological developments historically occurred to solve a problem that would make the lives of the people using it easier. However, as technology has caught up to modern problems, it has expanded to focus on trivial or non–existent problems, or problems that are not faced by a significant portion of the populace. The unbalanced distribution of technology adoption and the resultant ability to think associated with varying usage levels shows that the usage of technology does not impact one's ability to think. Ultimately, as people rely on technology more and more to solve their problems, they will increase their ability to think for themselves as they tackle more com-plex problems than the ones before.

55

Issue Task 56

Although innovations such as video, computers, and the Internet seem to offer schools improved methods for instructing students, these technologies all too often distract from real learning.

Write a response in which you discuss the extent to which you agree or disagree with the statement and explain your reasoning for the position you take. In developing and supporting your position, you should consider ways in which the statement might or might not hold true and explain how these considerations shape your position.

 Strategies

Restate the Issue:

Begin by restating the issue. Make the dependent clause the main clause of the sentence. Rearranging the clauses changes the focus and the connotation of each clause.

In other words:

Although technology all too often distracts from real learning, innovations such as video, computers, and the Internet seem to offer schools improved methods for instructing students.

Determine the question being answered by the statement.

What effect has technology had on teaching and learning?

The question may start you thinking about the way that you would answer it. Your own position may be taking shape. The question should help develop alternate points of view. The original issue statement is only one way to answer the question.

Now think about parts of the original issue statement that provide evidence you can affirm or refute.

◆ **innovations** – The root word, nova, means new. Innovations don't remain innovative for long. At one time, cars, telephones, television, and typewriters were innovative.

◆ **seem** – Seem is not a definitive word. It's not an absolute.

◆ **to offer** – One does not have to accept an offer. An offer implies choice.

56

◆ **improved** – This implies better, that what came before was not as good in some way.

◆ **distract** – This is the opposite of attract. Distract means to lead away from, while attract means to lead toward.

◆ **real learning**– Real is the opposite of artificial or fake. Is any learning artificial or fake?

Opposing viewpoint:

Innovations such as video, computer, and the Internet offer schools improved methods for instructing students and promote real learning.

Identify the parts of the opposing statement that provide evidence to refute or affirm.

◆ **promote** – Promote means to move forward. Technology helps learning to move forward. You may create a statement that qualifies the original or opposing viewpoint.

Alternative viewpoint:

Innovations such as video, computers, and the Internet have the potential to either offer schools improved methods for instructing students or to distract from real learning.

Identify the parts of the alternative viewpoint that provide evidence to refute or affirm.

◆ **potential** – The root of potential is potent, which means having power. Technology has the power to offer school improved methods for instructing students, or it has the power to distract from real learning.

Position:

With appropriate training, teachers and students can use technology such as videos, computers, and the Internet to enhance teaching and learning.

Examples:

a) **Record keeping** – teachers can use web-based grade books to keep track of assignments and student progress. Schools can allow students and parents access to those grade books, placing responsibility for completing assignments and awareness of problems on the student and parents.

b) **Communication** – Schools and/or individual teachers can create websites to communicate with students by placing assignments, special directions, etc. on the Internet. Teachers and/or schools can communicate with students and parents via email.

c) **Google docs** – web–based application that allows students to create office documents such as slide presentations, spreadsheets and compositions. This allows students to submit assignments without printing them; students can collaborate with each other or their teachers; and teachers can leave comments.

d) **Research** – multiple students can research the same topic simultaneously without worrying about books already checked out of the library. Teachers can use anti plagiarism programs.

 ## Sample Essay

In the early part of the twentieth century, people thought the car was a fad; they would never replace the trusty, hard–working horse. In the middle of the twentieth century, people thought television was a fad; it would never replace the radio. In the mid 1980's, people thought VCR's and video tapes were a fad; they would never replace the experience of going to the movies. Now we can drive in our cars and watch movies at the same time. Virtually everything that makes life more convenient will stay. We must accept that technology in the form of computers and the Internet are permanently entrenched in society.

What is the impact on teaching and learning? Teaching and learning have always been book and paper intensive. Teachers in every discipline assigned books to their students and used paper to keep track of which student had which book. Students used paper to complete assignments associated with those books and handed them in to their teachers, who carried those papers home to grade them. This process was repeated all over the country by millions of students and teachers every day for 36–40 weeks a year. Technology has the potential to allow students to complete a variety of work and submit it online.

Most notable of these applications is Google Docs where students can set up a free account and create writing pieces, spreadsheets, and slide presentations. Alternatively, they can upload those same documents from their home computers. Students share their work with their teachers who can insert comments, highlight elements, and assign grades. In fact, a student and teacher can work simultaneously on an assignment while "chatting" in a sidebar. Another benefit of Google Docs is the feature that saves a student's work instantaneously and keeps it on the Web. This application enhances the educational process through its accessibility and immediacy. When teachers can provide rapid feedback, students benefit.

Technology is a double–edged sword when it comes to research projects. On one side, information on any topic is available at the click of a mouse. On the other side is the temptation for students to cut and paste information directly from sources. There have always been students who plagiarize. Technology can make it easier, but it also is easier for teachers to uncover it using programs designed for that purpose or simply using Google's search function. Thanks to the Internet, gone are the days of creating Works Cited or References pages by hand

56

and agonizing over alphabetizing and citing correctly. There are both free and subscription services that do that for students. When students and teachers can focus on what the child has to say and how he says it, real learning happens.

The introduction of tablets is already revolutionizing learning. It is likely that future students will not be carrying backpacks crammed with books and binders. Rather, they will glide from class to class, carrying slim computers onto which they have downloaded their textbooks, and with which they will complete their classwork. As the accoutrements of education become easier to manage, there can be a clearer focus on leveraging these new technologies to better educate students. Therefore, while technology has the potential to distract students from learning if used poorly, its true potential lies in its ability to streamline classroom work and homework, giving students more time to learn about topics that may not have been covered otherwise.

56

Issue Task 57

Scientists and other researchers should focus their research on areas that are likely to benefit the greatest number of people.

Write a response in which you discuss the extent to which you agree or disagree with the recommendation and explain your reasoning for the position you take. In developing and supporting your position, describe specific circumstances in which adopting the recommendation would or would not be advantageous and explain how these examples shape your position.

 Strategies

Restate the issue, perhaps by reversing the order of the sentence components.

In other words:

Areas that are likely to benefit the greatest number of people should be the focus of scientists and other researchers.

Determine what question is being answered by the statement. This will help you begin to think how you would answer it and whether or not you agree with the original statement.

On what areas should scientists and other researchers focus their research?

Parts of the original statement that provide evidence that you can affirm or refute.

◆ **scientists** - This identifies someone with advanced education in some field of science.

◆ **other researchers** - Does this mean researchers in fields other than science? Education, perhaps?

◆ **focus** - Look closely at or select one subject

◆ **likely** - This suggests probability rather than certainty

◆ **benefit** - Scientists and other researchers should avoid areas that would cause harm. What type of benefit?

◆ **the greatest number of people** - Areas of research that benefit a small number of people should be abandoned. They should also abandon research that might benefit animals.

57

Next, create a statement that expresses the opposing viewpoint, using language similar to that of the original statement.

Opposing viewpoint:

Scientists and other researchers should not focus only on areas that benefit the greatest number of people.

◆ **not only -** Scientists and other researchers should work to benefit any size group.

Is there any other way to look at this issue? Can you qualify the original statement in some way? Is it possible to partially agree with the statement?

Alternative viewpoint:

Scientists and other researchers should first focus on areas that have the greatest urgency.

◆ **first -** Scientists should prioritize the subjects of their research.

◆ **greatest urgency -** Scientists must decide what can be postponed and what must be addressed immediately.

Examples:

57

a) Global warming or climate change - This qualifies as both urgent and having an effect on the greatest number of people.

b) AIDS - Failure to stop the spread or a cure threatens large numbers of people.

c) Autism Spectrum Disorders - The dramatic increase in the number of children diagnosed affects both families and schools.

d) Polio - Although it did not affect large numbers of people, scientists were compelled to eradicate it.

 Sample Essay

It is generally true that people make important choices in their lives based on deep interest or abiding passion. They may be influenced by a personal connection. A scientist, for example, may have watched his mother die from breast cancer, and, as a result, he dedicates his working life to discovering a cure. Another may have a sibling diagnosed with type I diabetes at an early age and then focuses his research on putting an end to that life–long, debilitating condition. A third may have had a beloved neighbor with Down syndrome and dedicates his career to discovering a means to repair or prevent chromosomal disorders. On the other hand, when scientists and re-searchers are required to work only on problems that affect the greatest number of people, they may be less like-ly to proceed with the required fervor to effect timely and far–reaching results. Scientists and other researchers should focus on areas that enable them to work tirelessly to relieve the ills of humanity, regardless of the number of people who benefit from their endeavors.

Scientists do not have crystal balls. They cannot predict which subject of research may ultimately benefit a great number of people. At one time, autism spectrum disorders were thought to be relatively rare, and little was done to improve the lives of those affected. They were isolated and given a pessimistic prognosis for any improve-ment in their condition or quality of life. Over the past few years, the rise in the number of those diagnosed with ASD has experienced a meteoric rise. Doctors claim that one in eighty children will be diagnosed with some form of autism, placing enormous burdens on families and schools. No one in the 1970's could have predicted that cases of ASD would increase at such a rapid rate. Once excluded from the world of work and education, most that have some form of autism today complete college and become productive citizens. Had scientists and other re-searchers ignored autism because it affected a supposedly low number of individuals, the progress that has been made would have been delayed by several decades, and our society would be poorer without the contributions of these people.

In the 1980's a disease emerged that created great concern and controversy around the world. When AIDS first came to the public's attention, it was regarded as a "gay" disease, present almost exclusively in homosexual men who had multiple sexual partners. The poster boy for this plague was Rock Hudson, the once strapping, hand-some leading man on both the big and small screens of America. The world watched as images of his haggard and wasted physique appeared in magazines and read of his desperate trips to France to seek any kind of treatment for his illness. His death provided fodder for those who think of homosexuality as an abomination; this plague was God's retribution. These attitudes and the apparently narrow scope of the disease may have delayed research for an effective treatment. When cases of AIDS began showing up in other segments of the population and its spread became rapid, researchers began to accelerate the process of finding a treatment or cure. Had the medical community relegated AIDS research to the back burner because it appeared to affect only people who engaged in risky behavior, the advances in treatment that prolong life and, in some cases, cure the disease might still exist only in the future.

Of great concern to scientists today is climate change. Most believe that human interaction with the environ-ment has created a variety of issues, including the hole in the ozone and the melting of the polar ice caps. Former Vice President, Al Gore, has been an outspoken critic of human practices that have led to global warming and has gone around the world with his documentary, An Inconvenient Truth, advocating for change. No other issue has effects as far reaching as this; every living human, animal, and plant is threatened in some way. Droughts, floods, desertification, and extinction challenge every society around the globe. No other issue affects a greater number of people, and failure to correct or reverse these changes spells doom for coastal communities as well as plant and animal species. The failure to focus research on the environment will have a deleterious effect on great num-bers of people around the world.

It is easy to identify concerns that currently affect the largest number of people. Focusing on those issues may cause scientists and other researchers to overlook problems that, although small now, may eventually have a negative impact on considerable populations. The world is smaller today. The ability of people to travel quickly and frequently to all corners of the globe makes once isolated issues a concern for everyone on the planet. Scientists and other researchers should be encouraged to perform their work in ways that benefit any group of humans.

57

Issue Task 58

The human mind will always be superior to machines because machines are only tools of human minds.

Write a response in which you discuss the extent to which you agree or disagree with the statement and explain your reasoning for the position you take. In developing and supporting your position, you should consider ways in which the statement might or might not hold true and explain how these considerations shape your position.

 Strategies

Restate the issue, perhaps by reversing the order of the sentence components.

In other words:

Because machines are only tools of human minds, the human mind will always be superior to machines.

Determine what question is being answered by the statement. This will help you begin to think how you would answer it and whether or not you agree with the original statement.

Why is the human mind superior to machines?

Parts of the original statement that provide evidence that you can affirm or refute.

◆ **always -** This absolute leaves no room for other options. Is it possible for something to always be true? Never true?

◆ **superior -** A superior position is above any other. It is higher, better.

◆ **only -** This can imply exclusivity, e.g. the only one. It also suggests a lack, e.g. only enough enough for two.

◆ **tools -** Humans have developed tools to make tasks easier. The ability to use tools has elevated some species and ensures their survival.

◆ **machines -** They are inanimate objects designed to serve man.

Next, create a statement that expresses the opposing viewpoint, using language similar to that of the original statement.

58

Opposing viewpoint:

Even though man has created machines, his mind is not always superior to machines.

Parts of the statement that provide evidence that you can affirm or refute.

- ◆ **even though** – This suggests exemptions or conditions under which the original statement may not be true.

- ◆ **not always** – This is also a conditional phrase.

Alternative viewpoint:

Man's failure to develop his mind can lead to the superiority of machines over man.

- ◆ **failure to develop** – not learning how to use or manipulate sophisticated machines

Examples:

a) 2001: A Space Odyssey – Hal begins to make independent decisions.

b) Watson, created by IBM to play Jeopardy!

c) Many people never learned to program their VCR's.

58

 # Sample Essay

When humans learned how to use tools, they increased their chances of survival. Humans were able to hunt more efficiently and plant crops, ensuring a food supply. Pulleys, levers, and wheels enabled men to lift heavy objects, move objects, and build shelters. Simple machines and tools were the servants of man. Over time, man modified his early tools and machines. By the middle of the twentieth century, humans were using tools and machines to accomplish virtually every daily task. Man had made all of these machines and was, therefore, superior to them. They did only what humans made them do. For the most part, they still do, but the advent of Artificial Intelligence may change that.

In 1968, 2001 A Space Odyssey introduced audiences to Hal, a computer with some human characteristics. Initially a tool used by space travelers Dave and Frank, Hal begins to behave independently of them. Frank and Dave eventually become concerned enough to hatch a plot that will deactivate Hal. Hal foils the plot and reveals to Dave that the precautions he and Frank took to discuss their plan out of Hal's hearing were futile, as Hal can read lips. Forty years ago, no one had a computer at home, so Hal's independent actions may have seemed both fantastic and frightening to movie audiences.

Two years ago, Jeopardy! fans tuned in to watch Watson, a computer designed with artificial intelligence, compete against two of the show's top winners. Despite some hiccups, Watson beat the former champs, including Ken Jennings, who won more than seventy games in his reign as champion. Although Watson, named for the original founder of IBM, had been designed and programmed by humans, he was able to think independently when answering each question on the show. He was not connected to the Internet, and, therefore, could not search for correct answers. Watson functioned like a thinking human brain.

Even though most of us have not had encounters with Artificial Intelligence, we have purchased machines that demonstrate our limits. When VCR's became readily available, nearly everyone applauded the ability to watch popular movies in the comfort of our own homes. Programming the machine, however, was beyond the skill of many homeowners. As a result, most VCR's sat on the shelf flashing 12:00 for the lifetime of the device.

Throughout the history of man, machines, both simple and complex, have been the tools of man. In fact, our sophisticated use of tools is what sets us apart from other animal species. It is difficult for those living in the twenty–first century to imagine what life was like for humans without the machines we use today. We can only imagine the time and labor involved in planting and harvesting crops before the advent of the cotton gin and the McCormack reaper, let alone the diesel–powered farm vehicles we see today. The working woman would not exist were it not for the labor–saving devices in her home: washing machines and dryers, vacuum cleaners and dishwashers. Today's students would find it quaint to complete math assignments without advanced calculators and English compositions without computers. Many schools have even gone paperless as students can submit their work online. For the purpose of making daily tasks easier, machines remain inferior to humans.

While it is true that the advanced machines that make our lives easier would not exist without the minds of the men who created them, our mindless use of them may be our downfall. Little thought goes into accomplishing either simple or complex tasks. Humans today run on autopilot. Without much consideration, we load the dishwasher, start the clothes washer, and set the house alarm before heading out the door to get into our cars that apply the brakes automatically if something is behind us as we back out of the driveway and parallel park when we reach our destinations. In many respects, every machine we own in turn owns us. We must clean , maintain, fuel, and insure them. We have created a symbiotic rather than dominant relationship with the machines in our lives today. How our relationship with machines evolves will determine whether or not the human mind will remain superior to them.

58

Issue Task 59

The primary goal of technological advancement should be to increase people's efficiency so that they have more leisure time.

Write a response in which you discuss the extent to which you agree or disagree with the statement and explain your reasoning for the position you take. In developing and supporting your position, you should consider ways in which the statement might or might not hold true and explain how these considerations shape your position.

 ## Strategies

Restate the issue, perhaps by reversing the order of the sentence components.

In other words:

Increasing people's efficiency so that they have more leisure time should be the primary goal of technological advancement.

Determine what question is being answered by the statement. This will help you begin to think how you would answer it and whether or not you agree with the original statement.

Why should the primary goal of technological advancement be to increase people's efficiency?

What benefits would result from technological advancements increasing people's efficiency?

Parts of the original statement that provide evidence that you can affirm or refute.

- **primary goal -** in other words, the first objective or the most important goal. This goal takes precedence over all others. It should be accomplished first.

- **technological advancement -** improved uses of technology. This could include greater speed or accuracy or new uses.

- **should be -** not exactly a mandate, more of a strong suggestion

- **increase people's efficiency -** implies greater speed and/or fewer errors

- **so that they have more leisure time -** time to relax, travel, pursue a hobby, etc.

Next, create a statement that expresses the opposing viewpoint, using language similar to that of the original statement.

Opposing viewpoint:

The primary goal of technological advancement should not be to increase people's efficiency so that they have more leisure time.

Increasing people's efficiency so that they have more leisure time should not be the primary goal of technological advancement.

Identify the parts of the opposing statement that provide evidence to refute or affirm.

◆ **not -** either the goal of technological advancement should be something other than increased efficiency or increased efficiency should result in something other than more leisure time.

Is there any other way to look at this issue? Can you qualify the original statement in some other way? Is it possible to partially agree with the statement?

Alternative viewpoint:

One goal of technological advancement should be increasing people's efficiency so that they have more leisure time.

◆ one - implies that other goals of technological advancement are also important

 # Sample Essay

To presume that technological advancements should serve the desires of humans for leisure is, at the very least, self–serving. Greater efficiency should make it possible for humans to accomplish more in a given period of time; however, advances in technology should improve not only the lives of humans in a variety of ways - but also other life forms and the earth itself. If any aspect of daily life on the planet is ignored by improvements in technology, some other aspect will suffer.

The advent of mechanization in the nineteenth century undoubtedly improved the efficiency of human activity. The cotton gin and the McCormack reaper changed agriculture forever by replacing backbreaking human labor with machine power. These advances enabled farmers to plant more crops and accomplish more work in less time. The steam engine enabled people to travel more quickly along the length of America's great rivers and across the country by train. Because more goods could move more efficiently, new factories arose and the demand for raw materials increased. Rather than creating more leisure time, mechanization created more jobs and a boost to the economies in countries that adopted it. In the twentieth century, mechanization entered the home, making it possible for housewives to complete household chores with greater efficiency. The vacuum cleaner eliminated the need to beat rugs hanging on a line in the backyard. The automatic washing machine replaced washboards and hand wringing of wet clothes. Eventually, the dishwasher and microwave would make short shrift of other kitchen chores. The upshot of these advances in technology had an effect contrary to creating more leisure time. Instead, women were able to enter the workforce. Greater efficiency in the home made possible the foray of housewives into the world of education, medicine, and business. Efficiency created by technological advances created time to complete more tasks rather than creating more leisure time.

Leisure time is not important when other aspects of life have not been improved by technological advances. The ability to spend leisure time traveling, for example, would have fewer benefits if all forms of travel had not been made safer. The frequency with which airliners crash and scores of people are killed has greatly diminished despite the fact that more planes and people take to the air every day. Going on vacation in the family car is safer because of airbags that make it more likely for passengers to survive a crash. Thanks to advances in communication technology, families can spend their leisure time enjoying any type of entertainment on their high–definition televisions.

More leisure time would be meaningless if technology had not made it possible to live longer, healthier lives. Implantable pacemakers and defibrillators enable people with heart disease to pursue active lifestyles. Those who previously were affected by debilitating osteoarthritis can have damaged joints replaced and enjoy their leisure time pain free. More children live to become healthy adults as a result of advances in vaccinations and treatment of childhood cancers.

Advances in technology have allowed scientists to monitor the climate conditions on earth. We know that human activity has contributed to the depletion of natural resources that affect the environment. The hole in the ozone layer caused by greenhouse gases has created an alarming increase in the incidence of skin cancer. Deforestation in the rainforests has led to the extinction of important plant and animal species. Climate change is melting the ice caps, imperilling the existence of polar bears and causing water levels to rise in coastal areas. Technological advances must address these conditions, or human leisure time will become meaningless.

59

Issue Task 60

Claim: *Researchers should not limit their investigations to only those areas in which they expect to discover something that has an immediate, practical application.*

Reason: *It is impossible to predict the outcome of a line of research with any certainty.*

Write a response in which you discuss the extent to which you agree or disagree with the claim and the reason on which that claim is based.

 ## Strategies

Restate the Claim:

Combine the claim and reason into one statement using a subordinate clause.

In other words:

Because it is impossible to predict the outcome of a line of research with any certainty, researchers should not limit their investigations to only those areas in which they expect to discover something that has an immediate, practical application.

What are the assumptions in the claim and reason? These will be statements that you can either refute or affirm.

Assumption 1: All research is valuable.

Assumption 2: The outcome of research is unpredictable.

Assumption 3: Research for research's sake has value.

Assumption 4: Research need not have practical, applicable results.

Opposing viewpoint:

Claim - *Researchers should limit their investigations to only those areas in which they expect to discover something that has an immediate, practical application.*

60

Reason - *The cost of research is prohibitive.*

What are the assumptions in the claim and reason? These will be statements that you can either refute or affirm.

Assumption 1: Not all research is valuable.

Assumption 2: Researchers must be practical.

Assumption 3: Research is too costly to conduct without a practical outcome.

Assumption 4: The goal of research should be financial reward.

 ## Sample Essay

Research is investigation that leads to discovery. Researchers are like the early explorers who set out to find new worlds. Even though the goals of those explorers might have been to discover gold or spices or other valuable resources, there was no guarantee that they would find what they sought. Kings and queens spared no expense as they outfitted sailing vessels whose voyages might or might not return with untold riches. Those sailors faced unknown dangers and the vagaries of winds and water in order to claim new territories for their sovereigns. Centuries later, there is very little left of a material nature to discover on earth. Exploration now takes place in outer space and in laboratories. Should all of these endeavors require practical and immediate results?

It has been nearly fifty years since President John F. Kennedy promised that the United States would land a man on the moon before the end of that decade. At the time, the only goal that seemed evident was to surpass the Soviet Union in the space race. What possible practical applications could result from that? The focus was on creating rockets powerful enough to propel a spacecraft outside of the earth's atmosphere and a capsule that would ensure the safety of its occupants. Scientists needed to create meals that could be dehydrated in order to fit the confines of the capsule. Numerous safety issues had to be addressed. As it turns out, many of the innovations developed for space travel did have practical uses for the general population. Space blankets come to mind. With an appearance similar to that of a piece of tinfoil, space blankets have become standard items in emergency kits because they can be folded into a very small square but have sufficient ability to keep someone warm who might be stranded on a highway in cold weather.

Men of a certain age around the world are thankful for the accidental application of a medication originally designed to treat heart disease. Without this medical research, the world would not have Viagra. Other conveniences are the result of mistakes made in the laboratory. Most practical among them are White Out, a liquid paper used for correcting typing or writing errors, and stick notes. A children's toy that used to be very popular is Silly Putty, another scientific flub. It came in a plastic egg and could be used to lift comic strips from a paper medium. Although some of these have had no real redeeming effect on mankind, they were commercial successes.

There is no debate about the cost of research. Setting up the environment in which research must take place involves expensive construction materials and specifications, proper equipment, and appropriately educated scientists to carry on the work. The work itself can be painstaking and long. Important discoveries are rarely made overnight. Spain's Ferdinand and Isabella probably complained about the cost of Christopher Columbus' journey across the ocean, and the returns were slight, but imagine what the world would be like today if they hadn't risked so much. The New World, itself, was an accidental discovery. Columbus bumped into it while seeking a shorter route to the Far East. If research is limited to investigations that will only lead to practical applications, other new worlds may be overlooked or missed entirely.

60

This page is intentionally left blank

Chapter **8**
Society

Issue Task 61

Some people believe that corporations have a responsibility to promote the well-being of the societies and environments in which they operate. Others believe that the only responsibility of corporations, provided they operate within the law, is to make as much money as possible.

Write a response in which you discuss which view more closely aligns with your own position and explain your reasoning for the position you take. In developing and supporting your position, you should address both of the views presented.

 Strategies

To get started, break down the statement and identify the assumptions made.

Statement Breakdown

- Corporations – the focus of the proposed viewpoints

- Responsibility – the focus of the topic of corporations

- Well-Being – the concept in question as related to responsibility

Assumptions

- Corporations are entities with responsibilities.

- Neglect of responsibility has ramifications on corporations.

- The operation of corporations intersects with both the law and the well-being of societies and environments.

After breaking down the statement and identifying assumptions, come up with pros and cons (or statements for and against) the topic given. You do not need to pick a side yet but knowing potential counterarguments will help you to develop a stronger essay once you do.

Pros and Cons

Pros (Supporting the former statement):

👍 Corporations will suffer from a reduced customer base if they do not ensure the well-being of societies and environments that they interact with.

👍 Corporations are made up of people, whose self-interest should lead them to want to preserve their societies and environments.

👍 Corporations will lose valuable resources if they do not protect the environments they interact with.

Cons (Supporting the latter statement):

👎 Corporations need to make money in order to remain functional.

👎 It is the responsibility of the law to determine the responsibility of corporations.

👎 Corporations that do not specialize in protecting societies or the environment should not be involved in doing so.

Examples

Include examples in order to make your essay as strong as possible. These are some potential routes you may take when choosing examples:

a) History contains many examples of arguments that support either side of this topic.

b) Corporations dealing with climate change and environmental protections contain examples of arguments for both sides of this topic.

c) Legal cases are another area where there are many examples of arguments for both sides of this topic.

Finally, come up with an outline of your essay. This may feel like it slows you down, but your essay will benefit from having an underlying structure.

 ## Sample Essay

Corporations have become increasingly ingrained into the societies and environments they interact with. In many cases, corporations that do not directly work to manage the well–being of the environment or the societies they interact with still have some tangible effect on those systems. Due to this, there has been much debate over

61

whether corporations have a responsibility to promote the well-being of these societies or environments they interact with, as corporations are currently only required to work within the bounds of the law. While promoting this well-being may not be legally required of corporations, they do have a responsibility to promote it, both to protect the people who interact with those communities and to protect their own self-interests.

As obesity increasingly becomes a health epidemic within the United States, backlash towards corporations that produce unhealthy or overly processed foods has increased in frequency. However, given that all of the foods sold by these corporations had been approved by the FDA, these corporations had no legal responsibility to make the products they sell healthier. In spite of this, many of these companies have launched campaigns to make their foods better for consumers and make the nutritional information associated with their products more apparent to consumers so that they can make healthier decisions when they shop for groceries.

If these corporations had not taken this path, it is entirely possible that the negative backlash from consumers may have driven them out of business, so they had a responsibility to promote the well-being of society to maintain the corporations' position in financial markets. Although this is not a legal responsibility, it connects back to the responsibility of companies to make as much money as possible, given that it furthers that end.

When BP spilled massive amounts of oil into the ocean during a mechanical failure of one of their pipeline systems, they were legally responsible for the monetary equivalent of the damages, but not for the cleaning and removal of the oil from the environment. However, the almost immediate backlash from environmental protection organizations, the media, and the general public placed this responsibility on BP for similar reasons to why food production corporations were forced to produce healthier foods. Because the negative backlash they were receiving would likely have had negative effects on their profits, preventing them from making as much money as possible.

While there is no legal precedent that requires corporations to promote the well-being of societies and the environment, doing so can help corporations remain within the limits of the law and maximize the amount of money they can make because it will make them look positive in the eyes of their customers, incentivizing increases in sales. In addition, destruction of societies or environments that corporations interact with will likely have negative consequences on the profits of corporations. Based on these facts, corporations do have a responsibility to promote the well-being of the societies and environments in which they operate in that this responsibility is connected to their ability to maximize the amount of money they can make.

61

Issue Task 62

The best way to solve environmental problems caused by consumer-generated waste is for towns and cities to impose strict limits on the amount of trash they will accept from each household.

Write a response in which you discuss the extent to which you agree or disagree with the claim. In developing and supporting your position, be sure to address the most compelling reasons and/or examples that could be used to challenge your position.

 Strategies

To get started, break down the statement and identify the assumptions made.

Statement Breakdown

◆ Environmental problems caused by consumer-generated waste – The target of the claim

◆ Limits on consumer waste production – The subject of the claim

◆ Households – The factor in the claim that should be controlled

Assumptions

◆ Environmental problems are caused by consumer waste.

◆ Households are the main source of consumer waste.

◆ Limiting the amount of waste households can generate is an enforceable approach.

After breaking down the statement and identifying assumptions, come up with pros and cons (or statements for and against) the topic given. You do not need to pick a side yet but knowing potential counterarguments will help you to develop a stronger essay once you do.

62

Pros and Cons

Pros

👍 Limiting the amount of consumer waste is likely to contribute to reductions in environmental problems.

👍 Households are typically populated by consumers who produce waste.

👍 Limits on the production of other types of waste have been implemented before.

Cons

👎 Imposing strict limits may not be feasible for households.

👎 It is unclear whether limiting consumer-generated waste will solve environmental problems.

👎 Trash that isn't accepted may be disposed of in a way that causes further environmental problems.

Examples

Include examples to make your essay as strong as possible. These are some potential routes you may take when choosing examples:

a) History contains many examples of arguments that support either side of this claim.

b) Past examples of local legislators curtailing waste disposal tend to support disagreements with this claim.

c) Legal cases are another area where there are many examples of arguments for both sides of this claim.

Finally, come up with an outline of your essay. This may feel like it slows you down, but your essay will benefit from having an underlying structure.

 Sample Essay

Environmental problems caused by consumer–generated waste are a serious problem affecting both the United States and the globe. Many approaches to solving these environmental problems have been attempted with little success. The claim proposed here postulates that imposing limitations on the amount of consumer–generated waste that will be accepted from an individual household will not only help to solve environmental problems caused by consumer–generated waste but is the best method to solve said environmental problems. This claim is clearly false for two main reasons: first, it is unclear whether limiting the consumer–generated waste

62

would actually solve the environmental problems (as opposed to halting the progress of the problems), and second, trash that is not accepted will likely be disposed of via alternative means, which will further environmental problems.

While consumer–generated waste is clearly linked to the propagation of environmental problems, past environmental research has shown that a reduction of the factors that cause environmental problems typically does not resolve these problems, only slows their progress. This can be seen in other policy measures such as the Paris Accords, a global agreement where almost all of the countries in the world agreed to reduce their carbon emissions in an attempt to slow the progress of climate change. There was no expectation that this agreement would solve the problem of climate change; instead, it was made in the hopes of giving researchers more time to discover other approaches to reversing the effects and progress of climate change. Given this, it is unlikely that limiting the amount of trash accepted per household will solve environmental problems. It is more likely that this approach will slow or halt the progress of these environmental problems, but active measures to counteract and resolve the environmental problems would have to be taken in order to fully solve the problems.

Historical regulations on waste disposal have shown that often when the amount of waste accepted by a certain entity decreased, this leftover waste was disposed of via non–standard methods that have severe environmental ramifications. Corporations that run factories which produce potentially harmful waste often dispose of the waste not accepted by traditional disposal organizations by releasing it into nearby bodies of water or local ecosystems. This causes severe negative consequences for these ecosystems that would not have otherwise happened without the implementation of this waste reduction policy.

While well–intentioned, the proposed policy would not be an effective approach to solving environmental problems caused by consumer–generated waste, as this policy would not solve the associated environmental problems at all. Instead, it may slow the progress of these environmental problems. Alternatively, the non–standard disposal of the trash not accepted by the disposal organization may be dumped in local ecosystems, speeding up the progress of the environmental problems this policy was meant to protect. There may not be a "best" way to solve environmental problems caused by consumer–generated waste, but making the populace that would be affected by these problems aware of the potential consequences they will have on their day–to–day life if the problems continue may be a good start.

62

Issue Task 63

To understand the most important characteristics of a society, one must study its major cities.

Write a response in which you discuss the extent to which you agree or disagree with the statement and explain your reasoning for the position you take. In developing and supporting your position, you should consider ways in which the statement might or might not hold true and explain how these considerations shape your position.

Strategies

Restate the issue, perhaps by reversing the order of the sentence components.

In other words:

Studying a society's major cities leads to understanding its most important characteristics.

Determine what question is being answered by the statement. This will help you begin to think how you would answer it and whether or not you agree with the original statement.

How can one understand the most important characteristics of a society?

Parts of the original statement that provide evidence that you can affirm or refute.

- **understand** – This implies more than identifying or listing. Understanding occurs at a deeper level.

- **most important** – The superlative –most- implies a selection process that eliminates less important characteristics. What process and how was it created?

- **society** – this can refer to any social entity, large or small.

- **major cities** – Major might refer to size of population, state capitals, centers of industry, number of educational institutions. How were cities identified as major?

- **study** – This implies a deep examination. What aspects of these cities should one study to gain understanding of society's most important characteristics?

Next, create a statement that expresses the opposing viewpoint, using language similar to that of the original statement.

63

Opposing viewpoint:

Studying its major cities is not a means to understanding a society's most important characteristics.

Identify the parts of the opposing statement that provide evidence to refute or affirm. In this case, the evidence is the same as that in the original statement except for the word not.

◆ **not** – In this case, it removes studying major cities as a means of understanding society's most important characteristics. Using this statement forces the writer to develop other means of understanding societal characteristics.

Alternatives

Is there any other way to look at this issue? Can you qualify the original statement in some way? Is it possible to partially agree with the statement?

New viewpoint:

To understand the most important characteristics of a society, one must study its major cities as well as small towns and rural communities.

Identify the parts of the new statement that provide evidence to affirm or refute.

◆ **one component** – This suggests that studying major cities does not illuminate all of a society's most important characteristics.

The following essay uses this balanced position. In other words, both major cities and smaller towns or rural areas have qualities that make them repositories of a society's important characteristics. List some examples to use as support. Because the issue does not mention what the important characteristics of a society are, you will have the freedom to suggest what they might be.

63

Examples:

a) Diversity – Cities are the likely repositories of this characteristic. Small towns are more homogeneous.

b) Culture – Major cities provide greater access to cultural events and displays, e.g., theater, symphony, museums.

c) Education – Access to a wide range of educational institutions exists in major cities.

d) Self–reliance – Lack of a variety of products and services makes residents of small towns more self–re liant.

Sample Essay

To claim that one can understand a society's most important characteristics by studying only its major cities ignores all the other social structures that exist within a country. A country as vast as the United States, for example, is made up of fifty states that act as independent entities in many respects. Within each of those states reside groups of citizens united or divided by race, ethnicity, religion, or social class. Some states do not even have what may be considered a major city. To presume that only major cities are worthy of study minimizes the contribution of smaller constructs to the characteristics of the larger society. On the other hand, many large cities are composed of smaller societies that may represent those that exist in the remote and far–flung areas of this large country.

Before determining where examples of a country's most important characteristics reside, one would need to identify those characteristics. If diversity is near the top of the list, then major cities would be the places to study it. New York City is home to neighborhoods like Little Italy, Chinatown, Spanish Harlem, and Hell's Kitchen. Additionally, residents of NYC live in neighborhoods that cater to lifestyle or economic class, such as Greenwich Village, SoHo, and Park Avenue. Small towns in rural America tend towards homogeneity, and their residents have little exposure to racial or ethnic diversity.

An appreciation for fine arts might rank high in importance as a societal characteristic, and, once again, cities are home to myriad institutions where the fine arts are displayed or performed. Only in major cities is one likely to find museums of art, symphonies, opera houses, and theaters for the live performance of plays and musicals. Residents of small towns may only have a high school band and access works of art on the Internet, thus limiting their exposure to and appreciation of the fine arts.

Physical access to institutions of higher learning elevates the citizens of a society and is universally considered to be important. Graduates of small–town high schools must generally leave home to obtain a college degree, whereas students in a major city need to travel only a few blocks to attend an Ivy League college, a state university, a design institute, or a school for the performing arts. Lack of access may even discourage children in remote areas from attending college, reducing the overall level of education in those towns and making them less desirable to study for identifying the important characteristics of society.

In contrast, small cities and rural towns may be better locations to study characteristics that are as important as the ones cited above. Residents of these communities are more likely to combine their efforts to support a member in need. One cannot miss the donation cans on convenience store counters that are used for collecting money to help a family that has lost everything to a fire or has a child undergoing expensive medical treatment. The local grocer has a community bulletin board where service clubs can post upcoming events to raise funds to send the high school baseball team to Florida for spring training or to build new dugouts at the town's playground. If concern for one's neighbors ranks high on the list of important characteristics, then small towns are suitable subjects of study.

Residents of rural towns retain some level of self–sufficiency, although the expansion of the Internet has had some impact on that quality. Vegetable gardens are common, and housewives still can and freeze their yields for future consumption. Husbands are jacks–of–all–trades. They mow their own lawns, paint their own houses, and use their own tools to repair broken machines or change a washer on a faucet. Kids on farms have chores as well as school work to complete each day. An important characteristic of any society might be hard work combined with ingenuity, and small towns are likely to be populated with people who display this.

On the whole, the original statement has veracity. Major cities are microcosms; their residents are representative of the society as a whole. Visitors to those cities can see people from all walks of life, from varied backgrounds and those who display talents and abilities that one may find isolated in smaller towns. Cities are growing while small towns are shrinking, so the important characteristics once unique to rural America are making their way into cities. However, when attempting to understand an entire society, one must examine all of its communities, including small towns and rural villages. Knowing the criteria used to create the original position would make affirming or refuting it a simpler task.

Issue Task 64

All parents should be required to volunteer time to their children's schools.

Write a response in which you discuss the extent to which you agree or disagree with the recommendation and explain your reasoning for the position you take. In developing and supporting your position, describe specific circumstances in which adopting the recommendation would or would not be advantageous and explain how these examples shape your position.

Strategies

Restate the Recommendation:

Attempt to use negative words to convey the same meaning as the original.

In other words:

No parent should be exempt from volunteering time to their children's schools.

Determine what question is being answered by the issue statement.

Which parents should be required to volunteer time to their children's schools?

Or: *Should all parents be required to volunteer time to their children's schools?*

Or: *How can parents become more involved in their children's education?*

    There may be several other questions that call for the answer in the original recommendation. Answering these questions can help you formulate a response or alternative recommendation. It can help you identify the circumstances in which adopting the recommendation would be advantageous or disadvantageous.

Now think about the parts of the original recommendation that provide evidence that you can affirm or refute.

◆ **All parents** – There are no exceptions. What about working parents? Non-custodial parents?

◆ **required** – Again, there are no exceptions. It's not an option.

◆ **time** – Does it have to be during the school day? This could be interpreted to mean cleaning the classroom on the weekend. Does it have to be time? Could they volunteer to supply snacks or tissues?

◆ **volunteer** – To volunteer is to give freely. Require and volunteer contradict each other.

Opposing viewpoint:

Not all parents should be required to volunteer time in their children's schools.

Identify the parts of the opposing statement that provide evidence that you can refute or affirm.

◆ **not all** – This implies that some should be required. For which parents should this be a requirement?

Alternatives:

Is there any other way to look at this recommendation? Can it be qualified in some way? Think about the absolute words like all and required. Can they be reduced to less than commands?

New viewpoint:

All parents should be encouraged to volunteer time in their children's schools.

Identify the parts of the new statement that provide evidence to affirm or refute.

◆ **all** – This leaves no one out. If volunteerism is encouraged, everyone should be invited to participate.

◆ **encouraged** – To encourage would involve building some flexibility into the time frame and types of volunteering required.

Examples and Reasons:

64

a) financial – Budget cuts have adversely affected the ability of teachers and schools to accomplish many tasks that aides or janitors used to do.

b) transparency – Volunteering is a great way to know what is happening in a child's school or classroom.

c) exceptions – Encouraging rather than requiring leaves an option for parents who have neither the time nor the desire to volunteer in their children's schools.

d) danger – Some children have parents who should not volunteer at their children's schools under any circumstances. Some parents are abusive or alcoholics or drug users. Their children are likely to feel safer at school than at home. Should volunteers have to undergo the same background checks as teachers?

 ## Sample Essay

Schools have always sought to involve parents in their children's educations\. For most parents, that involvement is receiving progress reports and rank cards. Some of them attend open houses or participate in parent/teacher conferences, although those numbers decline as the children leave elementary school. By the time they've reached high school, few parents ever cross the thresholds of the schools their children attend. If a child participates in sports or plays in the band, his or her parents may attend games or concerts. Many schools and teachers want parents to know what goes on in their schools and classrooms in order to develop transparency. After all, schools aren't– or shouldn't be – trying to hide anything. Today, schools are facing budget cuts that have decimated the ranks of teacher aides who performed tasks that teachers with their busy schedules don't have time to do. Custodial staffs are smaller, and schools aren't as clean or well–maintained as they used to be. Volunteerism seems the solution to a number of problems that schools face. However, requiring volunteerism is not a valid concept either in its phrasing or expectations.

Volunteerism by its definition is something done of one's free will; it is a choice. Requiring someone to volunteer changes the entire concept. How does one enforce mandatory volunteerism? What are the consequences for parents who can't or won't volunteer? When a requirement is not met, consequences do ensue. If one doesn't pay his/her taxes, the government levies a fine or sentences the violator to jail. Would schools fine parents who don't volunteer? Maybe they or their child would get detention. Clearly, the enforcement of such a policy would be difficult at best and unfair at worst.

There are bound to be parents who cannot, will not, or should not volunteer at their children's schools. It's probably safe to say that most parents work today. How would they fulfill the requirement to volunteer? The recommendation does not specify that the volunteerism must take place during the school day, but should working parents give up time with their families on their days off from work? Just as some children refuse to do their school work, there are parents who will simply refuse to volunteer at their children's schools. They pay their taxes to support the schools in their district, and that should be enough of a contribution. There are parents who, under no circumstance, should be allowed to volunteer at their children's schools. Some parents are physically, psychologically, or sexually abusive. Their children may think of school as an escape from a dangerous home, even if it is only for a few hours of the day. What would the impact be on those children if their parents were to show up in their classrooms on a regular basis?

Adults who work in school systems today, from the principal and teachers to the bus drivers must undergo fingerprinting and background checks before they can work around children. Shouldn't volunteers be subject to the same scrutiny? After all, we are letting them into spaces populated by our most vulnerable citizens. What is the liability to a school system when a volunteer becomes a danger to children? Teachers serve in loco parentis, in the parents' place while their children are at school. Parents trust that their children are safe, and it is the school's responsibility to see that they are.

School systems face a number of challenges today. Administrators and teachers are being asked to do more with less. Volunteerism seems a way to fill some of the needs not met by tight budgets. Some wonderful people do give freely of their time and talents to help out in their local schools, but the rewards aren't worth the risks of requiring all parents to volunteer in their children's schools.

Issue Task 65

The best way to understand the character of a society is to examine the character of the men and women that the society chooses as its heroes or its role models.

Write a response in which you discuss the extent to which you agree or disagree with the claim. In developing and supporting your position, be sure to address the most compelling reasons and/or examples that could be used to challenge your position.

 Strategies

Restate the Issue:

In this case, try inverting the clauses.

In other words:

Examining the character of the men and women that the society chooses as its heroes or its role models is the best way to understand the character of that society.

You could also determine what question is being answered by the issue statement.

What is the best way to understand the character of a society?

Or: What is revealed about a society by examining the character of the men and women that the society chooses as its heroes or its role models?

Considering how you would answer one or both of the questions may help you to decide to what degree you agree with the original issue statement.

Now think about the part of the original statement that provides evidence that you can affirm or refute.

- ◆ **best way** – Best is the superlative form of good. Any other way would be inferior or produce unsatisfactory results.

65

◆ **understand** – To understand does not mean to validate or agree with an idea. Does examination of the character of a nation's heroes lead to understanding the society? Is this information just one part of a country's character?

◆ **character of a society** – Character implies the breadth of morality displayed by a society. It can be negative or positive, strong or weak.

◆ **examine** – An examination involves close scrutiny. It means holding something under a microscope to view its smallest parts and then determining how those parts affect or fit into the whole.

◆ **chooses** – Choice implies free will. Does every society allow its men and women to choose their heroes and role models? What about countries that have dictatorships or autocracies?

◆ **heroes or its role models** – Listing them separately suggests that role models are not necessarily heroes and vice versa. Can someone act heroically and still have attributes that would not make him or her a suitable role model? Does heroism depend on special circumstances?

Opposing viewpoint:

Examining the character of the men and women that the society chooses as its heroes or its role models is not the best way to understand the character of that society.

Identify the parts of the opposing statement that provide evidence to affirm or refute. In this case, the only difference is the word, not.

◆ **not** – This can be read in two ways. On one hand, it could mean that one should avoid examining the character of the men and women that the society chooses as its heroes or its role models. On the other hand, the statement could imply that this is not the best way or the only way to understand the character of a society.

Alternatives

Is there any other way to look at this issue? Can you qualify the original statement in some way? Is it partially true? Do heroes and role models remain constant? Do they carry over from generation to generation?

65

New viewpoint:

One way to understand the character of a society is to examine the character of the men and women that the society chooses as its heroes or its role models.

Or: *Because heroes and role models are temporary, the character of a society based on its choice of heroes and role models can only be understood for a specific period in its history.*

Identify the parts of the alternate viewpoint that provide evidence to affirm or refute.

◆ **temporary** – People are fickle. Whom they consider to be heroes and role models today may not be the same as those they select tomorrow.

◆ **specific period in its history** – Events conspire to create heroes and role models. As the events change, so do the heroes and role models that arise from them.

Position:

Because heroes and role models are temporary, the character of a society based on its choice of heroes and role models can only be understood for a specific period in its history.

Examples and Reasons:

a) President Obama – His stature as a hero and/or role model has changed since he first decided to run for office.

b) Charles Barkley – One-time bad boy of the NBA who said, "I am not a role model."

 ## Sample Essay

Cultures throughout history have been analyzed based on the artifacts left behind, including architecture, art, writing, household items, and clothing. archaeologists have been able to extrapolate information about a culture's government, scientific knowledge, standard of living, diet, and cosmology. Burial mounds, pyramids, and cave drawings reveal the relative importance of and reverence accorded to individuals in the cultures that produced them. When history began to be recorded in a more systematic manner, writers left records of those who became heroes and role models. Those heroes and role models certainly influenced their cultures, from fashion to morals. That influence, however, was fleeting, and it was not long before someone new became the "flavor of the month". In fact, it may have been the events in history that influenced which men and women were elevated to the status of heroes and role models. The rapid pace of change today makes it nearly impossible to analyze a culture's character based on who is selected to represent the ideal, or as Andy Warhol is credited with saying, "Everyone will enjoy fifteen minutes of fame."

65

Charles Barkley, former NBA bad boy, said, "I am not a role model." Professional athletes have often been held to higher standards than people in the general population because of their visibility and high salaries. The paradigm for athletes has always been clean–cut, upstanding, and ethically superior. Before media coverage of every athlete's action became so pervasive, it is likely that those athletes did not always behave well in private or in public, but nobody knew about their bad acts. Parents held athletes up as examples of the kinds of people they wanted their children to become. After all, to reach the ranks of the pros, athletes had to be dedicated to their sport. Children were led to believe that if they adopted the work ethic and character of professional athletes, they, too, could become supremely successful. When Americans discovered that professional athletes have feet of clay, there was a huge outcry. Charles Barkley's statement was followed by his declaring that parents should be role models for their children. That works well for children whose parents do set a good example, but to whom do the others turn for lessons in good character? Certainly, not to Tiger Woods, whose string of infidelities led to pain and embarrassment for his family, nor to Ron Artest, who engaged in a brawl with a fan during a basketball game.

When the people of the United States became disenchanted with the direction that the government was taking during the most recent Bush administration, a young senator from Illinois took up the challenge to lead this country using the mantra of change. Barack Obama declared, "We can do it!" Since his election, the global econo-my has become precarious, and people in the US are unemployed and losing their homes to foreclosure. Citizens, once filled with hope for the future at the hands of this new president, became disillusioned, and Barack Obama is no longer seen as the hero they hoped he would be. Basing the character of the United States on the promises made by its presidential candidates is therefore clearly a poor metric, as these candidates do not truly know what kind of change they will be able to effect as president until they are elected into office. Additionally, candidates are likely to paint a picture of an idealized society during their campaigns, which may not reflect the current state of the society at the time.

What are the more likely subjects of analysis to determine the character of a society are those institutions or ideas that are more permanent. Rather than looking at the people who have temporarily held the position of hero or role model, look at the form of government that has served a population. Read its constitution. Do they allow the fair and equal treatment of a nation's citizenry? Are punishment and reward meted out in equal measure to citizens of all races, colors, creeds, and genders? The thread that runs through the history of a culture is a better indicator of that culture's character.

65

Issue Task 66

Claim: *It is no longer possible for a society to regard any living man or woman as a hero.*

Reason: *The reputation of anyone who is subjected to media scrutiny will eventually be diminished.*

Write a response in which you discuss the extent to which you agree or disagree with the claim and the reasons on which that claim is based.

 Strategies

Combine the claim and reason into one statement using a subordinate clause.

In other words:

Because the reputation of anyone who is subjected to media scrutiny will eventually be diminished, it is no longer possible for a society to regard any living man or woman as a hero.

What are the assumptions in the claim and reason? These will be statements that you can either affirm or refute.

Assumption 1: Media scrutiny diminishes reputations

Assumption 2: No living man or woman can be regarded as a hero.

Assumption 3: People who were regarded as heroes before media scrutiny became so intense can still be regarded as heroes.

Assumption 4: Only those who are dead can still be regarded as heroes.

Assumption 5: The media is the party responsible for diminishing reputations.

Next, create a statement that expresses the opposing point of view, using language similar to the original issue.

Opposing viewpoint:

Claim - *It is possible for a living man or woman to be regarded as a hero by society.*

Reason - *Media scrutiny enhances one's reputation.*

Assumption 1: Men and women living today can be viewed as heroes

Assumption 2: Media scrutiny can have a positive effect

Assumption 3: Media has an effect on reputations

Is there another way of looking at this claim and reason? Can both of the viewpoints expressed be true, or partially true?

Alternative claim:

It is possible for some men and women living today to be regarded as heroes, while others fail to gain that status.

Alternative reason: Media scrutiny brings to light the heroic actions of some men and women and diminishes the reputations of others.

Assumption 1: Some men and women survive or are even elevated by media scrutiny.

Assumption 2: Media scrutiny is not always a negative occurrence.

Assumption 3: The media can reveal heroic characteristics that might have gone unrecognized by society.

Now you must decide which point of view to address in your essay. Completing the prewriting activities has given you several choices and ideas for defending any of those choices. Even the viewpoints that are opposite of yours will have points that you can use in writing your response. As you review your notes, decide which of your ideas offer the strongest support for your position; you do not have to use all of them. Keep in mind that others may disagree with your position, so address their concerns in your response. Before you decide, carefully consider the following checklist. You will have addressed several of them in the exercises you have completed above.

◆ I have identified the central issue.

◆ I understand the instructions.

◆ I have decided that I agree/disagree/partially agree with the issue and why.

◆ I have identified the assumptions in the claim and determined whether or not they are reasonable.

◆ If necessary, I can explain how I interpret any or all of the concepts and terms used in the claim.

◆ I have identified my reasons for the position I have taken.

◆ I have compelling examples to support my position.

66

The next step should be listing the main reasons and support for your position. You may use any of the above prewriting activities as you prepare evidence for supporting your point of view. Remember that the GRE readers scoring your response are not looking for a "right" answer. The readers are evaluating your ability to address the specific instructions and articulate and develop an argument to support your understanding and evaluation of the issue.

Support for alternative claim and reason:

Example: News programs often have guests who are ordinary people who have committed extraordinary deeds. Some recent stories have included very young children who called 9-1-1 and saved a relative's life, or the coach who donated a kidney to an ailing player.

Example: Television, especially, has uncovered either bizarre or immoral behavior of famous people. Charlie Sheen has had more than his share of coverage related to his substance and sexual exploits.

Your notes do not have to be exhaustive. As you begin to write your essay, your brain will generate new ideas. Make certain that you keep the directions in mind as you develop your ideas. Use as many or as few paragraphs as you consider appropriate for your argument but create a new paragraph when you move on to a new idea or example of support for your position. The GRE readers are not looking for a specific number of ideas or paragraphs. Instead, they are reading to determine the level of understanding of the topic and the complexity with which you respond.

In this task, you are asked to write a response in which you discuss the extent to which you agree or disagree with the claim and the reasons on which that claim is based. You may completely agree or disagree with the statement, or you may agree under certain conditions. You are also instructed to explain your reasoning and consider ways in which the statement might or might not hold true and explain how these considerations shape your position.

You may use any organizational strategy or form of reasoning to present your position as clearly and succinctly as possible. You may recall writing strategies that you learned in high school or a writing-intensive course that you took in college, but it is not necessary to employ any of those strategies. It is important that your ideas follow a logical progression and display strong critical thinking.

 # Sample Essay

President Franklin D. Roosevelt, who had been stricken with infantile paralysis, began his leadership of the United States while America and the world were experiencing a great economic depression; and through three full terms in office, he oversaw the recovery from that depression and the entrance of the United States into World War II. Early in his fourth term as president, he died in Warm Springs, Georgia while in the company of his long–time mistress. Members of the media knew that President Roosevelt was confined to a wheelchair but out of respect for the high office he held, they never photographed the president in his wheelchair. The public saw the president seated behind his desk and at his inauguration, standing at the podium with the assistance of leg braces. Certainly, the members of the fourth estate and the secret service knew of President Roosevelt's mistress, but no one published any stories about the affair. The press recognized that there was little to be gained by portraying the leader of the free world as a man plagued by both physical weakness and marital infidelity.

Today, the public is aware that President Obama found it difficult to quit smoking cigarettes, that President Clinton tried smoking marijuana but never inhaled, and that Vice President Cheney nearly "smoked" a companion while bird hunting in Texas. The media's desire to sell a story and the public's insatiable appetite for sensationalism combine to create a toxic brew that everyone seems willing to swallow.

On the other hand, few people would be aware of the heroic deeds of otherwise ordinary people without the attention of the media. The public would be ignorant of the heroic behavior of miners trapped underground in Chile for several months or the herculean efforts of the engineers who constructed a means for their release. Their families and the entire world watched as each miner made the perilous journey through thousands of feet of rock, strapped in a narrow cage, to emerge from their dark prison into the light of day. Were it not for the media, we would remain ignorant about the crusade being waged by two Girl Scouts in an effort to preserve the rainforest habitat of the orangutan and other endangered species in Indonesia by having palm oil removed from the recipes for the cookies that the organization sells every year.

The media wields a double–edged sword. When swung one way, it cuts the feet off those who have stood in the spotlight by their own choice and reduces their stature to that of mere mortals. When swung the other way, it cuts a hole in the fabric of ignorance that prevents unlikely heroes from receiving the recognition they so richly deserve. It is unlikely that the press will revert to the respectful attitude it displayed in the first half of the twentieth century. Those, today, who choose to become public figures recognize the power of the media to unearth their weaknesses, flaws, and past mistakes, and they must prepare for that eventuality. Although we may lose qualified candidates for public office as a result of their fear of media scrutiny, we will certainly gain some heroes whose deeds would have otherwise remained unknown.

Issue Task 67

Society should identify those children who have special talents and provide training for them at an early age to develop their talents.

Write a response in which you discuss the extent to which you agree or disagree with the statement and explain your reasoning for the position you take. In developing and supporting your position, you should consider ways in which the statement might or might not hold true and explain how these considerations shape your position.

 Strategies

A good starting point is to break down the statement and identify the assumptions it makes. Look for ambiguous phrasing and consider all possible exceptions – they represent weak points that you can defend or attack depending on your chosen position

Statement breakdown:

- **Society** – what social structure would be responsible for this? Would it be official?

- **Identify** – through tests? At what age?

- **Special talents** – will they screen for all possible skills or just conventional ones?

- **Provide training** – in parallel with regular school? Completely different from regular curriculum? Individual training? General or just talent focused?

- **Early age** – how early would they start? Disrupting childhood?

Assumptions:

- Society is responsible for handling talented individuals

- Training is beneficial for children with special talents

- Regular curriculum is not challenging enough; represents a waste of talents

- Special talents should be cultivated from an early age

Pros and Cons:

Pros

👍 People are not equal, current system wants equal studies for unequal people

👍 Smart children are held back, to better fit in

👍 Talented students can become slackers; insufficiently challenging work means that they can get by with minimal effort

👍 They can focus on their talents, instead of trying to be sufficiently good at everything (including gaining knowledge they would likely never use again)

👍 Talented children can better reach their potential through special training programs than through regular education

👍 Currently, studying is based on age group instead of aptitude group

👍 Can better fit in with peers that can better understand them

👍 Currently teachers focus more on low achieving students, to help bring the norm up

👍 There are already programs that help gifted children (international Olympics and special schools)

Cons

👎 Prioritizing cognitive ability over emotional development

👎 Specialized training can isolate children (insufficient peer contact or having to fit in with older students)

👎 Talents in unconventional fields will be overlooked (some talents will be prioritized)

👎 Disruptive of natural growth process (starting at a too early age leads to stealing away their childhood)

👎 Special schools can instill superiority complexes

👎 Special training can mean not getting an all-around education (general education)

👎 Added pressure on the students to perform

👎 Parents can live vicariously through their children's achievements

👎 Can lead to feelings of inadequacy (children always having to prove themselves, having the feeling that love is conditional on achievements)

67

Examples:

a) Current examples of very talented people

b) Existing programs for talented people

c) Current teaching practices

d) Grades of talented students following the regular curriculum versus the ones following specialty training

e) Success rates of talented people

 Sample Essay

Great Great minds have always had a great impact on society, whether through scientific discoveries, artistic and cultural enrichment, or political reform. However, harnessing the potential of brilliant minds by providing specialized training for gifted students is not necessarily the most effective method of encouraging talent to flourish. This method can have seriously damaging consequences like increasing the pressure to succeed, instilling a sense of superiority in students and affecting their emotional development.

The first aspect to take into consideration is the fact that participating in specialized training does not provide a guarantee of success further in life. In fact, as Prof. Joan Freeman shows, the percentage of gifted children that become incredibly successful in life is currently at an incredibly low 5%. Despite having scholarships and participating in gifted programs, the talented students who were part of her study failed to achieve their potential. According to her findings, fate, personality and drive are just as important to success as is proper education. A nice example is Jocelyn Lavin, an extremely gifted child, who left university without a degree because she did not know what she wanted to do with her life. The same can be said for Ruth Lawrence, the math prodigy who went to Oxford at age 11. She has retired to Israel to raise her children "in a natural way".

Furthermore, providing specialized training would create an enormous pressure to perform. Talented students would not only have to contend with parental pressure but would also have to bear the burden of being labeled "gifted" and measure up to society's expectations of success that come with it. A culture of excellence that promotes value based on achievements leads to feelings of anxiety, perfectionism and worthlessness – the students end up viewing love as conditional upon their success. Failure in such a context is something world–shattering. A good example to illustrate this point is the rate of depression and suicide in Japanese children – almost triple than that of UK or USA. Aptly named, the main reason for suicide in students is the pressure of Shiken Jigoku (Exam Hell). The same can be said about India, where about 20 students kill themselves every day due to the stress related to exams, wanting to secure seats in prestigious schools, according to the National Crime Records Bureau.

Moreover, starting specialized training at an early age is likely to interfere with the emotional development of children. While gifted children can intellectually understand abstract concepts, they may be unable to deal with those concepts emotionally due to their age. According to Martha Morelock's study, gifted individuals are prone to asynchronous development – an uneven rate of development in the cognitive, affective and physical domains. Specialized training focused solely on a child's talents enhances the uneven development of the other domains and leads to a feeling of being "out of sync" with their age group peers. Moreover, Morelock has found that when education prioritizes cognitive ability over emotional development, the gifted students in question adopt unhealthy lifestyles that center on perfectionism and self–criticism often followed by depression and antisocial behavior. A perfect example is Sheldon Cooper, from the television series 'The Big Bang Theory". Sheldon who was a child prodigy fast–tracked his education and graduated college at the age of 14. While being extremely intelligent, Sheldon is also socially inept and possesses childlike qualities such as extreme stubbornness. Additionally, as in Sheldon's case, specialized training can isolate children, either through insufficient peer contact or having to fit in with older students. Nial Thompson is a real–life example; having started a math degree at Cambridge at age 15, he will graduate from university before his peers even start it. Unfortunately, due to the age disparity, he has only socialized once during his first year of university.

Lastly, starting a specialized training program from an early age can lead to students feeling like their childhood was stolen away. Andrew Halliburton, a math genius that did Mensa puzzles at age 11, confesses that "I feel like my childhood was sort of wasted, I didn't really get to go out as much as other kids...I never did learn to ride a bike." He further explains that being labeled a genius is a great burden because he always felt the pressure to live up to that expectation but never once thought that he could.

All in all, it seems that participating in specialized training programs not only damages the student's emotional development and adds an extreme pressure to perform, but it also has a low rate of success when it comes to student performances later in life.

Issue Task 68

It is primarily through our identification with social groups that we define ourselves.

Write a response in which you discuss the extent to which you agree or disagree with the statement and explain your reasoning for the position you take. In developing and supporting your position, you should consider ways in which the statement might or might not hold true and explain how these considerations shape your position

 Strategies

A good starting point is to break down the statement and identify the assumptions it makes. Look for ambiguous phrasing and consider all possible exceptions – they represent weak points that you can defend or attack depending on your chosen position.

Statement breakdown:

◆ **Primarily** – in what proportion is it responsible? What other ways of defining ourselves are there?

◆ **Identification** – ascribing to a group's values? Being identified as belonging to a certain group? Lying to ourselves?

◆ **Social groups** – does it include primary groups like family? Groups with or without a public agenda? Stated unifying values?

◆ **Define ourselves** – only self-identification or also how others define us? Honest? Accurate?

Assumptions:

◆ Social groups are the cornerstones of our identity

◆ We are conscious of our personality and the groups we belong to

◆ We define ourselves through external validation

Pros and Cons:

Pros

👍 You can reasonably accurately extrapolate a person's views based on groups of belonging

👍 Social groups have shared beliefs, goals, norms and values

👍 We are social by nature, we look for a sense of belonging

👍 Humans seek to conform (to preserve harmony; due to fear of exclusion; as a survival mechanism)

👍 The proximity effect – we are interested in those closest to us (in terms of distance, ideals, race, etc.)

👍 The imitation theory (people seek role models, especially when confronted with conflict; it is another survival mechanism)

👍 Subconscious imitation of those we like (gestures, speech patterns)

👍 Perception theory (we are always aware of how others see us)

👍 Perception theory (we are always aware of how others see us)

Cons

👎 People have contradictory natures

👎 People belong to more social groups at the same time

👎 People fall outside of the norms of a social group (they fit up to a point)

👎 Belonging to a group is only part of a person's identity

👎 People in denial can wrongly identify with a group

👎 People can ascribe to a group on the surface, for appearances

👎 Some groups you belong to automatically, from birth, but that doesn't mean you ascribe to their values (gender, religion, etc.)

👎 A person's identity is comprised of more than groups of belonging (culture, language, racial identity, socio-economic status, beliefs, philosophies, experiences)

68

Examples:

a) People that don't ascribe to the values of a group they are part of

b) Theories on identity formation

c) Groups of belonging based on birth (religion, gender etc.)

d) Social constructivism versus indeterminism

 ## Sample Essay

Identity has always been a delicate issue, even more so in recent times when people have gotten the courage to break away from socially-accepted norms and declare themselves as outsiders to the groups they have been relegated to since birth. Identity seems to require constant work, and it changes based on our personality, interactions and experiences. As Gabriel Garcia Marquez said, "He allowed himself to be swayed by his conviction that human beings are not born once and for all on the day their mothers give birth to them, but that life obliges them over and over again to give birth to themselves." The issue at hand here is not about establishing whether the process of identifying ourselves through social groups is appropriate but rather about observing the actual practices of identity formation. Currently, we can reasonably extrapolate a person's views based on the social groups they belong to; as long as we stick to general traits, and the person's association with the group was done voluntarily.

When looking at a self–proclaimed "foodie", we can deduce that they treasure experiences above material possessions, that they place a great deal of importance on food, especially its taste and presentation, and that they are quality-driven people (for them a meal is an experience, not a necessity). These extrapolations are easy to make because social groups tend to have shared beliefs, goals, norms and values – even more so when we are talking about official groups that make public statements about their values. In current times, even companies promote having a shared philosophy and work ethic. Creating social groups with shared values happens because we are social animals, like Aristotle said. We like living in groups, perhaps as a former survival mechanism based on the strategy of safety in numbers. Moreover, we do not look just for company, but for a sense of belonging – which is why social groups form based on commonalities.

The world, on the whole, is highly complex – there is too much information to process for our minds – which is also why a significant number of processes are subconscious or automated. This complexity leads to a so–called proximity effect; as individuals, we are primarily interested in those closest to us in ever widening groups (from family, to friends, to neighbors, to neighborhood and city, etc.). The closer the group, in terms of emotional attachments or similarity of values, the more impact the group would have in the way on which we define ourselves. This influence is especially noticeable in conflict situations when our identity is threatened. It is then that we look for models to either re–establish our identity or re–define ourselves, and the role models we use are those we know of (have acquaintance with).

People in general seek to imitate others – whether to conform to preserve harmony, out of fear of exclusion or as a learning mechanism. It is such an ingrained behavior, that it even occurs at a subconscious level. Studies have shown that in a conversation, people that like each other borrow gestures and speech patterns, even when it comes to people that they have just met. As individuals, we are always aware of how others see us, and we always strive to be liked – the concepts of shame or guilt only make sense in a social setting.

Given the attention and importance that we ascribe to the people around us, especially to the groups we identify with, it is no wonder that they play a major part in defining us. If you care about an opinion, you give the opinion maker power over you. And, as demonstrated above, we are constantly on the lookout for models and subconsciously imitate those around us. As Piaget discovered, our identity is formed through comparisons – careful selections of who we are and who we are not – and social groups provide the external validation that we crave.

68

Issue Task 69

Some people believe that in order to thrive, a society must put its own overall success before the well-being of its individual citizens. Others believe that the well-being of a society can only be measured by the general welfare of all its people.

Write a response in which you discuss which view more closely aligns with your own position and explain your reasoning for the position you take. In developing and supporting your position, you should address both of the views presented.

 Strategies

This issue already has two points of view. Begin by treating them separately. Restate the first opinion by reversing the order of the sentence components.

In other words:

A society must put its own overall success before the well-being of its individual citizens in order to thrive.

Determine what question is being answered by the statement. This will help you begin to think how you would answer it and whether or not you agree with the original statement.

Should a society put its overall success before the well-being of its individual citizens in order to thrive?

Parts of the original statement that provide evidence that you can affirm or refute.

◆ **some people** - This qualifier lets the reader know that the opinion is not universal. There is another side.

◆ **thrive** - This is a stronger idea than merely existing. Thriving involves great success.

◆ **society** - What comprises a society? A society is a group with common characteristics or goals. It can be large or small.

◆ **before** - Put overall success of a society chronologically ahead of individual needs.

◆ **well-being** - What type of well-being? Physical? Fiscal? Emotional?

◆ **individual citizens** - Each member of society separately

69

Opposing viewpoint:

Others believe that the well-being of a society can only be measured by the general welfare of all its people.

Restate the second opinion by reversing the order of the sentence components.

In other words:

The general welfare of all its people is the measure of a society's well-being.

Parts of the statement that provide evidence that you can affirm or refute.

◆ **general welfare -** What does this include? Does it refer to basic needs like food, shelter? What about employment, health care, safety?

◆ **measure –** In this case, determining factor

Is there any other way to look at this issue? Can you qualify the original statement in some way? Is it possible to partially agree with the statement?

Alternative viewpoint:

The well-being of a society can be measured by the general welfare of most of its people.

◆ **most –** some people's needs will not be met

Examples:

a) The working poor

b) Mother Teresa

c) How ignoring the poorest, least capable in a society affects progress

 ## Sample Essay

A nation's general welfare depends on the welfare of its individual citizens. When every citizen can free himself from dependency on government assistance and make his own contributions to the economy, the entire

population can benefit. The tax contributions of others can be abated leaving them with more discretionary income to purchase goods and services, funds to educate their children, and provide preventive health care for all family members. The providers of goods and services will react to increases in business by hiring more workers and ordering more inventory or raw materials. The trend is obvious; the general well–being of a society improves when all of its members are given the opportunity to advance.

Immigrants to the United States still believe its streets are paved in gold and that opportunities abound for anyone who is willing to work hard. However, many Americans fall into the demographic known as the working poor. According to research from earlier this year, America's total personal wealth is about $54 trillion. One percent of the population controls forty percent of that total. Eighty percent of the population controls a puny seven percent of the wealth. A significant portion of US citizens live below the poverty line, which is set at an income ranging from $11,000–$12,000 per year for a single person, less than someone working full time for the federal minimum wage of $7.25/hour. Those living at or near the poverty line must apply for Medicaid in their states of residence, a program supported by tax dollars. Those same individuals likely need food stamps, and they probably qualify for federally supplemented rental properties.

In her book, Nickel and Dimed, Barbara Ehrenreich writes about the working poor in America after experiencing firsthand the lives they lead. She left the comfort of her home in Florida to take on menial jobs in three locations around the country. She rented places to live based on the wages she would earn at each job with a goal of saving enough money to pay the next month's rent. In most cases, she had to work a second job just to make ends meet. She came to admire the hardworking people – mostly women– that she worked with and recorded their stories along with her own in her book. She came to the conclusion that the workers who do the jobs that make life easier for everyone else were undervalued. These people didn't have paid sick days or health insurance, so they went to work even when they were sick or injured. Losing a day's pay spelled financial disaster for them. When citizens of a society cannot afford adequate health care or earn wages that do not allow them to scrape out more than a meager living, they cannot contribute to the overall success of a society.

Today, the citizens of our country are engaged in a great debate about health care. President Obama had led the crusade for providing affordable health insurance for everyone in the United States. His opponents believed that the Affordable Health Care Act would be too costly, that businesses will suffer from being compelled to offer coverage to their employees, and that jobs will be lost. Republicans, for the most part, want to de–fund Obamacare, and to that end, Senator Cruz delivered the fourth–longest filibuster in the history of the country in an effort to convince his fellow senators to vote against funding the program. The deadlock in Washington threatens to shut down the government. On the surface, it appears that the Republicans believe that the overall success of society does not depend on the well–being of its individual citizens, while the Democrats and the president believe that the well–being of every individual in the country will ensure overall success for America.

When a country must supplement the basic lifestyles of a significant number of its citizens, that country cannot be considered to be thriving. When the general welfare of its citizens depends on raising taxes on middle–and high–income earners and postponing improvements to its infrastructure or military or educational institutions, the country begins to lose the ability to transport people and goods efficiently, to protect its citizens from enemies both foreign and domestic, and to provide skilled workers for essential occupations. Those whose general welfare is below par are a drain on society, and only by elevating them can the country achieve overall success.

69

Issue Task 70

Claim: *Many problems of modern society cannot be solved by laws and the legal system.*

Reason: *Laws cannot change what is in people's hearts or minds.*

Write a response in which you discuss the extent to which you agree or disagree with the claim and the reason on which that claim is based.

 Strategies

Combine the claim and the reason into one statement using a subordinate clause.

In other words:

Because laws cannot change what is in people's hearts or minds, many problems of modern society cannot be solved by laws and the legal system.

What are the assumptions stated or implied in the claim and reason? These will provide evidence that you can refute or affirm in your argument.

◆ Changing what is in people's minds and hearts will solve problems of modern society.

◆ Many of modern society's problems are not rooted in illegal actions.

◆ The problems of modern society are more troublesome than those of the past.

◆ People will follow their hearts rather than the laws.

Opposing viewpoint:

Claim: *Many problems of modern society can be solved by laws and the legal system.*

Reason: *Laws can override what is in people's hearts or minds.*

What are the assumptions stated or implied in the claim and reason? These will provide evidence that you can refute or affirm in your argument.

70

◆ The legal system is an effective agent of change.

◆ People's minds and hearts need not be changed to be subject to laws.

◆ The law has more authority than people's minds and hearts.

Alternative viewpoint:

Claim: *Many problems of modern society can be solved by laws and the legal system.*

Reason: *People can use what is in their minds and hearts to create or change laws.*

What are the assumptions stated or implied in the claim and reason?

◆ People can change laws that are not effective.

Sample Essay

Society must have laws. When nomadic peoples began living together in communal groups, the need for rules arose. Individuals could not steal from the group, kill other members of the group, or be dishonest. The great religions of the world created lists of prohibited actions, calling the commission of them sins against god. Christians have the Ten Commandments, and the laws in Christian countries reflect the prohibitions in those commandments. Because most people respect and obey the laws, the legal system can solve most problems of modern society.

When the problems of modern society are the result of people's attitudes or prejudices, laws are not effective in the short term, but evidence exists that they eventually create more just conditions for everyone. Just recently, the United States commemorated the fiftieth anniversary of Martin Luther King's I Have a Dream speech during the March on Washington. This action to protest unequal treatment of minorities eventually led to President Johnson's signing the Civil Rights Act. Despite this legislation, the hearts and minds of white Americans, particularly in the South, remained unchanged for decades. However, a recent survey revealed that 72% of Americans believe that progress has been made. The fact that voters elected a black man to serve as President of the United States is the most obvious example of that progress. The bias against women in leadership roles has changed, initially as a result of the passage of the Nineteenth Amendment that allowed them to vote. Decades later, laws made it possible for women to attend college at traditionally male institutions like Harvard, Yale, and military service academies. People's hearts and minds have changed sufficiently to make it acceptable for women to serve on the Supreme Court and run as vice presidential candidates. They serve as CEOs of major corporations. Most recently, some states have passed laws making it legal for same-sex couples to marry. Alternative lifestyles have become more acceptable.

Laws may be unable to change what is in people's minds and hearts, but people can use what is in their minds and hearts to change laws or even entire governments. In the early years of America, citizens lived under English law. England treated the colonies like a cash cow; every time Britain needed to raise funds, it levied a new tax or tariff on the colonists. When the taxes and tariffs became too burdensome, the colonists eventually revolted; and, in 1776, declared their independence from England. Today, Americans, like citizens in most democratic countries, have a means to change the laws. The representatives and senators –also referred to as lawmakers– on both the state and national level create new laws or amend old ones to reflect the needs and desires of their constituents. Laws have been changed to reflect what people think and feel. Not so long ago, it was against the law for people of different races to marry, but now it is common to see legally married couples of different races. Obtaining a divorce was virtually impossible, compelling couples to remain married long after they had stopped loving each other. Women were forced to remain in abusive marriages. Due to changes in those laws, people can follow their hearts and legally remove themselves from loveless relationships.

Laws may be an effective deterrent to crime. Fear of legal consequences certainly prevents most people from acting on feelings of anger or revenge. Would–be criminals are likely to avoid a life of crime if they know they will spend time in jail or be required to pay a hefty fine. The law may not change what is in a man's heart or mind, but it can change his course of action.

70

Issue Task 71

Unfortunately, in contemporary society, creating an appealing image has become more important than the reality or truth behind that image.

Write a response in which you discuss the extent to which you agree or disagree with the statement and explain your reasoning for the position you take. In developing and supporting your position, you should consider ways in which the statement might or might not hold true and explain how these considerations shape your position.

 ## Strategies

Restate the issue, perhaps by reversing the order of the sentence components.

In other words:

The reality or truth behind an image has become less important in today's society than creating an appealing image.

Determine what question is being answered by the statement. This will help you begin to think how you would answer it and whether or not you agree with the original statement.

Is creating an appealing image more important than the reality behind the image in contemporary society?

Parts of the original statement that provide evidence that you can affirm or refute.

◆ **Unfortunately** - implies that the statement reveals a negative consequence

◆ **contemporary society** - in the present time

◆ **creating** - involves some action on the part of the person desiring an image

◆ **appealing image** - It goes without saying that one would want an image that appeals to others

◆ **has become more important** - The need for an appealing image has grown.

◆ **reality or truth behind the image** - The image is false and does not portray the real character of the individual.

71

Society   *www.vibrantpublishers.com*

Next, create a statement that expresses the opposing viewpoint, using language similar to that of the original statement.

Opposing viewpoint:

In contemporary society, creating an appealing image has not become more important than the reality or truth behind that image.

Identify the parts of the opposing statement that provide evidence to refute or affirm.

◆ **has not become more important -** The image and the reality are the same.

Is there any other way to look at this issue? Can you qualify the original statement in some way? Is it possible to partially agree with the statement?

Alternative viewpoint:

In contemporary society, maintaining an appealing image has become more difficult because the reality behind that image can be more easily exposed.

Identify the parts of the alternative statement that provide evidence to refute or affirm.

◆ **Maintaining** – keeping up an image over time

◆ **More easily exposed** – social media broadcasts every mistake in an instant

 ## Sample Essay

Image is everything. Canon used this tag line in an advertising campaign in the 1990s featuring tennis great Andre Agassi, who changed the look of professional tennis with his long hair and unconventional clothing on the court. Fortunately for Canon and the tennis world, Agassi had the game to support his image. He is still considered one of the greatest to play the game. In contrast, Paris Hilton, who starred in The Simple Life with friend, Nichole Ritchie, has become known as a celebutante or "famous for being famous". Lacking any real talent, she has parlayed her inherited wealth into endorsing products she had not created. For Ms. Hilton, image isn't everything, it's the only thing. It is unfortunate that celebrities, athletes, and even giant corporations have created images that are contrary to the reality behind their façades.

Many athletes have gone beyond the boundaries of health and ethics to create images that have elevated them to the pinnacle of their individual sports and made them very wealthy. Perhaps no one in the twenty–first century has fallen more catastrophically than Lance Armstrong. A cancer survivor, Armstrong won seven

71

consecutive Tour de France races, the most difficult biking competition in the world. Millions of people adorned their wrists with the yellow bracelet imprinted with the Livestrong logo in support of Armstrong's cancer foundation. Just this year, the world watched as Lance Armstrong confessed in an interview with Oprah Winfrey that he was guilty of doping. He has been stripped of his titles and banned for life from professional cycling. It is fair to say that Armstrong was more concerned with his image than with the truth behind that image. Other athletes whose images have been tarnished by accusations of drug use include Roger Clemens, one of MLB's greatest pitchers, and Alex Rodriguez, whose career with the Yankees will likely end on a sour note.

The corporate world is not immune to the need for a positive image or concealing the truth behind that image. Walmart has parlayed its image of lower prices all the time into becoming the world's largest retailer. Television commercials show smiling, friendly employees touting the benefits of shopping for all of your needs at Walmart. When the corporation is planning a new store in a small town somewhere in America, it holds seminars for local businesses in which they reveal how these small businesses can survive and thrive after the new Walmart store opens. The image is one of cooperation. The truth behind the image is that many of those small stores will close in just a few years because they cannot compete with Walmart's low prices. An additional truth is that Walmart is a large recipient of corporate welfare. Their image as a great place to work belies the truth that great numbers of Walmart workers need public assistance to satisfy their basic needs.

Money is the biggest motivation for cultivating an image intended to mask the truth about an industry, a business, a star athlete, or a celebrity. In the 1950s, Rock Hudson was a tall, dark, and handsome leading man in some of the most popular movies made in that decade. He was also a homosexual. Although some in the movie industry suspected this, the studio that employed Hudson took measures to cover up the knowledge for many years, going as far as arranging his marriage to a woman. Those outside of the studio's top executives continued to adore Rock Hudson, and box office receipts for his movies continued to be high. When the truth about Mr. Hudson came out in the 1980's, he was dying of AIDS. Pictures showing his gaunt face and ravaged body replaced the image so carefully cultivated over several decades.

It is unfortunate that, today, image has become more important than the truth behind it. We have been told that the truth shall set you free and that if you always tell the truth, you don't have to remember what you have said to others. Those who attempt to conceal the truth – athletes, celebrities, giant corporations – must spend an inordinate amount of time and energy remembering which lies or half–truths they told and to whom they told them. It is additionally unfortunate that the general public must bear some of the responsibility for these false images. People's desire for bigger, better, faster, and cheaper have driven the fabrication of these images in the pursuit of fame and fortune on the parts of the famous and popular.

Issue Task 72

The well-being of a society is enhanced when many of its people question authority.

Write a response in which you discuss the extent to which you agree or disagree with the statement and explain your reasoning for the position you take. In developing and supporting your position, you should consider ways in which the statement might or might not hold true and explain how these considerations shape your position.

 Strategies

The best Analyze an Issue arguments are typically structured in a similar manner: 1 paragraph for the Introduction, 2-3 Body paragraphs that support your argument and 1 that opposes it, and 1 Closing statement. With only 30 minutes to complete your writing, spending 5 minutes to plan and structure your arguments is a critical step that will propel you to a top-scoring essay. Thus, it is best to start with a quick brainstorming session that presents 3-4 statements on either side of the argument. Take a look at ours:

Agree:

◆ Innovation results from questioning authority and from seeking ways around the "existing truth." Without the questioning of authority, people will simply become a hive mind dependent on the leader. While this may work reasonably well in very few cases (e.g., Singapore), it is extremely rare.

◆ In societies with freedom of speech where people can question authority, there is a system of checks and balances to ensure that those holding the power are doing the right thing. This is one pillar that separates progressive societies from traditional ones. As we are in the 21st century, it is time to move everyone toward a progressive society and better well-being.

◆ The ability to question authority on every level, including at the workplace, allows for a sort of "crowdsourced" decision-making. It is one where the ideas come from the bottom and not from the top – which is usually how great decisions are made. It is no mistake that great companies have a flat structure versus a hierarchical one, where everyone matters, and people believe that their contributions are important.

Disagree:

◆ The ability to question authority comes with a steep price: it is a time-consuming endeavor to respond to criticism. For societies or organizations under an emergency or crisis, this is not an option, as they need to move fast and exert complete control. The military is considered an extremely well-run organization, and it is extremely authoritative.

◆ Having many people question authority and leadership can be distracting and confusing. Furthermore, the reason people are in positions of authority is often because they are the most knowledgeable. Thus, to save time and make the best decisions, it is best to let authoritative figures run the show.

 ## Sample Essay

Factors comprising the well–being of a society include social mobility and equality, economic and technological progress, and quality of life. The best societies, then, are able to develop and enhance these areas and create happiness, health, and wealth among their people. Yet, finding a balance among these areas has often proven difficult, with gains in one area often resulting in sacrifices to another. One component of enhanced societal well–being under debate is the questioning of authority: is the well–being of a society enhanced or worsened when many people question authority? Although technocratic and authoritative environments may provide short–term success, we show that they are counterintuitive to long–term progress and happiness. Thus, the well–being of a society is enhanced when many people question authority.

We start by examining the short–term case. There are limited situations where an authoritative management style may be considered appropriate: under a crisis or emergency or in highly risky situations. Responding to criticism, second–guessing decisions, and investigating the outcomes of these decisions all take time. In these types of cases, decisions need to be made quickly (potentially sacrificing effectiveness). However, over a longer period and once the crisis or emergency has been averted, continued authoritative action tends to breed dissent and hatred, often leading to widespread protests or revolts (e.g., the Arab Spring or the American Revolution).

In contrast, in societies with freedom of speech where people can question authority, there is a system of checks and balances to ensure that those holding the power are acting appropriately and that those questioning authority are doing so in a reasonable fashion. Without the ability to question authority – sitting at the front of the bus rather than the back, protesting for civil rights, or questioning a leader's decision to act seemingly in contrast to best interests – social progress is hindered and stopped cold in its tracks. The ability to have a voice that matters is a key driver toward social equality and mobility, ultimately enhancing societal well–being.

Another advantage of the ability to question authority on every level is that it allows for a sort of "crowd-sourced" decision–making. For example, great companies have a flat structure versus a hierarchical one. That is, every individual matters and people's contributions are heard at all ranks of the company. After all, those best qualified to discuss improvements to a certain process are probably those working with the process on a daily basis rather than their manager's manager who has only a vague idea of what the process even does!

Moreover, innovation thrives when authority is challenged. Eric Schmidt, the CEO of Google, recently noted that Israel has a strong culture of innovation and entrepreneurship precisely because of its culture of questioning authority and challenging the status quo. A society that openly accepts the questioning of authority is essentially showing its members that taking risks and trying something new are acceptable, leading to bigger risk–taking activities by the people, driving progress.

Therefore, apart from some short–term cases, people should have the ability to question authority and scrutinize authoritative decisions carefully. Ultimately, this improves several key areas of well–being: decision–making is enhanced by allowing more voices to be heard, social and economic mobility and equality are increased through questioning of the status quo, and societal contentment is achieved by avoiding build–ups in dissent and hatred that come with an authoritarian leadership.

This page is intentionally left blank

Chapter **9**
Analyze an Argument Task

In the Analyze an Argument task, you will take an approach that differs from that in the Analyze an Issue task. You will not be asked to develop and defend a point of view. You will be asked to analyze an argument and the evidence and assumptions on which it is based. You will be presented with a brief passage that makes an argument either for taking some course of action, following a recommendation, or supporting a prediction. You should read the passage carefully to identify either stated or unstated assumptions or to determine the line of reasoning used by the author of the passage. The directions will instruct you to approach your analysis in any of several ways. You may be asked to state what additional evidence is needed to make the argument sound, what questions will need to be answered before accepting a recommendation, or whether a prediction based on the argument is reasonable.

As in the Analyze an Issue task, there is no "right" answer or approach. It is important to stay on topic, use sound reasoning and examples in your response, and strive to develop a coherent, cohesive, and fluent response. Remember that analysis is the act of breaking something down into its components to see how well they relate to each other. The components of the argument may include facts, statistics or other figures, and both stated and unstated assumptions. For example, the owner of Gemma's Jewelry store may predict that, based on the past two years' sales, the store will see an increase of 10% in next year's sales. One of the unstated assumptions is that the demand for luxury goods will increase despite whatever else may happen to the economy. Gemma's Jewelry doesn't say what will account for the increase in sales. Will the store add new lines of merchandise? Will the store increase its advertising? Will the store expand in size? Is a 10% increase significant? If sales were $40,000 last year, is an additional $4,000 dollars in sales meaningful?

Following is a list of the specific directions you will be asked to follow as you analyze an argument in your response.

- ❑ Write a response in which you discuss what specific evidence is needed to evaluate the argument and explain how the evidence would weaken or strengthen the argument.

- ❑ Write a response in which you examine the stated and/or unstated assumptions of the argument. Be sure to explain how the argument depends on these assumptions, and what the implications are for the argument if the assumptions prove unwarranted.

- ❑ Write a response in which you discuss what questions would need to be answered in order to decide whether the recommendation and the argument on which it is based are reasonable. Be sure to explain how the answers to these questions would help to evaluate the recommendation.

- ❑ Write a response in which you discuss what questions would need to be answered in order to decide whether the advice and the argument on which it is based are reasonable. Be sure to explain how the answers to these questions would help to evaluate the advice.

- ❑ Write a response in which you discuss what questions would need to be answered in order to decide whether the recommendation is likely to have the predicted result. Be sure to explain how the answers to these questions would help to evaluate the recommendation.

❑ Write a response in which you discuss what questions would need to be answered in order to decide whether the prediction and the argument on which it is based are reasonable. Be sure to explain how the answers to these questions would help to evaluate the prediction.

❑ Write a response in which you discuss what questions would need to be addressed in order to decide whether the conclusion and the argument on which it is based are reasonable. Be sure to explain how the answers to the questions would help to evaluate the conclusion.

❑ Write a response in which you discuss one or more alternative explanations that could rival explanation(s) can plausibly account for the facts presented in the argument.

You will not need knowledge in any specific discipline to analyze an argument. The topics are of general interest and are accessible to anyone regardless of previous course work. The GRE essay readers will be looking for your ability to reason and organize your thoughts in a logical way. The scoring guide that follows is reprinted from the Practice Book for the GRE Revised General Test, developed by Educational Testing Service.

Scoring Guide

Score 6

In addressing the specific task directions, a 6 response presents a cogent, well-articulated analysis of the issue and conveys meaning skillfully.

A typical response in this category:

❑ articulates a clear and insightful position on the issue in accordance with the assigned task

❑ develops the position fully with compelling reasons and/or persuasive examples

❑ sustains a well-focused, well-organized analysis, connecting ideas logically

❑ conveys ideas fluently and precisely, using effective vocabulary and sentence variety

❑ demonstrates facility with the conventions of standard written English (i.e., grammar, usage and mechanics), but may have minor errors

Score 5

In addressing the specific task directions, a 5 response presents a generally thoughtful, well-developed analysis of the issue and conveys meaning clearly.

A typical response in this category:

❑ presents a clear and well-considered position on the issue in accordance with the assigned task

❑ develops the position with logically sound reasons and/or well-chosen examples

❑ is focused and generally well organized, connecting ideas appropriately

❑ conveys ideas clearly and well, using appropriate vocabulary and sentence variety

❑ demonstrates facility with the conventions of standard written English but may have minor errors

Score 4

In addressing the specific task directions, a 4 response presents a competent analysis of the issue and conveys meaning with acceptable clarity.

A typical response in this category:

❑ presents a clear position on the issue in accordance with the assigned task

❑ develops the position with relevant reasons and/or examples

❑ is adequately focused and organized

❑ demonstrates sufficient control of language to express ideas with reasonable clarity

❑ generally, demonstrates control of the conventions of standard written English but may have some errors

Score 3

A three response demonstrates some competence in addressing the specific task directions, in analyzing the issue and in conveying meaning, but is obviously flawed.

A typical response in this category exhibits ONE OR MORE of the following characteristics:

❑ is vague or limited in addressing the specific task directions and/or in presenting or developing a position on the issue

❑ is weak in the use of relevant reasons or examples or relies largely on unsupported claims

❑ is poorly focused and/or poorly organized

❑ has problems in language and sentence structure that result in a lack of clarity

❑ contains occasional major errors or frequent minor errors in grammar, usage or mechanics that can interfere with meaning

Score 2

A two response largely disregards the specific task directions and/or demonstrates serious weaknesses in analytical writing.

A typical response in this category exhibits ONE OR MORE of the following characteristics:

- ❏ is unclear or seriously limited in addressing the specific task directions and/or in presenting or developing a position on the issue

- ❏ provides few, if any, relevant reasons or examples in support of its claims

- ❏ is unfocused and/or disorganized

- ❏ has serious problems in language and sentence structure that frequently interfere with meaning

- ❏ contains serious errors in grammar, usage or mechanics that frequently obscure meaning

Score 1

A one response demonstrates fundamental deficiencies in analytical writing.

A typical response in this category exhibits ONE OR MORE of the following characteristics:

- ❏ provides little or no evidence of understanding the issue

- ❏ provides little evidence of the ability to develop an organized response (i.e., is extremely disorganized and/ or extremely brief)

- ❏ has severe problems in language and sentence structure that persistently interfere with meaning

- ❏ contains pervasive errors in grammar, usage or mechanics that result in incoherence

Score 0

A typical response in this category is off topic (i.e., provides no evidence of an attempt to respond to the assigned topic), is in a foreign language, merely copies the topic, consists of only keystroke characters or is illegible or nonverbal.

The brief passages and directions in the Analyze an Argument task contain some complexity. In order to achieve a high score, you must understand the terminology. The following list is intended to help you clarify your written evaluation of the argument. Further, in this chapter, you will find Analyze an Argument tasks with elaborate strategies to write the response to a task as well as sample high scoring response or essay for each task.

Note that trained GRE readers evaluate your response based on how well you organize, develop and express your analysis. They give grades depending on the way you respond to the specific task instructions, identify and analyze key features of the passage, support your position with relevant reasons and/or examples and control the elements of standard English.

General Strategies

Although you do not need to know special analytical techniques and terminology, you should be familiar with the directions for the Argument task and with certain key concepts, including the following:

❑ Is there an alternative explanation for the events in question that can invalidate, either in whole or in part, the explanation given in the passage?

❑ How can I break the argument into its component parts to understand how they create the whole argument?

❑ Can I identify the line of reasoning used to create the argument?

❑ What does the author of the argument assume to be true for the argument to be true?

❑ Does the line of reasoning validate the conclusion?

❑ Can I imagine an example that refutes any or several of the statements in the argument?

❑ Am I able to evaluate the argument based on the quality of the facts and reasons presented in it?

Regardless of the approach you take, you must present a well–developed evaluation of the argument. You should take brief notes when you identify the argument's claims, assumptions, and conclusion. Jot down as many alternative explanations as you can along with additional evidence that might support or refute the claims in the argument. Finally, list the changes in the argument that would make the reasoning more solid. It is more important to be specific than it is to have a long list of evidence and examples. Use as many or as few paragraphs as you consider appropriate for your argument, but create a new paragraph when you move on to a new idea or example of support for your position. The GRE readers are not looking for a specific number of ideas or paragraphs. Instead, they are reading to determine the level of understanding of the topic and the complexity with which you respond.

You are free to organize and develop your response in any way you think will enable you to effectively communicate your evaluation of the argument. You may recall writing strategies you learned in high school or a writing–intensive course you took in college, but it is not necessary to employ any of those strategies. It is important that your ideas follow a logical progression and display strong critical thinking

Chapter **10**
Arts

1

Argument Task 1

The following appeared in a memo from a budget planner for the city of Grandview.

"It is time for the city of Grandview to stop funding the Grandview Symphony Orchestra. It is true that the symphony struggled financially for many years, but last year private contributions to the symphony increased by 200 percent and attendance at the symphony's concerts-in-the-park series doubled. In addition, the symphony has just announced an increase in ticket prices for next year. For these reasons, we recommend that the city eliminate funding for the Grandview Symphony Orchestra from next year's budget. We predict that the symphony will flourish in the years to come even without funding from the city."

Write a response in which you discuss what questions would need to be answered in order to decide whether the recommendation is likely to have the predicted result. Be sure to explain how the answers to these questions would help to evaluate the recommendation.

 Strategies

The first step in performing your analysis consists of identifying the texts' key point, recommendation, prediction or hypothesis. All the other arguments and assumptions are designed to support this central claim. In this case, the author attempts to demonstrate that "the symphony will flourish in the years to come even without funding from the city".

The next step would involve creating a statement that summarizes the text by including the central claim and its supporting arguments.

A budget planner from the city of Grandview predicts that the towns' orchestra will prosper in the coming years even without funding from the city since private contributions and orchestra event attendance have significantly increased.

When considering what questions are needed to evaluate the arguments outlined in the text, it is important to keep in mind that arguments are based on assumptions – points that are taken to be true, without need for proof. This is what you need to look for – explicit and implicit assumptions, since they lack the evidence required to prove their validity.

Assumptions

Explicit Assumptions	Implicit assumptions
An increase in ticket prices implies an increase in revenue	• People are willing to pay increased prices • The increase in prices outweighs the increase in costs • The increase in prices is significant
The tripling of private contributions and attendance provide sufficient revenue	• The additional amount of money covers the orchestra's budgetary needs • Maintenance and operation costs will stay fixed • A tripling of the previous amounts of money raised from private contributions and attendance is a big sum • "Concerts in the park" are the main orchestral event
Attendance and contributions will maintain their levels in the upcoming years	• A great percentage of investors will reinvest • Market will be stable • Last year's increase in private contributions and attendance was not due to a change in external factors

After having established your assumptions, you can find the questions that are needed to evaluate the argument by rephrasing each implicit assumption.

Questions

◆ Would people be willing to pay the increased ticket prices?

◆ Is the increase in ticket prices significant enough to cover the increase in costs?

◆ What percentage of the orchestra's budgetary needs was covered by the money garnered from the increase in contributions and attendance?

◆ Would the orchestra's running costs stay fixed for the next year?

◆ Does tripling the attendance and private contributions provide a significant sum of money?

- How many of the previous investors are likely to reinvest?

- Would the economical situation in the region remain unchanged?

- Were there no other external factors responsible for the increase in private contributions and attendance?

 ## Sample Essay

A budget planner from the city of Grandview predicts that the towns' orchestra will prosper in the coming years even without funding from the city since private contributions and orchestra event attendance have significantly increased. Decisions to eliminate funding are risky since the slightest miscalculation could send the orchestra into debt. The committee that would evaluate the budget planner's proposal would need to make sure that the assumptions that the prediction rests on are backed by facts and that the author has covered all aspects and key factors at play.

When making his case, the budget planner assumes that the tripling of private contributions and event attendance would provide sufficient revenue for the orchestra. The question that comes to mind in this instance is what percentage of the orchestra's budgetary needs in the past year was covered by the money garnered from the increase in contributions and attendance. Just because these factors increased, it does not mean that the orchestra has sufficient funding to keep running. If the added revenue only constitutes a small percentage of the running costs, then the measure to cut orchestra funding would be highly detrimental. Even if the reverse were true and the tripling of private contributions and event attendance would cover most of the budgetary needs, it would still not be justifiable to stop funding the orchestra. The reason is that the orchestra would still be in debt. However, should the extra money be enough to translate into profit without the city hall contribution, then the budget planner's prediction would have a greater chance of success, provided the economical conditions remain the same.

The idea that the current tripling of private contributions and event attendance would provide sufficient revenue for the orchestra rests on the assumption that the running costs for the upcoming year would remain fixed or increase just slightly. This begs the question of how much would the orchestra costs increase in the next year and if the current money gained from the tripling of contributions and attendance would be enough to cover it. Prices invariably fluctuate and, most often than not, costs end up increasing. Should the orchestra's running costs significantly increase in the upcoming year, it is highly likely that the current amount of extra money garnered from contributions and attendance would not be sufficient to cover the budgetary needs. In this instance, the author's recommendation to cut city hall funding would only serve to insure that the orchestra goes into debt. On the other hand, if the prices were to remain the same or only slightly increase then the idea that the orchestra could support itself would have more merit. However, without a further increase in the orchestra's revenue, it would still be difficult to say with any degree of certainty that the profits would end up outweighing the costs if the funding were to be cut.

The budget planner's optimistic prediction is based on the assumption that either the previous investors will reinvest, or enough new investors would be tempted to spend money on the orchestra. The author should take into account how many of the current investors have expressed a desire to reinvest. It is entirely possible that most of the private investments came from individuals interested in making a one-time donation, or they were spurred on by external circumstances. If the number of people that want to reinvest is low, it becomes less likely that the orchestra would be able to support itself without city funding or attracting new investors. With an uneven money distribution, if the small remaining percentage of private investors were also the biggest contributors, then the budget planner's recommendation would have a bigger chance at succeeding. Should most of the current investors be interested in reinvesting, it becomes more likely that the orchestra would be able to support itself. Although that statement would still be dependent on the amount of money people would be willing to contribute and the expected profit margins.

Another assumption at the core of the author's argument is the idea that increased ticket prices guarantee an increase of revenue. However, before making his prediction, the budget planner should bear in mind whether people would be willing to pay the increased ticket prices. It's possible that an increase in ticket prices can have the opposite of the desired effect and end up chasing people away. If people were to find the higher ticket prices to be too expensive, the attendance and overall revenue would decrease, so the author's argument that the orchestra can support itself would be weakened. On the other hand, if people would be more than willing to pay the higher prices and should attendance rates remain unchanged then the budget planner's prediction would be supported. The extra revenue might prove to be enough to make the orchestra flourish on its own – provided that the running costs don't rise too dramatically.

When predicting the orchestra's future well-being based on the existing conditions, the Grandview budget planner assumes that the increased attendance and contributions are not due to any external factors. It then becomes important to establish whether there were no other external factors responsible for the tripling of contributions and attendance. Given that the orchestra attendance rate increased for a specific event, namely the concerts in the park, it is likely that the weather had some influence. Unusually mild temperatures could have encouraged more people to join in outside activities. Regardless of the specifics, if the author were to discover that the increased attendance and contributions were due to external factors, then his assumption that levels of attendance and private donations would be maintained in the following year would be severely weakened. On the other hand, should external factors prove to not have had any hand in the past year's budget increase, it would become far more likely that the same performance could be repeated in the following year.

Overall, before making his prediction, the budget planner should take into account a multitude of other factors such as the likelihood of the investment and attendance rates continuing in the future and always rapport the increase in revenue to orchestra's running costs, or he would run the risk of sending the orchestra into debt, without the city's support.

2

Argument Task 2

Woven baskets characterized by a particular distinctive design pattern have previously been found only in the immediate vicinity of the prehistoric village of Palea and, therefore, were believed to have been made only by the Palean people. Recently, however, archaeologists discovered such a "Palean" basket in Lithos, an ancient village across the Brim River from Palea. The Brim River is very deep and broad, and so the ancient Paleans could have crossed it only by boat, and no Palean boats have been found. Thus it follows that the so-called Palean baskets were not uniquely Palean.

Write a response in which you discuss one or more alternative explanations that could rival the proposed explanation and explain how your explanation or explanations can plausibly account for the facts presented in the argument.

 Strategies

Regardless of the approach you take, you must present a well-developed evaluation of the argument. You should take brief notes when you identify the argument's claims, assumptions, and conclusion. Jot down as many alternative explanations as you can along with additional evidence that might support or refute the claims in the argument. Finally, list the changes in the argument that would make the reasoning more solid. It is more important to be specific than to have a long list of evidence and examples.

This argument cites recent archaeological discoveries and geological features to support the claim that these baskets were made not only by the Palean people.

In developing your response, you are asked to develop alternative explanations that could rival the explanation in the argument and explain how your explanation can account for the facts presented in the original explanation.

What conclusions and assumptions are either explicit or implied in the original explanation?

Facts and Assumptions:

◆ The Brim River is very deep and broad.

   The implication is that this has always been the case. The river may have changed course or become larger over time.

◆ The river could only have been crossed in boats.

here can be several ways to cross a wide, deep river.

◆ The Paleans had no boats.

This assumption is based on the fact that no evidence of the Paleans' having boats exists. That is not to say that at some point in the future evidence of boats will not be found.

◆ The Paleans could not have crossed the river.

This assumption underlies the claim that may need qualifying.

◆ "Palean" baskets have been discovered in Lithos.

This fact underlies the claim that the baskets are not unique to Palea. The river itself could have carried baskets from one side of the river to the other.

◆ The baskets are Palean in origin.

This assumption is supported by the discovery of the baskets in Palea prior to their being discovered in Lithos.

Alternative Explanations:

◆ Geography is always changing. The Brim River may have followed a different course or been shallower or narrower at some point in time. Climate changes throughout the year may affect the depth and width of the river. Does the river become shallower and narrower as the spring runoff recedes?

◆ The Paleans may have been terrific swimmers. Depending on other geographical features, the Paleans may have worked with the residents of Lithos to construct a bridge across the river.

◆ The materials that the Paleans used to construct their boats may have disintegrated over time, leaving no evidence of their having existed. As archaeologists continue their work, they may uncover evidence of boats.

◆ It is difficult to imagine that any group of people would have let a geographical feature, like a river, remain an obstacle. If there were resources that the Paleans needed or wanted on the other side of the river, they would have found a way to cross it. This is assuming that the river either existed at all or existed in its current state.

◆ Because the baskets have been discovered on both sides of the river does not mean that they were carried there by people. It is possible that during some flood, the baskets were lifted by the water itself and carried from one bank to the other.

◆ Because the baskets were discovered first in Palea, archaeologists assumed that they originated there. After their discovery in Lithos, it might be as correct to assume that the baskets originated there.

Your notes do not have to be exhaustive. As you begin to write your essay, your brain will generate new ideas. Make certain that you keep the directions in mind as you develop your ideas. Use as many or as few paragraphs as you consider appropriate for your argument, but create a new paragraph when you move on to a new idea or example of support for your position. The GRE readers are not looking for a specific number of ideas or paragraphs. Instead, they are reading to determine the level of understanding of the topic and the complexity with which you respond.

You are free to organize and develop your response in any way you think will enable you to effectively communicate your evaluation of the argument. You may recall writing strategies you learned in high school or a writing-intensive course you took in college, but it is not necessary to employ any of those strategies. It is important that your ideas follow a logical progression and display strong critical thinking.

 ## Sample Essay

Rivers are not static geographical features. Spring rains and snow melt swell rivers to their maximum width and depth. As warmer, drier months arrive, the thirsty land absorbs water from the river, and evaporation takes its toll. If we consider the mighty Mississippi River that makes its way from its headwaters in Minnesota in the north to its terminus in the Gulf of Mexico in the south, we know that spring floods are inevitable along its entire course. At those times, the width of the river and the speed of its currents make it difficult to cross even with a boat. After summer arrives, the Mississippi becomes narrower and slower, and both barges and pleasure craft ply its waters with ease. The explanation presented here fails to state if the Brim River is very deep and wide through-out the year. It is just as likely that the river behaves much like the Mississippi and travel across it is possible by means other than boats during the warmer, drier months of the year. The Paleans would have taken advantage of those conditions and used their unique baskets to carry goods to trade with the people of Lithos on the opposite bank.

To date no evidence exists to show that the Paleans had boats. For millennia, there was no evidence that Noah had built an ark, either, until what appeared to be the outline of a large vessel was found on the side of Mt. Ararat. Archaeological digs are ongoing events. Just as the baskets were found on the Lithosian side of the Brim River in recent times, it may be that evidence of Palean boats will be discovered as the study of the site continues. The boats were probably constructed of materials that would have disintegrated fairly rapidly if they existed at all. The assumption that they had none is based on missing evidence. Even assuming that the Brim River has always been wide and deep, means other than boats could have been used to cross it. Maybe the Paleans were terrific swimmers. Maybe they built rafts. Maybe they clung to logs and were carried across by the current. It is virtually impossible to prove or disprove any of these theories.

The fact that the baskets were found both in Palea and Lithos is open to a number of interpretations. Flooding of the river itself may be responsible for the migration of the baskets from one side to the other. The baskets may have been used at the river's edge to collect edible plants or fish, and some baskets may have been forgotten there. As the waters rose, the baskets were lifted and carried to the other bank. A shift in the course of the river may have divided what was once one village, leaving what became known as Palea on one side, Lithos on the other, and the distinctive baskets on both sides.

Archaeologists will likely continue to study this site. Until evidence is found to the contrary, their present conclusions may stand. That those conclusions are based on lack of evidence is not sufficient to abandon the search for artifacts that may alter them.

Argument Task 3

Two years ago, radio station WCQP in Rockville decided to increase the number of call-in advice programs that it broadcast; since that time, its share of the radio audience in the Rockville listening area has increased significantly. Given WCQP's recent success with call-in advice programming, and citing a nationwide survey indicating that many radio listeners are quite interested in such programs, the station manager of KICK in Medway recommends that KICK include more call-in advice programs in an attempt to gain a larger audience share in its listening area.

Write a response in which you discuss what questions would need to be answered in order to decide whether the recommendation is likely to have the predicted result. Be sure to explain how the answers to these questions would help to evaluate the recommendation.

 ## Strategies

The first step in performing your analysis consists of identifying the text's key point, recommendation, prediction or hypothesis. All the other arguments and assumptions are designed to support this central claim. In this case, the author attempts to demonstrate that "more call-in advice programs" will increase the station's listener ratings.

The next step would involve creating a statement that summarizes the text by including the central claim and its supporting arguments

The station manager of KICK recommends increasing the number of call-in advice programs being broadcasted in order to gain a larger audience, given that a similar strategy has worked for a radio station in another town, and a national survey indicates that people are interested in such programs

When considering what questions are needed to evaluate the arguments outlined in the text, it is important to keep in mind that arguments are based on assumptions – points that are taken to be true, without the need for proof. This is what you need to look for: explicit and implicit assumptions, since they lack the evidence required to prove their validity

Assumptions:

Explicit Assumptions	Implicit Assumptions
WCQP's increase in listeners is due to the additional call-in advice programs	• There were no other internal factors that could have contributed to WCQP's increase in listener ratings • There were no other external (economical) factors that could have contributed to the increase in listener ratings • The increase in listener ratings is for the call-in advice time slot • The increase in listeners was significant
The national survey accurately reflects the preferences of Medway's population	• Demographics of both Medway and the survey are compatible • The survey findings are conclusive
The strategy applied in Rockville is applicable in Medway	• Rockville and Medway have similar target audience demographics • WCQP and KICK have similar market situations • WCQP and KICK are comparable in terms of size and popularity
KICK's audience will increase with more call-in advice programs	• Medway's radio listener market size is big enough to support the potential audience growth • There is a need for call-in advice programs • The need for call-in advice programs was not met elsewhere

After having established your assumptions, you can find the questions needed to evaluate the argument by rephrasing each implicit assumption

Sample Essay

The station manager of KICK recommends increasing the number of call-in advice programs being broadcasted in order to gain a larger audience, given that a similar strategy has worked for a radio station in another town, and a national survey indicates that people are interested in such programs. Like all changes to a business' approach, the recommendation made by KICK's manager carries with it a risk of failure, and as such needs to be thoroughly analyzed before any decisions of implementing the suggested strategy are made.

In outlining his reasoning for the recommendation, the station manager of KICK rests his case on the assumption that WCQP's increase in listeners is due to the additional call-in advice programs. The first question that comes into mind, in this case is if there were any other internal and external factors that could have contributed to the increase in listeners, such as the shutdown of one of WCQP's major competitors, the start of a WCQP promotional campaign, or the station acquiring a popular radio host. Having a great number of other plausible explanations for WCQP's success would significantly weaken the premise that more call-in advice programs would have the desired effect on KICK's listener basis. However, should the answer to the question prove that the increase in call-in advice programs is the sole or major reason responsible for the listener audience boost, then it becomes plausible that WCQP's success can be replicated by KICK, given additional compatibility points like market analysis data.

The next inquiry point related to WCQP's success would investigate during which time slot the WCQP listener ratings increased and how significant was this increase. This data can serve to research whether the listener increase is statistically relevant. A rise in listener ratings of 1%, while technically still considered an increase, would mean that adding more call-in advice programs is a costly method with no substantial benefits, and the station managers should consider alternate means of bolstering listener ratings. From the other perspective, should it turn out that the increase in audience market shares is a dramatic one, then KICK's managers should give the WCQP's strategy due consideration.

When making his case for increasing the amount of call-in advice programs, the station manager cites the results of a national survey as compelling evidence that there is a great desire for programs of this type. When handling surveys and statistical data, it is always important to look not only at the results but also at the theoretical framework and methodology of the study being conducted to be able to ascertain whether the reasoning is sound, or if the scientists have missed some crucial aspect or mitigating factor. As such, the station manager should inquire as to how accurate the study findings are. Should the methodology be faulty, like having a small sample size with a big standard deviation or constructing the survey questions in a leading manner, the results would no longer be indicative of the people's desire for listening to call-in programs, and the station manager would have to find alternative means of estimating the potential market size, lest his argument becomes significantly weakened. A properly conducted survey can serve to strengthen the station manager's recommendation. In fact, most market analyses are based on such a type of direct information gathering.

If the survey findings are accurate, then the next step would be to determine whether these results are applicable to the population of Medway. The station manager should ask himself if the survey and Medway's demographics are compatible. If this assumption holds true, the manager has accurately pinpointed a current need of the Medway population and the recommendation to satisfy said need by changing their programs would be more warranted. But national studies deal with averages; therefore, it is possible that what might be true for the general population is not necessarily true for a particular subgroup. For instance, a national study that identified the preferred musical genres as rock and oldies might not be as applicable to specific cases, like towns in the bible belt. Should the demographics not be comparable, then the national survey at the center of the station manager's argument would not accurately reflect the preferences of the local population of Medway. In order to strengthen his argument, the station manager would have to look at radio preference indicators that are specific to Medway.

The station manager's assumption that the strategy applied in Rockville is applicable in Medway begets the question of how similar the Medway and Rockville markets and target audiences are to each other. If the target audience demographics and the market conditions like the number of competitors, market size or degree of popularity are relatively similar, implementing the suggested strategy would be a very good course of action, given the high likelihood of replicating WCQP's success. Not only that, but the similarity can make the strategy very cost effective and provide KICK with a ready-made implementation roadmap that has a high probability of increasing the company's profits. However, if the market and target audiences of the two cities are different, the assumption that the strategy applied in Rockville is applicable in Medway is significantly weakened because there is a high likelihood that WCQP's success strategy might not be suitable for the population of Medway. To deal with this possibility, the station manager would have to adapt the finer points of WCQP's strategy to the needs of the Medway population, in which case his recommendation might still be valid. Current trendsetting strategies also rely heavily on the reuse of successful strategies with adaptations made to suit each company's specific situation.

All in all, before arguing for the implementation of a strategy used by a different radio station, KICK's station manager should consider whether the market conditions in the two towns are similar enough to warrant making the suggested change. The manager should also consider how to adapt the strategies if the markets prove to be too different or completely reorient himself to other strategies, based on market demands.

Argument Task 4

The following appeared in a memorandum from the owner of Movies Galore, a chain of movie-rental stores.

"In order to reverse the recent decline in our profits, we must reduce operating expenses at Movies Galore's ten movie-rental stores. Since we are famous for our special bargains, raising our rental prices is not a viable way to improve profits. Last month our store in downtown Marston significantly decreased its operating expenses by closing at 6:00 p.m. rather than 9:00 p.m. and by reducing its stock by eliminating all movies released more than five years ago. Therefore, in order to increase profits without jeopardizing our reputation for offering great movies at low prices, we recommend implementing similar changes in our other nine Movies Galore stores."

Write a response in which you discuss what questions would need to be answered in order to decide whether the recommendation and the argument on which it is based are reasonable. Be sure to explain how the answers to these questions would help to evaluate the recommendation.

 Strategies

A good place to start your analysis is by creating a statement that reveals the main idea of the argument. Although the writer is creating an argument, he may ultimately be stating a position, making a recommendation, or making a prediction. It may be helpful for you to determine which of these formats is most evident in the argument.

The owner of Movies Galore is recommending the same changes in all of his stores that he made in his downtown Marston location as a means of reversing a decline in profits.

Assumptions:

- Reducing expenses is the best way for Movies Galore to increase profits.

- The changes made at the downtown Marston location will be successful at the other stores.

- Low prices are the major reason people patronize Movies Galore.

- Movies older than five years attract fewer customers than other genres or newer releases.

- The downtown Marston location is busiest between opening and 6:00 pm.

◆ The downtown Marston location is not busy enough between 6:00 and 9:00 pm to justify staying open during those hours.

Questions:

◆ Have profits declined at all or just some of the stores?

◆ Have profits increased at the downtown Marston store?

◆ During which hours is each store busiest?

◆ Has the owner tried other means of reducing expenses?

◆ Why do customers choose Movies Galore?

◆ Are older videos in high demand at any of the locations?

◆ Has the owner made some recent changes that have had a negative impact on profits?

After completing these steps, you should have enough material to write your analysis. Remember that you are not creating a position of your own; you are evaluating the strengths and weaknesses of the existing argument. You do not have to include all of the points that you have created in your prewriting. In fact, during the process of drafting your analysis, other ideas may come to mind, and if they strengthen your analysis, you should include them.

Sample Essay

The owner of Movies Galore has made a sweeping recommendation with a view to increasing profits for his business. Before adopting the recommendation at all of his locations, he or she needs to answer some pointed questions. One size may not fit all. Each location should be analyzed individually by examining the answers to the questions.

First, he should ask if each store is experiencing a decline in profitability. He may find that only one or two of the stores are creating the decline in profits. Those which are making money for the company should likely be left alone. Even though all of them may be losing money, each may need an individual, specific adjustment to reverse the trend. This owner should also ask what the successful stores may be doing that the others are not. The answer may lead him to make changes different from the ones in the argument.

Shortening the hours of operation and eliminating some inventory will certainly reduce expenses, but the tactic doesn't always contribute to greater profits. Has the downtown Marston store generated higher profits since the changes were made? If that store was not habitually busy between the hours of 6:00 and 9:00, then the relatively minor loss of revenue may be offset by a fairly significant decrease in operating expenses. Electricity, heat, and wages for three hours can be substantial and are aspects of a business operation that can be controlled. Was there very little demand for older videos in that location as well? If so, then money spent on inventory can be better used to stock videos in greater demand by customers in this particular store.

Assuming that the owner has made the correct business decisions for the downtown location, it might be logical to apply the same changes to the other Movies Galore stores. Do all of the other locations experience a lack of business after 6:00? Any stores located in or near a mall may be busiest during the evening hours. Malls are generally open until 9:00 at night, and a store that closes at 6:00 will not be able to take advantage of traffic generated by the other shops.

The owner of Movies Galore assumes that the low prices account for the stores' popularity, but is that really the reason that customers choose them? Movies Galore may have the best selection of the videos most in demand. The stores' locations may be convenient and have plenty of free parking. They may have a great selection of movie snacks. The staff may be friendly and helpful. Without surveying his customers, the owner could be holding onto an idea that has little to support it.

Has the owner attempted any other changes to improve profits? He could increase revenues by expanding the selection of movie snacks and training his associates to suggest patrons buy them with every rental. Customers may have abandoned Movies Galore because the videos are not organized logically, or the associates deliver poor service. Has the owner made some recent changes that have led to a temporary decline in profits? Upgrading heating systems or lighting fixtures, for example, can be costly one-time expenditures that can account for the current lack of profitability. The owner may have new employees or managers who are undercharging for rentals or who may be stealing from the company.

Are other, similar businesses in the area experiencing a similar decline in profits? If so, Movies Galore's owner may have to look at his problem in an entirely different light. The market may be over saturated with movie rental businesses. People's rental habits may have changed in recent years by using video-on-demand features through their television cable companies or by subscribing to services like Netflix. When he examines the answers to all of the questions, the owner of Movies Galore will make better-informed decisions about his business

Argument Task 5

The following was written as a part of an application for a small-business loan by a group of developers in the city of Monroe.

"A jazz music club in Monroe would be a tremendously profitable enterprise. Currently, the nearest jazz club is 65 miles away; thus, the proposed new jazz club in Monroe, the C-Note, would have the local market all to itself. Plus, jazz is extremely popular in Monroe: over 100,000 people attended Monroe's annual jazz festival last summer; several well-known jazz musicians live in Monroe; and the highest-rated radio program in Monroe is 'Jazz Nightly,' which airs every weeknight at 7 P.M. Finally, a nationwide study indicates that the typical jazz fan spends close to $1,000 per year on jazz entertainment."

Write a response in which you discuss what specific evidence is needed to evaluate the argument and explain how the evidence would weaken or strengthen the argument.

NOTE: The above topic has wording similar to Argument Task 9 of this book. However, if you read carefully you will notice that the task instructions are different. Hence, it is very important to read the topic as well as its instructions completely before you start to write your response.

Strategies

The first step in performing your analysis consists of identifying the texts' key point, recommendation, prediction or hypothesis. All the other arguments and assumptions are designed to support this central claim. In this case, the author attempts to demonstrate that "a jazz club in Monroe would be profitable"

The next step would involve creating a statement that summarizes the text by including the central claim and its supporting arguments.

The authors of the loan application argue that a jazz club in Monroe would be profitable because the town boasts a big jazz fan base and the nearest competitor is located very far away.

When considering the evidence that is necessary to support the arguments outlined in the text, it is important to keep in mind that arguments are based on assumptions – points that are taken to be true, without the need for proof. This is what you need to look for: explicit and implicit assumptions, since they require evidence that is not already listed in the text. Explicit assumptions can be broken down into or supported by implicit assumptions

Assumptions:

5

Explicit Assumptions	Implicit Assumptions
A jazz club in Monroe would be profitable	• The jazz market is profitable • The club will make a substantial profit • The market size is sufficient to support the club
A jazz club in Monroe would have the market all to itself	• The main competitor is too distant to attract the Monroe population • The Monroe inhabitants that are going to the distant jazz club will choose C-Note based on proximity • There are no other competing jazz venues (cafés, bars etc.)
There is a big jazz fan base in Monroe	• The number of festival attendants accurately reflects the size of the market in Monroe • The rating of Jazz Nightly accurately reflects the popularity of jazz in Monroe • National survey reflects local preferences
Jazz fans will be willing to spend money on the club	• A great size of the average sums fans spend on jazz during the year will go into clubbing • Monroe's inhabitants can afford the club prices

After having established your assumptions, you can find the evidence that is needed to evaluate the argument by considering what proof is necessary to validate each implicit assumption.

Evidence:

◆ National jazz market statistics

◆ C-Note's revenue and cash flow estimations compared with the costs of funding and operating the club.

◆ Comparison of the minimum viable population necessary to support the club with the Monroe population (jazz market size)

◆ Number of Monroe jazz fans frequenting the club situated 65 miles away from Monroe, reportedly the size of the local jazz market

◆ Number of jazz venues in the area

◆ The percentage from the festival attendants that reside in Monroe

◆ Jazz Nightly's audience ratings compared to Monroe's population size

◆ The jazz radio's ratings compared to those of the competing stations

◆ The percentage of money spent on clubbing from the estimated 1000 $ that the average jazz fan

◆ spends per year on jazz entertainment

◆ Monroe's income statistics reported to C-Note's ticket prices

◆ Comparison of the survey demographics with Monroe's demographics

 # Sample Essay

The authors of the loan application argue that a jazz club in Monroe would be profitable because the town boasts a big jazz fan base and the nearest competitor is located very far away. Before submitting the loan application, the group of developers would need to consider additional information, such as demographics, the competitor's prices, the real size of the Monroe jazz audience, and their willingness to spend money on jazz club entrance. Such an assessment would allow them to evaluate whether the business idea is viable in the first place.

The first bits of evidence lacking in the loan application are population statistics and their correlation with the club's funding and maintenance cost. The authors need to devise the minimum running costs and outline expected profit margins and then couple those with the potential size of the jazz market in Monroe. This data should outline whether Monroe's jazz market size is sufficient to support the club. If Monroe's population is not great enough to meet the minimum viable population criteria, then the claim that a jazz club in Monroe would be profitable is not sustainable. Should the population criteria be met, the recommendation of building a jazz club in Monroe would garner some merit, but further data would be needed to establish the profitability of the club. For this purpose, the group of developers should compare C-Note's revenue and cash flow estimations with the costs of funding and operating the club. This would help to establish the theoretical financial viability of the Jazz club. The developers should keep in mind that in addition to these types of estimations, profitability is also highly dependent on the overall state of the market. As such, national jazz market statistics will showcase people's interest and willingness to spend money on jazz entertainment and paraphernalia. If the jazz market is in decline, as a National Endowment for the Arts study has discovered, a jazz club in Monroe might not be profitable in the long run. On the other hand, if the market shows signs of improvement, then the developer's propositions would be greatly strengthened by this fact.

The group of developers bases their business idea on Monroe having a big fan base for jazz. They justify their assumptions by providing a local jazz festival attendance rate and the popularity of the local jazz radio station. The information they provide is incomplete – the investors evaluating this application will not be able to see what percentage of the jazz festival attendants were locals. This data would help better showcase the size of Monroe's jazz market. If a great number of the attendants were local residents, the assumption of a big jazz fan base in Monroe would be validated. If the data should reveal a low percentage of local residents from the total number of festival participants, the claim of a large jazz fan base in Monroe would be weakened, which in turn will affect the expected profitability of the club. The group of developers brings another argument in favor of the popularity of jazz in Monroe, namely the ratings of the local jazz radio station. To verify if the rating of Jazz Nightly accurately reflects the popularity of jazz in Monroe, the developers would first need to report those ratings to the population of the town.

This data would help them identify whether a significant part of the Monroe population listens to jazz, in which case their claims would be substantiated or whether the radio listening people form just a small part of the population, in which case, the high radio ratings would not be indicative of the entire population's preferences.

When making their argument, the group of developers also assumes that a jazz club in Monroe will have the market all to itself because the nearest competitor is located at a great distance. To establish whether this is the case, the loan applicants would have to compare C-Note and their competitor based on their prices, accessibility, and reputation. By assessing what percentage of Monroe's jazz fan base frequents the club situated 65 miles away the investors can ascertain what part of the market already belongs to the competitor. In addition to this evidence, the developers should also provide data about the number of jazz venues in the area such as jazz cafés or bars before concluding that the market would belong solely to the C-Note club. If indeed there are no other competitors in the area, C-note can enjoy market monopoly and the assumption that the club will be profitable becomes more plausible. However, should different jazz venues exist in the area, the developers would need to adjust their estimations and consider what size of the market belongs to the competitors and develop competitive strategies to be able to make the desired profits.

Another argument brought in to support the profitability of opening a jazz club in Monroe is a national survey that indicates the amounts of money the average jazz fan is willing to spend on jazz entertainment each year. To assess how this information is related to the Monroe audience, the author would need to compare the survey demographics to those of the Monroe population. This data should be able to reveal whether the people of the survey are indicative for the jazz club's intended target audience, a fact which would make the survey findings applicable, or whether the two groups of people are radically different, in which case the survey would have no bearing on how the jazz fan base of Monroe would spend their money.

Additionally, the authors should investigate what percentage of that money is spent for clubbing activities. Should it become evident that jazz fans like to spend a lot on clubs then that information would bode well for the future of C-Note. However, if the jazz fans in the study prefer to spend their money on different types of jazz events and paraphernalia, the developers would need to provide additional data that would demonstrate that the people of Monroe would be willing to attend C-Note and develop good market and pricing strategies to bolster attendance.

All in all, the group of developers that argue for the profitability of opening a jazz club in Monroe stands a better chance of supporting their claim by providing a thorough market analysis coupled with a financial plan. They would stand a better chance at gaining a loan by providing a complete business plan and developing competitive strategies that would show that they can not only identify business opportunities but also know how to make the best of them.

Argument Task 6

....

The following appeared in a memorandum from the manager of WWAC radio station.

"To reverse a decline in listener numbers, our owners have decided that WWAC must change from its current rock-music format. The decline has occurred despite population growth in our listening area, but that growth has resulted mainly from people moving here after their retirement. We must make listeners of these new residents. We could switch to a music format tailored to their tastes, but a continuing decline in local sales of recorded music suggests limited interest in music. Instead we should change to a news and talk format, a form of radio that is increasingly popular in our area."

Write a response in which you discuss what specific evidence is needed to evaluate the argument and explain how the evidence would weaken or strengthen the argument.

....

NOTE: The above topic has wording similar to Argument Task 13 of this book. However, if you read carefully you will notice that the task instructions are different. Hence, it is very important to read the topic as well as its instructions completely before you start to write your response.

 ## Strategies

Argument:

This argument uses a decline in listener numbers as justification for changing the radio station's format.

In developing your response, you are asked to identify what specific evidence is needed to evaluate the strength of the argument and explain how the evidence supports or negates the argument.

Facts and Assumptions:

◆ The fact is that there has been a decline in listener numbers. This leads to the assumption that the station needs to revise its format. Which demographic has caused this decline? Is the decline sudden or has it happened over a period of years? Are other stations in the area experiencing a similar decline in listeners?

◆ Local sales of recorded music have declined causing the station owners to assume that there is limited interest in music. Why has the sale of record music declined? Does the local store maintain sufficient inventory that includes a wide variety of genres? Has a dip in the general economy of the area contributed to the lack of sales? Has the radio station surveyed the local population to determine what type of music, if any, it is interested in? Has the growth of MP3 players affected the sales of recorded music? Satellite radio has changed the way people listen to music.

◆ The decline in listener numbers has led the owners to assume that a news and talk format would attract new listeners. Have the owners conducted a survey to determine if this is the case? If other stations are using this format, is the market saturated?

◆ The station owners have assumed that, since the rock-music format has lost its popularity, no other music genre should take its place.

Your notes do not have to be exhaustive. As you begin to write your essay, your brain will generate new ideas. Make certain that you keep the directions in mind as you develop your ideas.

Sample Essay

The station manager has assumed that a decline in listener numbers should lead to a change in format at WWAC. This is an executive decision based on lack of concrete evidence. He or she must find out why listeners are abandoning the station before making any drastic changes that could further alienate listeners.

The station manager contradicts the impact of the population growth in the area. On one hand, he implies that population growth should create more listeners; but, on the other hand, he implies that because most of the new residents are retirees, he doesn't expect them to become fans of the current format anyway. Despite that, he wants to make listeners of them and feels that changing the format will do the trick. This could very well alienate the station's faithful listeners.

This manager associates the low sales of recorded music with a decline in his station's listeners. He further assumes that people have a limited interest in music overall. The popularity of MP3 players contradicts this assumption. One only has to walk down the halls of any high school or the streets of any city to observe this phenomenon. People are going about their daily routines with wires trailing from earbuds that keep them tuned in. The online music store, iTunes, is doing a brisk business, and one can preview and buy music from the comfort of home. Satellite radio has cornered a portion of the listeners, as well. New cars come equipped with satellite receivers, and satellite dishes attached to homes in every neighborhood bring every genre of music imaginable into homes across the country. Those satellite connections and cable television may deliver several stations devoted to news and talk shows.

Local brick-and-mortar radio stations now face many challenges. They, indeed, may have to make some format adjustments, not only to attract new listeners, but to keep the ones that they have. This manager should discover the demographic of the area. Does one particular culture dominate? Does a large portion of the population speak Spanish or French? Are there a number of devotees of opera or classical music? It could be that the station doesn't offer enough variety. Switching to a talk format would still make WWAC a one-note station. If the manager is basing his decision on the popularity of talk shows already being broadcast in the area, is he moving into a market that is already saturated? It certainly won't make WWAC stand out among its competitors.

WWAC's manager may need to revisit what has worked for the station in the past. When were its listener numbers the greatest? What was the station doing at that time? Was it running a promotion? Were listeners able to call in and make requests for special songs? When did listener numbers begin to decline? Has the decline been gradual or sudden? Are other stations experiencing the same phenomenon? At the very least, the station manager should conduct a survey of residents in the station's broadcast range to find out their ages, interests, and tastes in music. If he tunes his listeners out, they won't tune in to WWAC.

Argument Task 7

The following is a memorandum from the business manager of a television station.

"Over the past year, our late-night news program has devoted increased time to national news and less time to weather and local news. During this period, most of the complaints received from viewers were concerned with our station's coverage of weather and local news. In addition, local businesses that used to advertise during our late-night news program have cancelled their advertising contracts with us. Therefore, in order to attract more viewers to our news programs and to avoid losing any further advertising revenues, we should expand our coverage of weather and local news on all our news programs."

Write a response in which you examine the stated and/or unstated assumptions of the argument. Be sure to explain how the argument depends on these assumptions and what the implications are for the argument if the assumptions prove unwarranted.

NOTE: The above topic has wording similar to Argument Task 10 of this book. However, if you read carefully you will notice that the task instructions are different. Hence, it is very important to read the topic as well as its instructions completely before you start to write your response.

Strategies

Argument:

Based on a decline in listener numbers, the business manager of a television station has recommended expanding coverage of weather and local news on all of its news programs.

In developing your response, you must examine the stated and/or unstated assumptions of the argument and how the soundness of the argument relies on them.

Facts and Assumptions:

◆ Over the past year, the station has devoted increased time to national news and less time to weather and local news. The assumption is that the station was responding to viewer demand. An additional assumption might be that it's easier to hook up to a national news feed than to produce a local news broadcast.

◆ During that time, customers complained about the station's coverage of weather and local news. Based on the previous statement, one might assume that customers want more coverage. However, customers may be unhappy with the time slot devoted to local news. Customers may simply not like the newscasters. They also may be complaining about lack of accuracy in the weather forecast. Most of the complaints are about news and weather. What are the other complaints?

◆ Local businesses have cancelled advertising contracts for the late-night news broadcast. It would be easy to assume that advertisers are expressing their displeasure with the late-night news show. On the other hand, they may have shifted their advertising dollars to other time slots. They may have had to make some economic decisions about advertising dollars.

◆ Expanding local news and weather on all of the station's news programs will prevent the loss of further advertising revenues. The business manager may be incorrectly assuming that this is the only point of dissatisfaction with the station.

Your notes do not have to be exhaustive. As you begin to write your essay, your brain will generate new ideas. Make certain that you keep the directions in mind as you develop your ideas.

Sample Essay

Television is facing stiffer competition than ever before in its history. New cable stations are popping up seemingly every day. In consequence, businesses are faced with deciding how to spend their advertising dollars. Do they maintain their focus on local stations or spread the money around on the cable networks that their customers also watch? The manager of the local television station is under the illusion that complaints about local news and weather coverage are his only problem; maintaining this illusion could lead him to make some fatal decisions.

Attracting more viewers may attract more advertising dollars. However, the assumption that increasing weather and local news coverage is the means to attract these viewers may be erroneous. Has the business manager spoken with his advertisers to find out why they cancelled their contracts? They could be looking for a better price or desire exclusivity in their time slot. The advertisers may not like the sound or graphics the station uses in their ads. There are many other potential reasons why these contracts were cancelled that have little to do with the station's approach to news coverage.

A second assumption arises from viewer complaints. Since most of the complaints are about weather and the local news coverage, the manager has decided to increase coverage of both on all of the station's news shows. The viewers might dislike the newscasters or desire more accuracy in the weather report. The television might be in the middle of farm country where accurate and frequent weather reports have a significant impact on planting and harvesting schedules. The business manager needs more details about the full nature of viewers' complaints. Those viewers may not be concerned about the amount of news coverage but by the content. They might appreciate more human-interest stories or segments about health or high school sports. The business manager's thinking may be too narrow in scope. The economy of the area may be experiencing a downturn. Advertisers' cancelling contracts may have nothing to do with programming and everything to do with their own bottom lines. Has the station manager considered discounting the advertising rates in an effort to entice the deserters to return? The economy may be contributing to the number of viewer complaints. More residents may be unemployed and watching more television. As a result, they are more aware of what is happening on their local television station.

The business manager might mistakenly assume that he can do anything to remedy the situation he finds himself in. The network that the station broadcasts may have an unpopular lineup of shows, and stations affiliated with that network around the county are in the same position. This is beyond the business manager's control unless he can convince the owners to apply to another major network.

Argument Task 8

The following appeared in a memorandum from the owner of Movies Galore, a chain of movie-rental stores.

"Because of declining profits, we must reduce operating expenses at Movies Galore's ten movie-rental stores. Raising prices is not a good option, since we are famous for our low prices. Instead, we should reduce our operating hours. Last month our store in downtown Marston reduced its hours by closing at 6:00 p.m. rather than 9:00 p.m. and reduced its overall inventory by no longer stocking any DVD released more than five years ago. Since we have received very few customer complaints about these new policies, we should now adopt them at all other Movies Galore stores as our best strategies for improving profits."

Write a response in which you discuss what specific evidence is needed to evaluate the argument and explain how the evidence would weaken or strengthen the argument.

 Strategies

A good place to start your analysis is by creating a statement that reveals the main idea of the argument. Although the writer is creating an argument, he may ultimately be stating a position, making a recommendation, or making a prediction. It may be helpful for you to determine which of these formats is most evident in the argument.

The owner of Movies Galore predicts that cost-saving measures taken at the downtown Marston location will prove successful in his other stores and sees reducing hours as preferable to increasing their famously low prices.

Assumptions:

◆ Reducing operating expenses will increase profits.

◆ Raising prices will have a negative effect on Movie Galore's reputation.

◆ What has worked for the downtown Marston store will work in the other locations.

◆ Measures taken in the downtown Marston store have increased profits.

◆ Customers have adapted to the changes in the downtown store.

◆ Customers choose Movies Galore because of its low price.

◆ The owner can make changes that will affect the stores' profitability.

Evidence needed to evaluate the argument:

◆ How other operating expenses have increased or decreased in the years that Movies Galore has been in operation?

◆ How Movie Galore's prices compare to those of other similar businesses?

◆ Why do people shop at Movies Galore?

◆ How the changes at the downtown Marston store have affected its profitability?

◆ Customer count before and after the changes in the downtown Marston store.

◆ What times of the day are busiest?

◆ How services such as Netflix or Red Box and the availability of cable or satellite stations affect movies Galore?

After completing these steps, you should have enough material to write your analysis. Remember that you are not creating a position of your own; you are evaluating the strengths and weaknesses of the existing argument. You do not have to include all of the points that you have created in your prewriting. In fact, during the process of drafting your analysis, other ideas may come to mind, and if they strengthen your analysis, you should include them.

 ## Sample Essay

Declining profits are a concern for any business, and Movies Galore is no exception. The owner of this chain of stores has taken some steps in the downtown Marston location that he believes should be applied at the other locations to reduce expenses and increase profits. Before rushing to judgment, this owner should evaluate several factors. Without sufficient evidence, he or she may make a fatal mistake.

It may be that the type of inventory and length of the business day contribute to the lack of profitability, but other operating expenses must not be overlooked. The owner must examine fixed expenses such as utilities, insurance, rent, and contributions to retirement accounts and compare the cost of each to their cost in previous years. Fixed expenses may have increased. A business owner is powerless when it comes to electricity rates or the cost of heating fuel. He or she should also consider any unexpected, one-time cash outlays that have affected the bottom line. One of the stores may have needed a new heating system or a new roof. Perhaps the stores needed to build ramps to comply with the Americans with Disabilities Act. Without a comprehensive financial picture, the owner may make changes that could lead to further financial decline for Movies Galore.

The owner assumes that Movies Galore's low prices are a big draw for the business. That may be true, but it is just as likely that the convenient hours of operation make his business popular. It should be simple to determine which hours of operation are the busiest in each location. The downtown location in Marston may thrive by closing at six, but mall or suburban locations may benefit from staying open later. Keeping low prices and cutting back hours may be counterproductive. How do his prices compare with those of his competitors? He may be able to raise his prices and keep them lower than theirs. Without operating hours that are convenient for each location, this business may see a decline in patronage. In some cases, he may be able to open later rather than close earlier. In addition, the owner has changed the stores' inventory by eliminating DVDs that were released more than five years ago. Chances are that those older DVDs cost less to purchase than new releases, enabling the owner to charge less for them. In some of the chain's locations, older movies may be very popular, and, by eliminating them, the stores could lose customers.

There are several reasons for the owner of Movies Galore to re-evaluate his decision to limit stocked films and store hours. While a change in the company's business model may be needed, this change should reflect the needs and desires of the local customers. By disregarding these needs, the owner risks sending his company into further financial ruin.

8

Argument Task 9

The following was written as a part of an application for a small-business loan by a group of developers in the city of Monroe.

"A jazz music club in Monroe would be a tremendously profitable enterprise. Currently, the nearest jazz club is 65 miles away; thus, the proposed new jazz club in Monroe, the C-Note, would have the local market all to itself. Plus, jazz is extremely popular in Monroe: over 100,000 people attended Monroe's annual jazz festival last summer; several well-known jazz musicians live in Monroe; and the highest-rated radio program in Monroe is 'Jazz Nightly,' which airs every weeknight at 7 P.M. Finally, a nationwide study indicates that the typical jazz fan spends close to $1,000 per year on jazz entertainment."

Write a response in which you discuss what specific evidence is needed to evaluate the argument and explain how the evidence would weaken or strengthen the argument.

NOTE: The above topic has wording similar to Argument Task 5 of this book. However, if you read carefully you will notice that the task instructions are different. Hence, it is very important to read the topic as well as its instructions completely before you start to write your response.

 Strategies

Regardless of the approach you take, consider the following steps:

◆ Is there an alternative explanation for the events in question that can invalidate, either in whole or in part, the explanation given in the passage?

◆ How can I break the argument into its component parts to understand how they create the whole argument?

◆ Can I identify the line of reasoning used to create the argument?

◆ What does the author of the argument assume to be true for the argument to be true?

◆ Does the line of reasoning validate the conclusion?

◆ Can I imagine an example that refutes any or several of the statements in the argument?

◆ Am I able to evaluate the argument based on the quality of the facts and reasons presented in it?

Based on your responses to all or some of these questions, you must present a well-developed evaluation of the argument. You should take brief notes when you identify the argument's claims, assumptions, and conclusion. Jot down as many alternative explanations as you can along with additional evidence that might support or refute the claims in the argument. Finally, list the changes in the argument that would make the reasoning more solid. It is more important to be specific than it is to have a long list of evidence and examples.

This argument uses facts, figures, and anecdotal evidence to obtain a loan for the purpose of establishing a jazz music club in Monroe.

In developing your response, you are asked to identify what specific evidence is needed to evaluate the argument and explain how that evidence would weaken or strengthen the argument.

What conclusions and assumptions are either explicit or implied in the original argument?

Facts and Assumptions:

◆ Over 100,000 people attended Monroe's annual jazz festival last summer. This fact leads to the assumption that at least as many people will attend the next festival in Monroe. This assumption underlies the claim that jazz is extremely popular in Monroe. The weather for last summer's jazz festival may have been perfect. There is no way to guarantee the conditions and, therefore, the attendance will remain the same every year. There may have been no competing events occurring at the same time.

◆ The typical jazz fan spends close to $1000 per year on jazz entertainment. This fact leads to the assumption that jazz fans will spend a portion of that money in Monroe. $1000 is a nationwide average. How much do the local residents spend on jazz entertainment?

◆ Because the nearest jazz club is 65 miles away, the C-Note would have the local market all to itself. This assumption underlies the claim that a jazz music club in Monroe would be tremendously profitable. Local citizens may travel to other jazz clubs for weekend getaways or to hear musicians not featured at the local club. How large is the local market? The town that is 65 miles away may have other amenities that draw jazz patrons: great restaurants, ease of parking, shopping, motels

◆ "Jazz Nightly", airing on the local radio station at 7:00 P.M., is the highest-rated show in Monroe. This fact leads to the assumption that most people in Monroe listen to jazz. This assumption underlies the claim that jazz is extremely popular in Monroe. Missing is information about the radio station's lineup of programs. A local station could have limited hours on the air, and the other programs may have little or no appeal to the local citizens. We also don't know how long the program lasts. If it runs until 10:00 P.M., it leaves little else for people to listen to. People may listen to other stations during the other hours of the day and tune in to the local station only during the jazz music show.

◆ Several well-known jazz musicians live in Monroe. The word several is open to interpretation. The implication is that these musicians will be happy to perform at the new club. These might be retired musicians; perhaps they live in a nursing home.

Your notes do not have to be exhaustive. As you begin to write your essay, your brain will generate new ideas. Make certain that you keep the directions in mind as you develop your ideas. Use as many or as few paragraphs as you consider appropriate for your argument, but create a new paragraph when you move on to a new idea or example of support for your position. The GRE readers are not looking for a specific number of ideas or paragraphs. Instead, they are reading to determine the level of understanding of the topic and the complexity with which you respond.

You are free to organize and develop your response in any way you think will enable you to effectively communicate your evaluation of the argument. You may recall writing strategies you learned in high school or a writing-intensive course you took in college, but it is not necessary to employ any of those strategies. It is important that your ideas follow a logical progression and display strong critical thinking

 ## Sample Essay

On the surface, the argument for developing a jazz music club in Monroe appears to be compelling. Monroe seems to have all of the requirements – location, musicians, and fan base – to make the club a success. Some of the information, however, is either insufficient or suspect. Investors should take a closer look at the information to determine its validity before deciding that the club is a good idea for Monroe.

In real estate, there are three factors to consider: location, location, and location. Because the nearest jazz music club is sixty-five miles away, Monroe seems to have the location all locked up. On the other hand, there may be amenities in the distant town that make it attractive enough to drive there for jazz performances. Perhaps it has great restaurants, shopping centers, and hotels that make it perfect for a weekend getaway. Have the developers selected a site in Monroe for the club? Will it interfere with other businesses or disturb nearby residents?

The fact that over 100,000 fans attended last year's jazz festival in Monroe is important if that is a figure that has been repeated over a number of years. If it were Monroe's first festival, the novelty may have been a draw. The weather may have been perfect as well. If there were no other jazz related events occurring during that time, Monroe's festival may have benefited from that. The weather and paucity of other entertainment likely won't hold true every year. If other towns are aware of the success that Monroe experienced, they could schedule competing events. Was the jazz music festival a profitable event for the town? The costs associated with hosting such an event may not have been recouped, despite the high attendance. The argument fails to mention whether those fans in Monroe had a satisfactory experience at the jazz festival. A survey that asks for information about the quality of performances, the ease of obtaining accommodations, the price of tickets, the variety of vendors, and the likelihood of returning next year would create a better basis for promoting the jazz music club. Unless those 100,000 people are residents of Monroe, continuous support for a club is likely to come from a much smaller number of people.

On a positive note, Monroe has what appears to be a strong fan base for jazz musicians. Several well-known jazz musicians live there, and the local radio station's jazz-based program is its most highly-rated broadcast. Because jazz musicians reside in Monroe is no guarantee of the club's success. Perhaps those musicians choose to live in Monroe to escape the pressure to perform and could, ultimately, resent the establishment of a club. They may be retired or living in a nursing home. The radio station could have limited hours of operation or air other shows for which there is no audience in Monroe. The broadcast of "Jazz Nightly" begins at 7:00 P.M., but it may air for the rest of the evening, leaving no opening for other types of music to go over the airways to the citizens of Monroe.

Finally, the fact about the spending habits of jazz music fans is misleading. The figure is based on a nation-wide survey. How many jazz fans are there in the country? How many of Monroe's citizens are jazz fans? A small portion, if any, of the $1000 will likely be spent in Monroe. A more realistic dollar amount could be discovered by surveying the local jazz fans.

Altogether there is too little specific information about the jazz climate in Monroe for the argument to carry sufficient weight with the bankers. The developers must do more research that is specific to Monroe to create a business plan that will make their proposal more realistic and have wider appeal to the investors.

Argument Task 10

....

10

The following is a memorandum from the business manager of a television station.

"Over the past year, our late-night news program has devoted increased time to national news and less time to weather and local news. During this time period, most of the complaints received from viewers were concerned with our station's coverage of weather and local news. In addition, local businesses that used to advertise during our late-night news program have just cancelled their advertising contracts with us. Therefore, in order to attract more viewers to the program and to avoid losing any further advertising revenues, we should restore the time devoted to weather and local news to its former level."

Write a response in which you discuss what specific evidence is needed to evaluate the argument and explain how the evidence would weaken or strengthen the argument

....

NOTE: The above topic has wording similar to Argument Task 7 of this book. However, if you read carefully you will notice that the task instructions are different. Hence, it is very important to read the topic as well as its instructions completely before you start to write your response.

 Strategies

The first step in performing your analysis consists of creating a statement that summarizes the text by including the central claim and its supporting arguments.

The business manager of a television station is arguing for reverting to the predominantly local weather and news coverage in a bid to increase viewer ratings and prevent further loss of funds from advertising cancellation.

When considering the evidence that is necessary to support the arguments outlined in the text, it is important to keep in mind that arguments are based on assumptions – points that are taken to be true, without the need for proof. This is what you need to look for: explicit and implicit assumptions, since they require evidence that is not already listed in the text. Explicit assumptions can be broken down into or supported by implicit assumptions

Assumptions:

Explicit Assumptions	Implicit Assumptions
Complaints about national weather and news coverage indicate a desire for more local programs	• The complaints are related to the national character of the weather and news coverage • Local coverage receiver less or no complaints • Complaints are linked to viewer ratings • The complaints are representative for the entire audience of the late-night news program
Advertising cancellations are due to the increase in time devoted to national news	• Add cancellations is not due to external circumstances • The rate of cancellations has increased • Local as opposed to national coverage has an impact on the local companies' business
Viewer ratings will increase by reverting to predominantly local news coverage	• Local coverage had higher viewer ratings than national coverage • The viewer's desires for local coverage are not met elsewhere • Late night news market has the potential for growth
Reverting to local news will prevent other businesses from cancelling their advertising contracts	• Local businesses would welcome the change • Businesses that have current ad contracts would not have other reasons for cancelling • The area will continue to be economically stable

Evidence:

◆ Precise nature of the complaints

◆ Comparison of the number of complaints received during local and national coverage

◆ Number of complaints throughout the years reported to the total number of late-night news viewers

◆ Comparison of the number of complaints received per type of program throughout the years

◆ Comparison of ad viewer ratings during national and local coverage

◆ Comparison of economic health of the region during local and national coverage

◆ Compare advertisement investment numbers for local businesses during the local and national coverage

◆ Compare advertisement cancellation rates during national and local coverage

◆ Compare viewer rates for local and national coverage

◆ Correlate the number of competitor programs offering local weather and news coverage with the size of the potential market

◆ Global viewer ratings for late night news programs in the area

◆ Profit and loss analysis of the local businesses currently under contract

◆ Survey or interviews with the local business owners currently under contract on how they perceive the change to more local coverage

 ## Sample Essay

The business manager of a television station is arguing for reverting to the predominantly local weather and news coverage in a bid to increase viewer ratings and prevent further loss of funds from advertising cancellations. Before implementing the manager's suggestions, the television station's board of directors needs to consider additional information. Undertaking such a change without careful consideration can run the risk of adopting costly yet ultimately unnecessary measures.

The manager's suggestions are based on the assumption that advertising cancellations are due to the increase in time devoted to national news and reverting to local news will prevent other businesses from cancelling their current contracts. A key bit of information needed to assess this claim is related to previous cancellations rates. The manager should compare advertisement cancellation rates during both national and local coverage. This evidence would help in establishing if the cancellations are a new phenomenon, in which case, it is possible that the national character of the news is responsible, or if cancellations are a regularly occurring phenomenon; as such, changing the nature of the late-night news coverage would have little to no effect. The manager should also analyze whether there were any other external factors that could have been responsible for the local businesses' decision to terminate their advertising contracts. A comparison of the economic health of the region during local and national coverage would help illustrate whether there are any other causes for the advertisement cancellations. Should that be the case, switching to a predominantly local coverage would not have the desired effect of preventing other businesses from cancelling their contracts.

Another key bit of evidence to consider when analyzing the assumption that reverting to local news will prevent other businesses from cancelling their current contracts is a comparison of ad viewer ratings during local and national coverage. This evidence would help establish if the national or local character of the coverage has an impact on the local companies' business.

The second part of the manager's argument focuses on the audience and is based on the assumption that viewer ratings will increase by reverting to a predominantly local news coverage. To support this claim, the manager cites that the majority of the complaints received by the television station are related to the coverage of local weather and news. Before considering the validity of this claim, the board of directors should first look at the nature of the submitted complaints. Based on this data, should the nature of the complaints be directly related to the fact that the late-night news program has a national instead of a local coverage, then the business manager's suggestion of reverting to the old model has increased merit. However, if the complaints received about the national coverage are more related to the anchormen or format of the show than the fact that it presents national and not local information, then switching to predominantly local coverage will not necessarily bring an increase in viewership.

10

When arguing that complaints about national weather and news coverage indicate a desire for more local programs, the television station's business manager assumes that the complaints received are representative for the entire audience of the late-night news program. To support that claim, the author should look into what percentage of the total number of late night news viewers is represented by people who complained about the national coverage.

The business manager centers his recommendation for reverting to a predominantly local coverage on the idea that viewer ratings will increase, and businesses will no longer cancel their advertising contracts. By comparing the viewer rates for local and national coverage, the author can establish if the viewers prefer local weather and news coverage to the national alternative. If that is indeed the case, barring external factors that could have influenced the results, the evidence would serve to corroborate the manager's theory that viewer rates will be restored once the station adopts the proposed change. However, if the opposite proves to be true and viewer ratings are higher during national rather than local coverage, then the manager's proposal runs the high risk of driving audiences away rather than increasing their ratings.

There is also the possibility that even if the population prefers local news, the market is saturated. To assess market readiness and availability, the television station's manager should correlate the number of competitor programs offering local weather and news coverage with the size of the potential market. Having the majority of the market cornered by competing local coverage programs would make the goal of increasing ratings significantly harder to reach. However, should the market be mostly free, then the manager's suggestion would have a great chance of being even more successful than expected.

All in all, when making such a potentially costly decision it is essential to thoroughly investigate the benefits and devise strategies that limit the risks. The television station manager needs to provide an accurate assessment of the market situation and conduct in depth research on the target audience, lest he run the risk of making a decision that would bring loss to the station.

Argument Task 11

The following appeared as part of a business plan developed by the manager of the Rialto Movie Theater.

"Despite its downtown location, the Rialto Movie Theater, a local institution for five decades, must make big changes or close its doors forever. It should follow the example of the new Apex Theater in the mall outside of town. When the Apex opened last year, it featured a video arcade, plush carpeting and seats, and a state-of-the-art sound system. Furthermore, in a recent survey, over 85 percent of respondents reported that the high price of newly released movies prevents them from going to the movies more than five times per year. Thus, if the Rialto intends to hold on to its share of a decreasing pool of moviegoers, it must offer the same features as Apex."

Write a response in which you discuss what questions would need to be answered in order to decide whether the recommendation is likely to have the predicted result. Be sure to explain how the answers to these questions would help to evaluate the recommendation.

 Strategies

A good place to start your analysis is by creating a statement that reveals the main idea of the argument. Although the writer is creating an argument, he may ultimately be stating a position, making a recommendation, or making a prediction. It may be helpful for you to determine which of these formats is most evident in the argument.

In an effort to increase profits and prevent the closing of the Rialto Theater, the manager recommends that the business take the same steps that the Apex took when it opened last year.

Assumptions:

◆ What works in a mall location will work in a downtown location.

◆ The Apex Theater is profitable.

◆ People went to movies more frequently when the prices were lower.

◆ Fewer people go to the movies now than in the past.

◆ The downtown location has always contributed to the Rialto's success.

Arts

Questions:

- ◆ Who responded to the survey, and how large was the sample?

- ◆ How profitable is the Apex?

- ◆ What types of movies are shown at each theater?

- ◆ Has attendance at the Rialto declined?

- ◆ What other factors may be contributing to the Rialto's predicted closing?

- ◆ Has the parking situation changed in the downtown area?

- ◆ Have businesses that used to attract people to the downtown closed or moved to the mall?

After completing these steps, you should have enough material to write your analysis. Remember that you are not creating a position of your own; you are evaluating the strengths and weaknesses of the existing argument. You do not have to include all of the points that you have created in your prewriting. In fact, during the process of drafting your analysis, other ideas may come to mind, and, if they strengthen your analysis, you should include them.

 Sample Essay

A good business plan depends on sufficient detailed information. Its creator must have answers to a number of questions to prove the reliability of the plan. The purpose of a business plan is generally to obtain funding, in this case to make significant changes to the Rialto Movie Theater. Before a bank or other investors open their checkbooks, the manager must answer questions about the Rialto's situation rather than provide general information about the competition.

The manager cites a survey about the cost of attending new releases and how it discourages movie goers from seeing more than five of them per year. Before making expensive changes based on this survey, the manager should ask who responded to the survey. The sample may be limited to a specific age group, for example. If the respondents were young families or senior citizens, they would have less discretionary income than some other age groups. Regardless of who completed the survey, if money prevents them from attending, adding attractions or improving the interior of the theater won't make them attend the movies more frequently. In fact, movie attendees' spending money on other attractions at the theater like a video arcade may reduce the amount that they can spend to actually purchase tickets to the show. It's always important to know who requested the survey and for what purpose. Missing from the survey is information about the types of movies the respondents prefer: what times of the year and days of the week they choose to attend movies. This information could help the Rialto tailor its movie selection and on which days to open and the number of times to show a film each day.

This business plan does not mention attendance numbers. Has attendance at the Rialto declined, or have other events led to the dire prediction of the theater's closing? Other than a decline in attendance, a rise in expenses can contribute to lower profits. Steady attendance at traditional prices means little if other costs of operation have increased. The cost of heating and/or cooling may be higher than last year. The same number of ticket buyers at the same prices as last year cannot support any unexpected expenses.

It appears that the downtown location has served the Rialto well for several decades. Has the downtown undergone some changes? Unfortunately, downtowns across the country have faced many challenges from mall development and big box stores. Independently-owned small businesses have been forced to close or move to the malls where traffic is heavier. Without business to drive citizens to the downtown, the Rialto may be unable to attract crowds large enough to make it profitable. Another possibility is that a large business of some type, a call center, for example, may have filled the empty buildings in the downtown. Operating 24 hours a day, the center's employees may be using parking lots or spaces that movie goers previously used. Without sufficient parking, the Rialto cannot hope to fill its seats.

Although the argument reveals the added attractions at the Apex, it does not reveal whether or not the Apex is profitable. Despite the video arcade, plush seats and state-of-the-art sound system, the Apex's expenses may make it unprofitable. It would be helpful to know if the video arcade contributes to the bottom line in a significant way or if people's patronizing the arcade has a negative effect on theater attendance.

Making big changes will require the Rialto to spend big bucks. Before going to that extreme, the Rialto must analyze all the results of the survey and how conditions in the downtown have changed in recent years. If there are insurmountable obstacles, the manager's recommendation may prove fruitless.

Argument Task 12

The following appeared on the Mozart School of Music Website.

"The Mozart School of Music should be the first choice for parents considering enrolling their child in music lessons. First of all, the Mozart School welcomes youngsters at all ability and age levels; there is no audition to attend the school. Second, the school offers instruction in nearly all musical instruments as well a wide range of styles and genres from classical to rock. Third, the faculty includes some of the most distinguished musicians in the area. Finally, many Mozart graduates have gone on to become well-known and highly paid professional musicians."

Write a response in which you examine the stated and/or unstated assumptions of the argument. Be sure to explain how the argument depends on these assumptions and what the implications are for the argument if the assumptions prove unwarranted.

Strategies

A good place to start your analysis is by creating a statement that reveals the main idea of the argument. Although the writer is creating an argument, he may ultimately be stating a position, making a recommendation, or making a prediction. It may be helpful for you to determine which of these formats is most evident in the argument.

The author of this website uses several claims about the Mozart School of Music to support the recommendation that parents choose the school for their children's music education.

Assumptions:

◆ Mozart School of Music is the best place for anyone who wants to learn to play a musical instrument.

◆ Students who attend Mozart are more likely to become successful musicians.

◆ Distinguished musicians are effective teachers.

◆ Other schools require an audition as part of the application process.

◆ Auditions are undesirable.

◆ Distinguished musicians teach at all ability levels.

◆ Mozart School of Music is affordable.

◆ The school has convenient hours of operation.

◆ All who apply will be accepted.

Alternative explanations:

◆ Mozart may be the only music school.

◆ Distinguished musicians are ineffective teachers.

◆ Distinguished musicians teach only advanced students.

After completing these steps, you should have enough material to write your analysis. Remember that you are not creating a position of your own; you are evaluating the strengths and weaknesses of the existing argument. You do not have to include all of the points that you have created in your prewriting. In fact, during the process of drafting your analysis, other ideas may come to mind, and if they strengthen your analysis, you should include them.

 ## Sample Essay

Of course, the owner of a business website is not going to include information that would discourage viewers from buying its product or service. The Mozart School of Music is no exception. In an effort to boost enrollment, the school cites some appealing facts that should lead those seeking music lessons for their children to assume Mozart School of Music can meet all of their needs. Visitors to the site may rely on incorrect assumptions when choosing the Mozart School of Music.

Based on the claims listed, parents may assume that their child will be in a class or lesson taught by a local, distinguished musician. The fact of the matter may be that distinguished musicians make up a small percentage of the total teaching staff, or they teach only advanced students. Those distinguished musicians may all be piano teachers, so anyone seeking to play the flute, saxophone, drums, etc. will not have one of these musicians as an instructor. These musicians may also be restricted to one style of music. If they are all jazz aficionados, children seeking to learn classical music will be in classes taught by less distinguished musicians. There is no guarantee that these musicians are effective instructors. They may have little patience for the stumbling, tentative attempts at music that young children are likely to display. Parents and/or students may demand to be placed with one of those distinguished musicians and go elsewhere if their demands aren't met. The website fails to reveal the qualifications of its instructors who are not distinguished musicians. Potential students need to know what kind of education and experience all of Mozart's instructors have.

No mention is made on the website about hours of operation, convenience of location, or the cost of lessons. Since children are in school all day, and most parents work, those seeking lessons may assume that the Mozart School of Music will accommodate families by offering lessons after school, in the evenings, and on weekends. Location is important. If the school is located in an out-of-the-way place or in an area that lacks parking, many potential students may not be able to get there. Parents may assume that the lessons are reasonably priced, or they may conclude, based on the information, that the lessons are too pricey. Parents should also ask if lessons with one of the distinguished musicians on staff cost more than lessons with other instructors. One might also ask if the school provides instruments, either for rent or sale and their cost. Lesson materials are another expense that prospective students will need to consider.

Parents may assume that all who apply to the Mozart School of Music will be accepted, since auditions are not required. This assumption may be unrealistic as the school is not likely to have unlimited space. It is also difficult to imagine how they place students in a class or individual lessons without an audition to determine their level of accomplishment. Parents and their children may be leery of a school that does not allow them to show what they know before being placed with an instructor. It smacks of desperation that the school accepts everyone who applies or can pay. Visitors to the website may assume that the school is neither very successful nor discriminating.

Mozart School of Music's claim of superiority may lead visitors to the site to assume there are several other schools that are inferior. Mozart, in fact, may be the only school. Conversely, it may be facing stiff competition from several other music schools, compelling its directors to make it sound attractive and emphasize the ease with which students are accepted. The fact that many of Mozart's graduates have gone on to become highly-paid professionals may actually deter some students from choosing this school. They may assume that the school applies pressure for its students to excel. This could intimidate students who want to learn to play an instrument for personal pleasure.

Parents of children who want music lessons should carefully examine the assumptions they might make after visiting Mozart School of Music's website. Without sufficient evidence, they could enroll their children in a school where distinguished musicians do little besides instruct the most superior students and whose cost and hours of operation make it an inconvenient choice.

12

Argument Task 13

The following appeared in a memorandum from the manager of WWAC radio station.

"WWAC must change from its current rock-music format because the number of listeners has been declining, even though the population in our listening area has been growing. The population growth has resulted mainly from people moving to our area after their retirement, and we must make listeners of these new residents. But they seem to have limited interest in music: several local stores selling recorded music have recently closed. Therefore, just changing to another kind of music is not going to increase our audience. Instead, we should adopt a news-and-talk format, a form of radio that is increasingly popular in our area."

13 Write a response in which you discuss what questions would need to be answered in order to decide whether the recommendation and the argument on which it is based are reasonable. Be sure to explain how the answers to these questions would help to evaluate the recommendation.

NOTE: The above topic has wording similar to Argument Task 6 of this book. However, if you read carefully you will notice that the task instructions are different. Hence, it is very important to read the topic as well as its instructions completely before you start to write your response.

 Strategies

A good place to start your analysis is by creating a statement that reveals the main idea of the argument. Although the writer is creating an argument, he may ultimately be stating a position, making a recommendation, or making a prediction. It may be helpful for you to determine which of these formats is most evident in the argument.

WWAC's station manager has tied a reduction in its listeners to the closings of local music stores and associates that with a lack of interest in music in general, leading to his recommendation to change the format of the station to news and talk shows.

Assumptions:

◆ The new residents have little interest in music.

◆ Stores have closed because the new residents have little interest in music.

◆ Changing its format will allow WWAC to attract more listeners.

◆ WWAC will be able to attract listeners from other news-and-talk format stations in the area.

◆ People in the area no longer listen to rock music.

◆ Retirees prefer news and talk shows.

Questions:

◆ Has WWAC made changes in its hours of operation that might account for a decline in listeners?

◆ Has another radio station gone on-air in the area, providing competition for WWAC?

◆ How much more popular is the talk-show format than it used to be?

◆ Do the rock music shows air when they can attract large audiences?

◆ Are news-and-talk shows popular with retirees?

◆ Has WWAC hired new on-air talent?

After completing these steps, you should have enough material to write your analysis. Remember that you are not creating a position of your own; you are evaluating the strengths and weaknesses of the existing argument. You do not have to include all of the points that you have created in your prewriting. In fact, during the process of drafting your analysis, other ideas may come to mind, and if they strengthen your analysis, you should include them.

 ## Sample Essay

News and talk shows have become pervasive on the radio and television airways over the past few decades. At virtually any time of day, one can tune in to a talk show either on radio or television. The number of stations focusing exclusively on news in each medium has also exploded. The advent of cable television, the Internet, and satellite radio puts news and talk at everybody's fingertips 24/7/365. The assumption that switching to this format based on the brief and vague information in the argument needs further verification before taking this drastic action.

Tying the closing of music stores to the apparent lack of interest in music may be a faulty assumption. Other explanations might be as valid. The proliferation of music competition shows on television and the longevity of these programs demonstrates a continued interest in music by people of all ages. If viewing audiences decline, advertisers may pull their sponsorship of these shows, and they will be off the air in short order. People are listening to music in different ways today. No longer does a jazz aficionado place an LP on a turntable; he downloads his favorite tunes from iTunes onto his iPod nano, plugs in his ear buds, and goes out for a run. Music of all genres is more accessible than it has ever been. If people didn't buy it, record companies would not produce it.

Brick-and-mortar music stores have not fared well in the twenty-first century but not as a result of declining interest in music.

Assuming that WWAC can make listeners of the retirees that have moved to the area by switching formats may be an exercise in futility. It is likely that many of them are living on fixed incomes and have little discretionary income to spend on entertainment. They might watch a lot of television and spend minimal time listening to the radio. This lack of spending money may contribute to the supposed lack of interest in music. They cannot afford to buy albums. On the other hand, they may have purchased all of the music they need before retiring. They either don't need or want to accumulate more possessions of any kind.

More people listen to the radio during drive time - the periods spent driving to and from work- than any other time of day. The assumption that retirees should be WWAC's target audience could eliminate a large number of listeners. Perhaps, WWAC should focus their appeal to those who work every day. Those commuters may prefer music of any genre to news reports that can be disturbing or talk shows that can be strident.

13 Just as they develop shopping habits, people develop listening habits. Attracting customers or listeners is generally a time-consuming and expensive proposition. Because there are already radio stations that have a news and talk-show format in the area, WWAC may have to go the extra mile to become successful in that market. The assumption that attracting new listeners is more cost effective than trying to maintain the listeners they already have could lead to unnecessary spending. They must offer shows that are different from and better than those already being aired. They will need to convince their sponsors that they can increase the number of listeners. If WWAC plans to use syndicated shows, the station will have to pay fees to the owners of those shows. Those listeners who currently tune in to hear rock music could abandon the station for another that plays rock. WWAC will not only need to attract new listeners, it will have to replace those it loses as a result of the change in format.

WWAC needs to conduct some market research before relying on the assumptions in the argument and abandoning its current format. A more varied mix of genres may help. Those retirees may, indeed, listen to the radio, but they prefer jazz or standards. The station may need to change its hours of operation. The local market may be saturated with talk and news shows. Without more detailed information, WWAC may make a decision that will lead to its going off the air.

Argument Task 14

The following appeared in an e-mail sent by the marketing director of the Classical Shakespeare Theatre of Bardville.

"Over the past ten years, there has been a 20 percent decline in the size of the average audience at Classical Shakespeare Theatre productions. In spite of increased advertising, we are attracting fewer and fewer people to our shows, causing our profits to decrease significantly. We must take action to attract new audience members. The best way to do so is by instituting a 'Shakespeare in the Park' program this summer. Two years ago the nearby Avon Repertory Company started a 'Free Plays in the Park' program, and its profits have increased 10 percent since then. If we start a 'Shakespeare in the Park' program, we can predict that our profits will increase, too."

Write a response in which you discuss what questions would need to be answered in order to decide whether the recommendation is likely to have the predicted result. Be sure to explain how the answers to these questions would help to evaluate the recommendation.

 Strategies

A good place to start your analysis is by creating a statement that reveals the main idea of the argument. Although the writer is creating an argument, he may ultimately be stating a position, making a recommendation, or making a prediction. It may be helpful for you to determine which of these formats is most evident in the argument.

The marketing director believes that imitating Avon Repertory Company's Free Plays in the Park program will increase attendance at Classical Shakespeare Theatre productions.

Assumptions:

◆ Profits are tied to attendance.

◆ The decline in attendance at Classical Shakespeare Theatre productions has occurred steadily over the past ten years.

◆ They are advertising in locations and publications that have worked for them in the past.

◆ Avon Repertory Company's profits have increased because of their Free Plays in the Park program.

Questions:

- ◆ Has Classical Shakespeare Theatre changed its repertoire?

- ◆ Should the company change its repertoire?

- ◆ Has the company changed the type of advertising it does?

- ◆ Has Avon Repertory Company taken other measures to increase profits?

- ◆ Does one particular year account for most of the decline?

- ◆ Do any particular plays draw larger audiences than others?

After completing these steps, you should have enough material to write your analysis. Remember that you are not creating a position of your own; you are evaluating the strengths and weaknesses of the existing argument. You do not have to include all of the points that you have created in your prewriting. In fact, during the process of drafting your analysis, other ideas may come to mind, and if they strengthen your analysis, you should include them.

 ## Sample Essay

Declining audience numbers is a legitimate concern for Classical Shakespeare Company. Efforts on the part of the company appear to have been ineffective, so they propose to duplicate the actions of Avon Repertory Company whose success appears to be on the rise. There is always danger associated with abandoning what one has always done. Change may be necessary, but the shape of that change must be carefully considered. One size does not always fit all. The marketing director needs answers to several questions before making the suggested changes.

An average is derived by adding a specific number of figures and dividing the total by that number. Some numbers are higher than the average, and some are lower. There may be a significant span between the highest and lowest numbers. Have some of Classical Shakespeare Theatre's productions had very poor attendance while others have standing-room-only attendance? This theater company may be able to solve attendance problems by discontinuing production of the plays that draw small audiences and increasing the number of performances of the plays that draw large audiences. The company may also benefit from changing the times of the performances. Are the largest reductions in attendance occurring consistently for performances on certain days of the work or specific times of the day? Changing days and times would be a relatively simple fix for the attendance problem. Avon Repertory Company may have been paying attention to these details and plays to full houses as a result.

Virtually all commercial enterprises use advertising to encourage the public to buy its product or use its service. Classical Shakespeare Company has used advertising in the past and has recently expanded its advertising in an effort to increase attendance at its productions. This tactic appears to have failed. Has the company changed the type of advertising it does or advertised in different publications? This theater company should research the reach of the advertising, perhaps by surveying their audience members. They may need to shift advertising dollars from print sources to radio or television. If the company has increased its television advertising, its ads may be appearing at times in the station's rotation when theater goers are not tuned in. If they are advertising upcoming productions that historically have had low attendance, they are likely to have wasted their money. The company may have changed advertising agencies, and the new agency has no experience creating ads for the entertainment industry.

Rather than look outside of the theater to improve attendance, the Classical Shakespeare Company might look at the condition of the theater itself. Has the company taken steps to ensure that the audience enjoys attending performances at its theater? The seats may be worn and uncomfortable. The heating and cooling system may work inefficiently. If the audience finds it difficult to sit in the seats, or they are too cold or too warm, they may abandon this company for another that has been renovated, making the theater experience more pleasurable. In fact, the condition of its theater may be the reason that Avon Repertory Company has increased profits rather than its Free Plays in the Park. Is the company's payroll too large? Employees are a big expense, and producing plays requires a variety of skilled workers in addition to the actors themselves. On-stage talent usually receive the biggest paychecks. This can be a double-edged sword. A theater company can hire better actors in an effort to draw bigger audiences, or it can hire lesser-known actors to reduce the overall payroll. If the payroll is smaller, the company's bottom line looks better. The risk is smaller audiences. Theater companies must strike a delicate balance when casting their productions.

A theater company experiencing financial uncertainty may only ensure its demise by taking on a project with no proven benefit. Before imitating Avon Repertory Company's Free Plays in the Park, the Classical Shakespeare Company should ask if that program directly contributes to Avon's increase in profits. Classical Shakespeare Company should scrutinize its past and current practices and answer some tough questions before adopting the suggestion in the argument.

Argument Task 15

The following was written as a part of an application for a small-business loan by a group of developers in the city of Monroe.

"Jazz music is extremely popular in the city of Monroe: over 100,000 people attended Monroe's annual jazz festival last summer, and the highest-rated radio program in Monroe is 'Jazz Nightly,' which airs every weeknight. Also, a number of well-known jazz musicians own homes in Monroe. Nevertheless, the nearest jazz club is over an hour away. Given the popularity of jazz in Monroe and a recent nationwide study indicating that the typical jazz fan spends close to $1,000 per year on jazz entertainment, a jazz music club in Monroe would be tremendously profitable."

Write a response in which you examine the stated and/or unstated assumptions of the argument. Be sure to explain how the argument depends on these assumptions and what the implications are for the argument if the assumptions prove unwarranted.

15

 Strategies

A good place to start your analysis is by creating a statement that reveals the main idea of the argument. Although the writer is creating an argument, he may ultimately be stating a position, making a recommendation, or making a prediction. It may be helpful for you to determine which of these formats is most evident in the argument.

Based on attendance at last year's jazz festival in Monroe and the average amount of money that jazz fans spend on entertainment each year, a group of developers propose to build a jazz club in Monroe which is home to several jazz musicians.

Assumptions:

◆ The attendance at the jazz festival indicates the genre's popularity in Monroe.

◆ The jazz festival draws large crowds every year.

◆ The jazz musicians perform regularly and would perform at a club in Monroe.

◆ Jazz fans will spend an average of $1000 per year at a jazz club in Monroe.

◆ Attendance at the jazz club will enable the owners to make a profit.

◆ There are enough jazz fans to support two jazz clubs an hour away from each other.

Alternative explanations:

- Last year's attendance at the jazz festival was much higher than normal.

- Jazz musicians prefer to live in a town different from the one(s) in which they perform.

- The jazz musicians in Monroe are retired.

- Monroe's jazz club will need popular artists to encourage fans to spend $1000 per year.

- A portion of the $1000 is spent on lodging and travelling rather than directly on jazz entertainment itself.

After completing these steps, you should have enough material to write your analysis. Remember that you are not creating a position of your own; you are evaluating the strengths and weaknesses of the existing argument. You do not have to include all of the points that you have created in your prewriting. In fact, during the process of drafting your analysis, other ideas may come to mind, and if they strengthen your analysis, you should include them.

Sample Essay

A group of developers has made some assumptions about conditions in Monroe that seem to favor opening a jazz club there. Any lending institution will want to test those assumptions before laying out a considerable sum of money to renovate an existing structure or build a new one for the purpose of entertainment. The developers will need to show that their assumptions are based on verifiable facts.

These developers first assume that the attendance at last year's jazz festival in Monroe proves the popularity of the genre in this geographic location. The basis of this assumption holds true only if 100,000 attendees is a typical total. A number of factors may have contributed to what appears to be a high number. The performers at last year's festival may have larger fan bases than groups in previous years. Unless the festival organizers can continue to attract popular jazz acts, the attendance may revert to lower numbers. The organizers may have offered special ticket prices last year in an effort to attract a larger audience. They may have to do the same this year or subsequent years to obtain high numbers of attendees. Other jazz festivals may have been cancelled or may have seen reduced attendance due to poor weather, leaving jazz fans hungry for entertainment, which they found in Monroe. The popularity of jazz in Monroe can be supported by the festival attendance only if a large portion of Monroe's population attended the festival. It may be held in Monroe because the town has a superior venue.

Revealing that a number of well-known jazz musicians live in Monroe leads to the assumption that they will perform at the jazz club. Upon further scrutiny, lenders might discover that those jazz musicians are either retired or booked for most of the year in other locations. These musicians may consider Monroe as a place to get away from it all and have no desire to perform in their hometown. Unless the developers can attract equally well-known and talented musicians to their club, they may find it difficult to be profitable.

Based on a survey revealing that the average jazz fan spends $1000 per year on jazz-related entertainment, the developers assume that jazz fans that live in or come to Monroe will also spend that amount every year. The truth about an average is that some fans spend more than $1000 per year and some spend less. The survey does not say that those fans spent that amount of money at jazz clubs. If the fans travel to visit clubs, a considerable portion of their spending could be for lodging, food, gas, or air fare. They may spend all or some of that money on recordings or music lessons. The Monroe club owners may have to provide a selection of jazz- related retail items to supplement the income from admission to the club.

The developers disclose that the closest jazz club is over an hour away to support the assumption that making jazz entertainment more convenient for the people in and around Monroe is a recipe for success. Before accepting this at face value, the lenders will need to know how many people live in the area. Monroe may be a small town, requiring the jazz club to draw attendees from a wide area. If traveling over an hour is an obstacle, the club in Monroe may suffer from a lack of nearby population. Regardless of distance, the other club may be very popular because of the quality of entertainment it offers, and the club in Monroe may not be able to equal its draw.

15

The lenders need more detailed information to prove or refute the assumptions inherent in the developers' argument. The risk inherent in any investment of this nature must be minimized before a bank or other investor opens its checkbook.

Argument Task 16

Woven baskets characterized by a particular distinctive pattern have previously been found only in the immediate vicinity of the prehistoric village of Palea and therefore were believed to have been made only by the Palean people. Recently, however, archaeologists discovered such a "Palean" basket in Lithos, an ancient village across the Brim River from Palea. The Brim River is very deep and broad, and so the ancient Paleans could have crossed it only by boat, and no Palean boats have been found. Thus it follows that the so-called Palean baskets were not uniquely Palean.

Write a response in which you discuss what specific evidence is needed to evaluate the argument and explain how the evidence would weaken or strengthen the argument.

 Strategies

The first step in performing your analysis consists of identifying the texts' key point, recommendation, prediction or hypothesis. All the other arguments and assumptions are designed to support this central claim. In this case, the author attempts to demonstrate that "Palean baskets were not uniquely Palean".

The next step would involve creating a statement that summarizes the text by including the central claim and its supporting arguments.

The author theorizes that the Palean baskets are no longer considered to be unique since a similar basket has been discovered in a different settlement that could only be reached by boat and the Paleans did not possess navigational means.

When considering the evidence that is necessary to support the arguments outlined in the text, it is important to keep in mind that arguments are based on assumptions – points that are taken to be true, without need for proof. This is what you need to look for – explicit and implicit assumptions, since they require evidence that is not already listed in the text. Explicit assumptions can be broken down into or supported by implicit assumptions.

Assumptions:

Explicit Assumptions	Implicit Assumptions
The basket found in Lithos was crafted there	• Lithos or the surrounding area has the raw materials necessary to make baskets • Lithos people have the woodworking skills required to make the baskets • The basket that was found in Lithos is made from raw materials that can be found in the area
The Brim River was broad and deep in the prehistoric period	• The prehistoric water levels of the Brim River were high • The prehistoric water levels of the Brim River were consistently high
Prehistoric deep river crossing could only be done by boat	• There were no other viable river crossing methods available at that time • From a geographical standpoint, Lithos could only be reached by crossing the river
Only Paleans could have transported the basket across the river	• Lithos is not a maritime community • Paleans did not trade with Lithos or any maritime communities • There are no other maritime communities in the area
Boat findings are a sufficient indicator of the presence or absence of a maritime culture	• The area's climate and geological history can preserve boat remains • There are no other sources that can indicate the existence of a maritime culture

Evidence:

◆ Historical or geological records indicating the presence of pliable or fibrous material in Lithos

◆ Weaving tool findings in Lithos

◆ The presence of artifacts crafted using similar woodworking techniques in Lithos

◆ Comparison of the Lithos basket materials with the raw materials available at the time in the area

◆ Geographical records of the prehistoric water levels of the Brim River (sedimentation, digital elevation etc.)

◆ Prehistoric rainfall records in the area

◆ River crossing methods available in the time period and area

◆ Geological map of the area in prehistoric times (cave systems, the river's paleo-shorelines)

◆ Boat findings in Lithos

◆ Historical records of the navigational means available in Lithos (written or oral history, carvings, cave paintings etc.)

◆ The presence of distinctively foreign artifacts in Palea belonging to settlements from across the river

◆ The number of Palean artifacts found in settlements from across the river

◆ Boat findings in the area

◆ Historical records of the navigational means available in the settlements in the area (written or oral history, carvings, cave paintings etc.)

◆ Comparison of the area's climate and geographical history with the conditions necessary for boat preservation

◆ Alternative historical sources related to the navigational means available in Palea

 ## Sample Essay

The author theorizes that the Palean baskets are no longer considered to be unique since a similar basket has been discovered in a different settlement that could only be reached by boat and the Paleans did not possess navigational means. More detailed information is necessary in order to be able to evaluate the truth of this claim.

The most compelling bit of evidence that is missing from the author's argument is related to the historical water levels of the Brim River. The writer assumes that since the Brim River is currently broad and deep the conditions must have been similar in the past. However, river levels fluctuate widely, and periods of drought can severely affect the breadth and depth of a river. In order to support his claim, the author should consider the geographical records of the prehistoric water levels of the Brim River and the prehistoric rainfall records in the area. Based on this data, should the Brim River prove to have been consistently high in the time period when the Palea village existed, it becomes less likely that the Palean style basket found in Lithos could have been carried across the river without the aid of a boat. Conversely, should the evidence show that the Brim River had low water levels in the prehistoric period, or the Palea region experienced periods of severe drought, then it becomes more likely that the Brim River could be crossed without a boat. In this case, the presence of a Palean basket in Lithos could be seen as evidence of trade rather than of Lithos developing a similar weaving style.

When making his case that the Palean basket was never transported across the river, the author assumes that deep river crossing is only possible with the aid of a boat. In order to be able to prove this claim, the author needs to look into what river crossing methods were available at the time and if there were any other geological possibilities of reaching Lithos, such as cave systems connecting the two banks of the river.

The next step in the author's argument relies on the assumption that only Paleans could have transported the basket across the river. In order to support this claim, the writer would need to show that neither Lithos nor any of the surrounding communities would have possessed the means of transporting the basket across the river. The most direct way to investigate this would involve looking at records of boat findings in Lithos or the surrounding area. Additional sources such as cave paintings, carvings or historical records depicting boats can also be used to determine whether the settlements in the area possessed a maritime culture. For instance, ancient Egypt, a civilization built on river trading, has many visual representations of boats and a history of nautical trading depicted in hieroglyphs. In the absence of boat findings or cultural evidence, trading records can also be used to demonstrate whether or not Palea had any contact with settlements from across the Brim River. Such trading evidence can come in the form of distinctively foreign artifacts in Palea belonging to settlements from across the river, or the other way around, Palean artifacts found in settlements from across the river. Should this evidence prove that it is possible that the basket found in Lithos is a result of trading, the main claim that the Palean baskets are not uniquely Palean would be severely weakened.

When arguing that the absence of boat findings in Palea shows that Paleans could not have transported the basket across the river, the author assumes that boat findings are a sufficient indicator of the presence or absence of a maritime culture. A comparison of the area's climate and geographical history with the conditions that are necessary for boat preservation would make it easier to state with certainty whether or not Paleans could cross the river.

Another assumption made by the author of the text is that the basket found in Lithos was crafted there. To assess the validity of this statement, the author should analyze whether or not the people of Lithos had the ability to produce the basket that was found there. He would first need to establish if the Lithos people had the necessary raw materials to produce the baskets. This can be accomplished by looking at historical or geological records indicating the presence of pliable or fibrous material in Lithos. This evidence would not be sufficient to either prove or disprove the claim. The author would further have to demonstrate that not just general weaving materials but also the specific materials required for the basket can be found in the area. However, the argument would still be incomplete without the data that demonstrates that the people of Lithos had the necessary skills to make the basket. Such evidence could be gained by examining records detailing the presence of weaving tools in Lithos or the presence of artifacts crafted using woodworking techniques similar to those required to make the basket.

All in all, additional evidence should make the author's claims harder to refute and help prevent him from drawing faulty conclusions based on inaccurate or incomplete data.

Chapter 11
Education

Argument Task 17

The following memo appeared in the newsletter of the West Meria Public Health Council.

"An innovative treatment has come to our attention that promises to significantly reduce absenteeism in our schools and workplaces. A study reports that in nearby East Meria, where consumption of the plant beneficia is very high, people visit the doctor only once or twice per year for the treatment of colds. Clearly, eating a substantial amount of beneficia can prevent colds. Since colds are the reason most frequently given for absences from school and work, we recommend the daily use of nutritional supplements derived from beneficia. We predict this will dramatically reduce absenteeism in our schools and workplaces."

Write a response in which you discuss what questions would need to be answered in order to decide whether the recommendation is likely to have the predicted result. Be sure to explain how the answers to these questions would help to evaluate the recommendation.

NOTE: The above topic has wording similar to Argument Task 23 and 27 of this book. However, if you read carefully you will notice that the task instructions are different. Hence, it is very important to read the topic as well as its instructions completely before you start to write your response.

17

 Strategies

The first step in performing your analysis consists of identifying the texts' key point, recommendation, prediction or hypothesis. All the other arguments and assumptions are designed to support this central claim. In this case, the author attempts to demonstrate that *"daily use of beneficia nutritional supplements would dramatically reduce absenteeism in schools and workplaces"*.

The next step would involve creating a statement that summarizes the text by including the central claim and its supporting arguments.

Based on a study that links beneficia with a reduction in cold reports and the fact that colds are the most commonly cited reason for absenteeism, the writers of the memo predict that daily consumption of beneficia nutritional supplements would dramatically reduce absenteeism in schools and workplaces.

When considering what questions are needed to evaluate the arguments outlined in the text, it is important to keep in mind that arguments are based on assumptions – points that are taken to be true, without need for proof. This is what you need to look for – explicit and implicit assumptions since they lack the evidence required to prove their validity.

Assumptions

Explicit Assumptions	Implicit assumptions
School and workplace absenteeism is mostly due to colds	• The greatest percentage of absenteeism is due to colds • People always give truthful reasons for their absences • People correctly identify their medical symptoms
The number of doctor visits in regards to colds indicates the actual population health	• People always visit the doctor when they have a cold • The number of doctor visits for colds was high before people started consuming beneficia • Visiting the doctor once or twice a year is low when compared to national averages
Beneficia consumption prevents or reduces colds	• No other drugs are responsible for the low number of colds • No other external factors are responsible for the low number of colds • Beneficia nutritional supplements retain the properties of the plant itself
The results of East Meria are applicable in West Meria	• The demographics for the two towns are similar

After having established your assumptions, you can find the questions that are needed to evaluate the argument by rephrasing each implicit assumption.

Questions

◆ What percentage of absenteeism is due to colds?

◆ How many people give the real reason for their absence?

◆ How many people can correctly identify their medical symptoms?

◆ What percentage of the town's people visit the doctor when they have a cold?

◆ What was the number of doctor visits in East Meria before beneficia consumption?

Education

◆ How does East Meria's number of doctor visits for colds relate to the national average of visits for the same reason?

◆ Did the people of East Meria use any other drugs that could have been responsible for the reduction in the number of colds?

◆ Are there any external factors that could have been responsible for the reduction of the number of colds in East Meria?

◆ How similar are the chemical properties of beneficia nutritional supplements to those of the plant itself?

◆ How similar are the two town's demographics?

◆ Are there any side effects to beneficia consumption?

◆ What is the toxicity threshold for beneficia consumption?

 ## Sample Essay

Based on a study that links beneficia with a reduction in cold reports and the fact that colds are the most commonly cited reason for absenteeism, the writers of the memo predict that daily beneficia consumption would dramatically reduce absenteeism in schools and workplaces. As a symbol of medical authority, the West Meria Public Health Council needs to be careful when evaluating proposals that might have an impact on people's health. Before making a dietary recommendation, the Public Health Council needs to take into consideration if there are any side effects of the plant's consumption, whether school and workplace absenteeism is serious enough to warrant such a change and if the correlation between beneficia and cold reduction is valid.

When making their prediction, the authors of the memo assume that school and workplace absenteeism is mostly due to colds. The first question that comes to mind in this instance is what percentage of absenteeism is due to colds. If the overall percentage is low, even if colds are the most cited reason for absenteeism, reducing the number of colds will only have a minimum impact on the overall workplace and school attendance. However, should colds prove to be a significant cause of absences, then the author's prediction of dramatically reduced absenteeism would be strengthened provided that beneficia nutritional supplements can be used to prevent colds.

The authors also assume that people's reports accurately reflect the cause of absence. In this case it becomes important to know how many people give the real reason for their school or workplace absenteeism. Since illness is less likely to bring admonitions from a teacher or employer, it is possible that students and employees alike would be more likely to report a cold as a reason for their absence, instead of the real cause. If that were the case and most people would wrongly state having a cold as a day for skipping work or school, then consuming a plant that is supposed to boost the immune system would do nothing in terms of drastically decreasing absenteeism. Should people give truthful accounts of their reasons for missing work or school, the author's argument that absenteeism is mostly due to colds would be strengthened. Provided that the consumption of beneficia is effective in preventing colds, the authors' recommendation for daily use of the nutritional supplements derived from the plant is likely to have a significant effect on school and workplace presence.

Another line of thought used by the authors to strengthen their claim about beneficia consumption is that the number of doctor visits in regards to colds indicates the actual population's health. When evaluating this claim, the West Meria Public Health Council should consider what percentage of the town's people visit the doctor when they have a cold. In modern days colds are often not considered a serious enough reason to go to the doctor, especially if the consultation comes with a fee. Instead, a lot of people could take 'over-the-counter' meds and treat themselves. If that were the case in East Meria also and people rarely visit the doctor if they had a cold, then the number of doctor visits would not really be able to reflect the population's health. Furthermore, it could also mean that beneficia consumption has no effect in regards to the treatment of colds, in which case introducing nutritional supplement derived from the plant in West Meria would do nothing to decrease school and workplace absenteeism.

Should people prove to always go to the doctor when they have a cold then that fact would strengthen the authors' argument that doctor visits reflect the condition of the population. However, their main claim that beneficia nutritional supplements consumption would decrease school and workplace absenteeism would only be marginally bolstered, as the results would still depend on whether or not the number of doctor visits in East Meria is due to using the plant.

Another question naturally arises from this line of thought, namely what was the number of doctor visits in East Meria before beneficia consumption. Answering this question would reveal whether the number of doctor visits is correlated with beneficia consumption or not. If people went just as much or even less to the doctor for cold treatments before they started eating beneficia, then the author's claim that daily consumption of nutritional supplements derived from the plant would have a drastic effect on absenteeism would be weakened. On the other hand, if the reverse would prove to be true and people would have had far more doctor visits for colds related reasons in the past, it would become more likely that using beneficia nutritional supplements would be able to prevent colds. School and workplace presence would still be dependent on whether or not people give truthful accounts for their reasons for cutting class or skipping work.

When claiming that beneficia consumption was responsible for the reduction of colds in East Meria, the authors of the memo assume there were no external factors that could have contributed to that result. Given that more people like to self-medicate nowadays, it becomes important to know if the people of East Meria use any other drugs that could have been responsible for the reduction in the number of colds. If the town's inhabitants make use of other cold prevention or treatment medicine like vitamins and paracetamol based drugs, it becomes less likely that the low number of doctor visits is solely due to beneficia consumption. Should the opposite be true, and the East Meria citizens were to use few if any drugs that could interfere with the results, the authors of the memo could claim with a greater degree of certainty that the plant is responsible for the reduction of colds.

Making diet changes that are bound to affect people's health comes at a risk. Before issuing their predictions, the authors of the memo should first consider whether there are any side effects to beneficia consumption and what is the plant's toxicity level. If there are no side effects to eating beneficia, the author's claims are not likely to be affected; however, should the plant prove to have harmful side effects then increased beneficia consumption could lead to even more absenteeism. In the end, the risks would outweigh the benefits and the town's inhabitants would stop taking the nutritional supplements based on the plant. In addition to that, the Public Health Council might face scorn for having proposed the measure in the first place. The same thing would happen if beneficia would have a low toxicity level since people would only be able to consume very small quantities before they would get sick. If the reverse were true, then the authors of the memo could safely recommend eating nutritional supplements derived from the plant, however that would have no bearing on its efficiency in curing colds.

When predicting that daily consumption of nutritional supplements derived from beneficia will help prevent or reduce the number of colds, the authors of the memo assume that the properties of the plant would be preserved through the process of making it into a dietary supplement. The question that comes to mind in that instance is just how similar are the chemical properties of beneficia nutritional supplements to those of the plant itself. The process of making a herbal based nutritional supplement often involves radical procedures such as tincturing, vacuum distillation, freeze drying and other measures of creating the plant extract. If, after this process, the chemical properties of the nutritional supplements are significantly altered from those of the plant from which they are derived, it becomes highly likely that the dietary supplements will not have the same effects as the plant. This would significantly weaken the claim that daily use of beneficia nutritional supplements would dramatically reduce absenteeism in schools and workplaces. However, if beneficia and the dietary supplements derived from it were to share the same chemical properties, it would strengthen the claim that daily consumption of the supplements would help reduce school and workplace absenteeism, provided that eating beneficia is an effective cold prevention method.

17

All in all, measures that affect public health are not to be taken lightly. The authors of the memo should properly investigate the causes of workplace absenteeism and the relationship between beneficia and the number of colds before they suggest measures that might prove to be ineffective.

Argument Task 18

The following is a recommendation from the personnel director to the president of Acme Publishing Company.

"Many other companies have recently stated that having their employees take the Easy Read Speed-Reading Course has greatly improved productivity. One graduate of the course was able to read a 500-page report in only two hours; another graduate rose from an assistant manager to vice president of the company in under a year. Obviously, the faster you can read, the more information you can absorb in a single workday. Moreover, Easy Read would cost Acme only $500 per employee - a small price to pay when you consider the benefits. Included in this fee is a three-week seminar in Spruce City and a lifelong subscription to the Easy Read newsletter. Clearly, Acme would benefit greatly by requiring all of our employees to take the Easy Read course."

Write a response in which you discuss what specific evidence is needed to evaluate the argument and explain how the evidence would weaken or strengthen the argument.

 Strategies

A good place to start your analysis is by creating a statement that reveals the main idea of the argument. Although the writer is creating an argument, he may ultimately be stating a position, making a recommendation, or making a prediction. It may be helpful for you to determine which of these formats is most evident in the argument.

Based on examples from other companies, the personnel director at Acme Publishing Company is recommending the Easy Read Speed-Reading course as a means of benefiting Acme Publishing Company.

Assumptions:

◆ Easy Read Speed-Reading Course increases productivity in the workplace.

◆ Graduates of the course are more likely to be promoted.

◆ People who read faster absorb more information.

◆ Benefits of taking the course outweigh the cost.

◆ Productivity needs to be improved at Acme Publishing Company.

Evidence needed:

- ◆ The ability for employees to read faster is important to productivity at Acme Publishing Company.

- ◆ The percentage of employees whose jobs require them to read rapidly.

- ◆ The manner in which employees are promoted at Acme Publishing Company.

- ◆ The focus of businesses that have seen greater productivity after their workers completed the speed-reading course.

- ◆ The cost of travel for employees of Acme Publishing Company to travel and stay in Spruce City.

- ◆ The effect on Acme Publishing Company of its employees' being gone for three weeks.

- ◆ Other factors in addition to speed reading that led to the employee's promotion

- ◆ Reading faster leads to greater knowledge.

- ◆ The productivity of Acme workers.

After completing these steps, you should have enough material to write your analysis. Remember that you are not creating a position of your own; you are evaluating the strengths and weaknesses of the existing argument. You do not have to include all of the points that you have created in your prewriting. In fact, during the process of drafting your analysis, other ideas may come to mind, and if they strengthen your analysis, you should include them.

 ## Sample Essay

Companies are always looking for ways to improve the efficiency of their workers. Time is money, and the more that employees can accomplish in a workday, the more money the company is likely to make. Methods to increase productivity must be tailored to the type of work being done and the results desired by the company. Acme Publishing Company's owners need evidence of the benefit to be derived from the speed-reading course before investing both time and money.

The ability to speed read is important in some occupations. Students doing research can benefit from quickly reading through documents to extract pertinent facts. Lawyers frequently wade through volumes of documents or case law, and the ability to speed read can save them a lot of time. Acme Publishing Company should determine how many of its employees actually need to read more quickly in order to perform more efficiently. The focus of the business may not include voluminous reading, so spending the money on the course for all of Acme's employees would not be a wise use of resources. Committing to a three-week retreat for all employees may be unrealistic. If the retreat is scheduled for only one three-week period, Acme Publishing Company would have to shut down to send all of its workers, potentially leading to a loss of business. The company may decide that some of its workers could become more productive after taking the speed-reading course and attending the retreat which would cost much less while, perhaps, making those employees feel more positive about their jobs.

The personnel manager cites examples of employees at one or more other companies who increased their reading speed or got promotions after taking the course. It would be helpful to know how rapidly the first employee read 500 pages before taking the course and whether or not reading faster was the main objective of his job. Evidence should also be forthcoming that the assistant manager's receiving a promotion was a direct result of taking the speed-reading course. That employee may have been in line to become vice president anyway based on his or her other qualifications. The president of Acme Publishing Company also needs evidence that the two employees cited work for a company whose goals and objectives are similar to those of Acme. If the other company involves vastly different work or product than Acme Publishing, then the examples are irrelevant. The ability to read rapidly may not be a factor in earning promotions at Acme Publishing. Evaluating the strength of this argument would be easier if the reader knows the criteria that Acme uses when selecting candidates for higher positions in the company.

Before accepting this recommendation, the company president should ask for evidence about his workers' level of productivity at all tasks required by Acme. The evidence may show that all of his workers meet established productivity levels, making the speed-reading course unnecessary. He may find that productivity levels are subpar in areas where the ability to read quickly is not a factor. On the other hand, he may find lower productivity in departments, where a course in speed-reading would help those workers perform better. This evidence can help the president determine which of his personnel can help the Company move forward by completing the recommended course.

The president of Acme Publishing needs evidence that speed reading leads to the absorption of more knowledge. Because more knowledge is important in virtually every industry, such evidence could prove the value of the course to the company and its employees. Lack of this evidence negates the personnel director's conclusion that the money spent on the speed-reading course would be a wise use of company resources.

18

Argument Task 19

Evidence suggests that academic honor codes, which call for students to agree not to cheat in their academic endeavors and to notify a faculty member if they suspect that others have cheated, are far more successful than are other methods at deterring cheating among students at colleges and universities. Several years ago, Groveton College adopted such a code and discontinued its old-fashioned system in which teachers closely monitored students. Under the old system, teachers reported an average of thirty cases of cheating per year. In the first year the honor code was in place, students reported twenty-one cases of cheating; five years later, this figure had dropped to fourteen. Moreover, in a recent survey, a majority of Groveton students said that they would be less likely to cheat with an honor code in place than without.

Write a response in which you discuss one or more alternative explanations that could rival the proposed explanation and explain how your explanation(s) can plausibly account for the facts presented in the argument.

Strategies

A good place to start your analysis is by creating a statement that reveals the main idea of the argument. Although the writer is creating an argument, he may ultimately be stating a position, making a recommendation, or making a prediction. It may be helpful for you to determine which of these formats is most evident in the argument.

The argument states the position that an honor code is a more effective means of curtailing cheating than close supervision by professors, and evidence at Groveton College appears to support the author's explanation.

Assumptions:

◆ Instances of cheating have declined since instituting an honor code.

◆ Between years one and five under the honor code system, instances of cheating continually declined.

◆ Enrollment at the college has remained the same during the five years of the honor code.

◆ Students are as likely to report cheating as are professors.

Alternative explanations:

◆ Students are less likely to report on their peers, thereby reducing the number of recorded cases of cheating.

◆ The college increased the severity of consequences for cheating when adopting the honor code.

◆ Students may not recognize some forms of cheating.

◆ Students don't have the opportunity to observe cheating.

◆ The school may have changed its grading system.

◆ Instructors may have adjusted their curriculum and assessments.

After completing these steps, you should have enough material to write your analysis. Remember that you are not creating a position of your own; you are evaluating the strengths and weaknesses of the existing argument. You do not have to include all of the points that you have created in your prewriting. In fact, during the process of drafting your analysis, other ideas may come to mind, and if they strengthen your analysis, you should include them.

Sample Essay

The argument promotes the effectiveness of using an honor code to prevent cheating and uses some scant evidence to justify its continued use. An apparent decline in the number of cheating incidents leads the reader to agree with the position, but other explanations may be more realistic.

Students are not as likely to observe, recognize, or report cheating as are their professors. In a testing situation, for example, students may be so focused on their own performance and completing the test on time that they are unaware of others around them. Given the opportunity to look at other students in the classroom, they might not recognize that a fellow test taker is cheating. Many of those who cheat have developed techniques that make their dishonest behavior invisible to the casual or inexperienced observer. Students who do see and recognize another's cheating are faced with a moral dilemma. On one hand, they have agreed to honor the code established by the college. On the other hand, they may risk losing a friend or causing the failure of an otherwise honest student. They may empathize with a classmate who chooses cheating as a means of passing a difficult course. Of course, cheating on a test is not the only form of academic dishonesty. Plagiarism rears its ugly head when students are under some pressure to meet a deadline for a research paper. The temptation to cut-and-paste and take credit for another's words or ideas is strong for college students who have run out of ideas before running out of time. Other students are not likely to see this type of work done by classmates and, therefore, cannot be expected to report it. The professors who do read and recognize the plagiarized writing are no longer compelled to report it. They may simply assign a grade of zero. These limitations can help to explain the lower number of reported incidents of cheating at Groveton College.

The adoption of the honor code by itself may not fully explain the apparent decline in cheating. School officials may have added new consequences or strengthened those that already exist if students are caught cheating in some manner. Fear of failure or expulsion would have created a greater incentive to remain academically honest at Groveton College.

In addition to instituting an honor code, Groveton College may have changed its grading system. They may have replaced a traditional 4-point measurement of excellence to pass/fail, for example. Relieved of the pressure to achieve based on rigid guidelines, students would feel less compelled to cheat in order to meet grading expectations. In addition, professors may have changed the nature of their assessments. Instead of administering tests in a pressurized classroom under time constraints, they may have given take-home tests that students can complete in the comfort of their own residences, using notes and other resources. They may have eliminated tests altogether, relying on measurements of knowledge that are less likely to create opportunities for cheating.

Perhaps the simplest explanation for a reduction in the number of reported instances of cheating would be a decline in student population at Groveton College. In fact, the college may have instituted the apparently popular honor code in an effort to attract more students to its campus. Depending upon the size of the student body, a reduction in the number of reported cases of cheating could be an increase in the percentage of students caught cheating.

19

Groveton's use of the survey results in which a majority of students said they would be less likely to cheat if an honor code exists may be short-sighted. The survey may not have included other incentives to curtail cheating. If the survey listed only an honor code as a choice, the conclusion is flawed and is not likely to explain the apparent reduction in reported cheating cases.

If any of these alternate explanations sufficiently account for the lower number of reported cases of cheating at Groveton College, the school must relinquish its belief that the honor code is an effective change in its academic philosophy. Further investigation by college administrators can uncover the real reason for an increase in academic integrity.

Argument Task 20

Fifteen years ago, Omega University implemented a new procedure that encouraged students to evaluate the teaching effectiveness of all their professors. Since that time, Omega professors have begun to assign higher grades in their classes, and overall student grade averages at Omega have risen by 30 percent. Potential employers, looking at this dramatic rise in grades, believe that grades at Omega are inflated and do not accurately reflect student achievement; as a result, Omega graduates have not been as successful at getting jobs as have graduates from nearby Alpha University. To enable its graduates to secure better jobs, Omega University should terminate student evaluation of professors.

Write a response in which you discuss what specific evidence is needed to evaluate the argument and explain how the evidence would weaken or strengthen the argument.

 Strategies

Argument:

This argument uses Omega graduates' difficulty obtaining jobs as a rationale for eliminating student evaluation of professors.

In developing your response, you must identify what specific evidence is needed to evaluate the writer's position and how that evidence weakens or strengthens that position.

What conclusions and assumptions are either explicit or implied in the argument?

Facts and Assumptions:

◆ Student grade averages have risen by 30 percent at Omega University. This fact leads to the assumption that professors have inflated their students' grades. Over the course of 15 years, a number of changes could have occurred that can account for higher student grades. Has the school changed its admissions' policy? Has the school become more selective, admitting students with higher test scores and high school GPAs? It may be that professors have improved their instructional practices and/or material in response to the evaluations, which has led to higher achievement.

◆ Omega graduates have had less success getting jobs than graduates of nearby Alpha University. The assumption that follows this fact is that the inflated grades have created a negative impression about

20

Omega students' real achievement. What courses of study does each school include? Perhaps Alpha University students have more desirable or marketable skills.

◆ Omega University instituted student evaluation of professors fifteen years ago. This fact led to the assumption that professors began inflating grades, ostensibly to receive better evaluations from students. Why did Omega U initiate this policy? Who evaluated the professors prior to this? What effect on professors do the survey results have? Do the results affect tenure? Retention? Remediation? What is the content of the evaluations?

◆ Omega University grades have risen by 30 percent, which has led to the assumption that professors have inflated student grades.

Your notes do not have to be exhaustive. As you begin to write your essay, your brain will generate new ideas. Make certain that you keep the directions in mind as you develop your ideas.

 ## Sample Essay

Employers have interpreted the rise in grades for Omega University graduates as an indication that professors are awarding higher marks in response to the institution's use of student evaluation. As a result, Omega graduates have more difficulty finding jobs than do the graduates of nearby Alpha University. In response to this unfortunate consequence, the writer posits that Omega University should terminate student evaluation of professors. If there is substantive evidence for this change, it has not been revealed in the passage.

Employers assume that professors have inflated grades to receive favorable evaluations from their students. Employers might benefit from knowing what aspects of the professors' pedagogy are evaluated. It may be that over the fifteen-year period that student evaluations have existed, professors have responded by improving their instructional techniques and curriculum materials. In consequence, students have found the classes more relevant and accessible and have had greater success than previous students. It is also unclear whether the evaluations of the professors have improved with the increase in grades. If it has not, this argument is invalid.

Another assumption that needs to be examined is that the quality of students has remained steady while grades have risen. Can evidence be uncovered that reveals a change in Omega University's admissions policy? The school may have instituted more stringent admissions requirements. The cohorts may have achieved higher scores on the SAT or taken Advanced Placement courses in high school. Omega University's increased selectivity could account for a rise in grades. It might be helpful to know if the student evaluation process replaced another type of evaluation. It could be that the professors, themselves, requested the student evaluation to help them critique their own effectiveness.

Finally, we must look at the 30 percent rise in grades. The reader may interpret this to mean that all of Omega University students have raised their GPAs or their actual numerical averages by 30 percent. Assuming that a student would need at least a 70 percent average to remain in school, a 30 percent increase would mean that every student has a minimum average of 91 percent. That would, indeed, be remarkable and a likely cause for skepticism on the parts of employers. However, if the statistic means that 30 percent of Omega students have increased their grade averages, it may not be a cause for concern. If Omega University has 1,000 students, then roughly 300 of them have raised their grades, a more realistic improvement. Employers should not write off these graduates without understanding the basis of the purported elevation of grades.

Omega University graduates' inability to secure employment may be due, in part, to suspicion about their actual achievement, but other factors may contribute to the dearth of jobs for them. Alpha University may offer majors in courses of study that are more marketable in today's economy.

Argument Task 21

According to a recent report, cheating among college and university students is on the rise. However, Groveton College has successfully reduced student cheating by adopting an honor code, which calls for students to agree not to cheat in their academic endeavors and to notify a faculty member if they suspect that others have cheated. Groveton's honor code replaced a system in which teachers closely monitored students; under that system, teachers reported an average of thirty cases of cheating per year. In the first year the honor code was in place, students reported twenty-one cases of cheating; five years later, this figure had dropped to fourteen. Moreover, in a recent survey, a majority of Groveton students said that they would be less likely to cheat with an honor code in place than without. Thus, all colleges and universities should adopt honor codes similar to Groveton's in order to decrease cheating among students.

Write a response in which you discuss what questions would need to be answered in order to decide whether the recommendation and the argument on which it is based are reasonable. Be sure to explain how the answers to these questions would help to evaluate the recommendation.

Strategies

21

Argument:

The writer recommends that all colleges and universities adopt an honor code similar to Groveton's.

In developing your response, you are directed to discuss what questions need to be answered before other colleges accept this recommendation.

Begin by identifying the facts and assumptions in the passage.

Facts and Assumptions:

◆ Cheating among college students is increasing. This reported fact should lead colleges to take some action to curtail cheating. The assumption accompanying this fact is that Groveton's policy provides the means to achieve this.

◆ Groveton has successfully reduced cheating. The writer assumes that this is a result of the honor code.

◆ The current honor code replaced teacher monitoring of students. The reader might assume that teacher monitoring became ineffective or burdensome. The administration may have wanted students to take more responsibility for their own learning.

◆ Under the old system, professors reported an average of 30 cases of cheating per year. The reader should assume that in some years there were more cases of cheating, and, in other years, there were fewer than thirty cases.

◆ In the first year of the newer policy, students reported 21 cases of cheating. The assumption is that there was less cheating immediately following adoption of the new policy. It is better than the previous practice.

◆ Five years after adopting the new policy, there were 14 cases of cheating. The assumption is that there has been a steady decline in the number of cheating cases. This assumption supports the administration's adoption of the new policy.

◆ Students report that they are less likely to cheat with an honor code in place. The reader assumes that an honor code is the best way to prevent or decrease the incidence of cheating.

Questions:

◆ Why do college students cheat? Which students cheat? Some students may feel greater pressure to achieve at a high level at some colleges. Students may have heavy, challenging course loads that prevent them from completing their work unless they cheat.

◆ Why did Groveton adopt an honor code to replace teacher monitoring? Whose idea was it? Was the change based on research?

◆ How many cases of cheating were there every year that the teachers monitored the students? What was the low number? The high number?

◆ How many cases of cheating were reported in years 2, 3, and 4 of the new system? There may have been enough cases to create an average similar to that of the old system.

◆ Why do students say they are less likely to cheat with an honor code in place? What questions were they asked? Were they asked if they prefer an honor code to teacher monitoring?

Considering how these questions might be answered will help you to evaluate the soundness of the recommendation.

Your notes do not have to be exhaustive. As you begin to write your essay, your brain will generate new ideas. Make certain that you keep the directions in mind as you develop your ideas.

Sample Essay

Why do students cheat? They do it at every level - elementary school through college and from the most gifted to the most challenged students. How does a school prevent cheating on the part of its students? Groveton College claims to have created a tool that decreases the number of cheating incidents by students on its campus. At Groveton College, students essentially monitor themselves by adhering to a recently instituted honor code. Under this system, students agree to avoid cheating and to report suspected cases of cheating to a faculty member. Before another college adopts Groveton's policy, the administration should ask why Groveton changed from its former practice of having teachers closely monitor their students. Is there some academic research that proves the efficacy of honor codes and peer reporting? Has Groveton responded to a petition by either or both its teachers and students?

The reported decline in the number of reported cheating incidents seems impressive on the surface. Another college looking at these statistics may agree that an honor code is the right policy to create on its own campus. That school would be advised to look further into the numbers. The report cited reveals an average number of cases reported when teachers were monitoring students but omits a yearly average for the years since the honor code has been in place. During the first year of the new practice, students reported twenty-one cases of cheating, and in the most recent year only fourteen cases. It would be easy to assume that there has been a steady decline in cheating at Groveton College. What were the numbers during the intervening years? It is possible that those numbers, when added to the first and last years' totals could average thirty, the same yearly average under the old system of monitoring.

Groveton has taken the additional step of surveying its students about the effectiveness of the new honor code. Students report that they are less likely to cheat with an honor code in place than without. Did the survey ask about other practices used to curtail cheating? Is an honor code preferable because the consequences are less severe? Did Groveton change the consequences for cheating when it allowed students to self-report? It is entirely possible that this response is biased by a fear of negative consequences resulting from cheating, making students unwilling to admit their true propensity to do so.

Colleges and universities agonize over the amount of cheating on their campuses. In response to the report that says cheating is on the rise, a college or university may be willing to try anything that appears to have some success. Reporting incidents of cheating is similar to closing the barn door after the horse has escaped. The cheating has already occurred. Any institution of higher learning might be better served by discovering why students cheat. Are the course loads and work requirements too cumbersome? Is there too much pressure to succeed at a high level? Is there too much competition to be admitted to graduate school or to get a good job? Society itself may have created an environment conducive to cheating by demanding that its college graduates be the best and the brightest.

Before accepting the recommendation to adopt Groveton's honor code, other colleges and universities should demand more information and scrutinize the practices that they have in place. Perhaps the best course of action is to stop cheating before it occurs. An ounce of prevention is worth a pound of cure.

Argument Task 22

The following appeared in a letter to the editor of Parson City's local newspaper.

"In our region of Trillura, the majority of money spent on the schools that most students attend - the city-run public schools - comes from taxes that each city government collects. The region's cities differ, however, in the budgetary priority they give to public education. For example, both as a proportion of its overall tax revenues and in absolute terms, Parson City has recently spent almost twice as much per year as Blue City has for its public schools—even though both cities have about the same number of residents. Clearly, Parson City residents place a higher value on providing a good education in public schools than Blue City residents do."

Write a response in which you discuss what specific evidence is needed to evaluate the argument and explain how the evidence would weaken or strengthen the argument.

Strategies

Argument:

Because Parson City has spent twice as much of its tax revenue as Blue City has on education, Parson City places a greater value on providing a good education as does Blue City.

In developing your response, you must determine what evidence the planning committee needs to uncover before making its final budget decisions for the amount it city can spend on its public-school students to demonstrate that it places more value on education than Blue City does

Facts and Assumptions:

◆ The majority of money spent on public schools in Trillura comes from city tax revenue.

◆ Parson City has recently spent almost twice as much per year as Blue City has for its public schools. The logical assumption that follows is that Parson City spends twice as much per student as Blue City does. Blue City may have more students in private schools. Parson City may have recently had to replace one of its schools, adding a significant amount to its yearly school budget. The word recently is a qualifier. Did Blue City spend more than Parson City in the past?

22

◆ Parson City and Blue City have about the same number of residents. This may lead to the assumption that each city has the same number of public-school students. In fact, Blue City may have a very different demographic than Parson City.

Your notes do not have to be exhaustive. As you begin to write your essay, your brain will generate new ideas. Make certain that you keep the directions in mind as you develop your ideas.

 ## Sample Essay

In this letter to the editor, the writer has taken the position that Parson City places a higher value on educating its children than does Blue City. The writer cites budget figures from the two cities to support his position. Since letters to the editor express an opinion, the reader should always accept the facts with a good deal of skepticism. Acknowledging that the writer's purpose is to persuade, the reader should demand some concrete evidence before accepting that opinion as fact.

The author's first statement is likely true. It is the case in most communities everywhere that local schools are supported, in large part, by local tax dollars and that the largest part of a community's budget is expended on its schools. However, to suggest that the amount of money that a community spends is a reflection of the value it places on education is misleading. A number of factors influence how much of a city's budget, both in real dollars and the percentage of the total budget, is to be allocated for public schools. The reader should seek evidence of the existence of any extenuating circumstances that would account for the greater amount spent in Parson City.

Consider the demographic of each community. The author states that both communities have about the same number of residents, a statement easily verified by looking at census results. The composition of each city's total may vary. Again, by scrutinizing census records, one can discover how many residents comprise each age group. If Parson City has considerably more school-age children than Blue City, the reason for the greater expenditure on public schools becomes patently obvious. Blue City, in fact, may be home to an ageing population. A large portion of that city's budget may go to services for the elderly.

In addition, Parson City may have had to replace an ageing school building, leaking roofs or windows, or an antiquated heating system. Any of those capital improvements would influence the school budget for a few years. The writer uses the word recently when comparing the two communities' public-school expenditures. Is there evidence that at some period in the recent past, Blue City spent more than Parson City on its schools? Blue City may have recently finished paying for capital improvements to its schools and, as a result, has been able to reduce its school budget.

A final assumption is that spending more money on education makes it better. More money can buy more books and the latest technology; it can build beautiful schools and reduce classroom size. However, only the school district's philosophy can create a good education. Many schools deliver an excellent education to its students while operating on a shoestring. Good education is measured by the achievement of students, not by the size of the budget.

In its current form, this letter to the editor provides too many vague statements and too little evidence for the reader to accept that Parson City places more value on education than does Blue City. Only if facts are uncovered to support the idea that Parson City is spending more per pupil than Blue City can the residents of Parson City feel a sense of superiority regarding education in its public schools.

22

Argument Task 23

The following report appeared in the newsletter of the West Meria Public Health Council.

"An innovative treatment has come to our attention that promises to significantly reduce absenteeism in our schools and workplaces. A study reports that in nearby East Meria, where fish consumption is very high, people visit the doctor only once or twice per year for the treatment of colds. Clearly, eating a substantial amount of fish can prevent colds. Since colds represent the most frequently given reason for absences from school and work, we recommend the daily use of Ichthaid - a nutritional supplement derived from fish oil - as a good way to prevent colds and lower absenteeism."

Write a response in which you discuss what specific evidence is needed to evaluate the argument and explain how the evidence would weaken or strengthen the argument.

NOTE: The above topic has wording similar to Argument Task 17 and 27 of this book. However, if you read carefully you will notice that the task instructions are different. Hence, it is very important to read the topic as well as its instructions completely before you start to write your response.

 Strategies

Argument:

The daily use of Ichthaid will prevent colds and lower absenteeism.

In developing your response, you must demonstrate what evidence is needed to support the recommendation that citizens of West Meria take the supplement, Ichthaid.

Facts and Assumptions:

◆ People in East Meria visit the doctor only once or twice per year for the treatment of colds. The writer assumes that this number is lower than elsewhere. The reader may wonder if the residents have colds for which they don't seek treatment.

◆ Fish consumption is high in East Meria. The writer has made a connection between high fish consumption and a presumed low incidence of colds. Are the residents taking some other preventive measure to reduce the number of colds? Are they eating a diet rich in vitamin C or taking Echinacea

23

supplements? They may be eating fish with lots of lemon, a fruit high in vitamin C. Does everyone eat fish? Do colds afflict non-fish eaters more than those who do eat fish?

◆ Colds represent the most frequently given reason for absences from school and work. The writer assumes that the workers and students have reported truthfully. Because colds are so common, they make a convenient excuse. The writer assumes that reducing the number of colds that people get, the less absenteeism there will be.

◆ Ichthaid is a nutritional supplement derived from fish oil. The writer assumes that this supplement will have the same supposed healthful effect as eating fish. Can the community force its residents to take this supplement? Will the cost of the supplement prevent some from taking it?

Your notes do not have to be exhaustive. As you begin to write your essay, your brain will generate new ideas. Make certain that you keep the directions in mind as you develop your ideas.

 ## Sample Essay

The author of this newsletter has combined two ostensibly unrelated facts to form a conclusion that is not supported by evidence. In addition, the writer has made a sweeping recommendation based on the original faulty assumptions. The residents of West Meria should scrutinize these statements before accepting the writer's recommendation to take the dietary supplement, Ichthaid.

According to the newsletter, the citizens of East Meria both eat a lot of fish and make few visits to the doctor for the treatment of colds. The writer assumes that this is an example of cause-and-effect. What evidence exists to support this? First, the reader should ask to know if East Meria's residents visit a doctor for treatment of every cold. It is likely that many people treat their colds themselves; after all, there is no cure. Next, they should ask how many of those cold sufferers are habitual fish eaters.

If East Merians do, in fact, contract fewer colds than average, they may be taking other preventive measures. Is there evidence that they take vitamin C or Echinacea? They may be eating large quantities of fresh fruits and vegetables, most of which are rich in vitamin C and other nutrients that contribute to good health. They may even be eating their fish with lots of lemon, a fruit known to be high in vitamin C.

The writer is probably accurate when he informs the reader that colds are the most often used excuse for absence from school and work. Since the cold is so common, it is a convenient excuse for anyone needing a day off from work or school. However, it is also common for students to avoid attending class by falsely claiming to be sick. How many students actually have colds? Even if colds can be prevented by taking the supplement, Ichthaid, can the same be said for absenteeism?

Nutritional supplements are popular and a seemingly harmless way to remedy deficits in one's diet. The citizens of West Meria should probably look for evidence of studies done on Ichthaid before accepting the recommendation in this newsletter. Supplements are neither always harmless nor effective. The expense and possible negative side effects should make them think twice, or to paraphrase Marie Antoinette, "Let them eat fish."

23

Argument Task 24

The following is part of a memorandum from the president of Humana University.

"Last year the number of students who enrolled in online degree programs offered by nearby Omni University increased by 50 percent. During the same year, Omni showed a significant decrease from prior years in expenditures for dormitory and classroom space, most likely because instruction in the online programs takes place via the Internet. In contrast, over the past three years, enrollment at Humana University has failed to grow, and the cost of maintaining buildings has increased along with our budget deficit. To address these problems, Humana University will begin immediately to create and actively promote online degree programs like those at Omni. We predict that instituting these online degree programs will help Humana both increase its total enrollment and solve its budget problems."

Write a response in which you discuss what questions would need to be answered in order to decide whether the prediction and the argument on which it is based are reasonable. Be sure to explain how the answers to these questions would help to evaluate the prediction.

Strategies

Prediction:

Humana's offering online degree programs will result in increased enrollment and solve its budget programs.

Facts and Assumptions:

◆ Omni University had a 50 percent increase in the number of students enrolled in its online programs over last year. The assumption is that this is a large number of students.

◆ Omni showed a significant decrease in expenditures for dormitory and classroom space. They don't need dorm and classroom space because instruction takes place via the Internet.

◆ Enrollment at Humana University has failed to grow over the past three years. One assumption is that Humana's offerings aren't attractive to prospective students. One might assume that students find Humana too expensive. Humana might have the capacity for no more students.

◆ The cost of building maintenance has grown along with its budget deficit. Perhaps the lack of growth has made it difficult for Humana University to meet its maintenance schedule and financial obligations.

Questions:

◆ How many students did Omni University have prior to the 50 percent increase? If that number were relatively small, a 50 percent increase isn't impressive.

◆ Why were Omni's expenditures for dorms and classrooms so much less than in previous years? The university may have upgraded those facilities a few years ago and have not had to do so in the past few years.

◆ Why did Omni begin offering online programs? The school may have been at capacity on campus and began offering online courses to meet the demand.

◆ Why has Humana University failed to grow? Its degree programs may not be as relevant as they used to be.

◆ Why has the cost of maintaining buildings increased at Humana? These costs may be cyclical. Maybe it has been several years since they have performed significant maintenance on the buildings.

◆ What has caused the budget deficit? The cost of doing business has increased while enrollment has remained flat.

◆ What evidence does Humana have that online degree programs will increase its enrollment? How will online programs reduce the budget deficit? There are expenses associated with developing online programs. They will need to offer high-demand programs to attract sufficient students to make a dent in the deficit.

Your notes do not have to be exhaustive. As you begin to write your essay, your brain will generate new ideas. Make certain that you keep the directions in mind as you develop your ideas.

Sample Essay

Humana University sees online degree programs as the silver lining in its cloud of financial challenges. The president cites the apparent success of nearby Omni University's foray into that market as justification for his recommendation and prediction. The president would be well-advised to look at some specifics and ask the hard questions before moving forward.

Humana's president should first investigate Omni University's apparent success with its online degree programs. Is a 50 percent increase in enrollment impressive? That depends on the original number of students. If Omni began with 10 students, a 50 percent increase would be 5 students, which is an insufficient number on which to base a new venture. On the other hand, if Omni began with 200 students and increased its enrollment to 300, that would be a rationale for wanting to replicate that success.

Next, the president should ask why Omni University decided to offer online programs in the first place. It may be a case of supply and demand. It may be that more students have demanded Omni programs than the school can meet in its campus location. Online offerings would be a logical solution to that enviable problem. If Humana University hasn't seen that same level of interest in its programs, it may be a prudent move for Humana's president to investigate further before jumping into that market.

Another reason that Humana's president proposes for taking on the challenge of online education is the recent maintenance costs of campus buildings. He assumes that Omni's reduction in those expenses is the reduced need for dormitory and classroom space on its campus. It could just as easily be that Omni had completed repairs and maintenance a few years ago and has not needed to repeat them in the last few years. Extensive renovation projects are likely to be cyclical, and Humana finds itself needing to complete those now.

Why has Humana's enrollment remained flat? The school may not be offering programs that reflect current trends in the job market. This, indeed, may be the crux of the problem at Humana. With more high school graduates than ever before going on to some form of higher education, Humana's enrollment should be increasing. Should Humana proceed with plans to offer online degree programs, it may find that students who enroll in those programs will be those who, otherwise, might have come to its campus. Humana may well be left with flat enrollment along with the expense of maintaining its dormitories and classroom buildings. The president's prediction of financial solvency may be a pipe dream.

Argument Task 25

The following is a recommendation from the Board of Directors of Monarch Books.

"We recommend that Monarch Books open a café in its store. Monarch, having been in business at the same location for more than twenty years, has a large customer base because it is known for its wide selection of books on all subjects. Clearly, opening the café would attract more customers. Space could be made for the café by discontinuing the children's book section, which will probably become less popular given that the most recent national census indicated a significant decline in the percentage of the population under age ten. Opening a café will allow Monarch to attract more customers and better compete with Regal Books, which recently opened its own café."

Write a response in which you discuss what questions would need to be answered in order to decide whether the recommendation is likely to have the predicted result. Be sure to explain how the answers to these questions would help to evaluate the recommendation.

 Strategies

Recommendation:

Monarch Books should open a café in its store.

Next, identify the argument's conclusions and the evidence that led to those conclusions.

Conclusions:

◆ Monarch Books will attract more customers if it opens a café in the store. Its rival, Regal Books, has opened a café.

◆ The children's book section will become less popular. The most recent national census shows a significant decline in the percentage of the population under ten.

◆ Monarch will be able to better compete with Regal books if it opens a café. Regal Books has already opened a café.

25

You should now be able to generate some questions whose answers will support or negate the recommendation.

Questions:

◆ What percentage of Monarch Books' current sales comes from the children's book section?

◆ Did Regal Books eliminate its children' book section when it added a café?

◆ What is the cost/benefit ratio of opening a café at Monarch Books? How many extra sales will need to be generated to offset the cost of opening the café?

◆ If Monarch Books is popular because of its wide variety of books, will eliminating the children's section have a negative effect on its current popularity?

◆ Did Monarch's current customers begin shopping there as children?

◆ Are children reading more or fewer books than in the past? What about authors like J.K. Rowling?

Your notes do not have to be exhaustive. As you begin to write your essay, your brain will generate new ideas. Make certain that you keep the directions in mind as you develop your ideas.

 ## Sample Essay

Monarch Books' board of directors has recommended that the store should open a café to attract more customers. The board further recommends that, to make room for the café, Monarch Books eliminate its children's books section. Many questions arise from this recommendation, and they should be answered before Monarch Books makes such a drastic and, perhaps, irrevocable decision.

Removing an entire genre from its inventory is a step that Monarch Books should not take lightly. They should certainly ascertain what percentage of their revenue derives from the sale of children's books. Has that portion of Monarch's sales declined appreciably in recent years? It is hard to imagine that with the popularity of J.K. Rowling's Harry Potter series, children are reading less than in the past. Has Monarch Books researched industry trends to determine if children's book sales have declined appreciably across the country? If they have not, this argument becomes invalid, because those book sales may be comparable to café sales.

The writer uses the results of a recent census that shows a decline in the percentage of the population under ten years of age to support replacing the children's book section with a café. He or she assumes that the same must hold true for the geographic area served by Monarch Books. How do the census figures apply here? It could be that the presence of a thriving book store attracts families with young children to settle in the area. Additionally, a decline in a segment of the population doesn't mean that the popularity of its activities will also decline.

Having fewer customers for a particular item shouldn't necessarily lead to eliminating that item; a store might simply stock fewer copies of it.

Another assumption is that Regal Books' addition of a café will draw customers from Monarch Books. Over the twenty years of Monarch's existence in its current location, the store has created a strong following because it carries a wide selection of books. Customers have formed a habit of patronizing this particular store, and retail experts will reveal that those habits are hard to change. Have Monarch customers requested a café? Have any of them defected to Regal Books? Monarch's owners should be able to study their sales figures or survey their customers to uncover their needs and areas of dissatisfaction.

While pondering the wisdom of eliminating their children's books in favor of adding a café, the store owners should study the retail area where the store is located. Does there appear to be a need for a café? Is there an abundance of restaurants in the area? Finally, they might want to know how Regal Books managed the addition of a café to its store. Did they eliminate their children's book section? Did they build an addition to their current structure to house the café?

When Monarch owners have answered the important questions, they may find that a café would enhance their business. On the other hand, they may decide that cafés are a passing fancy and the cost/benefit ratio doesn't make fiscal sense. If the reason for visiting a bookstore is, ultimately, to buy books, should Monarch limit the choices of genres available to its customers?

25

Argument Task 26

The following appeared in a letter to the school board in the town of Centerville.

"All students should be required to take the driver's education course at Centerville High School. In the past two years, several accidents in and around Centerville have involved teenage drivers. Since a number of parents in Centerville have complained that they are too busy to teach their teenagers to drive, some other instruction is necessary to ensure that these teenagers are safe drivers. Although there are two driving schools in Centerville, parents on a tight budget cannot afford to pay for driving instruction. Therefore an effective and mandatory program sponsored by the high school is the only solution to this serious problem."

Write a response in which you examine the stated and/or unstated assumptions of the argument. Be sure to explain how the argument depends on these assumptions and what the implications are for the argument if the assumptions prove unwarranted.

 Strategies

A good place to start your analysis is by creating a statement that reveals the main idea of the argument. Although the writer is creating an argument, he may ultimately be stating a position, making a recommendation, or making a prediction. It may be helpful for you to determine which of these formats is most evident in the argument.

The author of the letter to the Centerville school board uses some information regarding teenage drivers and accidents to recommend a mandatory driver education course at the local high school.

26

Assumptions:

◆ Teenage drivers caused all of the accidents in which they were involved.

◆ A school-sponsored driver education course is the only way to ensure that teens are safe drivers.

◆ Accidents involving teen drivers are a serious problem.

◆ The school-sponsored course can accommodate all students.

◆ Driver inexperience is the cause of most accidents.

◆ All teens want to learn to drive.

◆ Teens are worse drivers than those in other age groups.

◆ Parents are too busy to teach their teens to drive.

◆ Driving schools are too expensive.

Alternative explanations:

◆ Teens are not always at fault when involved in an accident.

◆ A small percentage of total accidents involve teen drivers.

◆ The school system cannot accommodate all students who wish to take the driving course.

◆ Distracted driving is the cause of most accidents.

◆ There has been considerable road construction during the past two years.

◆ Elderly drivers cause as many or more accidents than teens.

◆ Adopting a graduated driver's license program is an effective way to reduce accidents by teen drivers.

After completing these steps, you should have enough material to write your analysis. Remember that you are not creating a position of your own; you are evaluating the strengths and weaknesses of the existing argument. You do not have to include all of the points that you have created in your prewriting. In fact, during the process of drafting your analysis, other ideas may come to mind, and, if they strengthen your analysis, you should include them.

 # Sample Essay

Teenage driving is a frequent topic of discussion with parents, other authorities and insurance companies. Teen drivers in small towns know that the local cops are more likely to stop them than other drivers. These drivers know that they or their parents pay higher insurance premiums than do other drivers. One can only assume that teen drivers pose higher risks or drive less prudently than other drivers. Compelling all students at Centerville High School to take a driver education course through the school may not be the only or best way to reduce the number of accidents in the surrounding area.

The assumption that teens cause all of the accidents in which they are involved may be false. Even though teens are involved in an accident, the fault may be the other drivers. Even if each accident involving a teen driver is the teen's fault, the reader should not assume that they are a large portion of total accidents. Accidents caused by teen drivers may not result in serious injuries or extensive damage to cars or other property. During the two-year period mentioned in the argument, considerable road construction in the Centerville vicinity may have

Education

26

caused hazardous conditions for all drivers, so more accidents by all drivers occurred. The weather during this time span may have caused more dangerous driving conditions leading to a larger number of accidents involving teens and other drivers.

The author of the letter assumes that a mandatory driving course sponsored by the local high school is the only way to ensure that all teens learn to drive safely. There is no evidence that a high school course is more effective than other driving instruction for creating safe drivers. Requiring all students to take the course may be problematic. Some students may not be able to fit it into already challenging schedules. Some may not be interested in learning to drive. Many states have taken steps beyond driver education to reduce the number of accidents caused by teens. Some restrict new drivers to operating a vehicle only during daylight hours for the first six months. Others prohibit the teen driver from carrying passengers other than adults with licenses. These steps may be more effective in creating safer drivers than a mandatory course in high school.

The content of the letter leads to the assumption that teens are the worst divers on the road and that inexperience is the reason. Factors besides age influence a driver's ability to be safe. Good hearing and eyesight along with rapid reaction time keep drivers and others safe on our streets. Since it is the elderly drivers who may have poor vision and/ or reaction time, they may be the cause of as many accidents as teens are. Today, it is just as likely that a driver is distracted rather than inexperienced. More drivers of every age are using cell phones while operating a motor vehicle.

The conclusion that a high school course is the best solution is based in part on the assumptions that too many parents have no time to teach their teens to drive and that many families cannot afford the cost of the private driving schools. It would be helpful if the school board were given concrete numbers to support these assumptions. The number may be small enough to be significant; dedicating funds for the driver education course could put other programs at the school in jeopardy.

Drivers at any age can have accidents. Although experience prevents more serious accidents, other factors contribute to safety on the roads for everyone. Parents might be advised to buy the safest cars possible for their teens. Cars today have rear cameras that let drivers know of any obstacle behind them when they are backing up. Air bags save lives every day. When all of the factors are considered, the school board may decide that a course at the high school is the best decision, but they also may determine that other options are just as viable for creating safe, young drivers.

26

Argument Task 27

The following memo appeared in the newsletter of the West Meria Public Health Council.

"An innovative treatment has come to our attention that promises to significantly reduce absenteeism in our schools and workplaces. A study reports that in nearby East Meria, where fish consumption is very high, people visit the doctor only once or twice per year for the treatment of colds. This shows that eating a substantial amount of fish can clearly prevent colds. Furthermore, since colds are the reason most frequently given for absences from school and work, attendance levels will improve. Therefore, we recommend the daily use of a nutritional supplement derived from fish oil as a good way to prevent colds and lower absenteeism."

Write a response in which you discuss what questions would need to be answered in order to decide whether the recommendation and the argument on which it is based are reasonable. Be sure to explain how the answers to these questions would help to evaluate the recommendation.

NOTE: The above topic has wording similar to Argument Task 17 and 23 of this book. However, if you read carefully you will notice that the task instructions are different. Hence, it is very important to read the topic as well as its instructions completely before you start to write your response.

 Strategies

A good place to start your analysis is by creating a statement that reveals the main idea of the argument. Although the writer is creating an argument, he may ultimately be stating a position, making a recommendation, or making a prediction. It may be helpful for you to determine which of these formats is most evident in the argument.

The West Meria Public Health Council uses the low-frequency of doctor visits by residents of East Meria to support its recommendation that West Merians take a fish oil supplement.

27

Assumptions:

◆ High fish consumption in East Meria leads to fewer visits to the doctor for treatment of colds.

◆ Fewer colds will increase attendance at work and school.

◆ People always see a doctor for treatment of colds.

◆ A daily nutritional supplement from fish oil will have the same effect as eating fish.

◆ People are truthful about their reasons for missing school or work.

◆ People will willingly and consistently take the supplement.

◆ People in West Meria eat less fish than people in East Meria.

Questions:

◆ Does everyone see a doctor for treatment of every cold?

◆ Do citizens who eat the most fish have the fewest colds?

◆ Do residents of East Meria take any other steps to prevent colds?

◆ Are residents truthful with their employers about their reasons for missing work?

◆ Have East Meria's schools and workplaces seen a significant decline in absenteeism?

◆ Is the supplement affordable?

◆ How significant a problem is absenteeism in West Meria?

◆ Do East Merians have easy access to doctors?

◆ Do citizens of East Meria eat significantly more fish than those in West Meria?

After completing these steps, you should have enough material to write your analysis. Remember that you are not creating a position of your own; you are evaluating the strengths and weaknesses of the existing argument. You do not have to include all of the points that you have created in your prewriting. In fact, during the process of drafting your analysis, other ideas may come to mind, and if they strengthen your analysis, you should include them.

Sample Essay

The recommendation in this argument lacks sufficient support. A number of questions need answers before deciding on the efficacy of the recommendation that citizens of West Meria take a fish oil supplement each day to reduce the incidence of colds and improve attendance at work and school.

The first questions should attempt to clarify the reason for the implication that East Meria residents have fewer colds. Do they really have fewer colds or do they simply seek treatment less often than residents of West Meria? If a survey of East Meria residents shows that they do, indeed, have significantly fewer colds than people in West Meria, further investigation of lifestyle choices is warranted. On the other hand, survey results showing that they simply choose not to seek treatment for colds as often as people in West Meria invalidate the claim that eating fish makes East Meria residents less susceptible to colds.

Do East Meria residents take any other action that might result in fewer colds? They may avoid smoking tobacco, since smoking is linked to a variety of upper-respiratory illnesses. Perhaps they take daily supplements like Vitamin C or Echinacea, both of which purport to boost the immune system. East Merians may exercise regularly and maintain ideal weights. If any of these conditions exist, the argument and concomitant recommendation become weaker.

One may infer from the argument that absenteeism is a big problem in West Meria, but is that really the case? It is likely that people suffer colds more frequently than any other illness, but many go to work or school in spite of them. Without asking schools and businesses about their rates of absenteeism, it is impossible to determine the benefits of taking the fish oil supplement. Do workers and students in East Meria miss fewer days of work or school than residents of West Meria? Visiting the doctor fewer times each year does not necessarily indicate that East Merians have less absenteeism. In fact, residents of East Meria may contract more serious illnesses than do citizens of West Meria. Has the West Meria Public Health Council collected data on all types of illnesses?

How likely are West Merians to take the supplement? It may be too expensive or difficult to obtain. If they are not currently taking any action to avoid catching colds, they may balk at taking the supplement. Is there research that proves taking the supplement is effective in boosting the immune system? Residents may want to know how effective the supplement is before laying down any amount of money to purchase it.

Why is fish consumption so high in East Meria? Commercial fishing may be the main industry there, making easy access to fresh fish and prices low enough to make fish the protein of choice. Do East Merians in fact eat considerably more fish than West Merians? Residents of both towns may consume equal amounts of fish. What then accounts for the higher number of doctor visits in West Meria? They may have better health insurance that pays for those doctor visits. The citizens of East Meria may have to pay for doctor visits out-of-pocket and cannot afford to do so every time one has a cold.

Do colds account for the greatest number of absentee days? Although colds may be the most common reason for missing work or school, those suffering from them may miss only a day or two, whereas a more serious illness may require a longer absence from work. Are people always truthful about the reason they give for missing work? It's easier for people to say they have a cold than to admit they are hung-over or simply need a "mental health" day.

27

Until the citizens of West Meria have answers to the questions about the efficacy of a supplement derived from fish oil as a cold preventive or the impact of colds compared to other illnesses on absenteeism, they cannot commit to buying and taking a daily supplement.

Argument Task 28

The following appeared in a memo from the director of student housing at Buckingham College.

"To serve the housing needs of our students, Buckingham College should build a number of new dormitories. Buckingham's enrollment is growing and, based on current trends, will double over the next 50 years, thus making existing dormitory space inadequate. Moreover, the average rent for an apartment in our town has risen in recent years. Consequently, students will find it increasingly difficult to afford off-campus housing. Finally, attractive new dormitories would make prospective students more likely to enroll at Buckingham."

Write a response in which you discuss what specific evidence is needed to evaluate the argument and explain how the evidence would weaken or strengthen the argument.

 Strategies

A good place to start your analysis is by creating a statement that reveals the main idea of the argument. Although the writer is creating an argument, he may ultimately be stating a position, making a recommendation, or making a prediction. It may be helpful for you to determine which of these formats is most evident in the argument.

The housing director at Buckingham College recommends that the college build new dormitories to accommodate a projected growth in enrollment, make housing more affordable for students and to attract more students.

Assumptions:

◆ A large number of future students at Buckingham College will choose to live in dormitories.

◆ Living in dormitories is less expensive than renting apartments.

◆ Buckingham College enrollment will continue to grow at its current rate.

◆ Students select a college based on the attractiveness of its dorms.

◆ Existing dorm space is full to capacity.

28

Evidence needed to evaluate the argument:

◆ The percentage of Buckingham College students that live in dorms compared to the percentage that live in apartments.

◆ The cost of room and board at Buckingham College compared to the cost of living in an apartment.

◆ The rate of growth at the college over the past several years.

◆ The reasons that students attend Buckingham College

◆ Occupancy rate in the college dorms.

◆ National trends regarding college attendance.

◆ National population growth.

◆ Demographics of students enrolled at Buckingham. Are they older students? Married students?

After completing these steps, you should have enough material to write your analysis. Remember that you are not creating a position of your own; you are evaluating the strengths and weaknesses of the existing argument. You do not have to include all of the points that you have created in your prewriting. In fact, during the process of drafting your analysis, other ideas may come to mind, and if they strengthen your analysis, you should include them.

Sample Essay

The director of student housing is recommending the addition of considerable dormitory space at Buckingham College based on what appears to be continuing growth in enrollment at the college. More detailed information would help the college administrators make an informed decision. They should not rush into an expensive expansion without further research. Evaluating past and current trends, projected population growth, availability of off-campus housing and the cost/benefit of constructing new dormitories among other concerns will assist them in analyzing the current and future condition of campus housing.

An important piece of evidence missing from the recommendation is the current occupancy rate of the existing dormitories. The housing director has not revealed whether or not the rooms are fully occupied or if some double rooms have had to be converted to triples. Has the college had to refuse dormitory space to some students desiring it? In fact, the housing director's final reason for building new dorms suggests that the college lacks students rather than dorm space. His or her prediction is that attractive dorms will attract more students to the college. One is left to wonder whether the school needs more dormitory space or more students.

28

Does evidence exist showing that students select a college based on the attractiveness of its dormitories? One need only look at some of the oldest colleges and universities in the United States to question the veracity of that reason for building new dorms. Selective schools like Harvard, Yale, and Wellesley do not attract the top students from around the world because they provide luxurious living conditions. Students compete for a place at these schools because they will get the best education in the world, enabling them to become successful enough to build their own luxury homes. It would probably take relatively little time and effort to find survey results, listing the top ten reasons given by students for choosing a particular college or university.

Another reason given by the director for building new dorms is the apparently rising cost of apartments in the town. The director does not provide specific figures comparing the cost of room and board on campus to the cost of rent, food and utilities associated with off-campus living. Students are apt to have more options for living off-campus. The housing director doesn't cite a shortage of apartments as a reason for building new dorms, so one may believe that students have a variety of apartment sizes and rents from which to choose. Students can split the cost of off-campus living with one or more roommates, an option not available in college dorms where the cost for each resident is the same.

Before investing in new dormitories, decision makers should see information about the types of students who attend Buckingham College. A considerable portion of the student body may be non-traditional students. They are older or married or attend only part time. They could be commuters who live at home and travel to campus only to attend classes. These students will not live in dorms. On the other hand, a campus populated with traditional students generally requires more dormitory space.

Competition for students to fill classrooms and dormitories has increased. Today, anyone can earn a college degree at any level without ever leaving home. The University of Phoenix, for example, offers bachelor's through doctorate degrees in a variety of disciplines. Students can log on to their classes at a time convenient for them, participate in discussions with other students from around the country, complete assignments, take exams, and see their grades while still in their pajamas. Even traditional colleges offer online versions of courses for degree credit. If this trend continues, neither Buckingham College nor other institutions of higher learning will need to increase dorm space.

Undertaking a capital expense like new dormitories is never done lightly. The decision to do so should not be based on the assumptions in the housing director's recommendation without further research. If those assumptions prove to be too optimistic, the college will need to find other ways to attract new students and accommodate those it already has.

28

Argument Task 29

In a study of the reading habits of Waymarsh citizens conducted by the University of Waymarsh, most respondents said they preferred literary classics as reading material. However, a second study conducted by the same researchers found that the type of book most frequently checked out of each of the public libraries in Waymarsh was the mystery novel. Therefore, it can be concluded that the respondents in the first study had misrepresented their reading preferences.

Write a response in which you examine the stated and/or unstated assumptions of the argument. Be sure to explain how the argument depends on these assumptions and what the implications are for the argument if the assumptions prove unwarranted.

 Strategies

A good place to start your analysis is by creating a statement that reveals the main idea of the argument. Although the writer is creating an argument, he may ultimately be stating a position, making a recommendation, or making a prediction. It may be helpful for you to determine which of these formats is most evident in the argument.

It is the author's contention that the citizens of Waymarsh misrepresented their reading preferences on two surveys conducted by the University of Waymarsh.

Assumptions:

◆ Survey respondents got their literary classics from the library.

◆ Respondents lied on the survey.

◆ The survey sample was large.

◆ Respondents to both surveys were the same.

◆ Both surveys measured the same thing.

◆ The surveys were conducted in a short period of time.

◆ The survey was unbiased.

29

Alternative explanations:

- Respondents were different for each survey.

- Those who prefer to read the classics own the books.

- Respondents to the second survey misrepresented their choices.

- The surveys were conducted in different years.

- The surveys served different purposes.

- The survey samples were small.

- The libraries have more mystery novels available than classics.

- The libraries do not have classics on their shelves.

- The term, classic, was not clearly defined on the survey.

- Classics were checked out of the university's library.

- Respondents read the classics in the reading rooms at the public libraries.

After completing these steps, you should have enough material to write your analysis. Remember that you are not creating a position of your own; you are evaluating the strengths and weaknesses of the existing argument. You do not have to include all of the points that you have created in your prewriting. In fact, during the process of drafting your analysis, other ideas may come to mind, and if they strengthen your analysis, you should include them.

 # Sample Essay

The power of the survey must be used judicially. Without knowing what a survey is designed to measure, the results can be misinterpreted or manipulated. The surveys cited in this argument appear to reveal information about the reading habits of Waymarsh citizens, and on the surface appear to contradict each other. Closer analysis of the assumptions that led to the conclusion in the argument may bring alternative explanations to light.

The reader may assume that the surveys were conducted over a short period of time. However, given enough time between the two, it would be reasonable to expect that reading habits have changed. Even though the same group conducted the survey, they may have done the two projects four years apart. The respondents may have been the same, but, in a four-year span, they may have read all of the classics they wanted to and moved on to mystery novels.

29

The survey may not have provided a clear definition of the term, classic. Assuming that everyone has the same understanding of that term may have led to some faulty responses to the questions. Respondents to the survey may have had various understandings of the classic. The Maltese Falcon, for example, is often described as a classic detective novel; The Great Gatsby is a classic portrayal of the Roaring Twenties; The Grapes of Wrath is a classic depiction of the dispossessed. The creators of the survey may have had novels from the nineteenth century in mind. There is too little information in the argument to determine their intentions. On the other hand, it may have been clear to the respondents what constitutes a classic. The libraries in Waymarsh may have a limited number of classics on their shelves, so even those who prefer reading classics check out other types of novels when a classic that they have not read is unavailable.

Surveys must be free of bias to obtain accurate results. The wording of each question on the survey must avoid leading the respondents to select one answer over another. Qualifiers like better or worse can cause a respondent to select an answer that he thinks will please the creators of a survey. This invalidates the results.

Even though the same group conducted both surveys, assuming that each was designed for the same purpose, creates an unsustainable conclusion. The first survey may have been designed to determine the reading preferences of the respondents. It appears to have done that. The second survey may have sought to determine what genres are most frequently checked out of the local libraries. If so, it accomplished that goal. To presume that the respondents to the first survey misled the researchers fails if the surveys did not have the same goal.

The second survey discovered that mysteries were checked out of the public libraries more frequently than books of other genres. The readers of the survey may assume that respondents to the survey only use public libraries to obtain reading material. The argument does not mention whether there are other libraries in Waymarsh. Churches frequently have libraries. The city may have a literary society that provides copies of the classics to its patrons. The university itself must have a library. Any of these may provide copies of classics to the readers in Waymarsh. In fact, the readers of classics may not borrow the books from any source. They may choose to relax in the reading rooms of the various libraries. The public libraries may have the classics on CDs which borrowers may check out and listen to in their homes or cars.

Overall, too little information is present in the argument to support the conclusion reached by the researchers from Waymarsh University. It does not even reveal if the surveys were written or administered orally. One might assume that the researchers are from the English department of the university and use the information in the surveys to inform their curriculum or instruction. However, the researchers may be from the psychology or sociology department of the university, and they conduct the surveys to measure emotional responses to the questions. The argument cannot stand because of the missing information.

29

This page is intentionally left blank

Chapter **12**
Government & Politics

Argument Task 30

In surveys Mason City residents rank water sports (swimming, boating, and fishing) among their favorite recreational activities. The Mason River flowing through the city is rarely used for these pursuits, however, and the city park department devotes little of its budget to maintaining riverside recreational facilities. For years there have been complaints from residents about the quality of the river's water and the river's smell. In response, the state has recently announced plans to clean up Mason River. Use of the river for water sports is, therefore, sure to increase. The city government should for that reason devote more money in this year's budget to riverside recreational facilities.

Write a response in which you examine the stated and/or unstated assumptions of the argument. Be sure to explain how the argument depends on these assumptions and what the implications are for the argument if the assumptions prove unwarranted.

 Strategies

The first step in performing your analysis consists of identifying the texts' key point, recommendation, prediction or hypothesis. All the other arguments and assumptions are designed to support this central claim. In this case, the author attempts to argue that "The city government should devote more money to riverside recreational facilities".

The next step would involve creating a statement that summarizes the text by including the central claim and its supporting arguments.

Given the Mason City surveys ranking water sports as the favorite recreation activity of the residents and the upcoming river cleansing project that is thought to eliminate the cause for the low river usage, the author of the text argues for an increase in this year's budget devoted to riverside recreational facilities.

The easiest way to break down an argument into implicit assumptions is to look at the ideas that support each core (explicit) assumption. Ideally, it would be good to have at least three implicit assumptions for every explicit one. However, keep in mind that you likely won't have time enough to expound on all of them in your essay. When writing your argument, it's good to lay down the ideas like in the format below – it will help you easily determine which explicit assumptions are undermined/strengthened by the implicit argument you are analyzing.

30

Assumptions:

Explicit Assumptions	Implicit Assumptions
Survey accurately reflects people's opinions on water sports	• There are no biased or leading questions • The survey demographics are representative of the city (city and survey demographics are similar) • The studies have a low standard deviation (enough people participated, so that a small group's opinion cannot skew the results) • People who rank water sports as high will also participate in them
River pollution is responsible for the low usage of the city river	• The complaints are representative for the city • River pollution is the only reason why people do not use the river
Cleaning up the river will increase the usage of water sports	• There are no other outlets for water sports in the city • The smell of the river is due to pollution and not a naturally occurring event (sulphur) • The quality of the water is due to pollution and not a natural occurring event (mineral deposits) • Residents would like to use the river for water sports • The clean-up will end pollution/is extensive
The increase in usage is sufficient to justify increasing the budget for riverside recreational facilities	• A great percentage of people will go to the riverside • The people that go to the riverside need facilities • Riverside facilities are dedicated to water sports (and not other pursuits) • Current riverside facilities are insufficient • The clean-up of the river will happen in the short term (enough to justify making changes to this year's budget)

After After having established your assumptions you need to take care of the second part of your essay, namely the implications for the main claim should the assumptions be unwarranted. A good way to go about writing this part is to think of examples of situations that may contradict each implicit assumption. The

Government & Politics

30

examples are not vital; you can still build a case by directly stating "if assumption 'A' proves to be untrue, then..." However, including the contradicting situations will help enrich your essay and ultimately get you a higher score

The next step would be to create a "logic tree" to see how disproving an assumption will affect the other arguments down the line. The branch of the logic tree will follow this line: implicit assumption affects explicit assumptions which in turn relate to the main argument.

For instance, in our case:

Implicit Assumption	Contradicting Situations	Effect on Explicit Assumption	Effect on Main Argument
River pollution is the only reason why people do not use the river	• River is too distant • Very fast currents	• Somewhat weaken or disprove the assumption (people might still not use the river after it is cleaned)	• Building more facilities would become useless, if river usage will not increase • Waste of resources
The smell of the river is due to pollution and not a naturally-occurring event	• Sulfur • Natural gas leaks (Cattaraugus Creek)	• Cleaning the river will not remove the odor • Cleaning the river will not increase river usage	• Building more facilities would become useless, if river usage will not increase • Waste of resources
The complaints are representative for the city	• Low percentage of people complaining • An individual filing a large number of complaints	• The complaints do not reflect the resident's opinions about the river • River usage might not increase by solving the complaints	• Building more facilities would become useless, if river usage will not increase • Main cause of low river usage remains unknown

Sample Essay

Given the Mason City surveys ranking water sports as the favorite recreation activity of the residents and the upcoming river cleansing project thought to eliminate the cause for the low river usage, the author of the text argues for an increase in this year's budget devoted to riverside recreational facilities. The author of the proposal makes suggestions that can prove to be very costly especially if the assumptions upon which the case rests prove to be unwarranted.

When arguing for the increased revenue allocated to this year's budget for riverside facilities, the author draws upon data from surveys conducted in Mason City. One of the main assumptions that the case rests on is that the surveys conducted accurately reflect people's opinions on water sports. In taking this data at face value, the author further assumes that the survey demographics are representative for the entirety of the city. The most essential part of any research is the methodology. In this case, if the survey takers asked only people that live next to the river or only citizens of a certain age, that can very well mean that the rest of the citizens do not view water sports as a favorite activity, in which case, regardless of the river cleaning actions, the actual usage of the waterway will not increase.

Another implicit assumption related to the idea that the surveys accurately reflect people's opinions on water sports is the notion that the research methodology is sound, namely, there are no biased or leading questions. Phrasing survey questions is sometimes likened to an art – just like any activity that requires a considerable amount of skill and knowledge. Should the surveys contain badly phrased questions, like an option to choose between water sports or extreme activities, the results of the surveys would no longer be reliable. In this example, most people would choose water sports because it is the less extreme/unreasonable option and not because they would like to actively engage in this type of sporting activity.

In this case, a budgetary increase for riverside facilities could prove to be a waste of money, since people's interests lie elsewhere, and not with river-based activities. The same conclusion would apply if the questions were biased due to the personal interest of the survey researchers (a company providing water sports equipment can be unwittingly biased and skewer the results in favor of water sports activities simply by placing the focus of the questionnaire on said type of activity).

Another line of reasoning that the author uses to support his argument is the idea that river pollution and odor are responsible for the low usage of the city river. This argument is based on several other assumptions like the notion that the complaints received about river odor and pollution are representative of the city and the idea that there are no other possible explanations as to why the river usage is low. It is entirely within the realm of possibility that the overall number of complaints, when reported to the total number of citizens, is very low. Or, if the number of complaints is high, it may well be that only a small number of people are responsible for them (in the sense that a single person files a large number of complaints). In both these instances, the complaints prove not to be representative for the overall opinion of the citizens. If that is the case, and this assumption is unwarranted, then the upcoming cleaning of the river will not address the main cause of the low river usage, and the number of people engaging in sporting activities on the waterway will remain unaffected. As such, increasing the budget for riverside facilities would be pointless, not to mention costly.

30

The other assumption supporting the idea that the river pollution and odor are responsible for the low usage of the city river is the notion that there are no other possible explanations as to why the river usage is low. If there are other reasons why people don't like to use the Mason City river, like the distance to the river or the presence of strong currents, then the cleaning of the river would fail to address the people's main concerns with the waterway, and river usage will not increase.

These lines of inquiry lead directly to another main assumption on which the author rests his case for increasing the amount of money allocated to riverside facilities. The author assumes that cleaning up the river will increase the river's usage for water sports. When advocating for this line of thought, the author assumes that the smell and quality of the water are due to pollution and not naturally occurring events. Sulfur in the water can give it a rotten egg smell, or the presence of natural gas in the river banks can create a foul odor. As for the water quality, mineral deposits in the water or an abundance of underwater plant life can give the river an unappealing look. These are just some of the possible alternate explanations for the river's odor and water quality.

If there are natural causes for the look and odor of the river, cleaning the river will not get rid of either problem. Provided that most citizens consider the river's look and odor to be the main deterrent against doing sporting activities on the Mason City river, then river usage would not increase with the cleansing of the river. As such, the proposal to increase funds for riverside facilities would not be supported by a rise in actual usage of those facilities.

When proposing to increase the money allocated to the riverside facilities in Mason City, the author of the argument assumes there will be a sufficient increase in river usage to justify taking these budgetary measures. An implicit assumption of this argument is the idea that a great percentage of people will go to the riverside. If, for instance, there are a lot of water sport outlets in town, due to the river being unappealing and the residents of Mason City loving water-based activities, it's entirely likely that even after the river is made accessible, a great percentage of the population will continue to use those outlets (especially since they like to offer subscriptions). Should that be the case, and the number of people who go to the riverside is low, there would be no justification to increase the budget for riverside facilities.

All in all, when making the case for increasing the budget for the riverside facilities in Mason City, the author of the proposal makes a series of assumptions that are not backed by evidence and require further investigation. Spending taxpayer money always needs good justification;without a more thorough investigation, the author risks drawing inaccurate conclusions that will lead to making ineffective or costly suggestions.

30

Argument Task 31

The council of Maple County, concerned about the county's becoming overdeveloped, is debating a proposed measure that would prevent the development of existing farmland in the county. But the council is also concerned that such a restriction, by limiting the supply of new housing, could lead to significant increases in the price of housing in the county. Proponents of the measure note that Chestnut County established a similar measure ten years ago and its housing prices have increased only modestly since. However, opponents of the measure note that Pine County adopted restrictions on the development of new residential housing fifteen years ago, and its housing prices have since more than doubled. The council currently predicts that the proposed measure, if passed, will result in a significant increase in housing prices in Maple County.

Write a response in which you discuss what questions would need to be answered in order to decide whether the prediction and the argument on which it is based are reasonable. Be sure to explain how the answers to these questions would help to evaluate the prediction.

 Strategies

Prediction:

Limiting the development of existing farmland will result in a significant increase in housing prices in Maple County.

Argument:

Proponents point to similar measures being adopted in Chestnut County, resulting in only a modest increase in housing prices.

Opponents point to similar measures being adopted in Pine County resulting in housing prices more than double.

Questions:

◆ What is the median income in each of the other counties? How do they compare to the median income in Maple County?

31

◆ How do the school systems in the three counties compare?

◆ What was the housing inventory in the other two counties prior to development? What is the housing inventory in Maple County? This would include apartments, condominiums, town houses, as well as detached single-family homes.

◆ What incentive is there for people to move to any of the three counties? The counties may provide different services and facilities that make one county more desirable than the others.

◆ Is one of the counties home to a large city? Development around a large urban area may demand higher prices.

◆ What is the demographic of each county? It could be that Pine County residents are married couples

◆ with two incomes and growing families who need larger homes. Chestnut County residents may be retirees who are downsizing.

◆ Is there anything inherently wrong with increased prices for homes in Maple County? The residents of Maple County may benefit from a rise in real estate prices. The council may fear that higher housing prices will discourage people from moving to their county.

Your notes do not have to be exhaustive. As you begin to write your essay, your brain will generate new ideas. Make certain that you keep the directions in mind as you develop your ideas.

Sample Essay

In a backlash against urban sprawl, counties have created restrictions and parameters for development that require expanding their infrastructure and broadening the scope of their services. When a developer presents a plan for a new residential subdivision, he relies on the community to extend its water and sewer lines and lay down new streets. There are more structures for the fire department to cover, more area for police cruisers to patrol, and more roadways for plows to clear in winter. If families with children move into the new homes, the schools may become overcrowded. The expansion of the tax base may not offset increased costs to the city. Despite these additional demands, an expanded housing inventory tends to keep prices affordable and encourages people to move to the area. The council of Maple County would be wise to consider several questions before deciding either course of action regarding development.

The main objection to restricting development appears to be a fear that housing prices will increase dramatically. This is a likely consequence only if conditions that exist in Maple County are similar to those in Pine County. Why did housing prices more than double in Pine County? It may be that Pine County is a more desirable place to live, and there is a greater demand for homes there. Supply and demand always influence the price of any commodity. Pine County may be home to a large city that provides great career opportunities and cultural activities

31

that make its suburbs attractive to upper middle-class citizens. Pine County may have award-winning schools that attract young families desiring a high-quality education for their children. If Pine County does, indeed, possess these attributes, a lack of housing inventory would inflate the prices of existing homes.

In contrast, Chestnut County may lack the desirable characteristics that make an area attractive to people seeking a new place to live. Why did the prices of homes in Chestnut County experience only a moderate increase when officials limited development there? This county may be rural in nature, with significant distances between homes, eliminating the neighborhood structure that families find appealing. It may be that Chestnut County lacks opportunities for shopping, recreation, and cultural activities that attract well-educated, affluent families. Its schools may not be stellar, discouraging families with children from settling there. Even though Chestnut County has limited housing inventory, the demand for the homes that do exist simply isn't as high as it is in Pine County. As a result, any increases in prices there are likely due to inflation.

How does Maple County settle the argument about restricting development? Members of the council should complete a thorough analysis of the three counties to determine how Maple County is similar to or different from the other two. If Maple County has more in common with Pine County, they may want to lift restrictions on development and allow more homes to be built to keep housing prices affordable. On the other hand, if Maple County has more in common with Chestnut County, restricting development for the time being may be the wisest course. They will not have expended county funds to expand infrastructure and services for a county that is not likely to attract sufficient numbers of new residents to offset the cost of such improvement.

31

Argument Task 32

The following appeared as a recommendation by a committee planning a ten-year budget for the city of Calatrava.

"The birthrate in our city is declining: in fact, last year's birthrate was only one-half that of five years ago. Thus the number of students enrolled in our public schools will soon decrease dramatically, and we can safely reduce the funds budgeted for education during the next decade. At the same time, we can reduce funding for athletic playing fields and other recreational facilities. As a result, we will have sufficient money to fund city facilities and programs used primarily by adults, since we can expect the adult population of the city to increase."

Write a response in which you discuss what specific evidence is needed to evaluate the argument and explain how the evidence would weaken or strengthen the argument.

 Strategies

Argument:

Because of declining birth rates, the city can redirect funds it has habitually spent on facilities for young people to programs for adults.

In developing your response, you must determine what evidence the planning committee needs to uncover before making its final budget decisions for the next ten-year cycle.

Facts and Assumptions:

◆ Last year's birthrate was half that of five years ago. The assumption is that the birth rate has been declining steadily. Is last year's birthrate an anomaly? What was the birthrate in the intervening years? How many births were there five years ago? If there were only four births, for example, then half of that is not a huge drop. If there were 100 births five years ago, then half of that is cause for concern

◆ The committee assumes that the lower birth rate predicts a smaller school population. The committee reasons that the school budget can, therefore, be reduced. Does the committee have any figures on the number of families that may have moved to the town?

32

◆ The committee uses its assumption of a smaller school population to suggest that less money be spent on athletic playing fields and other recreational facilities. Even if the number of young people declines, won't those remaining still play sports and use the recreational facilities? Might residents be willing to pay to use the facilities to offset the cost of maintaining them? Are the facilities used only by children?

◆ The committee suggests diverting funds previously used on youth facilities to fund facilities and programs used primarily by adults. The assumption is that the adult population will increase as the youth population decreases. If there is a decline in the birth rate, won't there be a corresponding decline in the number of people who become adults? Have other towns had success doing this? How does the town attract new residents if it has let its facilities for young people decline in quality?

Your notes do not have to be exhaustive. As you begin to write your essay, your brain will generate new ideas. Make certain that you keep the directions in mind as you develop your ideas.

 ## Sample Essay

Unless one is planning a retirement community, catering to the needs of adults at the expense of the children is an unwise choice. It is sometimes easy to relegate children to the background when making budgetary decisions. Children don't vote or pay taxes. When there is an apparent decline in the number of children requiring services traditionally reserved for them in a town, it becomes easier to divert funds for their benefit to programs and facilities that focus on adults. Those voters and taxpayers whose own children have grown are now focused on their own needs and may see decisions that benefit them as the correct ones. City stakeholders must take a closer look at the facts presented by the planning committee before making any long-term decisions for the community.

The apparently drastic decline in the birthrate seems to justify the committee's recommendation. When citizens are told that the birth rate last year was just half of what it was five years ago, visions of empty classrooms and playing fields fill their heads. It would be logical to assume that fewer tax dollars will be needed to educate and entertain the young people of Calatrava. What these residents must do first is to more closely examine this statistic. How many children were born in Calatrava five years ago, and how many were born last year? A decline of fifty percent is alarming. However, if there were only four births in Calatrava five years ago, then last year's births totaled two. Two fewer births is hardly a cause to fire teachers, close schools, or let playing fields become decrepit. Upon further investigation, the committee may discover that five years ago, Calatrava recorded fifty births and last year only twenty-five births. Twenty-five children represent an average classroom population. This figure might justify eliminating an elementary school teaching position. The committee should also look at the intervening years. Was last year's birth rate a fluke? Was the birth rate of five years ago repeated or even surpassed in the years that followed? In addition to births, the population of children is affected by families moving in and out of Calatrava. The planning committee can access information about home sales and how many families have moved into or out of the city to get an accurate picture of the city's demographics.

32

Forestalling maintenance of athletic fields and recreational facilities may seem like a prudent move if, indeed, the population of children has declined significantly. The fact remains that the children of the town will still participate in school athletics and recreational activities. If the fields and facilities deteriorate, other towns may be reluctant to bring their teams to Calatrava to compete. Calatrava teams will have to travel more frequently to complete their athletic schedules, and this would be an expense that might offset the savings gained by ignoring the fields at home. Do adults in the community use these facilities? Does the town have an adult softball league that plays its games on the school athletic fields? Do adults as well as children use the community swimming pool?

Calatrava's planning committee must dig more deeply into the facts they have used to make their preliminary recommendations. The taxpayers should demand to know if their tax dollars are being spent in a way that benefits the greatest number of residents.

Argument Task 33

The following appeared in a recommendation from the planning department of the city of Transopolis.

"Ten years ago, as part of a comprehensive urban renewal program, the city of Transopolis adapted for industrial use a large area of severely substandard housing near the freeway. Subsequently, several factories were constructed there, crime rates in the area declined, and property tax revenues for the entire city increased. To further revitalize the city, we should now take similar action in a declining residential area on the opposite side of the city. Since some houses and apartments in existing nearby neighborhoods are currently unoccupied, alternate housing for those displaced by this action will be readily available."

Write a response in which you discuss what specific evidence is needed to evaluate the argument and explain how the evidence would weaken or strengthen the argument.

 Strategies

Argument:

To further revitalize Transopolis, the city should extend its urban renewal program to another declining residential area of the city.

In developing your response, you are asked to identify evidence that Transopolis needs to carry out its urban renewal plan.

Facts and Assumptions:

◆ Since Transopolis replaced substandard housing with an industrial complex, crime rates in the area have declined. The writer assumes that one action has led to the other. It is just as likely that an area with fewer people will have less crime. Has crime increased in other parts of the city?

◆ Tax revenues have increased for the entire city. Did the city have to expend any of its revenues to either buy out or relocate the former residents of the substandard housing? The new tax revenues may limply offset previous expenses. Will the city have to use its funds to develop the new proposed location?

33

◆ There is demand for more development in Transopolis. This assumption underlies the recommendation to remove a neighborhood in decline and repeat the development already completed on the other side of town.

◆ Some housing is available close to the proposed development for residents who will be displaced.

◆ The assumption that it makes more economic sense to relocate people to empty houses and apartments rather than locate the development there and leave the residents where they are.

Your notes do not have to be exhaustive. As you begin to write your essay, your brain will generate new ideas. Make certain that you keep the directions in mind as you develop your ideas.

 ## Sample Essay

Before moving forward with plans to develop an additional part of the city, planners should consider the real benefits of doing so. They should look for evidence to support the claims of reduced crime and increased tax revenues along with evidence of a need for more development. The current owners of the land and buildings or the contractors who complete the work may be the only beneficiaries.

The planning committee reports a reduction in crime because of the previous urban renewal project. That might be expected in an area that is now devoted to factories. The committee needs evidence that crime has not simply been moved to another part of the city along with the residents. Simply displacing crime is not a justification for further development. Is there evidence of significant crime in the location proposed for the new development? If not, that rationale won't fly. Moving crime to a different part of the city does not make residents safer or save the city any money.

The planners may be living with a field of Dreams mentality: if we build it, they will come. Does the city have manufacturers clamoring for space in Transopolis? If the city buys out the residents of the area and erects buildings on speculation, it may find itself a landlord of empty buildings with a sizable budget deficit. The taxpayers should demand to know that there is a guaranteed return on their investment. Otherwise, this development could wipe out any extra revenues from the previous urban renewal. Evidence is needed to support the choice of location for the new revitalization effort. The planner proposes moving residents of the declining neighborhood to nearby neighborhoods where some houses and apartments are unoccupied.

Further research may demonstrate that it would be more fiscally and humanely sound to place the new development where residences are already unoccupied. There is too little evidence in this passage to show that one location has advantages over the other. The city needs evidence of easy access to the proposed location. The original site is near the freeway, providing a means for workers and commercial vehicles to get there. Located on the opposite side of the city, the proposed site may require building new or widening existing roads. The result could be additional displacement of Transopolis citizens and/ or a reduction in property values.

33

All stakeholders of the city should complete more investigation of this proposal of the planning department before giving a green signal. It would be easy to get on board with the planning department considering the previous successes. However, Transopolis may have completed all the development it can presently handle or needs.

Argument Task 34

The following appeared in a memorandum written by the chairperson of the West Egg Town Council.

"Two years ago, consultants predicted that West Egg's landfill, which is used for garbage disposal, would be completely filled within five years. During the past two years, however, the town's residents have been recycling twice as much material as they did in previous years. Next month the amount of recycled material—which includes paper, plastic, and metal—should further increase, since charges for pickup of other household garbage will double. Furthermore, over 90 percent of the respondents to a recent survey said that they would do more recycling in the future. Because of our town's strong commitment to recycling, the available space in our landfill should last for considerably longer than predicted."

Write a response in which you discuss what specific evidence is needed to evaluate the argument and explain how the evidence would weaken or strengthen the argument.

 Strategies

The first step in performing your analysis consists of identifying the texts' key point, recommendation,

prediction or hypothesis. All the other arguments and assumptions are designed to support this central claim. In this case, the author attempts to demonstrate that "West Egg's landfill should last longer than predicted".

The next step would involve creating a statement that summarizes the text by including the central claim and its supporting arguments.

The West Egg Town Council chairperson predicts that due to a significant increase in material recycling the town's landfill space should last longer than the five years that were estimated by experts.

When considering the evidence that is necessary to support the arguments outlined in the text, it is important to keep in mind that arguments are based on assumptions – points that are taken to be true, without the need for proof. This is what you need to look for: explicit and implicit assumptions, since they require evidence that is not already listed in the text.

Assumptions:

Explicit Assumptions	Implicit Assumptions
Increased recycling means significantly less material is sent to the landfill	• Recycled material constitutes a great percentage of the monthly waste production per household
Increased household garbage pickup fees will stimulate recycling	• Recycling can be greatly increased
Residents declared pro-recycling attitude will translate into facts	• Household waste production rates will not change
The filling rate of the West Eng landfill has dropped	• Stable population growth • Reduction in "other household garbage" collection means less trash will go to the landfill • Garbage pickup fees are an effective measure • The survey respondents are representative for the population • West Egg landfill is currently emptier than predicted

Evidence:

◆ Percentage of material currently being recycled out of monthly waste production rates

◆ Percentage of non-recyclable material out of the monthly waste production

◆ Comparison of the amount of waste that can be recycled with the amount of waste that is recycled

◆ Waste production rates over the years compared with recycling rates

◆ Population expansion rates compared to recycling rates

◆ Percentage of improperly sorted material that is non-recyclable and will end up in the landfill

◆ Survey on primary motivations for recycling

◆ Percentage of survey respondents out of the total city population

◆ Survey demographics compared to the town's demographics

◆ Current infrastructure waste handling capacity reported to the expected increase in recycling

34

Government & Politics

◆ Current assessment of how full the landfill is compared to the predicted assessment

 ## Sample Essay

The West Egg Town Council chairperson predicts that due to a significant increase in material recycling the town's landfill space should last longer than the five years that were estimated by experts. To accurately assess the prediction, the town council would require data about the current landfill occupation levels. This information will serve to prove or disprove if the filling rate matches the councilperson's predictions. Should the fill rate prove to be slower than the expert's estimation, the chairperson's assessment of the future of West Egg's landfill would be undermined, although this evidence would have no definitive bearing on whether recycling is responsible for the positive results. Having the data reveal the opposite, that the landfill's occupancy rate matches or exceeds the expert's evaluation, would cast doubt on the effectiveness of recycling and the optimistic outcome envisioned by the chairperson. In this case, alternative measures would have to be taken to ensure that the occupancy rate of the town's landfill decreases to more manageable levels.

West Egg's chairperson invokes other arguments when making his prediction, chief among them being the fact that an increase in recycling would mean that significantly less waste material is sent to the landfill. The chairperson rests this argument on the assumption that recycled material constitutes a great percentage of the monthly waste production per household. As such, to validate the claim, the author would have to provide evidence related to the percentage of material currently being recycled out of monthly waste production rates. This evidence can showcase whether the amount of material being recycled is sufficient to prompt a drop in the landfill rates or whether the total amount of recycled material is low enough not to warrant such optimistic forecasts about the future of the town's landfill – a doubling of a low percentage would still constitute a low percentage.

When discussing the increase of recycling and its effects on the town, the chairperson needs to take into consideration the measure's potential for growth, namely, to what percentage out of the total amount of waste can recycling be increased. This information would help establish whether recycling can be greatly increased, in which case the town would have to focus its efforts on campaigns and infrastructure centered on it or if the percentage of material that can be recycled would soon hit a plateau, which would mean that the chairperson would have to research alternative measures of waste management to meet the prediction about the landfill rate.

Another assumption made by the chairman in his prediction is centered on the idea that some of the parameters of the equation will remain unchanged, namely the fact that household waste production rates do not change, and the population size is stable. If population expansion rates were to reveal a drastic increase in the number of residents in West Egg, the amount of waste material produced would also increase. The author of the prediction would have to consider this new data and factor it against recycling rates to determine whether the filling rate has remained constant or if recycling needs to be increased even more to deal with the surplus of waste material. However, if the data were to reveal that the population is stable or decreasing, then the chairman's predictions would not be affected by the outcome. The relative stability of waste production rates also comes into play when assessing the future effects of recycling. A stable monthly waste production rate would mean that any increase in recycling would reduce the amount of material being sent to the landfill. However, if people were to produce more waste each month, an increase in recycling might end up evening out with the surplus of material and not having any effect on the amount of garbage being sent to the landfill. The chairman should support his prediction with more data about the makeup of the monthly household waste rates and population information if he wants to make a more accurate estimate of the future landfill occupancy.

The chairman cites survey findings as a basis for predicting an increase in recycling rates in West Egg. When handling surveys and statistical data it is always important to look not only at the results but also at the theoretical framework and methodology of the study being conducted to be able to ascertain whether the reasoning is sound, or if the scientists have missed some crucial aspect or mitigating factor. The chairman needs to take into consideration how comparable are the demographics of the survey participants to those of the general population of West Egg. If the general population is not accurately represented by the survey respondents, it would become more difficult to support the claim that recycling will increase in the future. However, if the beliefs of the town's residents are accurately reflected by the cited survey, it becomes more likely that the predicted increase in recycling will match the expected rates.

All in all, the chairperson needs to take a lot more evidence into consideration to ensure that the landfill predictions have a solid factual basis. The author should also take measures to ensure that the increase in recycling can be easily supported by the infrastructure.

34

Argument Task 35

The following appeared in a memo from a budget planner for the city of Grandview.

"Our citizens are well aware of the fact that while the Grandview Symphony Orchestra was struggling to succeed, our city government promised annual funding to help support its programs. Last year, however, private contributions to the symphony increased by 200 percent, and attendance at the symphony's concerts-in-the-park series doubled. The symphony has also announced an increase in ticket prices for next year. Such developments indicate that the symphony can now succeed without funding from the city government, and we can eliminate that expense from next year's budget. Therefore, we recommend that the city of Grandview eliminate its funding for the Grandview Symphony from next year's budget. By doing so, we can prevent a city budget deficit without threatening the success of the symphony."

Write a response in which you discuss what questions would need to be answered in order to decide whether the recommendation is likely to have the predicted result. Be sure to explain how the answers to these questions would help to evaluate the recommendation.

Strategies

A good place to start your analysis is by creating a statement that reveals the main idea of the argument. Although the writer is creating an argument, he may ultimately be stating a position, making a recommendation, or making a prediction. It may be helpful for you to determine which of these formats is most evident in the argument.

Based on information about new revenues for the Grandview Symphony Orchestra, the budget planner for Grandview concludes that the city can eliminate its traditional funding of the orchestra and avoid a budget deficit.

Assumptions:

◆ Increased donations and higher ticket prices will enable the Grandview Symphony Orchestra to function without funding from the city.

◆ Those who attended concerts in the park will pay to attend regular performances.

◆ Eliminating funding for the symphony will prevent a budget deficit.

35

◆ People will pay higher prices for tickets.

◆ Private donations will remain at the increased level.

◆ Avoiding a budget deficit relies on eliminating funding for the symphony orchestra.

Questions:

◆ What percentage of the symphony's expenses is covered by private donations?

◆ What percentage of the symphony's expenses is covered by ticket sales?

◆ How will an increase in ticket prices affect sales?

◆ What was the total of private donations prior to the increase?

◆ How much money is raised by the concerts in the park?

◆ What portion of the city budget is dedicated to the symphony orchestra?

◆ How important is the orchestra to the city?

After completing these steps, you should have enough material to write your analysis. Remember that you are not creating a position of your own; you are evaluating the strengths and weaknesses of the existing argument. You do not have to include all of the points that you have created in your prewriting. In fact, during the process of drafting your analysis, other ideas may come to mind, and if they strengthen your analysis, you should include them.

 ## Sample Essay

Cities are responsible for allocating tax dollars to institutions and services that provide the most benefit for their citizens. They fund police and fire departments, schools, and public works. They may also contribute to libraries, recreation departments, and museums. When budgets are tight, those in control may have to decide between repairing the streets and putting a new roof on the library. They may ask the school department to eliminate positions or public works to cancel overtime. Grandview's budget planner appears to have sufficient evidence that demonstrates the likelihood of continued success for the Grandview Symphony Orchestra. He predicts that the city can eliminate its usual funding of the orchestra and, thus, avoid a budget deficit. The strength of his prediction relies on the answers to several questions.

What portion of the orchestra's budget comes from the various sources? First, consider the city's contribution. If it is a small portion, losing the money may not have any impact on the ability of the orchestra to survive. On the other hand, if it is a large portion of the orchestra's operating budget, losing it, even with the increase in

35

donations and higher ticket prices, may cause the orchestra to fail. Second is the portion provided by private donations. The size of it determines whether or not a 200 percent increase is significant. If private patrons formerly supplied 10 percent of the orchestra's budget, the increase would represent a current 30 percent of the budget. That increase alone may enable the orchestra to survive easily without a contribution from the city.

In contrast, private money that formerly constituted only two percent of the total operating budget would now be six percent, which may still leave the orchestra in need of city money. It would appear that the increase in donations is insufficient to ensure the financial health of the orchestra. Ticket prices also contribute to the orchestra's finances, and the group has plans to increase them. What effect will higher prices have on ticket sales? Lower sales could offset any gains made by increased prices. How many people attended the concerts in the park before the audience doubled in size, and did they pay an admission fee? Doubling becomes more meaningful the higher the base number is. If that audience paid no admission fee, the number of people in it doesn't matter because the series is not a source of revenue for the orchestra. In fact, people who can attend free concerts in the park may forgo buying tickets for an inside performance, dismissing the revenue stream for the orchestra.

How important is the orchestra to the city? The Grandview City Orchestra may be a highly regarded institution that brings people to the city from surrounding towns. They may have dinner in local restaurants before the performance. Some may travel from far away and need to stay in a hotel. The revenue generated by concert goers may more than offset the orchestra's cost to the city.

What portion of the city budget is dedicated to the symphony orchestra? Is it a large enough expenditure that eliminating it will make a significant difference in the city's budget? The actual contribution by the city may be a fraction of one percent of the total budget. Depending on the size of the forecasted deficit, the money given to the orchestra may make little difference, or it may be just enough to prevent the deficit.

What happens if the orchestra falls on hard times in the future? Will the city be able to reinstate its contribution, or will the symphony orchestra be forced to shut down? If this should occur a few years down the road, the city may have committed the funds it formerly gave to the city orchestra to some other facility in the city. The likelihood of the city's finding that money again is slim. The orchestra may leave behind an empty building that will be difficult to sell and, thus, create an unattractive appearance in its neighborhood.

Too many questions are left to be answered before the city leaders make what may be an unwise and irrevocable decision about the future of the Grandview City Orchestra. When they have sufficient information, the council or mayor can make a more informed choice about the funding. The predicted result of avoiding a budget deficit by not funding the orchestra may be proven false.

35

Argument Task 36

The following appeared in a memo from the vice president of a company that builds shopping malls around the country.

"The surface of a section of Route 101, paved just two years ago by Good Intentions Roadways, is now badly cracked with a number of dangerous potholes. In another part of the state, a section of Route 40, paved by Appian Roadways more than four years ago, is still in good condition. In a demonstration of their continuing commitment to quality, Appian Roadways recently purchased state-of-the-art paving machinery and hired a new quality-control manager. Therefore, I recommend hiring Appian Roadways to construct the access roads for all our new shopping malls. I predict that our Appian access roads will not have to be repaired for at least four years."

Write a response in which you discuss what questions would need to be answered in order to decide whether the recommendation is likely to have the predicted result. Be sure to explain how the answers to these questions would help to evaluate the recommendation.

 Strategies

A good place to start your analysis is by creating a statement that reveals the main idea of the argument. Although the writer is creating an argument, he may ultimately be stating a position, making a recommendation, or making a prediction. It may be helpful for you to determine which of these formats is most evident in the argument.

The writer argues that Appian Roadways will be a better choice than Good Intentions Roadways for paving the access roads to his new shopping malls and predicts that the pavement should remain free of repairs for at least four years.

Assumptions:

◆ Routes 101 and 40 handle the same amount and type of traffic.

◆ Both routes have the same type of pavement.

◆ Mall access roads will experience the same traffic conditions as Route 40.

◆ New machinery guarantees good work.

◆ Weather conditions are identical in both parts of the state.

36

◆ Appian Roadways does better work than Good Intentions Roadways.

◆ Good Intentions Roadways uses outdated equipment.

Questions:

◆ How does the traffic on Route 101 compare to the traffic on Route 40?

◆ Are weather conditions the same in both parts of the state?

◆ Why did Appian Way buy new equipment?

◆ Does Appian Way's paving generally last longer than that of other companies?

◆ How has Good Intentions performed on other paving projects?

◆ Are the malls in question located in various parts of the state?

After completing these steps, you should have enough material to write your analysis. Remember that you are not creating a position of your own; you are evaluating the strengths and weaknesses of the existing argument. You do not have to include all of the points that you have created in your prewriting. In fact, during the process of drafting your analysis, other ideas may come to mind, and if they strengthen your analysis, you should include them.

 ## Sample Essay

Targument reveals information that makes it appear that Appian Way provides road paving that lasts longer than that of Good Intentions Roadways. All things being equal, that may be true. The scant information in this argument raises several questions that must be answered before selecting a paving contractor, and the mall developer may discover inequities that affect his decision.

Are weather conditions the same in both parts of the state mentioned in the argument? Many states are large enough or varied enough in geography to experience varied weather conditions at any time of the year. Northern parts of the state may have a long winter season, leading to frost heaves which crack the pavement in the spring. Warmer parts of the state may have large amounts of rain that cause washouts and undermining of the pavement. Has there been any unusually severe weather event along Route 101 during the past two years that could account for its state of disrepair? A hurricane or tornado could have caused more-than-normal wear on a stretch of highway. Route 101 may follow the winding course of a river or curve around geographical formations such as mountains causing more rapid wear and tear on the pavement. In contrast, Route 40 may pass through a portion of the state, where the average temperature is moderate, and no geographical impediments stand in the way of the road's running flat and straight.

Is traffic different on both roadways? The volume of traffic on Route 101 might be considerably higher than the volume of traffic on Route 40. Even if the number of vehicles along both highways may be the same, the types of vehicles traveling on each may affect the durability of each road's surface. Large numbers of heavy trucks can cause more wear and tear on a road's surface in a shorter period of time than the same number of passenger vehicles. Concerns about the efficacy of one paving company over the other can be allayed by answering these questions.

Why did Appian Way buy new equipment? Does the company regularly update to the newest equipment? A company that demonstrates careful attention to quality by updating its equipment is an attractive choice on the surface. On the other hand, a company that allows its equipment to fall into disrepair and must replace it may have the same negligent attitude toward the work it does. Does Good Intentions also have the latest equipment? If so, the state of either company's equipment is not a sufficient reason to choose one over the other. One should also ask why Appian Way has hired a new quality-control manager. Has Appian Way received complaints about the quality of their work? The nature of the work done on Route 40 may not be typical of the company's paving ability. Likewise, the subpar work on Route 101 may not be representative of the quality that Good Intentions normally produces. How has each company performed over time? Knowing that one or the other of the paving concerns has an exemplary record for quality and durability would help the mall developers choose the best candidate for their projects.

Are the malls in question located in various parts of the state? Depending upon their locations, the malls may be subject to traffic and weather conditions that will affect the durability of the paving on their access roads. Predicting that Appian Way's paving will not need repair for at least four years may be overly optimistic. Adopting the recommendation and accepting the prediction that follows should be done only after answering several questions.

37

Argument Task 37

Since those issues of Newsbeat magazine that featured political news on their front cover were the poorest-selling issues over the past three years, the publisher of Newsbeat has recommended that the magazine curtail its emphasis on politics to focus more exclusively on economics and personal finance. She points to a recent survey of readers of general interest magazines that indicate greater reader interest in economic issues than in political ones. Newsbeat's editor, however, opposes the proposed shift in editorial policy, pointing out that very few magazines offer extensive political coverage anymore.

Write a response in which you discuss what questions would need to be answered in order to decide whether the recommendation and the argument on which it is based are reasonable. Be sure to explain how the answers to these questions would help to evaluate the recommendation.

 Strategies

A good place to start your analysis is by creating a statement that reveals the main idea of the argument. Although the writer is creating an argument, he may ultimately be stating a position, making a recommendation, or making a prediction. It may be helpful for you to determine which of these formats is most evident in the argument.

In order to revive sales of Newsbeat, the publisher, against the advice of the editor, suggests shifting the magazines' focus from politics to economics and personal finance.

Assumptions:

◆ Political news on the cover rather than other content is responsible for decreased sales of certain issues of the magazine.

◆ Readers of general interest magazines will begin to read Newsbeat if the magazine changes its focus.

◆ Sales of Newsbeat magazine will rise if it features more stories about economics and personal finance.

◆ There is room in the marketplace for another magazine with a focus on economics and personal finance.

◆ Sales of magazines that feature articles on economics and personal finance are higher than sales of Newsbeat.

Questions that need answers in order to decide whether the recommendation and argument are reasonable:

◆ What other factors may have contributed to lower sales of those issues?

◆ Were those poorest-selling issues published in the same year, or were they evenly distributed over the three-year period?

◆ Has the magazine surveyed its own readers to learn their preferences?

◆ How many issues feature political news on their covers?

◆ Were any of those years' election years?

◆ Does Newsbeat have staff writers capable of writing about economics and personal finance?

◆ Is there a market for another magazine that focuses on economics and personal finance?

◆ Have magazines that feature articles about economics and personal finance continued to sell well?

◆ Why is there an apparently strong interest in information about economics and personal finance?

After completing these steps, you should have enough material to write your analysis. Remember that you are not creating a position of your own; you are evaluating the strengths and weaknesses of the existing argument. You do not have to include all of the points that you have created in your prewriting. In fact, during the process of drafting your analysis, other ideas may come to mind, and if they strengthen your analysis, you should include them.

 ## Sample Essay

The publisher of Newsbeat magazine should not be too hasty to change the format of the publication. Using a survey of readers of general interest magazines to determine the future course of Newsbeat is akin to comparing apples to oranges. Before making costly changes, this publisher should ask several important questions that will help her determine the editorial decisions she should make to improve Newsbeat's circulation.

Did the three-year dip in sales occur in the period between national elections? It's logical to expect that interest in political news would peak during election years and wane in the other three years. The publisher does not reveal whether or not this three-year dip is typical throughout the magazine's history. If that is, indeed, the case, the publisher and editor should make decisions about some changes in focus during the dips and continue to focus on politics during the fourth year. The focus on politics may not be the real reason for the dip in sales. Are the articles poorly written, or do they express unpopular opinions? They may not be objective enough, offending half of the potential readers. The articles may not be timely, or they may be too regional in nature.

Has Newsbeat conducted its own survey of its readers? If Newsbeat wants information about the preferences of its reader, the magazine should conduct its own survey. The questions on the survey cited in the argument may have been worded to elicit specific answers. Using survey results out of context can be misleading. Just because readers of general interest magazines prefer articles about economics and personal finance to articles about politics may not indicate that the same is true for the readers of Newsbeat. In fact, the respondents may prefer articles about fashion or entertainment above all others, and articles about economics may be very near the bottom of their list of favorites. They may not buy Newsbeat whatever its focus.

Focusing on economics and personal finance may increase Newsbeat's circulation, but that may be short-lived if the articles are poorly written. Does Newsbeat have writers on its staff that are capable of writing in depth about those topics? If Newsbeat is forced to hire writers whose expertise is in the field of finance, the expense may not be offset by increased sales. Alternatively, the publisher may be forced to lay off seasoned political writers to hire finance writers, and, when she needs them during election years, they will not be available. This strategy could result in a death spiral for Newsbeat.

Looking at the periodicals section of a grocery store or bookstore reveals the wide variety of genres available. There's something for everyone. As a corollary, there must be someone for everything. There must be an audience for a news magazine. The method used by that audience to gain access to magazines has changed. Has Newsbeat tried another format to attract readers? Like so many other publications, Newsbeat may have to create an online presence. They may have to use some form of social media to increase exposure to the magazine. If Newsbeat has not made subscriptions available in the past, perhaps they should do so now.

Are poor sales of issues with political topics featured on the cover a cause for great concern? If the magazine is published every month, thirty-six issues would have appeared in a three-year span. If one or two per year featured political stories, the lower sales of those particular issues should not be the only reason to change the magazine's focus. For any issue to have the poorest sales in any given year, the sales total only has to be one dollar less than the next- lowest-selling issue. The publisher may be overstating her case for change.

Based on current trends in periodicals and the manner in which people gain access to information of any kind, not only Newsbeat, but every magazine may be in peril. Any change that the publisher and editor can agree on should be taken with caution. Depending on the answers to important questions, they may be saving this magazine, and they may be throwing good money after bad in an effort to increase circulation.

Chapter **13**
Science & Technology

Argument Task 38

An ancient, traditional remedy for insomnia—the scent of lavender flowers—has now been proved effective. In a recent study, 30 volunteers with chronic insomnia slept each night for three weeks on lavender-scented pillows in a controlled room where their sleep was monitored electronically. During the first week, volunteers continued to take their usual sleeping medication. They slept soundly but woke up feeling tired. At the beginning of the second week, the volunteers discontinued their sleeping medication. During that week, they slept less soundly than the previous week and felt even more tired. During the third week, the volunteers slept longer and more soundly than in the previous two weeks. Therefore, the study proves that lavender cures insomnia within a short period of time.

Write a response in which you discuss what specific evidence is needed to evaluate the argument and explain how the evidence would weaken or strengthen the argument.

 ## Strategies

The first step in performing your analysis consists of identifying the texts' key point, recommendation, prediction or hypothesis. All the other arguments and assumptions are designed to support this central claim. In this case, the author attempts to demonstrate that *"lavender completely cures insomnia in a short time"*.

The next step would involve creating a statement that summarizes the text by including the central claim and its supporting arguments.

Following a three week trial involving 30 volunteers, the writer claims that lavender has been shown to cure insomnia, given that the use of lavender has improved both the quality and soundness of sleep of the subjects.

When considering the evidence that is necessary to support the arguments outlined in the text, it is important to keep in mind that arguments are based on assumptions – points that are taken to be true, without the need for proof. This is what you need to look for: explicit and implicit assumptions, since they require evidence that is not already listed in the text. Explicit assumptions can be broken down into or supported by implicit assumptions

Assumptions

Explicit Assumptions	Implicit assumptions
Lavender does not just alleviate, but cures insomnia	• Insomnia completely disappears with the use of lavender
A thirty- person study is representative for the population	• The study subjects accurately represent the demographics of Mentia • 30 people are sufficient to prevent statistical anomalies
Lavender is the only explanation for the third week increase in the length and quality of sleep	• There were no other external contributing factors in the control room • The patients were not under the influence of any interfering drugs • Environmental changes are not responsible for the effect • The effects of the sleeping pills wore off during the second week • The volunteers followed the methodology without fail
A short term study is conclusive for long term effects	• The length of studies is sufficient to determine the effects of lavender • The effects of lavender will persist over time and multiple uses
Lavender improves the quality and length of sleep	• The length of sleep has significantly increased • The quality of sleep has significantly increased

After having established your assumptions, you can find the evidence that is needed to evaluate the argument by considering what proof is necessary to validate each implicit assumption.

Evidence

◆ Comparison of the sleep data (EEG, oximeter, REM length) between people with regular sleep patterns and the data gathered from the chronic insomniacs that have used lavender

◆ Demographic compatibility between the subjects of the study and the population of Mentia

◆ Minimum viable number of subjects necessary to conduct a study of this nature

◆ Standard deviation

◆ Comparison between the list of known sleep remedies and the elements available in the control room

◆ Comparison with a control group that undergoes the same trial in terms of length and sleeping quarters and continues to make use of sleeping pills

◆ The subjects daily drug test results for the duration of the study

◆ Differences in noise and luminosity between the control room and the subjects' own sleeping quarters

◆ The advertised kick-off time of the sleeping pills compared to the kick-off time proposed by the study

◆ Average duration of sleep studies

◆ Follow-ups on the buildup tolerance of lavender

◆ Percentage of sleep increase during third week compared to the first week

 ## Sample Essay

Following a three week trial involving thirty volunteers, the writer claims that lavender has been shown to cure insomnia. When dealing with short term studies that provide seemingly miraculous cures to modern ailments potential users should consider a host of supplementary information regarding the sample size, methodology, theoretical framework and side effects of the purported treatment.

The author's claim that lavender cures insomnia rests on the assumption that a thirty-person study is representative of the population. Therefore, the first things a potential user should consider are volunteer demographics like age and gender. A demographic comparison between the study's subjects and national population statistics would reveal whether the two groups are compatible and therefore the results of the study are applicable. If the two groups would turn out to be incompatible, the claim that lavender cures insomnia would become less plausible, given that there would be no data linking the demographic segments that were not featured in the study to the effects of lavender. For instance, a treatment tested solely on people under 40 is likely to have different effects on users above sixty, especially since there are different health conditions to take into account. However, should the two groups be demographically compatible, then this evidence would serve to strengthen the credibility of lavender as a cure for insomnia, as long as the study methodology is viable. Even if the volunteer group would be reasonably balanced in terms of demographics, potential lavender users should consider the minimum viable number of subjects necessary to conduct a study of this nature, related to the standard deviation. What this means is that if the number of subjects is considered to be too low, then minor effects would get amplified because each incidence would carry a greater statistical weight. This would mean that the study results could have been skewed by a small group of people that reacted very well to lavender and as such greatly influenced the statistical outcome of the result, making the claim that lavender cures insomnia less accurate. If the minimum requirement of study participants was met, and the overall standard deviation was low, potential users of lavender could more safely conclude that the study results are more likely to be viable. For a greater degree of certainty, potential users would also have to examine how the study was conducted.

The writer assumes that lavender is the only explanation for the third week increase in the length and quality of sleep. To assess the validity of that claim, readers should consider the necessary evidence to exclude any other explanations. Results of drug test controls performed regularly on the volunteers would be useful in establishing whether or not the increase in sleep quality and quantity was due to the effectiveness of lavender or whether the effects were caused by other drugs such as muscle relaxants and mild traces of sedatives present in medicine not related to sleeping pills. Should any of these drugs be detected in the subjects' system, the results of the study would fall under severe doubt, and the researchers would have to perform additional tests to be able to exclude the influence of these factors on the results. However, if nothing was detected following the drug tests, the researchers' findings would be strengthened, as the likelihood of external influences would be reduced.

Additionally, to exclude other potential environmental interactions, control group results should be examined – for instance people who have slept without lavender for the third week. This would serve to showcase whether the soundness of sleep is due to the fact that people have adapted to the environment or if the effect of lavender is producing the results. P The researchers should also consider how the environmental differences between the control room and the subjects' own bedrooms might affect the results of the test. If the subjects' home environment is much noisier or brighter than the control room, it can be said that their sleep improvement is due to the ambiance (lack or decrease of insomnia-inducing stressors) rather than the lavender. Were the data to reveal that there are no significant changes in the sleeping environment in terms of sleep inducing factors, then the resulting increase in sleep quality would likely be due to the existing variable, namely lavender.

When proposing lavender as a cure for insomnia, the author claims that the volunteers experienced an increase in sleep quality and duration. In examining this claim, readers should first assess the number of hours of sleep per week and per patient. Should the sleep duration during the second and third week not be significantly different, the argument would be weakened. A ten-minute sleep difference, for instance, even if it indicates an increase in sleep duration, does not constitute a sufficient basis for claiming to have cured insomnia. An increase of upwards of an hour, however, would mean that the subjects are getting significantly more sleep, making it more likely that lavender has a big impact on quality of sleep.

It is also important to relate the study findings to the population with regular sleep patterns. The data on the people who participated in the sleep study matches that of a control group constituted by people with regular sleep patterns, the study can more strongly conclude that lavender is a cure for insomnia. However, if the subjects of the study were not able to match or reach the vicinity of regular people when it comes to sleep quality, then lavender should not be considered a cure, but a treatment, since it did not eradicate the condition, but merely ameliorated it.

Overall, the study needs to present more evidence in regard to the methodology employed by the researchers to be able to exclude any other potentially influencing factors. To this effect, the addition of more control groups would significantly bolster the credibility of the results.

Argument Task 39

The vice president for human resources at Climpson Industries sent the following recommendation to the company's president.

"In an effort to improve our employees' productivity, we should implement electronic monitoring of employees' Internet use from their workstations. Employees who use the Internet inappropriately from their workstations need to be identified and punished if we are to reduce the number of work hours spent on personal or recreational activities, such as shopping or playing games. Installing software on company computers to detect employees' Internet use is the best way to prevent employees from wasting time on the job. It will foster a better work ethic at Climpson and improve our overall profits."

Write a response in which you discuss what specific evidence is needed to evaluate the argument and explain how the evidence would weaken or strengthen the argument.

Strategies

The first step in performing your analysis consists of identifying the texts' key point, recommendation, prediction or hypothesis. All the other arguments and assumptions are designed to support this central claim. In this case, the author attempts to demonstrate that "Internet monitoring will improve productivity and profits".

The next step would involve creating a statement that summarizes the text by including the central claim and its supporting arguments.

The vice president for human resources at Climpson Industries recommends implementing internet monitoring coupled with punishments for personal use in an effort to increase employee productivity and subsequently improve the company's profits.

When considering the evidence that is necessary to support the arguments outlined in the text, it is important to keep in mind that arguments are based on assumptions – points that are taken to be true, without need for proof. This is what you need to look for: explicit and implicit assumptions, since they require evidence not already listed in the text. Explicit assumptions can be broken down into or supported by implicit assumptions.

Assumptions

Explicit Assumptions	Implicit assumptions
Internet monitoring and sanctions against personal use will improve productivity	• Productivity is determined by the amount of time spent working on a task • Restricted access will be effective • Internet monitoring is guaranteed to increase productivity • People use the internet for personal reasons during work hours
Time not spent on the internet for personal reasons will be spent working	• There are no other time wasting activities • People will redirect the newfound additional time towards work
Personal internet use is the main time wasting activity	• People do not waste time offline • Time wasted online is much greater than the amount of time wasted offline • Time spent working is always productive
Internet monitoring will increase the company's profits	• Internet monitoring is economically viable • The increase in productivity will be significant

After having established your assumptions, you can find the evidence that is needed to evaluate the argument by considering what proof is necessary to validate each implicit assumption.

Evidence

◆ Productivity breakdown based on the most important components and the ranking of time spent working among them

◆ Percentage of people owning phone or tablets with internet

◆ Percentage of people already using their phones or tablets for personal internet browsing

◆ Comparison of productivity data in companies with and without the internet monitoring policy

◆ Division and ranking of work time based on the activities it is spent on

◆ Amount of time wasted online compared to amount of time wasted in offline activities

◆ What are the hourly intervals when employees use the internet for personal matters

◆ The amount of time wasted online compared to the individual's work length day

◆ Amount of time spent on non-productive work related activities

◆ Cost of installing and maintaining the monitoring system reported to the percentage of expected increase in productivity

 Sample Essay

The Vice President for Human Resources at Climpson Industries recommends implementing internet monitoring coupled with punishments for personal use in an effort to increase employee productivity and subsequently improve the company's profits. Before embarking on a costly venture, the company's president needs to have additional information in relation to the project's cost benefit analysis and the overall effectiveness of such a measure.

The Vice President claims that implementing electronic internet monitoring devices would ultimately lead to an increase in the company's profits. By looking at the cost of the monitoring system reported to the percentage of the expected increase in productivity, the company's president can determine if the venture will be profitable. It is possible that the cost of purchasing, installing and maintaining the monitoring system far outweighs the expected revenue increase due to the boost in monthly productivity. In this case, the result of the policy change would have contrary results to the predicted increase in profits. Should the cost of the internet monitoring system be recovered in a timely manner from the expected productivity increase, the venture would pass financial muster.

The author further claims that electronic monitoring of internet usage will positively affect productivity. To assess this statement, the President should examine evidence related to the current recreational methods used by employees during work hours, in terms of the amount of time spent, the time slot dedicated to such activities, and the amount of activities occurring online or being performed on personal devices. When trying to establish the efficiency of the internet monitoring system, the Director should first look into the percentage of the work day that is spent on personal internet use in order to determine if said amount of time is sufficient enough to warrant the implementation of the system. If the amount is on average less than 30 minutes per day (5% out of the 8 work hours), it is highly unlikely that productivity will be significantly bolstered by internet monitoring. However, if it turns out that employees are regularly spending over an hour on recreational activities during work, a means of reducing said amount of wasted time would have a positive impact on the company's productivity. The Director would also have to consider how effective the internet monitoring system would be in preventing browsing for personal reasons. Here is where the percentage of people owning phones or tablets with internet comes into play. This evidence would serve to indicate whether internet monitoring of the workstations would prevent people from using the internet for personal browsing. There are a number of studies that show that a great majority of people would switch to browsing on their personal devices should their workstations be monitored. If a great percentage of the company owns tablets and smartphones, it is highly likely that internet monitoring will not have much of an effect in stopping the amount of time people spend on the internet for personal reasons. Even if the majority of people do not possess personal devices with access to the internet, implementing an internet monitoring measure is not guaranteed to increase the amount of time employees spend working, given that they could redirect their attention toward offline-based time wasting activities.

Which brings us to the next point: the author assumes that browsing is the sole or major time-wasting opportunity available for the people in the company. Thus, comparing the amount of time wasted online with the time spent on non-productive offline activities can provide an accurate gauge of which activity is the most wasteful and, therefore, more deserving of efforts directed towards preventing it. The Vice President needs this data to demonstrate that browsing is the main non-productive activity prevalent in the company, in which case finding ways of stopping it would prove beneficial for the company. Should the balance lean the other way, and the preferred way of wasting time be related to the offline environment, like socializing with colleagues, the Vice President's suggested solution would be focusing on the wrong problem, and the company's productivity would not increase.

The view that internet monitoring and sanctions against personal use improve productivity rests on the assumption that the time spent working is productive time. By analyzing the amount of time spent on non-productive work related activities, the Vice President should be able to see if the extra work time the employees would gain through internet monitoring will be spent in a productive manner or not. Should people spend a great part of their work day on non-productive activities like meetings, a far more effective and less costly method of increasing productivity would be to reduce the number of meetings. However, if all the time spent working proves to be spent productively, it would be reasonable to conclude that the Vice President's suggested policy change can positively impact the company's productivity rates.

Before making a potentially costly decision, Climpson's board of directors can analyze the potential effects without taking on the risk of implementing the policy change by comparing productivity data from companies that have already implemented internet monitoring, with that of companies managing without it. For instance, Google allows employees additional recreational time beside the standard lunch hour and encourages people to work on personal projects. According to Google's reports, after implementing these methods, productivity skyrocketed. Following this example, implementing internet monitoring might actually prove detrimental to the company's productivity rates, and the more profitable avenue would be to implement an employee-autonomy work schedule. Alternately, the example of other companies might demonstrate the effectiveness of internet monitoring in bolstering productivity and the Vice President's suggestion would be validated by external proof of concept.

Ultimately, before making a case for implementing internet monitoring policies the Vice President should consider alternate methods of bolstering productivity before settling on a single method. His decision would be greatly aided by gaining a better understanding of the makeup and importance of time wasting activities so as to prevent spending resources on the wrong or lesser problem.

Argument Task 40

The following appeared in a recommendation from the President of the Amburg Chamber of Commerce.

"Last October, the city of Belleville installed high-intensity lighting in its central business district, and vandalism there declined almost immediately. The city of Amburg, on the other hand, recently instituted police patrols on bicycles in its business district. However, the rate of vandalism here remains constant. Since high-intensity lighting is clearly the most effective way to combat crime, we recommend using the money that is currently being spent on bicycle patrols to install such lighting throughout Amburg. If we install this high-intensity lighting, we will significantly reduce crime rates in Amburg."

Write a response in which you discuss what questions would need to be answered in order to decide whether the recommendation is likely to have the predicted result. Be sure to explain how the answers to these questions would help to evaluate the recommendation.

 ## Strategies

The first step in performing your analysis consists of identifying the texts' key point, recommendation, prediction or hypothesis. All the other arguments and assumptions are designed to support this central claim. In this case, the author attempts to demonstrate that "If we install this high-intensity lighting, we will significantly reduce crime rates in Amburg."

The next step would involve creating a statement that summarizes the text by including the central claim and its supporting arguments.

Based on the crime prevention success of high intensity lighting in the city of Belleville and the unchanged vandalism rates following the measures implemented in Amburg, the president of the Amburg Chamber of Commerce recommends redirecting funds from bicycle police patrols to high intensity lighting in a bid to significantly reduce the crime rates of the town.

When considering what questions are needed to evaluate the arguments outlined in the text, it is important to keep in mind that arguments are based on assumptions – points that are taken to be true, without the need for proof. This is what you need to look for: explicit and implicit assumptions since they lack the evidence required to prove their validity.

Assumptions

Explicit Assumptions	Implicit assumptions
The measures applied in Belleville will have the same results in Amburg	• Vandalism makes up most of the crime rate in Amburg • The two cities' demographics are similar • Belleville and Amburg face the same type of criminal problems
High intensity lighting is more effective than police patrols	• Police bicycle patrols have been implemented for a sufficient length of time to start showing results • High intensity lighting is more effective than police patrols at stopping other types of crimes than just vandalism
The high intensity light in Belleville had a significant impact on the crime rate	• The crime rate in Belleville was high • The crime rate was reduced throughout the city • Vandalism constitutes the greatest percentage of crimes
High light intensity is the only measure responsible for the reduction in vandalism in Belleville	• There were no external causes (like economical health) that could have influenced the outcome • There were no other crime prevention methods being deployed at the same time

After having established your assumptions, you can find the questions that are needed to evaluate the argument by rephrasing each implicit assumption.

Questions

◆ What is the minimum time necessary for police bicycle patrols to start showing results?

◆ How effective is high intensity lighting vs police patrols at stopping crimes other than vandalism?

◆ What percentage of Amburg's crime rate is constituted by vandalism?

◆ How high was the crime rate in Belleville before the introduction of the high intensity lighting?

◆ With the introduction of the high intensity lighting was the crime rate reduced also throughout the city?

Science & Technology

40

◆ Are there any other external causes such as economical health that could have influenced the outcome in Belleville?

◆ Were there other crime prevention methods used at the same time as the high intensity lighting?

◆ How comparable are Amburg and Belleville's demographics?

◆ How similar are the types of criminal problems both cities have to face?

 ## Sample Essay

Based on the crime prevention success of high intensity lighting in the city of Belleville and the unchanged vandalism rates following the measures implemented in Amburg, the president of the Amburg Chamber of Commerce recommends redirecting funds from bicycle police patrols to high intensity lighting in a bid to significantly reduce the crime rates of the town.

Since the measure proposed by the author of the argument is not meant to supplement but replace one form of protection with another, it becomes essential to have a proper evaluation of the effectiveness of both measures. This additional data can be obtained by answering a few basic questions about the assumptions made by the author.

One such question deals with the assumption that the introduction of high intensity lighting in Belleville had a significant impact on the town's crime rate. Since the lighting was introduced mainly in the business center of the town, the first question that comes to mind is if the crime rate was also reduced throughout the city or only mainly in the area where the lighting was introduced. If the overall crime rates were lowered, that would make the high intensity lighting a very effective measure, provided that the results stay constant for a long period of time (and the criminals don't figure out new ways around them). In this case, the argument made by the president of the Amburg Chamber of Commerce would be significantly strengthened - and more so since the proposal argues for introducing this measure throughout the city. Should the crime rates stay the same in the parts of town not covered by high intensity lighting, that would not affect the argument of the author since, as stated above, the plan is to introduce high intensity lighting throughout the city.

Another way of evaluating the success of the high intensity lighting in preventing crime in Belleville is to inquire just how high the crime rate was before the introduction of high intensity lighting and what constitutes a significant increase. Following that line of thought, if the crime rate before the introduction of the high intensity lighting was very low, the results could be due to chance and not any real effectiveness on the part of the implemented measure. It is always the case when dealing with statistics of any kind. Of note, low numbers tend to come with a high standard deviation (meaning that, in small groups, each occurrence of an event holds greater weight). However, a high crime rate would strengthen the validity of the conclusions drawn from the Belleville example, provided there were no other factors that could have influenced the results. In this case, the main argument would not be affected much, since it depends on a whole host of other, more significant assumptions.

When describing the effectiveness of the high intensity lighting in Belleville, the author of the argument draws attention to the reduction in the rates of vandalism occurring in the area where the measure was instated. There is not much data about the impact of high intensity lighting on other types of crimes. This begs the question of what percentage of Amburg's crime rate is constituted by vandalism. If most of the crimes committed in the city of Amburg are related to forms of vandalism, that fact would strengthen the proposal to introduce high intensity lighting in the city since the measure was shown to be particularly effective for this type of crime. However, should vandalism constitute only a small percentage of the types of crimes committed in the city of Amburg, that would significantly weaken the assumption that crime rates would be reduced by installing high intensity lighting since it is entirely possible that the method is not effective against the other types of crimes.

When making his case for the introduction of high intensity lighting in the town, the president of the Amburg Chamber of Commerce assumes that this measure was the only one that was responsible for the reduction in vandalism in Belleville. Before launching a proposal that could have no effect on the town's safety, the author should wonder if there were any other external causes that could have influenced the outcome in Belleville. It is entirely possible that at the time, the economical health of the region improved alongside the overall well-being of the citizens which triggered a reduction in petty crimes. Should there be any other reasons for the decrease in crimes, like the one mentioned above, it becomes highly likely that introducing the high intensity lighting in Amburg will not have the desired effect.

However, if there is no other external explanation for the drop in crime rates, then that would significantly strengthen the bid of the president of the Chamber of Commerce to add high intensity lighting, provided there were also no other crime reduction methods in place at the time. If the town of Belleville had run other crime prevention methods like police patrols in parallel with the high intensity lighting program, it would become questionable to introduce only one part of the equation in Amburg without considering the exact role that each measure had to play in reducing the crime rate. However, should the opposite be true, then high intensity lighting would have increased credibility as a crime reduction method and the author's proposal to introduce it in Amburg would gain more merit.

The president of the Amburg Chamber of Commerce recommends installing high intensity lighting by diverting funds from the existing bicycle police patrols, based on the assumption that it would be more effective than the police patrols at reducing the crime rate. The author compares a fully-fledged program (the one in Belleville) with a newly instated one. The question in this case is what is the minimum time necessary for police bicycle patrols to start showing results reported to how long the measure was instated in Amburg before being evaluated. If the police bicycle patrols require much more time to be effective than the period that passed between their introduction and evaluation, that fact would weaken the assumption that high intensity lighting is more effective than police patrols at reducing crime, simply because the data about the patrols is inaccurate. In this case, replacing the patrols with the high intensity lighting might be an unnecessary move. However, if the reverse is true and the results of introducing police bicycle patrols should be visible immediately, then the author of the argument would have been correct in assuming that high intensity lighting is the more effective measure, provided that the data from Belleville is accurate.

When making the suggestion to replace bicycle patrols with high intensity lighting, the president of the Amburg Chamber of Commerce assumes that the measures that were applied in Belleville will have the same results

40

in Amburg. To be able to claim that with any degree of certainty, the author of the argument should inquire into just how comparable are the types of criminal problems the two cities have to face. Should both Amburg and Belleville have very similar types of crimes they face, that bit of information would strengthen the argument that the measures applied in Belleville can be expected to have the same results in Amburg. The main claim that introducing high intensity lighting will significantly reduce crime rates would only be slightly strengthened, since it depends more on whether or not the measure is actually effective. Should the cities face completely different types of crimes, it would not do well to assume that the same crime fighting measure would be effective in both cities. For instance, if Belleville mainly has to deal with vandalism, while Amburg is rife with organized crime, then installing high intensity lighting on the streets would have no effect on the high level crimes being committed in Amburg, especially since a lot of these types of crimes are committed in broad daylight, when high intensity lighting is superfluous.

All in all, the president of the Chamber of Commerce of Amburg should take more time to investigate the effectiveness of both high intensity lighting and police bicycle patrols before suggesting one measure over the other. Without the proper information, the author of the argument might suggest a course of action that could prove to be ineffective and/or costly.

Argument Task 41

The following appeared in a memorandum from the planning department of an electric power company.

"Several recent surveys indicate that homeowners are increasingly eager to conserve energy. At the same time, manufacturers are now marketing many home appliances, such as refrigerators and air conditioners, that are almost twice as energy efficient as those sold a decade ago. Also, new technologies for better home insulation and passive solar heating are readily available to reduce the energy needed for home heating. Therefore, the total demand for electricity in our area will not increase - and may decline slightly. Since our three electric generating plants in operation for the past twenty years have always met our needs, construction of new generating plants will not be necessary.

Write a response in which you examine the stated and/or unstated assumptions of the argument. Be sure to explain how the argument depends on these assumptions and what the implications are for the argument if the assumptions prove unwarranted.

 Strategies

Argument:

Because of the availability of energy-saving appliances and new technology for better home insulation and heating, the current power plants will not need to be replaced.

In developing your response, you are asked to examine the stated and unstated assumptions in the argument and explain how the arguments depend on the assumptions' soundness to sustain the argument.

Facts and Assumptions:

◆ Surveys show that homeowners are increasingly eager to conserve energy. The assumption derived from this fact is that the home owners will conserve energy and will take steps to make that possible.

◆ Many manufacturers are producing home appliances that are almost twice as energy-efficient as those sold a decade ago. The writer assumes that consumers, in an effort to reduce their energy consumption, will buy these new appliances. Appliances are a big expense. How long will it take the home owners to recoup the cost of the appliances through energy savings? Homeowners are likely to keep a new appliance for more than ten years, so if they bought their current inefficient appliances just before manufacturers changed their designs, they may not be ready for new ones.

◆ New technologies exist for better home insulation and passive solar heating. Again, the writer assumes that homeowners are going to install new insulation or passive solar heating devices. The cost/return factor may come into play here, as well.

◆ The total demand for electricity in the area will not increase. This assumes that no new factories will be built and that no new residents will move to the area. Every existing condition would have to remain the same for demand for electricity to remain the same.

◆ The current three electricity-generating plants have served the needs of the area for twenty years and will not have to be replaced. The assumption here is that these twenty-year-old plants have technology that will continue to produce electricity efficiently. Again, this assumption is based on zero-population growth and industry and business remaining what it is today.

Your notes do not have to be exhaustive. As you begin to write your essay, your brain will generate new ideas. Make certain that you keep the directions in mind as you develop your ideas.

 ## Sample Essay

This memorandum claims that there is no need to construct more electric plants due to an increased interest from the local population in energy conservation. The claims rely on several assumptions being correct, and the writer uses some facts about energy use in the area to support these assumptions. This writer is also relying on the behavior of others to make a recommendation for the future of the electric company. In reality, the only behavior one can predict is his own.

Building a new electricity-generating plant is expensive and time- consuming. Most companies would rather avoid having to do so. The writer in this case appears to have done some research to support his proposition that the three existing plants will be sufficient into the future. The first fact derives from a survey that reports homeowners' desires to conserve energy. The writer does not say how homeowners plan to accomplish that, nor does it reveal in which areas they want to save that energy. Do they want to reduce their electricity usage, or cut back on the amount of heating fuel they consume? They may decide to install a wood or pellet stove to heat their homes instead of reducing their electricity use.

The writer goes on to cite the move on the part of manufacturers to produce and market more energy-efficient appliances as a rationale for maintaining the status quo. It is probably true in every case that, when consumers today shop for new appliances, they look for the energy star and nod with satisfaction when buying a refrigerator that uses only $60.00 worth of electricity each year. In calculating their savings, they must determine how many years it will take to recoup the cost of that new refrigerator, which, in most cases, will cost upwards of $1000. If the benefit isn't great enough, they may postpone that purchase. Those building new homes may opt for those new appliances, but the planning department would need to know how much of their total energy usage is demanded by new construction. In addition, new technologies in the insulation and passive solar heating sector have encouraged the planning department to estimate less or static energy demand from their current generators. Retrofitting older homes to take advantage of these new technologies is expensive, and homeowners will once again calculate the cost/savings ratio before making those changes. Passive solar technology is only effective in an area with sufficient sunlight. Is that true of the area where this energy company operates?

After considering the availability of appliances and technologies available to consumers who want to reduce their energy use, the planning committee has concluded that energy use will not increase and may even decline in the future. This conclusion precludes any type of growth in the area. For energy use to remain static, no new factories or homes could be built. In contradiction to this idea is the likelihood that local town and city planners are recruiting new businesses and families to move to their communities.

The final solution proposed by the planning department is to forego any plans for a new power plant and to remain with the three existing plants that have served them well for the past twenty years. This proposal relies on the assumptions' having sound foundations and the lack of growth in the area. To presume that twenty-year-old machinery will not need upgrading or replacing could lead to unsound financial decisions on the part of the power company. The charge this writer should be making to the power company is to act prudently and plan for future growth.

Argument Task 42

The vice president of human resources at Climpson Industries sent the following recommendation to the company's president.

"In an effort to improve our employees' productivity, we should implement electronic monitoring of employees' Internet use from their workstations. Employees who use the Internet from their workstations need to be identified and punished if we are to reduce the number of work hours spent on personal or recreational activities, such as shopping or playing games. By installing software to detect employees' Internet use on company computers, we can prevent employees from wasting time, foster a better work ethic at Climpson, and improve our overall profits."

Write a response in which you examine the stated and/or unstated assumptions of the argument. Be sure to explain how the argument depends on these assumptions and what the implications are for the argument if the assumptions prove unwarranted.

 Strategies

Argument:

Monitoring employees' Internet use will improve productivity by keeping them from wasting time on personal and recreational activities. The result will be increased company profits.

Assumptions:

◆ Climpson Industries has assumed that its employees are using the Internet for personal business. How did this suspicion arise? Has Climpson heard this complaint from other businesses?

◆ They have also assumed that personal Internet use has caused a loss in productivity. If employees are not as productive as the company would like, there may be reasons other than Internet use. Does the company provide ongoing training? Are there incentives for increased productivity

◆ Monitoring Internet use will improve company profits.

◆ Employees are wasting time. Is there sufficient meaningful work to keep them busy throughout the work day?

◆ Employees have a poor work ethic. Has this been demonstrated by employees' arriving late for work or leaving early? Do they call in sick on a regular basis?

◆ Punishment will increase productivity. This is rarely the case. Positive reinforcement or incentives are more likely to increase productivity. Employees need to know what's in it for them. Punishment is generally a short-term solution.

Your notes do not have to be exhaustive. As you begin to write your essay, your brain will generate new ideas. Make certain that you keep the directions in mind as you develop your ideas.

Sample Essay

Climpson Industries, to improve its overall profits, is proposing to monitor its employees' Internet use. Although there appears to be no concrete evidence, the company assumes that its employees are wasting time on the Internet for personal and recreational activities during work hours. The vice president of human resources is suggesting a Big Brother approach to ensure that company employees are doing what they're supposed to be doing in the workplace.

The company assumes that its employees are using the Internet for personal and recreational activities. Simply asking the employees about Internet use may be more efficacious than assuming the worst? Done in a respectful and professional manner, an interview with each employee may confirm or belay the company's suspicions. A lack of productivity would result in deadlines being missed or orders being left unfilled. Is that happening at Climpson? If not, then current productivity is not in question. If the company seeks to improve productivity, it would do so in response to an increased demand for its products or services.

In conjunction with the assumed lack of productivity is the belief that employees are wasting time. Do the employees have enough meaningful work to fill their days? If current quotas are being met, the employees must be working efficiently. If they have time to waste, it is because their time is not filled by employer demands. The additional assumption of a poor work ethic would also be reflected in work going undone. Employees with a poor work ethic are apt to call in sick, arrive late to work, take extended lunch breaks, and/or leave early at the end of the day. If such behavior exists at Climpson Industries, it would be blatantly obvious and easy to check by reviewing time cards.

The desire to punish the slackers on the company payroll is counterproductive. What form would the punishment take that would not have deleterious consequences for the company itself? It would, in the long term, cause discontent and dissatisfaction with the managers. Knowledgeable and profitable employers know that incentives are a more effective means of increasing productivity and employee loyalty. In turn, company profits are likely to increase.

Changes in technology over the past couple of decades have created new challenges for business. A proactive approach would be to adopt policies before implementing changes. Does Climpson Industries have a policy manual that outlines what are and are not acceptable activities regarding Internet use? When the rules are clear, employees will generally have no trouble obeying them. Rather than taking on the role of Big Brother, the management would be better served by acting as coaches and leading their employees and, concomitantly, their company to greater success.

42

Argument Task 43

The following appeared in a memo from a vice president of Quiot Manufacturing.

"During the past year, Quiot Manufacturing had 30 percent more on-the-job accidents than at the nearby Panoply Industries plant, where the work shifts are one hour shorter than ours. Experts say that significant contributing factors in many on-the-job accidents are fatigue and sleep deprivation among workers. Therefore, to reduce the number of on-the-job accidents at Quiot and thereby increase productivity, we should shorten each of our three work shifts by one hour so that employees will get adequate amounts of sleep."

Write a response in which you examine the stated and/or unstated assumptions of the argument. Be sure to explain how the argument depends on these assumptions and what the implications are for the argument if the assumptions prove unwarranted.

 Strategies

Argument:

Shortening each shift at Quiot Manufacturing will reduce the number of workplace accidents.

Assumptions:

◆ The workers at Quiot Manufacturing are fatigued. Are the employees found sleeping on the job?

◆ The workers at Quiot Manufacturing suffer from sleep deprivation. Have studies been done to confirm this?

◆ Fatigue and/or sleep deprivation are the cause of on-the- job accidents at Quiot Manufacturing. Is the work environment safe? Do employees follow appropriate safety measures?

◆ Panoply Industries has fewer accidents because their workers are better rested. Do workers there perform the same kind of tasks as the workers at Quiot?

◆ If work shifts are shortened, workers will get more sleep. Workers are just as likely to use the extra time to go shopping, socialize, or watch television.

Your notes do not have to be exhaustive. As you begin to write your essay, your brain will generate new ideas. Make certain that you keep the directions in mind as you develop your ideas.

 ## Sample Essay

43

Quiot Manufacturing's vice president has used faulty reasoning to reach the conclusion that shortening work shifts will reduce the number of on-the-job accidents at the plant. Fatigue and sleep deprivation certainly can contribute to workplace accidents, but so can several other factors. Before deciding to shorten the work shifts, the managers should consider all the conditions that affect safety at Quiot Manufacturing.

The vice president of the company assumes that worker fatigue is the culprit behind the high number of on-the-job accidents. Is there evidence of fatigue? Are workers falling asleep on the job? Are they coming to work late? Has anyone surveyed the employees? Without answers to these questions, his assumption may be erroneous. He may be basing his assumption on the fact that Panoply Industries, with its shorter work shifts, has fewer workplace accidents. The writer should examine the reasons behind Panoply's lower incidence of accidents at its facility.

If it turns out to be true that the workers at Quiot Manufacturing are sleep deprived, what is the cause? Most work days are eight hours, likely the length of each shift at the company. If Quiot workers are not spending more time than the average worker on the job, the length of the work day is not the most logical cause of their fatigue. The nature of the work may be tiring. Is it arduous, physically taxing, or is it monotonous and boring? Regularly scheduled breaks may solve that.

Quiot Manufacturing should examine its own culpability for creating an unsafe workplace. Has the company installed safety equipment that reduces accidents? Have the workers been trained to follow appropriate safety procedures? If the managers at Quiot were to question Panoply Industries, they may find that Panoply has recently reduced the number of accidents occurring at its plant. They may have installed safety features and instituted employee training that account for the lower incidence of accidents. On the other hand, safety features and training may be identical at both businesses and the shorter shifts have led to a reduction in accidents.

This writer must discover the actual figures behind the thirty percent more accidents at Quiot Manufacturing. How many accidents did each company report? If Panoply reported three on-the-job accidents, and Quiot had thirty percent more than that, then Quiot reported four accidents. This is hardly a number worth changing the structure of work shifts at the plant. On the other hand, if Panoply Industries reported thirty accidents, then Quiot Manufacturing would have had thirty-nine accidents. An additional nine would be cause for concern, and the company should investigate the cause.

Shorter shifts may not improve either workplace safety or productivity. The vice president assumes that workers will rest more if they work less. The workers are just as likely to use the extra time to go shopping, socialize with friends, or watch television. Introspection may be a better approach than innovation to ensure worker safety and increased productivity.

Argument Task 44

Milk and dairy products are rich in vitamin D and calcium - substances essential for building and maintaining bones. Many people therefore say that a diet rich in dairy products can help prevent osteoporosis, a disease that is linked to both environmental and genetic factors and that causes the bones to weaken significantly with age. But a long-term study of a large number of people found that those who consistently consumed dairy products throughout the years of the study have a higher rate of bone fractures than any other participants in the study. Since bone fractures are symptomatic of osteoporosis, this study result shows that a diet rich in dairy products may actually increase, rather than decrease, the risk of osteoporosis.

Write a response in which you discuss what specific evidence is needed to evaluate the argument and explain how the evidence would weaken or strengthen the argument.

 Strategies

Argument:

The results of a long-term study demonstrate that a diet high in dairy products increases the risk of osteoporosis.

In developing your response, discuss the specific evidence needed to support the writer's position.

Facts and Assumptions:

◆ Vitamin D and calcium are essential for building and maintaining bones, and dairy products are rich in these substances. The natural assumption is that one must eat these foods to develop and maintain strong bones. Many foods in the plant family are also good sources of calcium and vitamin D.

◆ Osteoporosis is linked to both environmental and genetic factors. Did any study participants have genetic markers for osteoporosis? Did any of them live in areas with environmental conditions that could have promoted the development of osteoporosis? These areas could include parts of the world where there are long periods of little sunshine or daylight.

◆ A long-term study revealed that participants who consumed dairy products more consistently than other participants suffered more bone fractures. The assumption is that the dairy products contributed to this tendency. It would serve the reader well to know if those participants are ones with genetic markers or who may have lived in the northern latitudes where long, sunny days are few.

◆ Bone fractures are symptomatic of osteoporosis. A correlate might be that osteoporosis is the chief cause of bone fractures. Lifestyle is a great contributor to bone fractures. Those who are active and/or risk takers are apt to suffer more fractures than those who live more sedately.

Your notes do not have to be exhaustive. As you begin to write your essay, your brain will generate new ideas. Make certain that you keep the directions in mind as you develop your ideas.

 ## Sample Essay

There is no doubt that sufficient levels of calcium and vitamin D contribute to bone health in humans. Many foods are good sources of these nutrients, but the ones that come most readily to mind are milk and other dairy products. Regular exposure to sunlight is also required to enable the body to synthesize vitamin D. The study cited in this passage suggests that consuming milk and dairy products is detrimental to bone health and may contribute to osteoporosis. The author makes some leaps from the incidence of bone fractures to conclusions about the deleterious effects of milk and dairy products. Assumptions are not sufficient to establish a position. This writer needs evidence to support the argument.

Generalities in the passage need more specificity. A long-term study with a large sample size doesn't tell the reader much. Over how long a period was the study conducted? How many subjects participated in the study? What were the ages and geographic locations of the subjects? These details are important for determining the veracity of the claims in the passage. The passage doesn't even make clear that the study was about the effect of eating dairy products on bone strength. The writer should discover which participants in the study consumed dairy products on a regular basis. If they were young people, it could help to explain the high rate of bone fractures as young people tend to be more active than older subjects. On the other hand, if the sample population was largely made up of senior citizens, their propensities for osteoporosis may result in higher fracture rates.

Assuming that researchers were studying the effects of a diary rich in milk and dairy products, the reader should ask to know how much of each participant's diet consisted of dairy products and which dairy products they were encouraged to consume. Maybe they took to heart the recent campaign that states, "Milk: it does a body good" and drank lots of that beverage. Were their diets replete with cheeses, sour cream, and/or yogurt? The subjects may also have consumed food or drink that has negative effects on calcium absorption. Carbonated beverages have been shown to leach calcium from bones, making them weaker and more susceptible to fractures and osteoporosis.

The author cites the fact that developing osteoporosis is linked to either or both genetic and environmental factors. Some subjects in the study may live where pollutants in the air or water affect calcium absorption. Others may live in the northern latitudes where the sunshine necessary for the synthesis of vitamin D is absent for long periods of the year. Some may be genetically destined to develop osteoporosis. Lifestyle changes may postpone the onset of some chronic conditions, but chances are, if the subjects' parents had osteoporosis, so will they.

Overall, those who conducted this study need to seek and reveal more information about their subjects. The final and, perhaps, most telling statistic is the age of the participants. At the very least, they were considerably younger when the study began than when it ended. Add this to environmental and genetic factors and you have a rationale for the development of osteoporosis, not for the condemnation of milk and dairy products as part of a dietary regime.

44

Argument Task 45

The following appeared in a letter to the editor of a journal on environmental issues.

45

"Over the past year, the Crust Copper Company (CCC) has purchased over 10,000 square miles of land in the tropical nation of West Fredonia. Mining copper on this land will inevitably result in pollution and, since West Fredonia is the home of several endangered animal species, in environmental disaster. But such disasters can be prevented if consumers simply refuse to purchase products that are made with CCC's copper unless the company abandons its mining plans."

Write a response in which you examine the stated and/or unstated assumptions of the argument. Be sure to explain how the argument depends on these assumptions and what the implications are for the argument if the assumptions prove unwarranted.

 Strategies

Argument:

The writer exhorts the readers to boycott Crust Copper Company until the company abandons its mining plans in West Fredonia.

In developing your response, you must identify both the stated and implied assumptions in the argument and explain how the veracity of the assumptions affects the argument.

Facts and Assumptions:

◆ CCC has purchased over 10,000 square miles of land in West Fredonia. The writer assumes that, because CCC is a mining company, it will open a mining operation on this land. There is no direct statement in the passage that CCC does have plans for a mine.

◆ Mining on this land will cause pollution. Again, there is no evidence in the passage to support this conclusion. Has CCC been guilty of pollution in the past? Even if the company does open a mine, it may have measures in place to abate the pollution that results.

◆ West Fredonia is home to several endangered animal species. The writer assumes that any mining activity on the part of CCC will further endanger those species.

◆ The environmental disasters can be prevented if the readers boycott CCC products until the company abandons its plans. The assumption that CCC plans to mine on this piece of land is not proven in the passage. There is also the assumption that consumers know which products are made with CCC copper.

Your notes do not have to be exhaustive. As you begin to write your essay, your brain will generate new ideas. Make certain that you keep the directions in mind as you develop your ideas.

Sample Essay

The author of this letter to the editor has used pathos in the hope that readers will overlook the glaring lack of support for his assumptions. Hot-button words like pollution and endangered species are almost guaranteed to get a desired reaction from the audience. Visions of burning rain forests and dead animals fill their brains, and they are ready to do whatever it takes to stop this destruction and carnage. Although fired up and ready to go, readers must look for the omissions in reasoning created by the author before taking action that could have a catastrophic effect on a mining company.

The author of this letter has chosen his audience carefully by submitting it to a journal on environmental issues. The readers may take his assumptions to be facts. It is a fact that Crust Copper Company has recently purchased over 10,000 square miles of land in the tropical nation of West Fredonia. It is an easy leap from there to assume that the company will open a mining operation at that location. If that eventuality comes to pass, an environmental disaster will ensue. The writer proposes that pollution is inevitable. CCC may have adopted mining practices that reduce or eliminate harmful pollution.

The author also implies that CCC's purchase of land in West Fredonia is an imminent threat to several endangered species that make their home there. This is a large tract of land. If CCC opens a mining operation, it may be nowhere near any endangered animals. It is even possible that CCC has purchased this particular tract of land to establish an animal preserve. The author has purposely left out information that does not serve his intention.

Finally, we have the author's call to action. It is always the goal of persuasion to get the audience to believe in a certain way or to take some action. In this case, the readers are encouraged to boycott goods made with CCC's copper unless the company abandons its mining plans. The problem with this exhortation is the assumption that CCC has plans to mine this tract of land. The other difficulty might be identifying the products that contain the company's copper. It is unlikely that a copper mining company manufactures anything at all. The writer of this letter has provided just enough information to let the readers create their own assumptions about CCC's intentions in West Fredonia.

Argument Task 46

A recently issued twenty-year study on headaches suffered by the residents of Mentia investigated the possible therapeutic effect of consuming salicylates. Salicylates are members of the same chemical family as aspirin, a medicine used to treat headaches. Although many foods are naturally rich in salicylates, food-processing companies also add salicylates to foods as preservatives. The twenty-year study found a correlation between the rise in the commercial use of salicylates and a steady decline in the average number of headaches reported by study participants. At the time when the study concluded, food-processing companies had just discovered that salicylates can also be used as flavor additives for foods, and, as a result, many companies plan to do so. Based on these study results, some health experts predict that residents of Mentia will suffer even fewer headaches in the future.

Write a response in which you discuss what questions would need to be answered in order to decide whether the prediction and the argument on which it is based are reasonable. Be sure to explain how the answers to these questions would help to evaluate the prediction.

NOTE: *The above topic is same as Argument Task 51 in this book. However, if you read the solution carefully you will notice that it is solved differently. This helps you get a different perspective to approach the same task.*

 Strategies

Regardless of the approach you take, consider the following steps:

◆ Is there an alternative explanation for the events in question that can invalidate, either in whole or in part, the explanation given in the passage?

◆ How can I break the argument into its component parts to understand how they create the whole argument?

◆ Can I identify the line of reasoning used to create the argument?

◆ What does the author of the argument assume to be true for the argument to be true?

◆ Does the line of reasoning validate the conclusion?

◆ Can I imagine an example that refutes any or several of the statements in the argument?

◆ Am I able to evaluate the argument based on the quality of the facts and reasons presented in it?

Based on your responses to all or some of these questions, you must present a well-developed evaluation of the argument. You should take brief notes when you identify the argument's claims, assumptions, and conclusion. Jot down as many alternative explanations as you can along with additional evidence that might support or refute the claims in the argument. Finally, list the changes in the argument that would make the reasoning more solid. It is more important to be specific than it is to have a long list of evidence and examples.

This argument - *to promote the use of salicylates as a flavor enhancer* - cites evidence collected in a twenty-year study of the effect of salicylic preservatives in food on the frequency of headaches in Mentia.

In developing your response, you are required to generate questions that will help you decide if the prediction and the argument on which it is based are reasonable and then explain how the answers to your questions would help evaluate the prediction. It might be helpful to isolate the prediction.

Prediction:

Residents of Mentia will suffer even fewer headaches in the future.

Next, identify the argument's conclusions and the evidence that led to those conclusions.

Claims and evidence:

◆ The argument claims that adding salicylates to processed food decreases the incidence of headaches in Mentia. The evidence to support this claim appears to arise from the results of the study.

◆ Food additives are preferable to natural sources of salicylates. This unstated assumption arises from the decrease in headaches after the addition of salicylates to processed food rather than from an increase of the consumption of foods naturally rich in salicylates.

◆ If the amount of salicylates already added to food improves one's health, more additives would be even better. This unstated assumption underlies the prediction that the citizens of Mentia will experience even fewer headaches once they begin consuming food with more salicylates.

Questions:

◆ How has the population of Mentia changed over the last twenty years? Perhaps the citizens who suffered from headaches were older and have since died, leaving a younger, healthier population.

◆ Have the subjects of the study remained the same over the twenty-year period?

◆ What caused the headaches? Some may have been the result of allergies, and, when those people treated their allergies, the headaches declined in number. Some headaches may have occurred due to stress. Lifestyle changes could have eliminated some of those headaches.

◆ Many headaches are idiopathic. They come and go for no apparent reason. How can their disappearance be attributed to the addition of salicylates?

◆ Have the residents of Mentia changed their diets to include more of the foods that are naturally rich in salicylates?

Your notes do not have to be exhaustive. As you begin to write your essay, your brain will generate new ideas. Make certain that you keep the directions in mind as you develop your ideas. Use as many or as few paragraphs as you consider appropriate for your argument, but create a new paragraph when you move on to a new idea or example of support for your position. The GRE readers are not looking for a specific number of ideas or paragraphs. Instead, they are reading to determine the level of understanding of the topic and the complexity with which you respond.

You are free to organize and develop your response in any way you think will enable you to effectively communicate your evaluation of the argument. You may recall writing strategies you learned in high school or a writing-intensive course you took in college, but it is not necessary to employ any of those strategies. It is important that your ideas follow a logical progression and display strong critical thinking.

 ## Sample Essay

The salicylate issue is much like the current addition of fiber to foods. Since studies have shown that fiber in one's diet can lower cholesterol and improve bowel health, food companies have rushed to add fiber to everything from cereal to yogurt. The wisdom seems to be that, if some fiber is good, more fiber is better. Marketing of many prepared foods now focuses on the added fiber. As in the case of salicylates, many natural foods are rich in fiber, and eating them, in the long run, is probably better for the consumer than relying on added fiber in processed foods. The question here is how much is enough? If the residents of Mentia have been experiencing a steady decline in headaches over the last twenty years, isn't that trend likely to continue, even without more salicylate additives?

What other variables may have contributed to the decrease in headaches? Because headaches arise from a number of causes, changes other than the addition of salicylates may account for some of the decline in the number of headaches. Headaches can occur as the result of stress. Some Mentia residents may have made lifestyle changes that reduced the stress in their lives, thereby reducing the incidence of headaches or eliminating them altogether. They may have changed jobs, taken up a hobby, or found other ways to relax. Other headaches may arise from allergies. If those residents began treatment for their allergies, their headaches may also have disappeared. Still other headaches are idiopathic and come and go for no apparent reason. It is unlikely that either the presence or absence of salicylates in processed food had any effect on them. Mentians may simply have begun eating more foods that are naturally rich in salicylates.

Has the environment of Mentia undergone any changes in the last twenty years? Maybe factories have closed or implemented improved methods of reducing or cleaning up their emissions. As a result, the air in Mentia is

46

cleaner, providing relief to headache sufferers. The city may have cut down trees, eradicated ragweed, and taken other steps to reduce pollen producers that plague allergy sufferers. Until these factors have been taken into account, attributing the reduction in headaches to the addition of salicylates to processed food is premature.

Food processing companies are likely to add the flavor-enhancing salicylates to their products and tout not only their improved taste but also the benefits to those who suffer headaches. The decline in headaches will eventually reach a bottom point. Some residents will continue to have headaches as a result of some pathology or other. It may be acceptable to predict that as a result of more additives, fewer people will suffer headaches, but from a scientific standpoint, several questions require answers before attributing all of the benefits to added salicylates.

46

Argument Task 47

The following appeared in a health magazine published in Corpora.

"*Medical experts say that only one-quarter of Corpora's citizens meet the current standards for adequate physical fitness, even though twenty years ago, one-half of all of Corpora's citizens met the standards as then defined. But these experts are mistaken when they suggest that spending too much time using computers has caused a decline in fitness. Since overall fitness levels are highest in regions of Corpora where levels of computer ownership are also highest, it is clear that using computers has not made citizens less physically fit. Instead, as shown by this year's unusually low expenditures on fitness-related products and services, the recent decline in the economy is most likely the cause, and fitness levels will improve when the economy does.*"

47

Write a response in which you examine the stated and/or unstated assumptions of the argument. Be sure to explain how the argument depends on these assumptions and what the implications are for the argument if the assumptions prove unwarranted.

Strategies

The first step in performing your analysis consists of identifying the texts' key point, recommendation, prediction or hypothesis. All the other arguments and assumptions are designed to support this central claim. In this case, the author attempts to argue that "the recent decline in the economy is most likely the cause, and fitness levels will improve when the economy does".

The next step would involve creating a statement that summarizes the text by including the central claim and its supporting arguments.

The author of the text published in the health magazine predicts that fitness levels in Corpora will rise once the economy improves. These conclusions are based on the opinion of medical experts that claim that the fitness standards in Corpora have declined, when compared to 20 years prior. To make the case more compelling, the author also excludes computer usage as a cause for the decrease in fitness, by relating areas with high levels of computer ownership to high levels of fitness.

The easiest way to break down an argument into implicit assumptions is to look at the ideas that support each core (explicit) assumption. Ideally, it would be good to have at least three implicit assumptions for every explicit one. However, keep in mind that you likely won't have time enough to expound on all of them in your essay. When writing your argument, it's good to lay down the ideas like in the format below – it will help you more easily determine which explicit assumptions are undermined/strengthened by the implicit argument you are analyzing.

After having established your assumptions you need to take care of the second part of your essay, namely the implications for the main claim should the assumptions be unwarranted. A good way to go about writing this part is to think of examples of situations that may contradict each implicit assumption. The examples are not vital, you can still build a case by directly stating "if assumption 'A' proves to be untrue, then…" However, including the contradicting situations will help enrich your essay and ultimately get you a higher score.

Assumptions:

Explicit Assumptions	Implicit Assumptions	Contradicting Statement
The physical fitness level of Corpora citizens has declined	• Current standards are the same as 20 years ago • Corpora demographics are unchanged • Fitness measurements are relevant	• Different standards due to advances in medical technology • Different demographics (more elderly or very young people) • Measuring exercise time instead of intensity • Based on BMI instead of muscle to fat ratio
Computer usage is not to blame for low fitness levels	• Computer owning can be equated to computer usage	• Person having PCs at work and at home • Person owning PCs used by other members of the family
The economic decline is responsible for the fitness decline	• There are no other factors responsible for the decline in fitness equipment purchasing • Equipment purchase is indicative of equipment usage • Fitness equipment is indicative of fitness levels	• People working from at home • Gyms offering reductions • People that already bought the more expensive equipment/necessary equipment • People working without equipment • People doing sports that does not require a lot of equipment
The economic increase will result in more fit people	• Fitness standards will not change in the meanwhile • People will spend the money on fitness	• Fitness standards might become harsher • People can get used to a more sedentary lifestyle • People can spend the money on entertainment

47

The next step would be to create a "logic tree" to see how disproving an assumption will affect the other arguments down the line. The branch of the logic tree will follow this line: implicit assumption affects explicit assumptions which in turn relate to the main argument.

For instance, in our case:

Implicit Assumption	Effect on Explicit Assumption	Effect on Main Argument
Computer owning can be equated to computer usage	• Weakens the assumption (even if the people own a lot of computers, if they use them very little, there is no valuable correlation between low/normal levels of computer usage and high fitness) • Does not completely invalidate it – even if the highest levels of fitness would be correlated with the lowest PC usage (there could be other factors involved)	• Somewhat weakens it (while it's not the only one, the economy might still be one of the major factors that contributed to the low fitness levels)
Corpora demographics are unchanged	• Weakens the assumption (the two demographics need to be comparable – the fitness levels should be compared per demographic category) • Does not invalidate it – even with a completely different demographic makeup, it's possible that comparing within similar categories, the fitness levels have declined	• Weakens the assumption (if the levels have not declined, then economy has no bearing on fitness levels, and changing it will not bring about any increase in fitness)

47

Sample Essay

The author of the text published in the health magazine predicts that fitness levels in Corpora will rise once the economy improves. These conclusions are based on the opinion of medical experts that claim that the fitness standards in Corpora have declined, when compared to twenty years prior. To make the case more compelling, the author also excludes computer usage as a cause for the decrease in fitness, by relating areas with high levels of computer ownership to high levels of fitness. Any prediction is only as strong as its supporting arguments; the author's assumptions prove to be unwarranted, then it becomes highly likely that the prognosis will not come to pass, in which case, the author's reputation might suffer some damage.

One of the main assumptions made by the author is that the physical fitness levels of the citizens of Corpora have declined, when compared to those from twenty years prior. The main pillar of support for this idea is the notion that current standards are the same as twenty years ago. As with pretty much everything in life, fitness standards are subjected to change. With the growth of knowledge on the inner workings of the body, measuring techniques evolve to encompass this new understanding. For instance, the better understanding of how the heart functions has reduced heart attack deaths by 40% when compared to twenty five years ago. The same could be the case in terms of fitness;it is possible that today's standards of fitness are much harsher and more encompassing, so that people of twenty years ago would have had the same fitness levels, if judged by modern standards. Should the standards of twenty years ago and now be different, that would have a significant impact on the assumption that the physical condition of people in Corpora has declined. If the standards were lower in the past, it would significantly weaken the claim from above and subsequently the main argument.

If the fitness levels have not declined, the economy has no bearing on fitness levels, and an improved economy will not bring about any increase in fitness. On the other hand, should the fitness standards prove to be harsher in the past, it would strengthen the idea that the physical levels of the citizens of Corpora have declined. Overall, however, it would not have much bearing on the main claim that an economical increase will see a surge in fitness levels, since that idea also depends on whether economy is the major factor for the fitness levels decrease in the first place.

The assumption that the demographics of Corpora are the same as twenty years ago has a similar, if somewhat lesser effect. It is entirely possible that the low levels of fitness are simply due to the population make up, for instance, if, when compared to the past, there are much more elderly people in Corpora today (such as some towns in Florida have been transformed into retirement places). Should that be the case, then even if the elderly were to be fit for their age, their overall level of fitness will be judged to be lower than that of the middle aged, average inhabitant. The comparison between modern and past Corpora demographics would then yield inaccurate results. Regardless of specifics, if the assumption that Corpora demographics are similar to those of twenty years ago were to be invalidated, then that would significantly weaken the claim that the citizens' levels of fitness have declined. To get accurate results, the fitness levels should be compared per demographic category. However, that does not completely invalidate the notion that the physical fitness levels in Corpora have dropped – even with a completely different demographic makeup, it's possible that within similar categories, the modern-day fitness levels have declined when compared to the past. Should that be the case, then the main claim would be weakened - if the physical levels have not declined, the economy has no bearing on fitness levels, and improvements will not bring about any increase.

When arguing that the economical drop is the major cause for the drop in physical fitness noticed in Corpora, the author contradicts the medical expert's opinion that computer usage is to blame for the population's lack of fitness. In doing so, the author equates computer usage with computer owning by relating areas with high levels of computer ownership to high levels of fitness. It may well be that a person has a PC for at work and one for at home, but does not spend much time on them, or that the person that owns multiple computers has bought them for family use (parents own computers, but children are the main users).

If owning computers is unrelated to the amount of time a person spends on the computer, that fact weakens the assumption that computer usage is not to blame for low fitness levels. Even if the people own a lot of computers, if they use them very little, then there is no valuable correlation between low/normal levels of computer usage and high fitness. However, the lack of direct proportionality between computer owning and usage does not mean that the authors' assumption is invalidated, and the computers are to blame for the fitness levels, like medical experts argue. Even if the highest levels of fitness would be correlated with the lowest PC usage, there could still be other factors involved (such as the economic downturn).

Indeed, the author attributes the decline of fitness levels in Corpora to the economic decline in the region. When doing so, the author assumes that there are no other factors responsible for the decline in fitness expenditures. It's possible that people have already bought the necessary equipment and have no current needs to make big purchases. It's also likely that people exercise at home, instead of at the gym, or perform sports that do not require a lot of equipment. In all the scenarios above, the common thread is the idea that fitness purchases do not directly relate to how much the people exercise or how fit they are. If that is the case and the decline in fitness expenditures is not due to the economy, then the assumption that the economy is responsible for the fitness decline would be somewhat weakened, provided the amount of fitness expenditures is not indicative of how much people exercise. Should that notion also prove to be unwarranted, and fitness purchases were not to be indicative of the amount of time people spend exercising, the idea that the economic decline is responsible for the fitness decline would be severely weakened. In that case, an economic improvement, unlike what the author suggested, would have little to no effect on the fitness levels of people in Corpora.

Even if the economy were to be responsible for the dip in fitness levels, there is no guarantee that the author's assumption will come true, and an economic increase will bring about a surge in fitness levels. The author assumes that people will spend their extra money on fitness, however, in the meanwhile, it's possible that people have gotten used to a more sedentary lifestyle and are unwilling to spend money on activities that require more effort. It's also possible that people will just spend their extra money on entertainment if the economic dip had them cut fun activities and instead focus on necessities. Either way, should the people prove to be unwilling to spend money on fitness, that would somewhat weaken the main claim that economic welfare would bring about a rise in fitness – it would not, however, invalidate it, since, like mentioned above, it is entirely possible that people can exercise without having to purchase any equipment.

All in all, the author rests his case on baseless assumptions and should seek to consolidate them with facts before making any recommendations derived from them.

Argument Task 48

Arctic deer live on islands in Canada's Arctic regions. They search for food by moving over ice from island to island during the course of the year. Their habitat is limited to areas warm enough to sustain the plants on which they feed and cold enough, at least some of the year, for the ice to cover the sea separating the islands, allowing the deer to travel over it. Unfortunately, according to reports from local hunters, the deer populations are declining. Since these reports coincide with recent global warming trends that have caused the sea ice to melt, we can conclude that the purported decline in deer populations is the result of the deer's being unable to follow their age-old migration patterns across the frozen sea.

Write a response in which you discuss what specific evidence is needed to evaluate the argument and explain how the evidence would weaken or strengthen the argument.

48

 Strategies

Argument:

This argument uses facts about the deer's migration pattern along with supposed global warming trends and anecdotal reports from hunters to explain a purported decline in the deer population in Canada's Arctic region.

In developing your response, you are asked to identify what specific evidence is needed to evaluate the strength or weakness of the argument and explain how that evidence would weaken or strengthen the argument.

What conclusions and assumptions are either explicit or implied in the original argument?

Facts and Assumptions:

◆ Arctic deer travel across the ice from island to island to reach their food source. This fact leads to the assumption that an inability to reach some of these islands has led to a decline in deer population.

◆ Global warming trends have caused sea ice to melt. There is no evidence in the passage that the ice between the islands used by the deer has melted. The reader also doesn't know when it melted.

◆ Hunters report that deer populations have declined. Perhaps the deer have migrated to other feeding grounds. Tagging deer with radio devices would help to track their movements and deaths. The deer populations could have declined for other reasons. They may have become infected with the deer tick that affects their brains and, ultimately, causes their deaths. Hunting itself may have caused the decline. Some states in the US severely limit the number of does that can be tagged each year in an effort to preserve the deer population.

Your notes do not have to be exhaustive. As you begin to write your essay, your brain will generate new ideas. Make certain that you keep the directions in mind as you develop your ideas.

 ## Sample Essay

This argument posits that the deer population in the Arctic region of Canada has declined due to melting ice caused by global warming. However, this argument is replete with vague suppositions and anecdotal information that cannot support either the actual decline in the deer populations or the reasons for that purported decline. Maybe global warming trends caused sea ice to melt, preventing the deer's traveling between islands in search of food. There is no evidence to support this. The writer needs to demonstrate that the habitat of the Arctic deer was, indeed, affected by sea-ice melt. It appears that, for some of the year, the ice does melt, and that has always been the case. Considering the number of environmental watch-dog groups in existence, one should be able to find concrete evidence of where and when Arctic ice melt has occurred. That evidence would support the argument in the passage or cause the writer to look for other factors or events that could affect the deer population.

What else could have caused a decline in the deer population? Wild animals are susceptible to danger from several fronts. Most animals have natural predators. Deer may be prey to wolves or coyotes. Is there evidence of an increase in the numbers of those animals in the Arctic deer habitat? Deer populations have also fallen victim to the deer tick, a parasitic insect that takes up residence in the deer's brain and eventually causes its death. Necropsy clearly discovers the presence of this tick. Alternatively, humans are also deer's natural enemy. It could be that the human residents have over-hunted the deer. Many areas have severely restricted the hunting of does to sustain their deer populations. Evidence of increased predation, deer ticks, or over hunting could weaken the argument proposed in this passage.

Despite the reports of local hunters, there is no concrete evidence that the deer population has declined. Has a census been conducted? It is not uncommon to tag wild animals with radio transmitters that allow officials to track their movements and their deaths. Such tactics might reveal that the deer have not returned to their traditional feeding grounds or that they have died off for some reason. A reduction in the deer's food supply would compel them to move or remain elsewhere. Alternatively, increased hunting in certain locations may compel deer to move to different locations, resulting in the appearance of a reduced population.

Neither the author nor his purpose for the argument has been identified. What is the writer's interest in the Arctic deer population? The writer's agenda may influence his willingness to accept the unfounded information presented in the passage. The reader requires more empirical evidence before accepting the conclusions presented in this argument.

Argument Task 49

The following appeared in a letter from a firm providing investment advice to a client.

"Homes in the northeastern United States, where winters are typically cold, have traditionally used oil as their major fuel for heating. Last year that region experienced 90 days with below-average temperatures, and climate forecasters at Waymarsh University predict that this weather pattern will continue for several more years. Furthermore, many new homes have been built in this region during the past year. Because these developments will certainly result in an increased demand for heating oil, we recommend investment in Consolidated Industries, one of whose major business operations is the retail sale of home heating oil."

Write a response in which you discuss what questions would need to be answered in order to decide whether the recommendation and the argument on which it is based are reasonable. Be sure to explain how the answers to these questions would help to evaluate the recommendation.

49

 Strategies

A good place to start your analysis is by creating a statement that reveals the main idea of the argument. Although the writer is creating an argument, he may ultimately be stating a position, making a recommendation, or making a prediction. It may be helpful for you to determine which of these formats is most evident in the argument.

An investment firm is recommending that a client invest in Consolidated Industries based on the predicted use of heating fuel in new homes being built in the northeastern United States.

Assumptions:

◆ Newly constructed homes will heat with oil.

◆ Below-average temperatures will continue for several years.

◆ The price for home heating oil will remain high.

◆ Oil is a significant portion of Consolidated Industries' holdings.

◆ Profits from the oil business will offset any potential losses in other Consolidated Industries' holdings.

Questions:

◆ What portion of Consolidated Industries business is oil?

◆ What type of heating systems have been installed in the new-construction homes?

◆ How far below-average were the temperatures last year?

◆ How have investments in Consolidated Industries performed in the past?

◆ What are the client's investment goals?

◆ Has the company's advice paid off in the past?

◆ Does the client have the money to make the investment?

After completing these steps, you should have enough material to write your analysis. Remember that you are not creating a position of your own; you are evaluating the strengths and weaknesses of the existing argument. You do not have to include all of the points that you have created in your prewriting. In fact, during the process of drafting your analysis, other ideas may come to mind, and, if they strengthen your analysis, you should include them.

 ## Sample Essay

The average working man or woman has too little time or knowledge to navigate the ins and outs of the stock market, and most rely on the advice of a financial planner. It is easier to simply put one's money where the planner recommends. The smart investor asks questions, and he or she should before buying stock in Consolidated Industries. The answers to those questions will lead the investor to agree with the planner or decide to dive into another industry altogether.

The investment adviser assumes that new homes built in the northeast will use oil for heat. Are other types of heating systems becoming more prevalent? The rising cost of heating fuel has led homeowners to supplement oil with pellet stoves or heat pumps or, perhaps even solar panels. Builders of new homes may have to install these in order to appeal to modern consumers, many of whom want to reduce this country's dependence on foreign oil.

Have the home builders taken any other steps to reduce heating costs? They may have oriented the homes to take advantage of passive solar heat so that, on sunny days, the rooms where families spend most of their time will be warmed by the sun, reducing the number of hours that homeowners will need to run the furnace. Builders are able to select from a variety of components that reduce energy consumption. Double-pane, low-E windows prevent heat from escaping the house in the winter; a variety of insulating materials keep cold air out.

How far below average were the temperatures last year, and did those days occur during the winter? If those days were one degree below average, they did not make a significant contribution to heating costs. If a chunk of those days occurred during the summer months, they probably had little impact on oil consumption. If they occurred during the winter months and were several degrees below average, they would have increased the amount of time that homeowners turned their furnaces up, causing more gallons of fuel to be burned.

In addition to answers about the likelihood of increased oil sales in the northeast, the investor needs answers to questions about Consolidated Industries itself. How big a portion of the company's holdings are in heating fuel? Even though the financial planner cites heating oil as one of Consolidated's major holdings, he may have failed to mention that it is one of many major industries in which Consolidated has an interest. How is Consolidated Industries performing overall? Even though its oil division may be very profitable, its other holdings may be under performing, making an investment in Consolidated an unwise decision. In contrast, Consolidated's other holdings may be profitable enough to make it a sound investment even if heating oil experiences either a dip in price or a decline in consumption.

Once this client has answers to these questions, he or she can make a more informed decision about the investment. Before jumping on board this investor should also consider how his advisor has performed for him or her in the past and how an investment in Consolidated Industries fits with the other stocks in his or her portfolio. How does this investment help or hinder the client's financial goals? Will it help him send his children to college or make possible an earlier, more comfortable retirement? The client may want a rapid return in order to meet some short-term goals. Does the client even have the necessary funds to invest? He may have other commitments to meet at present. If the answers are satisfying, he should hand his money over to the financial planner.

Argument Task 50

The following appeared in the summary of a study on headaches suffered by the residents of Mentia.

"Salicylates are members of the same chemical family as aspirin, a medicine used to treat headaches. Although many foods are naturally rich in salicylates, for the past several decades, food-processing companies have also been adding salicylates to foods as preservatives. This rise in the commercial use of salicylates has been found to correlate with a steady decline in the average number of headaches reported by participants in our twenty-year study. Recently, food-processing companies have found that salicylates can also be used as flavor additives for foods. With this new use for salicylates, we can expect a continued steady decline in the number of headaches suffered by the average citizen of Mentia."

Write a response in which you discuss what specific evidence is needed to evaluate the argument and explain how the evidence would weaken or strengthen the argument.

50

 Strategies

Argument:

Salicylates as flavor enhancers as well as preservatives will have an even greater ability to reduce the incidence of headaches in Mentia.

Facts and Assumptions:

◆ Salicylates are members of the same chemical family as aspirin. The assumption is that they would act in the same manner as aspirin, that salicylates are pain relievers.

◆ Many foods are rich in salicylates. One might assume that eating a diet comprised of those foods would help to prevent pain.

◆ Food processing companies have been adding salicylates to food as preservatives for several decades.

◆ There has been a steady decline in the number of headaches reported by participants in a twenty-year study. The fact that this is a long-term study lends credence to any results reported out of it. The assumption is that the food additive has had a palliative effect on headaches.

◆ The rise in the commercial use of salicylates correlates with a reduction in headaches reported by participants in the study. This is an example of cause and effect.

◆ Food companies have discovered that salicylates can be used as flavor additives for foods. The assumption is that the companies will begin using salicylates in this manner and that headaches will decline in greater numbers. An additional assumption is that people will buy these foods, perhaps in response to their greater curative powers.

Your notes do not have to be exhaustive. As you begin to write your essay, your brain will generate new ideas. Make certain that you keep the directions in mind as you develop your ideas.

Sample Essay

Although the results of the study suggest a direct link between the addition of salicylates as a food preservative and a reduction in the reported number of headaches by participants in a study, blanks remain to be filled. Headaches can be annoying for some but debilitating for others. Treating headaches medically is a multi-million dollar industry. Treating headaches with a product that people are going to buy and consume as a matter of course would save individuals considerable amounts of money. The strength of the argument relies on evidence to support it.

The author of the study cited here purports that a reduction in headaches is linked to the addition of salicylates as a preservative in processed foods. The reader needs evidence that the participants in the study actually ate a large amount of those foods on a regular basis. A question that arises concerns other treatments for headaches. Did the study participants use any analgesics to treat the headaches? Did they eat foods naturally high in salicylates in addition to the processed foods? The participants may have sought alternative treatment such as acupuncture to relieve their headaches.

Will there be a further decline in the number of headaches when food processing companies use additional salicylates in their products? It may be that the effectiveness of salicylates has reached a saturation point. Compare this to the effectiveness of the humble aspirin. If two aspirin relieve a headache, would three be more palliative? What about side effects? Does the consumption of salicylates in processed food cause some of the same complications as aspirin does? Some people are discouraged from taking aspirin because of its blood-thinning properties. Should the same caution be attached to salicylates?

How does the addition of salicylates affect the cost of processed food? Will adding even more, further raise prices? If that is the case, consumers may be reluctant to buy the products. Another factor to consider is the current move to natural and organic foods. Headache sufferers may decide that foods grown and processed without additional chemicals may have beneficial health effects.

At the very least, the reader needs more details about the lifestyles of the study participants to determine if salicylates in processed food are the real heroes in this scenario. When all is revealed, the prediction about a further decline in headaches may not hold water.

Argument Task 51

A recently issued twenty-year study on headaches suffered by the residents of Mentia investigated the possible therapeutic effect of consuming salicylates. Salicylates are members of the same chemical family as aspirin, a medicine used to treat headaches. Although many foods are naturally rich in salicylates, food-processing companies also add salicylates to foods as preservatives. The twenty-year study found a correlation between the rise in the commercial use of salicylates and a steady decline in the average number of headaches reported by study participants. At the time when the study concluded, food-processing companies had just discovered that salicylates can also be used as flavor additives for foods, and, as a result, many companies plan to do so. Based on these study results, some health experts predict that residents of Mentia will suffer even fewer headaches in the future.

Write a response in which you discuss what questions would need to be answered in order to decide whether the prediction and the argument on which it is based are reasonable. Be sure to explain how the answers to these questions would help to evaluate the prediction.

NOTE: The above topic is same as Argument Task 46 in this book. However, if you read the solution carefully you will notice that it is solved differently. This helps you get a different perspective to approach the same task.

 Strategies

The first step in performing your analysis consists of identifying the texts' key point, recommendation, prediction or hypothesis. All the other arguments and assumptions are designed to support this central claim. In this case, the author attempts to demonstrate that "the population of Mentia will suffer from fewer headaches in the future".

The next step would involve creating a statement that summarizes the text by including the central claim and its supporting arguments.

Based on a twenty-year study on headaches, some health experts predict that the population of Mentia will suffer from fewer headaches in the future, given that salicylates, which are similar to aspirin, will be increasingly used in commercial food productions, and studies have shown a correlation between this increase and the reduced number of headache reports.

When considering what questions are needed to evaluate the arguments outlined in the text, it is important to keep in mind that arguments are based on assumptions – points that are taken to be true, without the need for proof. This is what you need to look for: explicit and implicit assumptions since they lack the evidence required to prove their validity.

Assumptions:

Explicit Assumptions	Implicit Assumptions
The study is representative for Mentia	• The sample population meets the minimum viability criteria • The demographics of the study participants and the makeup of the city's population are similar
The increase of salicylate use in commercial foods is responsible for the decrease in headaches reported	• People did not take any other drugs that could have been responsible for the drop-in headaches • There are no other external factors responsible for the decrease of headaches (natural environment changes, area stress levels) • People's willingness to report headaches remained constant • The decrease in headaches was significant
Increasing the commercial use of salicylates will decrease headaches in Mentia	• The increase in the commercial use of salicylates will be substantial • People of Mentia consume enough products containing flavor additives • There will be no change in the external factors responsible for causing headaches • Large quantities of salicylates have no adverse effects
Salicylates can cure headaches since they belong to the same chemical family as aspirin	• Members of a chemical family share all properties • Members of the same chemical family have similar effectiveness

51

After having established your assumptions, you can find the questions that are needed to evaluate the argument by rephrasing each implicit assumption.

Questions:

◆ Does the study sample population meet the minimum viability criteria for research of this nature?

◆ How similar are the demographics of the study participants to those of Mentia?

◆ Did the study participants consume any other drugs that could have been responsible for the drop-in headaches?

◆ Are there any other external factors that could have caused the decline in reported headaches?

◆ How constant was the people's willingness to report headaches throughout the 20-year study?

◆ How significant was the decrease in headaches?

◆ How big is the expected increase in the commercial use of salicylates?

◆ How many products containing flavor additives does the average citizen of Mentia consume?

◆ What is the likelihood that the external factors responsible for causing headaches will remain constant?

◆ Are there any adverse effects to consuming salicylates in large quantities?

◆ Do members of a chemical family share all properties?

◆ Do members of a chemical family have similar effectiveness rates?

51

 ## Sample Essay

Salicylates, which are similar to aspirin, will be increasingly used in commercial food productions in the coming years. Studies have shown a correlation between this increase and the reduced number of headache reports. Based on a twenty-year study on headaches, some health experts predict that the population of Mentia will suffer from fewer headaches in the future due to the novel discovery that salicylates can be used in food as a flavor additive. As with any prediction, it is important to assess the validity of the claims being made by a thorough investigation of the premises that form its basis.

The health experts base their assessment of the efficiency of salicylates in treating headaches on its similarities with aspirin, a well known headache remedy. This assumption begs the question if the aspirin's properties are transferable to salicylates just on the basis that they belong to the same chemical family. Should that prove to be true, then the health experts' main assumption that increased salicylate consumption can lead to fewer headaches is greatly strengthened, provided that the quantities of salicylates to be added as flavor additives will be sufficient to be effective. However, if the opposite were true, this would significantly weaken the premise that aspirin's properties are transferable to salicylates because members of the same chemical family share all properties. The answers would not invalidate the prediction that salicylates can cure headaches if the researchers have evidence of the direct effectiveness of the compound, regardless of its relation to aspirin.

In this vein, the health experts draw on additional evidence to support their prediction, specifically, a twenty-year study that correlates the increase of salicylates in commercial food usage with a decrease of reported headaches. To evaluate the validity of this assumption, it becomes necessary to ask if there are any other external factors that could have caused the decline in reported headaches. Some studies found that daily stress is the major contributor to headaches. Changes in the stress level of the area where the study was conducted can have a significant impact on the number of reported headaches. Other influencing factors can be tied to changes in the natural environment - like the reduction in air pollution due to the implementation of more ecologically friendly policies.

According to researchers, weather and air pollution are significant triggers of severe headaches. If there are any other external changes, like the ones mentioned above, that can be responsible for the decrease in the number of headaches then the conclusions of the study would be severely weakened. The same would happen to the claim of the health experts with regard to the reduction of headaches in Mentia since their whole case rests on the validity of the twenty-year study. However, should the health experts show that there were no other factors that could have contributed to the reduction in headaches, it would strengthen their claim that increased salicylate consumption in Mentia will result in fewer headaches, provided that the study participants did not take any painkillers or other drugs that can reduce headaches.

This is a particularly poignant issue for our current times since there has been a significant rise in self-medication over the years coupled with an equal rise of prescription drug usage. This trail of thought leads us straight to the next line of inquiry tied to the health expert's assumption that the increase of salicylate use in commercial foods is responsible for the decrease in headaches reported. What the authors of the argument should ask themselves is whether the study participants consumed any other drugs that could have been responsible for the decrease in headaches. If, according to the increased medicine consumption trend, the participants in the study took any drugs that could have headache curing properties like Ibuprofen, aspirin and Valium (to name just a few), then the results of the study would be completely invalidated since the researchers would not be able to say with any degree of certainty that the salicylates, and not the other drugs, were responsible for the reduction of headaches. This fact would significantly weaken the health experts' argument that an increase in salicylate consumption would result in fewer headaches in Mentia. However, should the opposite be true, the authors of the argument can further strengthen their main claim. If salicylates are shown to be the only headache reducing drug taken by the people in the study, then it becomes more likely that salicylates do have headache curing properties.

The validity of the twenty-year study, on which the health experts base their prediction, is also dependent on the assumption that the headache reports present in the study are accurate. This creates an interesting avenue of debate. The health experts should wonder just how constant was the people's willingness to report headaches throughout the twenty-year study. Twenty years is a very long time for people to keep records. If people are consistently willing to report their headaches, then the scientists would have a more accurate representation of the changes in the levels of aches experienced by the study subjects, provided that the methodology for the data collection is sound. This would strengthen the claim that salicylates can be used to cure headaches if the researchers also show that there were no other factors that could have been responsible for the results. However, as stated, twenty years is a long time;if people are a lot less willing to report headaches year after year, it becomes very likely that the reduction in headache reports is not due to any curative properties of salicylates. This idea would throw into question the whole premise that salicylates can be used to cure headaches, in which case an increased consumption of salicylates would have little to no effect on the headache rates in Mentia.

When arguing that increased salicylate consumption will reduce the number of headaches in Mentia, the health experts assume that the study results are also applicable to Mentia. Before making any predictions on the outcome of the increased usage of salicylates in Mentia, the authors of the statement should inquire how similar are the demographics of the study participants to those of Mentia? If the two demographics are similar, this would slightly strengthen the argument that increased salicylate usage in Mentia will reduce headaches, if people will consume the products that contain the additives based on salicylates. However, if the demographics are different, then the health experts would need to determine to what extent the study findings are applicable. Should the selection criteria for the participants be biased towards people that are less likely to suffer from headaches then the results would not be applicable to the whole population of Mentia. For instance, if the study was conducted with young people while Mentia's population consists mainly of elderly people (retiree towns like Florida), it's highly likely that the results of salicylate consumption would be different. The elderly take a lot of other drugs that could interfere and are generally more prone to headaches. Should the demographics of the study not match those of the town, the health experts would need to do more research before advocating for the use of salicylates. However, this idea would not significantly weaken the prediction that there would be fewer headaches in Mentia unless there is also a significant dip in effectiveness for the specific demographic categories of Mentia when compared to those of the study.

51   The health expert's prediction that the people of Mentia will suffer from fewer headaches rests on the idea that an increase in the commercial use of salicylates can cure headaches. The problem with the statement above is that it's rather ambiguous in terms of quantities to be used by the companies including salicylates in their food additives and shopping statistics for Mentia (percentage of products containing flavor additives that are bought by the people). Two main questions would arise from this issue, namely, how big is the expected increase in the commercial use of salicylates and how many products containing flavor additives does the average citizen of Mentia consume.

These questions are relevant for determining whether the increase of salicylate usage for commercial purposes is also followed by a significant increase in the consumption of salicylates, enough to be considered effective. Should the companies add just traces of salicylates in their additives, not enough to be considered effective, it would significantly weaken the suggestion that an increase in salicylates usage for commercial purposes will reduce the number of headaches in Mentia. It would not, however, completely invalidate the conclusion should the people of Mentia prove to be big consumers of products containing flavor additives. In this case, even if an individual food portion containing salicylates might not be effective, the mass consumption of such foods will ensure that enough of the substance will be present in the people's bodies, for it to be effective.

All in all, before making predictions about the health of Mentia, the health experts should take into consideration other factors that might influence the accuracy of their estimates. While they are not outright suggesting that people should consume more salicylates, their position of authority in the health field lends weight to their words and people that read the short snippet might be swayed by their argument. Given the potential impact, the health experts should take all adverse effects into account and consider studies that can corroborate or disprove the findings of the twenty-year study.

Chapter **14**
Society

Argument Task 52

The following appeared in a letter from the owner of the Sunnyside Towers apartment building to its manager.

"One month ago, all the showerheads on the first five floors of Sunnyside Towers were modified to restrict the water flow to approximately one-third of its original flow. Although actual readings of water usage before and after the adjustment are not yet available, the change will obviously result in considerable savings for Sunnyside Corporation, since the corporation must pay for water each month. Except for a few complaints about low water pressure, no problems with showers have been reported since the adjustment. Clearly, restricting water flow throughout all the twenty floors of Sunnyside Towers will increase our profits further."

Write a response in which you discuss what questions would need to be answered in order to decide whether the recommendation is likely to have the predicted result. Be sure to explain how the answers to these questions would help to evaluate the recommendation.

52

Strategies

Analysis consists of identifying the texts' key point, recommendation, prediction or hypothesis. All the other arguments and assumptions are designed to support this central claim. In this case, the author attempts to demonstrate that *"restricting water flow throughout all the twenty floors of Sunnyside Towers will increase our profits further."*

The next step would involve creating a statement that summarizes the text by including the central claim and its supporting arguments.

Based on the low number of complaints following a one month trial where water flow was reduced on the first five floors, the owner of the Sunnyside Towers apartment building predicts that further reducing water flow throughout all the floors of the tower will increase their profits.

When considering what questions are needed to evaluate the arguments outlined in the text, it is important to keep in mind that arguments are based on assumptions – points that are taken to be true, without the need for proof. This is what you need to look for: explicit and implicit assumptions since they lack the evidence required to prove their validity.

After having established your assumptions, you can find the questions that are needed to evaluate the argument by rephrasing each implicit assumption.

Assumptions

Explicit Assumptions	Implicit assumptions
People living in the apartment building are not bothered by the water flow change	• All the people that were bothered sent complaints • The number of complaints constitutes a small percentage of the first five floor's inhabitants • The water pressure will stay the same at the higher floors
Reduced water flow implies reduced water usage	• We can predict water usage even without the readings • People spend the same amount of time in the shower with and without reduced water flow • Showering is the main water consuming activity • Overall water usage will be reduced significantly
Water flow restrictions will increase profits	• Water costs are high • Water costs constitute a significant part of the overall building costs • The cost of the showerhead modifications will be covered by the expected profits • Showering is the main water consuming activity

52

Questions

◆ Did all the people that were bothered by the water flow change send complaints?

◆ What percentage of the first five floor's inhabitants sent complaints?

◆ Is the water pressure constant throughout the entire twenty floors?

◆ How accurate is the water usage prediction?

◆ How much time is spent in the shower when water flow restrictions are in place, compared to the amount of time spent before the restrictions?

◆ What percentage of the total water consumption is represented by showering?

◆ What percentage of the overall building costs is represented by water costs?

◆ Does the expected profit from the water flow restriction cover the costs of the showerhead modifications?

Sample Essay

Based on the low number of complaints following a one month trial where water flow was reduced on the first five floors, the owner of the Sunnyside Towers apartment building predicts that further reducing water flow throughout all the floors of the tower will increase their profits. Like all changes to a business' approach, the owner's prediction carries with it a risk of failure, and as such needs to be thoroughly analyzed before any decisions of implementing the suggested strategy are made.

In outlining his reasoning for the recommendation, the owner of the Sunnyside Towers apartment building rests his case on the assumption that the people living in the building are not bothered by the water flow change, since there were few complaints. The first question that comes to mind in this instance is whether all the people that were bothered by the new policy sent complaints to the building manager. Should the answer to this question prove to be positive, then the owner can state with a greater degree of certainty that implementing the new measures would not be faced with much opposition.

If it turns out that most of the people that had issues with the reduced water flow did not send any official complaints, then it is possible that extending this measure to the rest of the building will be faced with opposition. In this case, his main assumption that people living in the apartment building are not bothered by the water flow change would be severely weakened. It remains however unclear to what extent the owner's central argument about the company's profits would be affected, given that it would be difficult to establish if the inhabitant's issues with water flow reduction are serious enough for them to take action.

This line of thought naturally leads to the next avenue of inquiry, namely how much are the people bothered by the low water pressure. This question is essential in establishing whether the reduced water flow constitutes a minor issue, in which case the building manager can extend the new policy to the rest of the building with little opposition, or whether the low water pressure is a serious enough issue that could end up affecting his profits. If people are extremely bothered by the new measure, then extending it could lead to increased complaints, petitions to change the showerheads to their previous levels, or, in extreme places, people moving to a different apartment building. In this case, the new policy would prove to be detrimental to the company's expected profit increase.

The manager's assumption that people will not be bothered by the water flow change is also based on the idea that the water pressure is the same throughout the entire building, therefore the reduced water flow will affect all floors the same. If, like in most apartment buildings, the water pressure is lower on the higher floors, then the amount of complaints the building manager receives is bound to increase with each floor number. However, should the opposite prove to be true, then the owner can be reassured in his assumption that the low number of complaints received from the first five floors would be applicable to the rest of the building.

Another idea at the core of the arguments presented by the building owner is the assumption that reduced water flow implies reduced water usage. The main question that arises is how accurate is the owner's prediction when compared to water readings from before and after the measures. This question should help determine if the building owner was correct in his prediction or not. In the first scenario, the data would support the claim that

52

the reduced water flow implies also less water usage, which in turn bring about reduced water costs. Should the second scenario prove to be true, and the data would invalidate the owner's assumption, then the entire claim would be severely weakened. If people's water usage has remained the same or even increased, then not only would the measure be ineffective in terms of increasing the profits, but it would also bring an increase in costs.

The author's claim that reducing water flow in the shower heads will significantly reduce water usage rests on the idea that showering is the main water consuming activity. In order to support this claim, the author should investigate what percentage of the total water consumption is represented by showering. Taking a bath, using the washing machine or dishwasher are all activities that utilize water that is not restricted by the modified showerheads. If the bulk of water usage is represented by other activities than showering, then restricting water flow with the new showerheads would have little effect on the amount of water consumed by each household, and subsequently the company's water costs would not experience any significant change. However, should showering prove to be the main water consuming activity, then it becomes more likely that limiting the showerhead water flow will have an impact on the total amount of water consumed, if people's showering habits were to remain unchanged.

This brings to the fore another question, namely, how much time is spent in the shower when water flow restrictions are in place, compared to the amount of time spent before the restrictions. If people adapt to the new measure by spending more time in the shower, then the end result will bring little or no change in the amount of water usage, and the policy would be ineffective in increasing the company's profits. However, if the opposite were true and the building's inhabitants were to spend the same or less amount of time in the shower, then Sunnyside Tower's water usage would decrease.

The profitability of the owner's prediction, doesn't rest solely on water usage but also depends on water costs in general. Before implementing the change, the building's manager should evaluate the possible benefits of the water flow reduction by analyzing what percentage of the overall building costs is represented by water costs. If water costs represent a significant percentage of the building's monthly costs, then reducing water flow, even if it only brings a small amount of actual water usage reduction, should still make a significant difference for the company's profits. However, if water costs prove to be very low, then extending the measure to the rest of the building might prove to be more costly than beneficial, especially when considering the cost of labor and equipment necessary to make these changes.

The last idea brings to the fore another line of inquiry, namely whether the expected profit from the water flow restriction cover the costs of the showerhead modifications. If the cost of the modifications is too great or the expected profit is too small, then at the end of the day the company risks being at a loss. It would still be possible for the Sunnyside Tower's owner to profit, but the investment would have to be long term. If the opposite were to be true, then the owner would have all the more reason for implementing the change, given that the necessary investment would be covered by the profits.

Overall, the owner of Sunnyside Towers should make a thorough cost benefit analysis and conduct more inquiries about the opinions of the building inhabitant before implementing measures that would have an impact on their living conditions. In addition, the building owner should rest his claims on facts rather than supposition, otherwise he would run the risk of instating a new policy that could prove to be detrimental.

Argument Task 53

Twenty years ago, Dr. Field, a noted anthropologist, visited the island of Tertia. Using an observation-centered approach to studying Tertian culture, he concluded from his observations that children in Tertia were reared by an entire village rather than by their own biological parents. Recently another anthropologist, Dr. Karp, visited the group of islands that includes Tertia and used the interview-centered method to study child-rearing practices. In the interviews that Dr. Karp conducted with children living in this group of islands, the children spent much more time talking about their biological parents than about other adults in the village. Dr. Karp decided that Dr. Field's conclusion about Tertian village culture must be invalid. Some anthropologists recommend that to obtain accurate information on Tertian child-rearing practices, future research on the subject should be conducted via the interview-centered method.

Write a response in which you discuss what questions would need to be answered in order to decide whether the recommendation and the argument on which it is based are reasonable. Be sure to explain how the answers to these questions would help to evaluate the recommendation.

 Strategies

Regardless of the approach you take, consider the following steps:

◆ Is there an alternative explanation for the events in question that can invalidate, either in whole or in part, the explanation given in the passage?

◆ How can I break the argument into its component parts to understand how they create the whole argument?

◆ Can I identify the line of reasoning used to create the argument?

◆ What does the author of the argument assume to be true for the argument to be true?

◆ Does the line of reasoning validate the conclusion?

◆ Can I imagine an example that refutes any or several of the statements in the argument?

◆ Am I able to evaluate the argument based on the quality of the facts and reasons presented in it?

Based on your responses to all or some of these questions, you must present a well-developed evaluation of the argument. You should take brief notes when you identify the arguments claims, assumptions, and conclusion. Jot down as many alternative explanations as you can along with additional evidence that might support or refute the claims in the argument. Finally, list the changes in the argument that would make the reasoning more solid. It is more important to be specific than it is to have a long list of evidence and examples.

This argument cites the results of two studies concerning child-rearing practices on the island of Tertia and the group of islands that includes Tertia and makes a recommendation about further research.

In developing your response, you are required to generate questions that will help you decide if the recommendation and the argument on which it is based are reasonable and then explain how the answers to your questions would help evaluate the recommendation. It might be helpful to isolate the recommendation.

Recommendation:

To obtain accurate information on Tertian child-rearing practices, future research on the subject should be conducted via the interview-centered method.

Next, identify the argument's conclusions and the evidence that led to those conclusions.

Claims and assumptions:

◆ Dr. Field's conclusion about Tertian village culture must be invalid. This assumption supports the recommendation to conduct further studies using the interview-based approach. Later studies seem to negate Field's findings.

◆ The observation – centered approach yields inaccurate results. This unstated assumption underlies the recommendation that, in order to obtain accurate results, further studies should be conducted using the interview-based approach.

◆ The interview-centered method yields accurate results. The conclusions in Karp's research seem to justify this conclusion. This assumption supports the recommendation.

◆ Some anthropologists recommend the interview-centered approach for future research.

◆ You should now be able to generate some questions that could clarify or weaken the argument.

Questions:

◆ If the interview-centered approach had been used before the observation-centered approach, would the second results have invalidated those first results?

◆ What kinds of questions were included in the interviews?

◆ What outside influences may have arisen in the twenty years between the two studies? Have the women in the islands gone outside of the home to work? Have television and/or the Internet become available? Think about the ways in which your own community has changed in the last twenty years.

◆ Has the family structure undergone any changes in the twenty years between the two studies? Are families having fewer children?

◆ What other islands were included in Dr. Karp's study? Were child-rearing practices similar on all of the islands?

◆ Are the results of each study both valid and reliable? Did the studies indeed measure what they were intended to measure? If the same study were done again, would the results be the same?

◆ Did Dr. Fields' study make the people of Tertia reconsider their method of child-rearing? His questions may have caused them to reflect upon the way they perform this task.

Your notes do not have to be exhaustive. As you begin to write your essay, your brain will generate new ideas. Make certain that you keep the directions in mind as you develop your ideas. Use as many or as few paragraphs as you consider appropriate for your argument, but create a new paragraph when you move on to a new idea or example of support for your position. The GRE readers are not looking for a specific number of ideas or paragraphs. Instead, they are reading to determine the level of understanding of the topic and the complexity with which you respond.

You are free to organize and develop your response in any way you think will enable you to effectively communicate your evaluation of the argument. You may recall writing strategies that you learned in high school or a writing-intensive course that you took in college, but it is not necessary to employ any of those strategies. It is important that your ideas follow a logical progression and display strong critical thinking.

 ## Sample Essay

Change in virtually every society around the world is occurring at almost lightning speed. Tertia and the group of islands to which it belongs are not likely to be immune to change. If we assume that Dr. Field's conclusions were appropriate twenty years ago, we must ask ourselves if events during the intervening years may have changed the child-rearing practices that he observed. Exposure to other people visiting the island, access to television and the Internet, and even people leaving the island would influence future studies of the culture. Dr. Field's study, alone, could have caused the residents of Tertia to question their child-rearing practices and, as a result, modify them. Dr. Karp's recent study, regardless of the technique he used, could not fail to yield different results than the earlier study. Playing devil's advocate for a moment, let's reverse the order of the studies. Assume that Dr. Karp completed his study using the interview-centered approach and that, twenty years later Dr. Field arrived at the island and used his observation-centered approach to complete his study. The results would most certainly still disagree with each other. In this case, do Dr. Field's results invalidate those of Dr. Karp?

The scope of each study appears to be different, as well. Dr. Field allegedly studied only the families on the island of Tertia while Dr. Karp visited the group of islands that includes Tertia. The fact that the subjects were different for each event is enough to nullify one's superiority over the other. It also appears that Dr. Field observed the culture of Tertia as a whole, while Karp focused on child-rearing practices. Having used two variants of research procedures, the anthropologists were destined to achieve unreliable results.

We should take a closer look at the approaches that each anthropologist adopted. As Field employed the observation- centered method to study the culture of Tertia, what did he observe in addition to child-rearing practices? One could infer that those practices were a small, perhaps even minor, portion of his entire project. On the other hand, Karp's project, using an interview-centered method, seems to have ignored other aspects of the culture. Why would a group of scientists use these disparate studies as a basis for further research?

Overall, the results of these studies have too much dissimilarity and leave too many questions unanswered to use them as justification for more research using either one of the methods mentioned in the argument. The author of the argument may have more information than he has seen fit to reveal and, thus, may be qualified to sit in judgment of the methods and the results. However, based on what has been revealed here, the recommendation is based on flawed reasoning.

53

Argument Task 54

Nature's Way, a chain of stores selling health food and other health-related products, is opening its next franchise in the town of Plainsville. The store should prove to be very successful: Nature's Way franchises tend to be most profitable in areas where residents lead healthy lives, and clearly Plainsville is such an area. Plainsville merchants report that sales of running shoes and exercise clothing are at all-time highs. The local health club has more members than ever, and the weight training and aerobics classes are always full. Finally, Plainsville's schoolchildren represent a new generation of potential customers: these schoolchildren are required to participate in a fitness-for-life program, which emphasizes the benefits of regular exercise at an early age.

Write a response in which you examine the stated and/or unstated assumptions of the argument. Be sure to explain how the argument depends on these assumptions and what the implications are for the argument if the assumptions prove unwarranted.

 Strategies

54

Argument:

The argument uses information about healthful activities in Plainsville to support Nature's Way's opening its next franchise in Plainsville.

In developing your response to the topic, you must identify and examine both the stated and unstated assumptions of the argument to determine how the argument depends on those assumptions and how the argument fails if the assumptions prove to be incorrect.

Assumptions:

◆ Nature's Way should be very successful in Plainsville. The writer assumes that the residents of Plainsville will purchase products from Nature's Way. This underlies the claim that Nature's Way will be successful in Plainsville. Since the residents are already health conscious, they may be buying health food somewhere else. Is there another health food store in Plainsville?

◆ Nature's Way franchises tend to be profitable in areas where the residents lead healthy lives. "Tend" is a qualifying word; it is not absolute. Are some Nature's Way stores not profitable in areas where residents lead healthy lives? What might cause that lack of success?

◆ The assumption that the children of Plainsville will be future customers of Nature's Way underlies the claim that Plainsville citizens lead healthy lives. There is no evidence that the children eat healthy food, just that they must participate in an exercise program. How many of these children will live in Plainsville as adults?

◆ The residents of Plainsville lead healthy lives. The writer uses health club memberships and sales of running shoes and exercise clothing to support this assumption. It would be helpful to know how many of those club memberships are new and how many are renewals. How many times per week do the members go to the club to work out? What time of year is it? After the New Year's holiday, people make resolutions to lose weight, eat healthier, and exercise. Those resolutions rarely stick. The stores may be having after-Christmas sales, and the reduced prices have prompted the citizens to replace worn out sneakers and clothing.

Your notes do not have to be exhaustive. As you begin to write your essay, your brain will generate new ideas. Make certain that you keep the directions in mind as you develop your ideas.

 ## Sample Essay

The writer of the passage has listed facts about the lifestyle of Plainsville residents that support the likely success of a Nature's Way franchise that is opening in that town. On the surface, this litany of healthy behaviors appears to be sufficient to bolster the position in the argument. Any good salesman would use a similar pitch to promote his product. However, several questions arise that could undermine the assumptions in this passage.

The first questions surround the reported increases in gym memberships and sales of sneakers and exercise clothing. It is no mystery that gym memberships increase at the beginning of each year. Adults make New Year's resolutions to lose weight, eat healthier food, and exercise more, resulting in upticks in the purchases of gym memberships, increased traffic at healthy food stores, and increased purchases of fitness clothing. After-holiday sales might also account for the increase in sales of sneakers and exercise clothing. After all, those new gym members need something to wear.

The argument also posits that future sales at Nature's Way are guaranteed as the children become healthier in Plainsville. They are required to participate in a program that emphasized the benefits of regular exercise at an early age. However, it is unclear whether this program requires them to exercise or eat healthy food, or how this might be enforced. Participation in the program does not guarantee participation in healthy activities. Their parents' food and exercise habits are more likely than a school program to influence the children's behavior. How many of those children will remain in Plainsville as adults? Merchants in other parts of the state or country are apt to benefit from the buying habits of these children when they become productive adults.

The assumption that any new business will be successful in any town is risky. Even WalMart locations have failed in areas where the residents have no need to shop there. What is the median income in Plainsville? Are the residents college-educated? Specialty health-food stores cater to a relatively high socioeconomic group. Is there already a health-food store in Plainsville? What does Nature's Way have that will set it apart from businesses that already exist? Are the prices at Nature's Way low enough to attract a large customer base? Unless the store provides superior product or service, or a lower price point, it will not stand out in any appreciable way.

Finally, the author's use of the word tend should lead the reader to question the soundness of the assumptions in the passage. What happens to Nature's Way when it turns out that Plainsville residents don't stick to their resolutions to become healthier? They will find good excuses to skip going to the gym this week, and they'll rationalize their way through a pan of brownies. When all is said and done, the author's statement that Nature's Way should be successful may be correct. If the people of Plainsville are serious about leading healthy lives, they should shop at Nature's Way. That doesn't mean that they will.

54

Argument Task 55

The following appeared in an article written by Dr. Karp, an anthropologist.

"Twenty years ago, Dr. Field, a noted anthropologist, visited the island of Tertia and concluded from his observations that children in Tertia were reared by an entire village rather than by their own biological parents. However, my recent interviews with children living in the group of islands that includes Tertia show that these children spend much more time talking about their biological parents than about other adults in the village. This research of mine proves that Dr. Field's conclusion about Tertian village culture is invalid and thus that the observation-centered approach to studying cultures is invalid as well. The interview-centered method that my team of graduate students is currently using in Tertia will establish a much more accurate understanding of child-rearing traditions there and in other island cultures."

Write a response in which you discuss what specific evidence is needed to evaluate the argument and explain how the evidence would weaken or strengthen the argument.

 Strategies

Argument:

The interview-centered method will establish a more accurate understanding of child- rearing traditions in Tertiary than did the observation- centered approach.

In developing your response, you are asked to identify specific evidence that Dr. Karp needs to sustain the validity of his position.

Facts and Assumptions:

◆ Twenty years ago, Dr. Field observed that children in Tertia were reared by an entire village rather than by their own biological parents.

◆ Recently, Dr. Karp visited the group of islands that includes Tertia and used the interview-centered method to study child-rearing practices. Readers of this passage might assume that he interviewed residents of Tertia to compare practices from twenty years ago to those of today.

◆ The children interviewed by Dr. Karp spent more time talking about their biological parents than other adults in the village. The assumption is that child- rearing practices may have changed over the last twenty years or that Dr. Field's conclusions were incorrect.

◆ Dr. Karp did conclude that Dr. Field's conclusions must be invalid. The assumption is that Dr. Karp's methods yield more accurate results.

Questions:

◆ Why did Dr. Field choose the observation-center method to study the people of Tertia? Did he have good results with that method in previous studies?

◆ What prompted Dr. Karp to visit this group of islands? Did he actually visit and interview the residents of Tertia?

◆ What types of questions did Dr. Karp use with the children he interviewed? Did he ask them about all adults, or did he restrict his questions to those about their parents?

◆ Have child-rearing practices changed in the twenty years between the two visits?

Your notes do not have to be exhaustive. As you begin to write your essay, your brain will generate new ideas. Make certain that you keep the directions in mind as you develop your ideas.

Sample Essay

Ever since Margaret Mead journeyed to study the Samoans in the early part of the twentieth century, anthropologists have continued to investigate the social mores of remote groups around the world. Each anthropologist is bound to have a preferred method for confuting research, and they may alternate those methods depending on what aspect of the culture they are investigating. To evaluate Dr. Karp's recommendation, the reader requires evidence that his interview-centered method is superior to Dr. Field's observation-centered approach.

The first piece of evidence should reveal the purpose of each anthropologist's visit to the area of Tertia. It is not even clear that Dr. Karp actually visited Tertia itself. The passage implies that each of them purposely studied child-rearing practices since no mention is made of other results. However, it could be that those results are ancillary to the real purpose of each visit. The studies may have had a broader scope than is revealed in this passage. In addition, if Dr. Karp pursued this study in reaction to the data,he saw from Dr. Field's work, he may have made assumptions about the study's conclusions that would bias his experimental design.

Dr. Karp currently has a team of graduate students using the interview-based method to study child- rearing practices in Tertia. The content of an interview can be designed to elicit specific types of responses. Do the questions lead the children of Tertia to talk about their parents rather than other adults on the island? There is a world of difference between asking, "When do your parents feed you?" and "When do you eat your meals?" Are the graduate students using questions developed by Dr. Karp, or have they created their own questions? Grad students may not have enough experience to write questions that are objective.

Twenty years have passed since Dr. Field visited and observed the residents of Tertia. Is there evidence of any outside influences on village life since his visit? The rapid growth of technology has created the global village, and it is difficult to imagine that Tertia has not been, at least tangentially, affected. Satellites have made access to the World Wide Web possible from virtually anywhere on the globe. Cellular phones are ubiquitous. It is even possible that Dr. Field's visit, itself, influenced the behavior of the Tertians. In fact, it would be unrealistic to believe that child-rearing practices have remained static anywhere.

The one piece of evidence that is clear is that Dr. Karp wrote the article. It is doubtful that this anthropologist has maintained an objective point of view while contrasting the two research methods. An opinion delivered by a scientist with no vested interest in the outcome might be the strongest evidence for evaluating the strength of the argument.

55

Argument Task 56

The following appeared in a letter to the editor of a local newspaper

"Commuters complain that increased rush-hour traffic on Blue Highway between the suburbs and the city center has doubled their commuting time. The favored proposal of the motorists' lobby is to widen the highway, adding an additional lane of traffic. But last year's addition of a lane to the nearby Green Highway was followed by a worsening of traffic jams on it. A better alternative is to add a bicycle lane to Blue Highway. Many area residents are keen bicyclists. A bicycle lane would encourage them to use bicycles to commute, and so would reduce rush-hour traffic rather than fostering an increase."

Write a response in which you discuss what specific evidence is needed to evaluate the argument and explain how the evidence would weaken or strengthen the argument.

NOTE: The above topic has wording similar to Argument Task 65 of this book. However, if you read carefully you will notice that the task instructions are different. Hence, it is very important to read the topic as well as its instructions completely before you start to write your response.

 Strategies

Argument:

Based on the results of adding an additional lane to the Green Highway, the writer argues that adding a bike lane to the Blue Highway is a better alternative to an additional traffic lane.

Claims and Assumptions:

◆ The writer claims that commuting time between the suburbs and the city have doubled on the Blue Highway. The assumption is that the highway does not have sufficient lanes to handle the volume of traffic. Another assumption might be that more vehicles than before are traveling on this road during rush hours. The reader needs to know why there is an apparent increase in traffic. Has there been an interruption in public transportation? Are fewer commuters carpooling? Did a Park and Ride close? Is all of the rush-hour traffic attributed to people going to and from work? Has an attempt been made to actually count the cars?

◆ The writer also claims that, since the addition of a lane on the Green Highway, there have been worsening traffic jams. The assumption here is that an additional lane may have been the cause of the traffic jams. One is left to wonder why there appears to be increased traffic difficulties on both highways. Do traffic jams continue to be a problem on Green Highway?

◆ Many area residents are bicycle enthusiasts. The writer assumes that, if there were a bike lane, many of those cyclists would ride their bikes to work. Can commuters travel in this manner year-round? Will they bike to work in the rain? What about when the days are shorter, and they must travel in the dark? Are there enough places to store or park bikes safely during the work day? Which area residents are keen bicyclists?

Your notes do not have to be exhaustive. As you begin to write your essay, your brain will generate new ideas. Make certain that you keep the directions in mind as you develop your ideas.

Sample Essay

The writer of this editorial is expressing his opinion about a way to relieve apparent traffic jams on Blue Highway. Either the writer or people he has spoken to complain that commuting time between the suburbs and the city center has doubled. The motorists' lobby proposes adding a lane to the highway, but the writer, citing trouble on Green Highway since it added a lane for cars, suggests that a bike lane would be a better solution to the problem on Blue Highway. Decision makers need more evidence about the traffic situation on both highways before opting for either choice.

The reader assumes that a doubling of commuting time must mean a doubling of the number of cars traveling on Blue Highway. An increase in the number of vehicles may be partially responsible, but it could be that the highway department reduced the speed on the highway as well. Where have the extra vehicles come from? The decision makers may discover that another traffic artery is partially or completed closed for construction, and the increased traffic may be temporary.

Comparing Blue Highway's problems to those of Green Highway in unproductive. The two roads carry traffic from different areas and, maybe, for different purposes. To support the addition of a bike lane, the writer must present evidence that bike lanes effectively reduce automobile traffic in cities where there is a large volume of commuters. That should be a simple matter of contacting other urban areas that have bike lanes used by commuters.

For commuters to agree that biking is a suitable alternative to driving to work, they will need evidence of security for their bikes in the city. Are there now or will there be in the future facilities where bicyclists can safely park their bikes during the work day. They also might need some incentive to ride bikes rather than drive cars to work each day. What have other cities done if anything? After all, these cyclists are helping to reduce pollution and rush-hour traffic jams. Shouldn't there be some reward? Has the author surveyed cyclists to determine their number

56

and their willingness to commute by bike? Has he checked a meteorological survey to discover how many days a year, on average, are suitable for traveling by bike?

Can this writer provide evidence that the city can save construction costs by adding bike lanes rather than another lane for vehicles? One might imagine that the specifications for a bike lane would be less onerous than that for a lane of traffic expected to carry thousands of passenger cars and heavy commercial vehicles. Because bikes travel in the same direction as motorized vehicles, the city would need to build a lane on each side of the highway. Is there room on both sides of the highway for a bike lane?

In a culture that has a continuing love affair with the automobile, the author will need a raft of evidence to support the building of bike lanes rather than an additional lane for cars and trucks. He also needs evidence to show how an additional lane for vehicles is not the answer to alleviating the commuter dilemmas on Blue Highway.

56

Argument Task 57

The following appeared in a memo from the vice president of a food distribution company with food storage warehouses in several cities.

"Recently, we signed a contract with the Fly-Away Pest Control Company to provide pest control services at our fast-food warehouse in Palm City, but last month we discovered that over $20,000 worth of food there had been destroyed by pest damage. Meanwhile, the Buzzoff Pest Control Company, which we have used for many years, continued to service our warehouse in Wintervale, and last month only $10,000 worth of the food stored there had been destroyed by pest damage. Even though the price charged by Fly-Away is considerably lower, our best means of saving money is to return to Buzzoff for all our pest control services."

Write a response in which you discuss what specific evidence is needed to evaluate the argument and explain how the evidence would weaken or strengthen the argument.

NOTE: The above topic has wording similar to Argument Task 61 of this book. However, if you read carefully you will notice that the task instructions are different. Hence, it is very important to read the topic as well as its instructions completely before you start to write your response.

 Strategies

A good place to start your analysis is by creating a statement that reveals the main idea of the argument. Although the writer is creating an argument, he may ultimately be stating a position, making a recommendation, or making a prediction. It may be helpful for you to determine which of these formats is most evident in the argument.

As a result of food spoilage in the Palm City warehouse, the vice president of the company recommends a return to using Buzzoff pest control services.

Assumptions:

◆ Conditions at both warehouses are identical.

◆ The same type of pest is present at both warehouses.

◆ The food stored in both warehouses is equally attractive to pests.

◆ Both warehouses are the same size and require the same amount of pest-control product.

◆ The higher cost of Buzzoff services will be offset by a reduction in food spoilage.

◆ The amount of the loss is greater than in previous years.

Evidence needed to evaluate the argument:

◆ The types of food stored at each facility

◆ The types of pests present at each facility

◆ Other conditions that may have resulted in spoilage

◆ Why the company decided to use a different company for its facility in Palm City

◆ How much food is stored at each warehouse?

◆ The percentage of the food that was spoiled at each warehouse

After completing these steps, you should have enough material to write your analysis. Remember that you are not creating a position of your own; you are evaluating the strengths and weaknesses of the existing argument. You do not have to include all of the points that you have created in your prewriting. In fact, during the process of drafting your analysis, other ideas may come to mind, and, if they strengthen your analysis, you should include them.

57

Sample Essay

Food is perishable. It must be stored at correct temperatures and humidity. Even when those conditions are managed correctly, pests are still a threat. Some may arrive with the food from its country of origin, while others invade at its arrival point. This company has hired two companies to control the pests at its warehouses, and, according to the manager, one has been more successful than the other. Before the owners of the company take the suggestion to return all of the pest control to Buzzoff, they need more evidence of Fly Away's inability to keep their products free from pests.

First, the owners should know what prompted the switch to Fly Away. There might be evidence that Buzzoff had not been as successful in Palm City as they had been in previous years or in the company's other locations. Buzzoff may have been too busy to continue servicing the Palm City warehouse and may not even be able to do so if asked in the future. On the other hand, Fly Away may have approached the food company and made promises that they could not keep. If that is the case, the company is justified in returning to Buzzoff.

Some foods are more susceptible to invasions of pests. The strength of the recommendation may rest on knowing the types of food at each location. Palm City stores fast food, but the argument does not reveal what type of fast food. In fact, if this warehouse provides storage for ground beef, temperature, rather than pests would be the likely culprit for spoilage. Fly Away may have been effective in eliminating pests, but a refrigeration problem would cause the bacteria already present in ground meat to cause its breakdown. The warehouse in Palm City may have some structural damage that could allow pests like rats or raccoons to get into the building and feast on the product within. Fly Away may not have been instructed to poison or trap these critters. The warehouse in Wintervale may store frozen food exclusively, so pests are not a big problem. The $10,000 loss could have resulted from a malfunction in a unit or even an issue with a delivery truck. On the other hand, both warehouses may be perfectly maintained, store the same type of food, and Fly Away did an inferior job at pest control in Palm City. It would be important to know how much food is stored at each warehouse. The argument provides the dollar amount of loss at each location, but not the percentage of total inventory lost to pests. It appears that the $10,000 loss in Wintervale is not as alarming as the $20,000 loss in Palm City. If, however, the Palm City warehouse stores $200,000 worth of product, and the Wintervale warehouse stores $100,000 worth of product, the percentage of loss is the same. Companies that deal with perishable merchandise usually have some level of acceptable loss, but that information is not present in the argument. In fact, they may have had bigger losses last year. This year's loss to pests might be average.

Environmental anomalies could account for Fly Away's apparent failure to protect the food stored in the Palm City warehouse. Temperatures may have been much higher or lower than usual. There may have been significantly more rain or humidity. Some insect populations are cyclical. Fly Away may have contracted to do the job for a specific price that was suitable for average conditions. If the conditions were extraordinary in some way, any company would have found it difficult or impossible to prevent the loss. Additionally, conditions in Wintervale may have been more favorable than normal, helping to make the loss there significantly smaller.

The loss of product in either or both warehouses may have been beyond the company's control regardless of which pest service it used. The pest problem may have originated with the company's suppliers. The vice president doesn't reveal if he or one of his managers decided to buy product from a new supplier. If the loss to pests this year is unacceptable, the company needs clearer evidence that Fly Away rather than some other contingency is the cause. It may turn out that Fly Away is an excellent choice for pest control, and the easiest way to save money is to use them for all the company's warehouses.

57

Argument Task 58

The following appeared in a memo from the new vice president of Sartorian, a company that manufactures men's clothing.

"Five years ago, at a time when we had difficulties in obtaining reliable supplies of high-quality wool fabric, we discontinued production of our alpaca overcoat. Now that we have a new fabric supplier, we should resume production. This coat should sell very well: since we have not offered an alpaca overcoat for five years and since our major competitor no longer makes an alpaca overcoat, there will be pent-up customer demand. Also, since the price of most types of clothing has increased in each of the past five years, customers should be willing to pay significantly higher prices for alpaca overcoats than they did five years ago, and our company profits will increase."

Write a response in which you discuss what specific evidence is needed to evaluate the argument and explain how the evidence would weaken or strengthen the argument.

 Strategies

Argument:

Based on the ability to obtain high quality fabric and an opportunity to corner the market, Sartorian will reintroduce its alpaca overcoat.

In developing your response, reveal the specific evidence that Sartorian needs to decide whether or not reintroducing its alpaca coat is a sound idea.

Facts and Assumptions:

◆ Five years ago, Sartorian discontinued production of its alpaca overcoat because it lacked a reliable supply of high quality wool fabric. There must be very few suppliers of alpaca wool fabric.

◆ Sartorian has a new supplier of fabric. A new producer has come about or the quality of a previous supplier has improved enough to satisfy Sartorian.

◆ Sartorian has not offered an alpaca coat for five years. The company assumes that its customers are eager for the company's new coat.

58

◆ Sartorian's major competitor no longer makes an alpaca coat. Sartorian may assume that the competitor's coat did not measure up, and customers stopped buying it. Sartorian needs to consider that the competitor's coat may have been lovely, but demand for alpaca coats or the cost of production made it unwise to continue producing them.

◆ The price of most types of clothing has increased in each of the past five years. The assumption is that customers have become used to higher prices and will be agreeable to higher prices for the alpaca coat. Sartorian believes that higher prices for its coat will increase company profits.

Your notes do not have to be exhaustive. As you begin to write your essay, your brain will generate new ideas. Make certain that you keep the directions in mind as you develop your ideas.

 ## Sample Essay

Sartorian appears eager to jump back into the alpaca coat market after a five-year absence. The company must have a strong emotional attachment to the coat they used to make and sell with some success. One is left to wonder if discontinuing the coat left a gap in their clothing line that it has been unable to fill with another garment. The lack of competition in the alpaca coat market seems a further incentive to resume production. Sartorian has drawn some conclusions that bear further scrutiny before taking what is probably an expensive step.

The clothing manufacturer assumes that its customer loyalty guarantees the success of its alpaca coat. The stores who formerly sold the coat may have replaced it with other outer garments with which they are very satisfied. As a result, those stores may not have the money to stock the new alpaca coats. Sartorian should survey the buyers for retail outlets that sold their previous coat as well as any new stores. The manufacturer may discover that it cannot generate sales sufficient to justify reintroducing the alpaca coat.

58

Sartorian seems encouraged by the lack of competition in the alpaca coat market. Its only competitor has ceased production of its own coat. Sartorian would be well-advised to interview the other manufacturer to uncover the reason for stopping production. The truth of the matter may be that alpaca coats have fallen completely out of favor. The pent-up customer demand that Sartorian is anticipating may not exist.

The final justification that Sartorian cites is the overall increase in clothing prices over the past five years. The company assumes that they will be able to demand higher prices for its alpaca coat, which will help the company's bottom line. The truth may be that individual clothing budgets may be strained by the rise in prices, and there is no money left over with which to buy an expensive alpaca coat.

Sartorian's vice president has some research to do before jumping back into the alpaca coat market. He needs evidence of continuing demand for the product. Cornering the market for a clothing item that won't sell would not be a feather in this vice president's hat.

Argument Task 59

A recent sales study indicates that consumption of seafood dishes in Bay City restaurants has increased by 30 percent during the past five years. Yet there are no currently operating city restaurants whose specialty is seafood. Moreover, the majority of families in Bay City are two-income families, and a nationwide study has shown that such families eat significantly fewer home-cooked meals than they did a decade ago but at the same time express more concern about healthful eating. Therefore, the new Captain Seafood restaurant that specializes in seafood should be quite popular and profitable.

Write a response in which you discuss what specific evidence is needed to evaluate the argument and explain how the evidence would weaken or strengthen the argument.

NOTE: The above topic has wording similar to Argument Task 64 of this book. However, if you read carefully you will notice that the task instructions are different. Hence, it is very important to read the topic as well as its instructions completely before you start to write your response.

 Strategies

Argument:

Based on the apparent popularity of seafood dishes, the new Captain Seafood restaurant should be popular and profitable in Bay City.

In developing your response, you must identify what evidence is needed to show that the new restaurant will indeed be both popular and profitable.

Facts and Assumptions:

◆ The consumption of seafood dishes in Bay City restaurants has increased by 30 percent during the past five years. The assumption is that the consumption of seafood dishes is very high. The truth of that depends on the level of consumption five years ago. Sales of these dishes have increased by roughly one-third, so any restaurant that used to sell 3 seafood dishes each day is now selling 4.

◆ There are currently no operating restaurants that specialize in seafood. Were there seafood restaurants in the past? What happened to them?

59

◆ Bay City has a large number of two-income families, and studies show that this type of family eats significantly fewer home-cooked meals than they did a decade ago. The assumption is that these families eat out frequently. They are just as likely to buy prepared food at the grocery store. What does significantly mean? Again, the reader needs to know the level of home-cooked meals that these families ate a decade ago.

◆ These same families express more concern about healthful eating. One assumption implied by this statement is that those families actually are eating more healthy meals. Another assumption is that the seafood dishes being served in restaurants are healthy.

Your notes do not have to be exhaustive. As you begin to write your essay, your brain will generate new ideas. Make certain that you keep the directions in mind as you develop your ideas.

Sample Essay

The writer offers the reader some statistics that presume to prove a significant increase in the popularity of seafood dishes in Bay City's restaurants even though none of those eateries specialize in seafood. Some might mistakenly understand that seafood entrées comprise 30 percent of restaurant sales, and that would be impressive. In actuality, the sale of such dishes has increased by 30 percent, or roughly 1/3, over the past five years. If we know that restaurant A sold 6 seafood dishes each day five years ago, then we can calculate that the same restaurant sells 8 per day now. An increase of two dishes per day is not cause for celebration. Should we discover, however, that restaurant A sold 30 seafood dishes every day five years ago, a 30 percent increase would now be 40 dishes per day. Depending on the restaurant's overall volume, an additional 10 seafood dishes might be meaningful.

Another statistic employed by the writer relates to the domestic habits of the two-income families that comprise most of Bay City's population. Nationwide studies show that families in this demographic eat significantly fewer home-cooked meals than they did a decade ago. Significant is a subjective term. What is significant for one family may be trifling for another. The reader would be wise to apply the logic from the previous paragraph to this fact. In addition, the fact that they eat fewer home-cooked meals does not lead inevitably to the conclusion that they are not eating at home. These families may very well be purchasing prepared or frozen meals at the local supermarket. Counting on their patronage to ensure the popularity and profitability of a new restaurant would be a mistake without further evidence about their dining habits.

The same study cited in the previous paragraph reveals that two-income families express more concern about healthy eating. Expressing concern and taking some action are two widely different concepts. Many people are concerned about heart disease but continue to smoke. In the context of this passage, the writer would lead the reader to assume that seafood entrées are more healthful than other dishes. A fillet of haddock smothered in buttered bread crumbs or served with a cream sauce is no healthier for a dinner than a lean piece of beef cooked on the grill. The writer should examine the menus at the restaurants to determine the ingredients and cooking

59

methods used for the seafood dishes. If the entrées are baked, steamed, or poached and served with lemon and fresh vegetables, they could be considered more healthful than dishes that naturally have more animal fat and cholesterol.

Finally, the writer claims that the current lack of a restaurant specializing in seafood in Bay City is certain to ensure the success of the new Captain Seafood restaurant. Was there a seafood restaurant in Bay City at one time? If so, why did it close? If a seafood restaurant closed in the city, which could account, at least in part, for the increase in seafood entrées' popularity in the other eateries. A closer examination of some of the facts and assumptions in the passage reveals that the popularity and profitability of Captain Seafood is not a foregone conclusion. It relies on evidence that easily could be obtained to support the writer's claim.

Argument Task 60

The following appeared in a letter from a homeowner to a friend.

"*Of the two leading real estate firms in our town - Adams Realty and Fitch Realty - Adams Realty is clearly superior. Adams has 40 real estate agents; in contrast, Fitch has 25, many of whom work only part-time. Moreover, Adams' revenue last year was twice as high as that of Fitch and included home sales that averaged $168,000, compared to Fitch's $144,000. Homes listed with Adams sell faster as well: ten years ago I listed my home with Fitch, and it took more than four months to sell; last year, when I sold another home, I listed it with Adams, and it took only one month. Thus, if you want to sell your home quickly and at a good price, you should use Adams Realty.*"

Write a response in which you examine the stated and/or unstated assumptions of the argument. Be sure to explain how the argument depends on these assumptions and what the implications are for the argument if the assumptions prove unwarranted.

Strategies

Argument:

The writer tells his friend that he should use Adams Realty if he wants to sell his house quickly and at a great price. He claims that Adams Realty is superior to Fitch Realty.

You are instructed to create a response in which you examine the explicitly stated assumptions and the implied assumptions of the argument and tell how the argument's validity relies on these assumptions. You must also explain how the argument would be affected if any or all of the assumptions prove incorrect.

Assumptions:

◆ The assumption that more agents create a better real estate business underlies the claim that Adams Realty had twice as much revenue last year as did Fitch Realty.

◆ The assumption that full-time agents are better than part-time agents also supports the claim that Adams Realty had greater revenues.

60

◆ There is the implied assumption that the housing market is the same today as it was ten years ago. The writer creates this assumption by contrasting his own experiences with selling his homes.

◆ Also implied is that the real estate companies have made no changes in their businesses, also supported by the writer's contrasting his experiences.

◆ The assumption that the writer sold two virtually identical homes underlies the claim that his current sale occurred more quickly and at a better price.

Your notes do not have to be exhaustive. As you begin to write your essay, your brain will generate new ideas. Make certain that you keep the directions in mind as you develop your ideas.

Sample Essay

The author of this argument has experience using two local real estate agencies to sell his two homes in a period of ten years. On the surface, his recommendation to his friend must carry some weight. However, he has overlooked some important information while making his assumptions about the effectiveness of Adams Realty being superior to that of Fitch Realty. To accept the author's argument, the reader needs more substantial reasons to accept the assumptions.

The author would have us believe that a bigger real estate agency is better than a smaller one as he reports the number of agents working at each agency and that Fitch Realty has many part-time agents. Based on that information, the reader assumes that all or most of Adams Realty agents work full time. Additionally, there is the assumption that full-time employees are more productive or effective as realtors than part-time employees. Should we find that is not the case, the assumption would prove false.

The author would also have his friend believe that Adams Realty secures higher prices than Fitch Realty for the homes they sell based on the average price each company reveals. There are several weaknesses inherent in this assumption. An average is derived from totaling the amount that each house sold for and dividing the total by the number of units sold. It could very well be that Fitch Realty sold several houses at a very high price and several houses for very low prices, whereas Adams Realty could have sold most of its inventory at very similar prices. Houses have appraised values; there is no evidence that one or the other of the real estate companies is better than the other at selling houses at or close to their appraised values. The author also fails to reveal whether the clients of each company were happy with the service and/or prices they received for their homes.

An implied assumption in this letter is that the real estate market has not changed in the intervening ten years since the author sold his first home. The reader must also assume that the two real estate agencies have not undergone any changes. They must have the same agents and marketing strategies that they employed ten years ago. Considering what has happened to the housing market in the last few years, as well as economic trends such as inflation and social trends such as gentrification, it is unlikely that either or both agencies has not altered its approach to the sale of houses.

Virtually all business is predicated on the law of supply and demand. Ten years ago, the writer's house may not have been in high demand. There may have been glut of houses just like his on the market and very little demand for that type of house. In the current market, the type of house that he sold may be very popular with plenty of potential customers seeking the features that his house had. There is no guarantee that the writer's friend will have the same experience either with Adams Realty or getting a fast sale and a high price for his home.

Argument Task 61

The following appeared in a memo from the vice president of a food distribution company with food storage warehouses in several cities.

"Recently, we signed a contract with the FlyAway Pest Control Company to provide pest control services at our warehouse in Palm City, but last month we discovered that over $20,000 worth of food there had been destroyed by pest damage. Meanwhile, the Buzzoff Pest Control Company, which we have used for many years in Palm City, continued to service our warehouse in Wintervale, and last month only $10,000 worth of the food stored there had been destroyed by pest damage. Even though the price charged by Fly-Away is considerably lower, our best means of saving money is to return to Buzzoff for all our pest control services."

Write a response in which you discuss what questions would need to be answered in order to decide whether the recommendation and the argument on which it is based are reasonable. Be sure to explain how the answers to these questions would help to evaluate the recommendation.

NOTE: The above topic has wording similar to Argument Task 57 of this book. However, if you read carefully you will notice that the task instructions are different. Hence, it is very important to read the topic as well as its instructions completely before you start to write your response.

 Strategies

A good place to start your analysis is by creating a statement that reveals the main idea of the argument. Although the writer is creating an argument, he may ultimately be stating a position, making a recommendation, or making a prediction. It may be helpful for you to determine which of these formats is most evident in the argument.

As a result of pest damage in the Palm City warehouse, the vice president of the food distribution company recommends a return to Buzzoff Pest Control for pest control in Palm City.

Assumptions:

◆ Buzzoff Pest Control is more effective than FlyAway.

◆ Conditions at both warehouses are identical.

◆ Both warehouses contain the same product.

61

◆ A larger percentage of food was lost in Palm City than in Wintervale.

◆ The amount of loss this month was greater than in previous months.

Questions:

◆ Why did the food distribution company change pest-control companies at its Palm City location?

◆ What types of food does the company store at each facility?

◆ What percentage of the total value of food stores at each facility was destroyed by pests?

◆ Is the $20,000 loss in the Palm City facility higher than normal?

◆ How much product is generally lost to pest each year at each location?

◆ What conditions exist at the remainder of the company's several locations?

After completing these steps, you should have enough material to write your analysis. Remember that you are not creating a position of your own; you are evaluating the strengths and weaknesses of the existing argument. You do not have to include all of the points that you have created in your prewriting. In fact, during the process of drafting your analysis, other ideas may come to mind, and, if they strengthen your analysis, you should include them.

Sample Essay

It appears that the vice president of the food distribution company has had a change of heart concerning his choice of pest control at the Palm City warehouse. The facts that he presents, on the surface, appear reasonable. Upon closer examination of the information in the recommendation, the reader may identify several questions that need answers before agreeing with the vice president.

61

The vice president should ask himself why he changed companies in the first place. Without more detailed information, one might assume that this vice president was dissatisfied with the service provided by Buzzoff in the Palm City location. Other, similar businesses may have recommended Fly Away as an alternative, and this vice president, seeing the reduction in price, may have accepted the recommendation without carefully examining Fly Away's record of performance. The storage company has several other locations in addition to those in Palm City and Wintervale. Which pest control companies provide services for those warehouses? How successful are they at preventing losses? If Buzzoff successfully prevents pest damage in these other locations, the company would be advised to rehire them in Palm City. It may be that the warehouse company uses one or more other companies altogether. Answers to these questions may provide evidence that the vice president's recommendation is correct, or they may show that another company altogether would be a better candidate for pest control at Palm City.

How does last month's $20,000 loss compare to losses from prior months or the same month in previous years at the Palm City location? If it is significantly higher than the average of losses in the past, the warehouse company may be justified in making the recommendation to return to Buzzoff's service. If the figure represents an average loss for that month, however, the $20,000 figure becomes irrelevant to the argument and recommendation. The same scrutiny should be applied to the Wintervale loss of product. Is a $10,000 loss typical, lower than average, or higher than average?

For the comparison between the two locations to be valid, these questions must be answered. Is the $20,000 loss significant at all? If the company stores two million dollars' worth of food in Palm City, the loss is only 1%. How much product is stored at each of the two facilities? If both warehouses have products with the same dollar value, then Palm City has lost twice as much as Wintervale to pest damage during the same period of time, a fact that would lead to further scrutiny of both pest control companies' practices. If Wintervale stores considerably less product than Palm City, the $10,000 loss may represent a greater portion of the total lost to pest damage and raises the question of Buzzoff's ability to provide sufficient protection against pests.

Could some other event explain the loss at Palm City? The pest damage may have occurred prior to the product's arrival at the warehouse. Containers may have been improperly closed, or refrigeration functioned defectively. If so, Fly Away cannot be held responsible for the resulting pest damage, and should not be replaced. Workers at the warehouse itself may have mishandled the product, again relieving Fly Away of responsibility for the loss of product. The county in which Wintervale is located may have initiated an aerial spraying program that made it easier, perhaps even unnecessary, for Buzzoff to control pests and incur less damage. Conversely, the county that Palm city calls home may have suspended an aerial spraying program making it more difficult to control pests in that location.

The food distribution company owns several warehouses in a variety of locations, and pest control is important for profitability. The answers to the questions will help the owner make a considered decision about the most effective means of eliminating loss in Palm City. It may turn out that they should retain Fly Away, rehire Buzzoff or use another company entirely.

61

Argument Task 62

The following appeared in a letter from the owner of the Sunnyside Towers apartment complex to its manager.

"One month ago, all the showerheads in the first three buildings of the Sunnyside Towers complex were modified to restrict maximum water flow to one-third of what it used to be. Although actual readings of water usage before and after the adjustment are not yet available, the change will obviously result in considerable savings for Sunnyside Corporation, since the corporation must pay for water each month. Except for a few complaints about low water pressure, no problems with showers have been reported since the adjustment. Clearly, modifying showerheads to restrict water flow throughout all twelve buildings in the Sunnyside Towers complex will increase our profits further."

Write a response in which you discuss what specific evidence is needed to evaluate the argument and explain how the evidence would weaken or strengthen the argument.

 Strategies

A good place to start your analysis is by creating a statement that reveals the main idea of the argument. Although the writer is creating an argument, he may ultimately be stating a position, making a recommendation, or making a prediction. It may be helpful for you to determine which of these formats is most evident in the argument.

The owner of Sunnyside Corporation is touting the money-saving benefits of installing low-flow shower heads in all of the units at Sunnyside Towers as a means of increasing profits.

62

Assumptions:

◆ Water used for showers is a significant contributor to total water usage.

◆ Residents will spend the same amount of time showering as they did before installation of the new shower heads.

◆ Reducing water usage is the best way to increase profits.

◆ Residents take showers rather than baths.

◆ Residency rates and types will remain constant.

Evidence needed:

- The portion of total water usage attributed to showering.

- Water consumption before and after installation of the new shower heads.

- How much time residents spend showering after installation of the new shower heads as opposed to time spent before doing so?

- Occupancy rate in the three buildings with new shower heads.

- Other steps the owner may have taken to save money.

- How the owner determined that shower head replacement is a good way to save money?

- If the owner pays any other utilities like heat or cable, etc.

- How much water is used for other tasks, like laundry, dishwashers, or a pool?

- Whether or not other costs of operation have increased.

- The month during which the new shower heads were in use.

After completing these steps, you should have enough material to write your analysis. Remember that you are not creating a position of your own; you are evaluating the strengths and weaknesses of the existing argument. You do not have to include all of the points that you have created in your prewriting. In fact, during the process of drafting your analysis, other ideas may come to mind, and if they strengthen your analysis, you should include them.

 ## Sample Essay

Making a profit is the key to remaining in business. The owner of Sunnyside Towers has taken what he declares to be an important step to insuring the solvency of his business. Gathering more evidence about the cost of operations at Sunnyside Towers may lead the owner to decide he could have taken more or other steps to reduce expenses and increase profitability.

Of course, the most helpful piece of evidence, which the owner says is not yet available, is the water usage before and after installing the new shower heads. In the meantime, other evidence may shed light on the savings likely to be incurred by completing the conversion. The owner might begin by determining how much of the total water usage in the buildings is attributed to showers. Other appliances that use water include toilets, dishwashers, and washing machines. Knowing how much water the tenants use to complete these activities may lead the owner to seek savings in other areas. Some tenants may prefer baths to showers, so low-flow shower heads will have little impact in those apartments. In addition to household appliances, the owner may have installed a lawn sprinkler; the complex may have a pool. Those amenities might account for a great deal of total water usage in the complex. If the weather has been warmer and/or drier than normal, the sprinklers and pool may be used more than in an average year.

Another piece of evidence that would be helpful is a maintenance log. Each unit in the complex has a kitchen and at least one bathroom. If only half of them have leaky faucets, gallons of water are wasted every day. The owner may discover that repairing the faucets is more cost-effective both in materials and water saved. The maintenance log may also reveal that several steps, such as repairing leaky faucets, have already been taken and replacing the shower heads is the next logical step.

Knowing the occupancy rates in the buildings would help to evaluate the argument. Low occupancy in the three buildings that have had shower heads replaced might account for the low number of complaints about water pressure. It would be helpful to know if those complainants are taking longer showers to compensate for the reduction in pressure. Full occupancy might lead to more complaints. In fact, knowing the occupancy rates of all twelve buildings would help to make decisions about changes that increase profitability. If several apartments in each building are empty, replacing the shower heads is not likely to have much impact on profits. If most units are full, however, the savings realized from each shower head will be multiplied.

Evidence relating to all operating expenses will help determine what changes, if any, should be made at the apartment complex to increase profits. If the owner pays for heat as well as water, he has likely seen an increase in the cost of doing so. Oil prices have risen, and the owner may find greater savings by turning down the thermostats a couple of degrees or adding insulation to the walls. The cost to mow the lawns or plow the driveways may have risen. Without investigating all costs associated with the apartment buildings, the owner may discover that the money he saves on water usage is offset by greater expenditures in other areas.

Knowing which month the shower heads were in use would help to evaluate the argument. If it was a winter month, overall water usage may be less because sprinklers are idle. During the summer, several residents may be away on vacation, so water used for showers would be reduced. Evidence about rainfall totals and frequency may help him decide to change or reduce the amount of time that the sprinklers are in operation.

Attributing savings to shower heads may be incorrect. In fact, any savings or extra expenditures at any time of the year may be difficult to credit to the installation of the shower heads unless some of the water meters for the complex are dedicated to measuring water used for showering. The owner of Sunnyside Towers needs more evidence about water usage before declaring that new shower heads will create a significant savings.

62

Argument Task 63

The following appeared in a memo from the marketing director of Top Dog Pet Stores.

"Five years ago Fish Emporium started advertising in the magazine Exotic Pets Monthly. Their stores saw sales increase by 15 percent after their ads began appearing in the magazine. The three Fish Emporium stores in Gulf City saw an even greater increase than that. Because Top Dog Pet Stores is based in Gulf City, it seems clear that we should start placing our own ads in Exotic Pets Monthly. If we do so, we will be sure to reverse the recent trend of declining sales and start making a profit again."

Write a response in which you examine the stated and/or unstated assumptions of the argument. Be sure to explain how the argument depends on these assumptions and what the implications are for the argument if the assumptions prove unwarranted.

Strategies

A good place to start your analysis is by creating a statement that reveals the main idea of the argument. Although the writer is creating an argument, he may ultimately be stating a position, making a recommendation, or making a prediction. It may be helpful for you to determine which of these formats is most evident in the argument.

Based on an increase in sales for Fish Emporium after it advertised in Exotic Pets Monthly, the marketing director of Top Dog Pet Stores recommends that they advertise in the same publication in order to make the business profitable again.

Assumptions:

- ◆ Advertising in Exotic Pets Monthly will increase sales for Top Dog Pet Stores.

- ◆ Fish Emporium continues to experience higher sales.

- ◆ Fish Emporium sales increased as a direct result of placing ads in Exotic Pets Monthly.

- ◆ The increase in Fish Emporium sales in Gulf City stores was significantly higher than the 15% increase in their other stores.

- ◆ Failure to advertise in Exotic Pets Monthly is the reason for declining sales and lack of profit for Top Dog Pet Stores.

- ◆ All Top Dog Pet Stores have declining sales and profits.

Alternative explanations:

◆ After the first rise in sales, Fish Emporium's sales have remained flat.

◆ Fish Emporium made other changes at the same time that they began advertising in Exotic Pets Monthly.

◆ The additional increase in profits in Fish Emporium's Gulf City stores was too small to be significant.

◆ Top Dog Pet Stores may have made decisions or taken action that has resulted in a decline in sales.

◆ Some Top Dog Pet Stores are profitable.

After completing these steps, you should have enough material to write your analysis. Remember that you are not creating a position of your own; you are evaluating the strengths and weaknesses of the existing argument. You do not have to include all of the points that you have created in your prewriting. In fact, during the process of drafting your analysis, other ideas may come to mind, and if they strengthen your analysis, you should include them.

Sample Essay

The owner of Top Dog Pet Stores has created some assumptions about Fish Emporium's increase in sales that he believes apply to his own business. He should examine his assumptions to ensure that no other explanations for the increased sales exist before taking actions that may be costly and ineffective.

The The owner of Top Dog Pet stores assumes that Fish Emporium increased its sales by placing ads in Exotic Pets Monthly. In fact, Fish Emporium may have made some other changes at the same time that are the real reason for greater sales. The owner may have added new products that are in high demand. They may have rearranged their displays to make higher priced goods more visible. Perhaps they cleaned up the store or hired more knowledgeable employees who made it easier for customers to find everything they needed. In contrast, Top Dog Pet Stores may have failed to take similar actions to improve sales. The stores may be dirty, stocked with old or outdated merchandise, and manned by associates who have little knowledge about the products in the stores. In that case, no amount of advertising in any publication is likely to have any lasting positive effect on Top Dog's sales or profits.

The first rule of real estate is "location, location, location". The same is very often true in business. Customers must be able to find the store and park nearby. Fish Emporium's stores may be in ideal locations in Gulf City. They may be in popular malls or busy downtown shopping areas with plenty of free parking. Top Dog Pet Stores might be off the beaten path, making it difficult for customers to find them. The owner of Top Dog Pet Stores assumes that Gulf City is an ideal location for improving his business, and he bases his belief on the apparent success of Fish Emporium. Fish Emporium may have saturated the pet store market in Gulf City making Top Dog's success unlikely at best.

63

A fifteen percent increase in sales sounds significant. Whether or not it is depends on what sales were when Fish Emporium began its advertising campaign in Exotic Pets Monthly. The owner of Top Dog Pet Stores may assume that the increase is on top of already satisfactory sales. If sales had fallen to an all-time low before the advertising campaign, the increase may have simply returned sales to previous levels. However, if sales were good prior to the ads, then the increase is something to celebrate. The even greater increase in sales at the Gulf City stores might be minor, in which case, Top Dog should not base its decision to run a similar campaign on that increase. Fish Emporium could have run a special promotion when it advertised in the magazine, attracting new customers and leading to a temporary uptick in sales. They may not have sustained the increase over the five-year time span even though the argument may lead to that assumption.

The reader may assume that all Top Dog Pet Stores are experiencing a decline in sales and profits. Companies with stores in different locations are servants to the vagaries of the marketplace. Some stores may be located in towns that are experiencing an economic downturn, and people cannot afford to spend money on pets and pet supplies. In contrast, other stores may be located in towns or cities where the economy is booming, and residents have the discretionary income to spend on treats for their pets. The owners may be better off by advertising in local newspapers or on local radio and television stations where sales have fallen off. Tailoring its advertising for each location may be a better strategy than relying on one outlet for its promotions.

It is common to assume that the steps to success for one business apply to all businesses or, at least, all similar businesses. This assumption can lead to costly mistakes. All conditions should be examined before spending money on any advertising.

63

Argument Task 64

A recent sales study indicates that consumption of seafood dishes in Bay City restaurants has increased by 30 percent during the past five years. Yet there are no currently operating city restaurants whose specialty is seafood. Moreover, the majority of families in Bay City are two-income families, and a nationwide study has shown that such families eat significantly fewer home-cooked meals than they did a decade ago but at the same time express more concern about healthful eating. Therefore, the new Captain Seafood restaurant that specializes in seafood should be quite popular and profitable.

Write a response in which you discuss what questions would need to be addressed in order to decide whether the conclusion and the argument on which it is based are reasonable. Be sure to explain how the answers to the questions would help to evaluate the conclusion.

NOTE: The above topic has wording similar to Argument Task 59 of this book. However, if you read carefully you will notice that the task instructions are different. Hence, it is very important to read the topic as well as its instructions completely before you start to write your response.

 Strategies

A good place to start your analysis is by creating a statement that reveals the main idea of the argument. Although the writer is creating an argument, he may ultimately be stating a position, making a recommendation, or making a prediction. It may be helpful for you to determine which of these formats is most evident in the argument.

The author predicts that a new Captain Seafood restaurant in Bay City should be very profitable based on an apparent increase in the consumption of seafood dishes at local restaurants.

Assumptions:

64

- ◆ Seafood dishes are healthier than other types of entrées.

- ◆ A seafood restaurant will be successful in Bay City.

- ◆ All restaurants in Bay City have seen a 30 percent increase in the sales of seafood dishes.

- ◆ A 30 percent increase in the consumption of seafood dishes is significant.

- ◆ Restaurants in Bay City are selling fewer meat and poultry entrées.

Questions:

- ◆ Have seafood restaurants opened and closed in Bay City?

- ◆ Do seafood dishes generate as much profit as meat and poultry dishes?

- ◆ Is a 30 percent increase in the consumption of seafood dishes significant?

- ◆ What percentage of total sales is represented by seafood dishes?

- ◆ Are seafood dishes inherently healthier than other meat dishes?

After completing these steps, you should have enough material to write your analysis. Remember that you are not creating a position of your own; you are evaluating the strengths and weaknesses of the existing argument. You do not have to include all of the points that you have created in your prewriting. In fact, during the process of drafting your analysis, other ideas may come to mind, and if they strengthen your analysis, you should include them.

 ## Sample Essay

Anyone relying on the conclusion in this argument should first seek answers to several questions before conceding that the new Captain Seafood restaurant will be successful in Bay City. Any restaurateur needs more details about the facts offered in this scant list of reasons that support the promise of profitability in serving seafood to the residents of the town.

The survey reveals that consumption of seafood dishes in Bay City restaurants has increased by thirty percent during the past five years. The percentage is significant, but how does that translate into dollars? For example, suppose that sales of seafood dishes five years ago totaled $500. A thirty percent increase would mean that the most recent sales total $650. On the other hand, sales of $50,000 five years ago would be $65,000 today. Determining the success of the new Captain Seafood eatery based on an increase in sales would depend on which answer is correct. The significance of the increase would also depend on how high or low the percentage of sales was in previous years. What was the percentage of sales represented by seafood dishes? If it were five percent, a thirty percent increase would mean that current sales are six and a half percent, hardly enough to declare that Captain Seafood will be profitable. If previous sales accounted for twenty percent of total sales, today they are twenty-six percent of the total. Now, one in four orders is for seafood dishes, perhaps a significant number to make the author's conclusion reasonable.

Does an increase in the sales of seafood dishes translate into higher profits? If, for example, the restaurant serves lobster, it must have a tank in which to keep those crustaceans alive. Some are likely to die anyway, and they must be discarded, and those sales are lost. Seafood tends to be more delicate in nature than beef, pork, or

64

chicken and may require more labor-intensive handling and preparation which increases overhead. Pricing sea food dishes to make them as attractive as other entrées may have a negative effect on the bottom line.

Why are there no seafood restaurants currently operating in Bay City? The use of the word currently, itself, may give pause to anyone considering this enterprise in the city. If such restaurants existed in the past, one should seek to know why they closed. If they closed as a result of poor management, developing a strong business plan should, indeed, enable a restaurateur to presume success in a new venture. If, however, those restaurants closed because the citizens were not interested in seafood or could not afford the dishes, the start-up might not be a good idea. Relying on past restaurant's success rates may not be sufficient for making a decision. Have the demographics of Bay City changed significantly? The age and socioeconomic status of Bay City residents may have risen or declined. If the average age is lower and the median income higher, families may have more expendable income to spend on dining out and ordering what may be pricier seafood entrées. On the other hand, an elderly population with a lower median income creates more risk for the new Captain Seafood restaurant.

Are seafood dishes more suitable for a health-conscious diet than other types of dishes? Before using this rationale to predict success for a seafood restaurant in Bay City, one must also ask what method has been used to prepare the most popular dishes in the local restaurants. If battered, deep-fried fish and clams are the most frequently ordered main courses, the impetus to order them is unlikely to be reduced fat and calories. Conversely, if the most popular dishes are steamed or poached fish fillets, the question may be answered in the affirmative.

The answers to these questions should help to evaluate the author's prediction of success for Captain Seafood in Bay City. Relying solely on the insufficient and, perhaps, anecdotal information in the argument might lead the reader to an erroneous conclusion about the likelihood of the new restaurant's ability to thrive.

64

Argument Task 65

The following appeared in an editorial in a local newspaper.

"Commuters complain that increased rush-hour traffic on Blue Highway between the suburbs and the city center has doubled their commuting time. The favored proposal of the motorists' lobby is to widen the highway, adding an additional lane of traffic. Opponents note that last year's addition of a lane to the nearby Green Highway was followed by a worsening of traffic jams on it. Their suggested alternative proposal is adding a bicycle lane to Blue Highway. Many area residents are keen bicyclists. A bicycle lane would encourage them to use bicycles to commute, it is argued, thereby reducing rush-hour traffic."

Write a response in which you discuss what questions would need to be answered in order to decide whether the recommendation and the argument on which it is based are reasonable. Be sure to explain how the answers to these questions would help to evaluate the recommendation.

NOTE: The above topic has wording similar to Argument Task 56 of this book. However, if you read carefully you will notice that the task instructions are different. Hence, it is very important to read the topic as well as its instructions completely before you start to write your response.

 Strategies

Argument:

The city should add a bike lane to Blue Highway to reduce congestion on the highway during rush hours.

In developing your response, you are asked to discuss what questions need to be answered before the city takes this step and how the answers to those questions will affect the decision.

65

Facts and Assumptions:

◆ Commuters are complaining that traffic during rush hour on Blue Highway has doubled their commuting time between the suburbs and the city center. The assumption is that the highway doesn't have sufficient room for all of the commuters.

◆ The motorists' lobby wants to widen the highway by adding another lane. They assume that an additional lane will lessen commuting time by providing more space for the cars on the highway.

◆ Worsening traffic jams followed the addition of a lane to Green Highway last year. The assumption is that an additional lane is not the answer to commuter problems.

◆ Many area residents are keen bicyclists. The writer assumes that many of them would like to ride their bikes to work.

Questions:

◆ How much of an increase in traffic is there? Why has commuting time doubled?

◆ Is Green Highway still experiencing traffic jams? Was it a temporary situation?

◆ Who are the opponents to the proposed extra lane? Are they homeowners who may be displaced by the expansion or whose homes will be too close to the road when it is expanded? Are they developers

◆ who have other ideas for using the land over which the new lane will travel?

◆ Who are the keen bicyclists? Are they children or adults?

◆ How practical is a bike lane for commuters? Are bikers willing to travel in the dark during the winter months? Does the area experience cold, snowy winters? Will commuters travel by bike in the rain? Will traveling by bike take more time each way?

Your notes do not have to be exhaustive. As you begin to write your essay, your brain will generate new ideas. Make certain that you keep the directions in mind as you develop your ideas.

Sample Essay

An editorial is usually written by an editor to express the position of the newspaper on a particular topic. The excerpt provided here simply presents both sides of an issue. On one side are motorists who are frustrated by the increased traffic and commuter travel time on Blue Highway and think that an additional lane would relieve the problem. On the opposing side are those who point to problems on Green Highway since the addition of a lane there and think that the addition of a bike lane is the answer. A number of questions need answers before planners take either action.

The reader knows that motorists are in favor of an additional highway lane. Who are the opponents? Several groups come to mind. Homeowners who live near the highway may fear being displaced or encroached upon by a highway expansion. They may be worried about the increased noise. It could lower property values, and the homeowners could face challenges when trying to sell their houses. Commercial developers may have their sights set on the land that would be needed for a highway expansion. The possibility of new jobs and a broader tax base may trump commuter comfort.

65

Is a bike lane a viable option? It may be if this highway is in a part of the country where the daylight hours are always long, and the sun always shines. If the highway is in a location where the days are shorter in the winter months, workers may jump in their cars to travel safely in the dark. When it rains or snows or gets cold, commuters are likely to opt for their cars in favor of bikes. If one of the aims is to reduce commuting time, a bike route may not be the answer. Bikes do not travel at the same speeds as cars.

Is Green Highway still experiencing traffic jams? Was the additional lane the cause of traffic jams, or was traffic diverted to the newly expanded Green Highway as a result of road construction elsewhere? It may have been a temporary situation. Because it happened on Green Highway is no guarantee that traffic will snarl on Blue Highway. All of these questions deserve consideration before any final decisions are made regarding any type of expansion of Blue Highway.

65

Argument Task 66

....

The following appeared in a memorandum written by the vice president of Health Naturally, a small but expanding chain of stores selling health food and other health-related products.

"Our previous experience has been that our stores are most profitable in areas where residents are highly concerned with leading healthy lives. We should therefore build one of our new stores in Plainsville, which clearly has many such residents. Plainsville merchants report that sales of running shoes and exercise equipment are at all-time highs. The local health club, which nearly closed five years ago due to lack of business, has more members than ever and the weight-training and aerobics classes are always full. We can even anticipate a new generation of customers: Plainsville's school children are required to participate in a program called Fitness for Life, which emphasizes the benefits of regular exercise at an early age."

Write a response in which you discuss what specific evidence is needed to evaluate the argument and explain how the evidence would weaken or strengthen the argument.

....

 Strategies

A good place to start your analysis is by creating a statement that reveals the main idea of the argument. Although the writer is creating an argument, he may ultimately be stating a position, making a recommendation, or making a prediction. It may be helpful for you to determine which of these formats is most evident in the argument.

Based on reports from local merchants and health club owner, the vice president of Health Naturally proposes building one of their new stores in Plainsville.

Assumptions:

- Plainsville citizens will continue to attend the health club in the same numbers in the future.

- The health club has always offered weight-training and aerobics classes.

- The current population of school children will remain in Plainsville

- The health club has substantially greater membership than it did five years ago.

- There are no stores in Plainsville that sell health foods and other health-related items.

66

◆ Plainsville has a population large enough to support a Health Naturally store.

◆ People who exercise buy health foods.

Alternative explanations:

◆ The increase in numbers occurred at the beginning of the year- New Year's resolutions

◆ The health club may have upgraded its equipment and added new classes.

◆ Competing health clubs may have closed.

◆ The health club is open during more convenient hours.

◆ Residents are able to buy health foods at the local grocery store.

◆ The all-time high in sales of running shoes and other exercise equipment is a very small increase over the second-best year.

After completing these steps, you should have enough material to write your analysis. Remember that you are not creating a position of your own; you are evaluating the strengths and weaknesses of the existing argument. You do not have to include all of the points that you have created in your prewriting. In fact, during the process of drafting your analysis, other ideas may come to mind, and, if they strengthen your analysis, you should include them.

 ## Sample Essay

Health Naturally is expanding and like any well-run company, has researched existing conditions before deciding which towns to select for its new stores. Using past experience, Health Naturally has determined that Plainsville is a suitable location. The company vice president has loaded his memo with highly charged words in an effort to persuade others to adopt his recommendation. "All-time high", "more than ever", and "always full" make the future in Plainsville sound very promising. These descriptors mean little or nothing when taken out of context.

When Plainsville merchants claim that sales of running shoes are at an all-time high, they don't reveal by how much in dollars or how many units sold. Sales in total dollars would just have to be one dollar higher than the previous best year to be considered an all-time high. The high dollar amount might be a result of an increase in the prices of running shoes. The merchants may actually have sold fewer pairs of shoes. The number of units sold might be a better measure of greater-than-ever success, but, again, selling one more pair of shoes than in the previous best year should not determine the health consciousness of Plainsville residents. If the conditions stated here are true, they do not support the argument put forth by Health Naturally's vice president.

66

The health club in Plainsville also appears to be thriving, claiming more members than ever before. A total membership of one more than the previous best year supports this claim, but one additional member is not sufficient to justify the expense of building a Health Naturally store in this location. In fact, this company should seek to know why the health club had so little business five years ago. There may have been several other clubs in the area that actually have closed in the intervening years, leaving this club as the only one still standing. When members of the closed clubs sought another place to exercise, they had no other choice but the club in Plainsville.

This same situation explains why the aerobics and weight-training classes are always full. On the other hand, the health club may have reduced the number of classes, causing those who want to attend to crowd in to those available. Membership in the health club may fluctuate throughout the year. Some of the most popular New Year's resolutions are to lose weight and to adopt a healthier lifestyle. If Health Naturally interviewed the merchants and the health club owner shortly after the beginning of the New Year, their numbers may be inflated. If those interviews took place in May or September, for example, the numbers reported could be a reason for optimism.

A presumption in this argument is that people who exercise will buy health foods, and they will buy them at a Health Naturally store. If the residents of Plainsville buy natural foods, they must already have a source for it, maybe even the local grocery store. Getting people to change their shopping habits is expensive and time consuming and, ultimately, may not be possible. Knowing the socioeconomic status of Plainsville residents would help Health Naturally make a decision about locating there. Natural foods are generally more expensive than foods carried in typical grocery stores. If the income levels in Plainsville are too low, the new health store will probably fail.

Finally, the vice president of the company assumes that the children of Plainsville are sure to become future customers of the store. Because the children must participate in a Fitness for Life program, they will continue to practice what they learn. A piece of information that would help determine the veracity of this assumption is the employment picture in Plainsville. Unless today's children can be assured of employment as adults, they will have to leave to seek their fortunes elsewhere.

The vice president of Health Naturally needs more detailed evidence to support his proposal to establish one of the company's new stores in Plainsville. It may turn out that this town is indeed health conscious and would welcome a store offering products that enhance their lifestyle choice. In contrast, further evidence may reveal the shallow nature of the apparent healthy behavior in Plainsville, and the decision to locate a new store in another location would be the wisest one.

Argument Task 67

There is now evidence that the relaxed pace of life in small towns promotes better health and greater longevity than does the hectic pace of life in big cities. Businesses in the small town of Leeville report fewer days of sick leave taken by individual workers than do businesses in the nearby large city of Masonton. Furthermore, Leeville has only one physician for its one thousand residents, but in Masonton the proportion of physicians to residents is five times as high. Finally, the average age of Leeville residents is significantly higher than that of Masonton residents. These findings suggest that people seeking longer and healthier lives should consider moving to small communities.

Write a response in which you examine the stated and/or unstated assumptions of the argument. Be sure to explain how the argument depends on these assumptions and what the implications are for the argument if the assumptions prove unwarranted.

 Strategies

A good place to start your analysis is by creating a statement that reveals the main idea of the argument. Although the writer is creating an argument, he may ultimately be stating a position, making a recommendation, or making a prediction. It may be helpful for you to determine which of these formats is most evident in the argument.

By comparing the small town of Leeville to the neighboring large city of Masonton, the author of this argument concludes that living in a small town promotes better health and longevity.

Assumptions:

◆ Residents of smaller towns are healthier than residents of large cities.

◆ Residents of small towns have less serious illnesses than those in large cities.

◆ A relaxed pace of life is healthier than a hectic pace.

◆ Small towns have a more relaxed pace of life than do large cities.

◆ Workers call in sick only when they are genuinely ill.

◆ One doctor is sufficient to treat the one thousand residents of Leeville.

67

Alternative explanations:

◆ Leeville is a retirement community.

◆ Masonton is home to more than one college.

◆ Masonton has a large medical center.

◆ People from Leeville seek medical treatment in Masonton.

◆ Doctors may live in Masonton and work in other towns.

After completing these steps, you should have enough material to write your analysis. Remember that you are not creating a position of your own; you are evaluating the strengths and weaknesses of the existing argument. You do not have to include all of the points that you have created in your prewriting. In fact, during the process of drafting your analysis, other ideas may come to mind, and if they strengthen your analysis, you should include them.

Sample Essay

The author of this argument uses the small town of Leeville and the large city of Masonton as examples of evidence that shows life in a small town is better for one's health than is life in a large city. The assumptions in the argument are based on some vague generalities without real numbers or statistics to clarify them. A number of alternatives can shoot holes in the substance of this position.

The argument assumes that people live longer in Leeville because it is a small town. It may simply be that older people have chosen to live in a small town rather than in the large city of Masonton. Anyone traveling up and down either coast of Florida, especially during the winter months, will pass through dozens of small towns where the average age is considerably higher than the average age in the cities of that state. In fact, those towns are largely populated by the elderly, at least for several months of the year. They are retirement communities. Senior citizens from colder states flock there each autumn and stay until late spring.

Without facts to the contrary, one could assume that Leeville, also, is a retirement community. There may be covenants that prohibit people under a certain age, say fifty-five, from living there. Residents of Leeville may not have selected this community because the pace of life is slower; they have, in fact, created that pace simply by living there. In contrast, large cities are bound to have a broader demographic and a lower average age as a result. The population will be a mix of young singles, families with young children, along with some senior citizens.

The higher proportion of doctors to residents in Masonton could arise from the presence of one or more medical centers in the city. In fact, it would be hard to name or imagine a large city without several health care facilities. Therefore, assuming that the larger number of doctors in Masonton derives from the greater number of

67

sick people there may be erroneous. The elderly almost always require visits to a number of specialists, especially cardiologists, oncologists, and rheumatologists. A town of one thousand residents is not likely to have physicians practicing in those specialties. The one doctor in Leeville can probably provide sufficient care for minor ailments, but serious conditions must be treated in Masonton. Older citizens may prefer to live in smaller towns with a slower pace of life but desire comprehensive medical care to be in close proximity.

The assumption that Leeville's citizens are much older than the citizens of Masonton needs some further examination. The significant difference in median age between Leeville and Masonton may be a result of Masonton's having an unusually large percentage of young people. It would not be unreasonable to expect that Masonton has one or more colleges; most large cities do. When classes are in session, the average age of Masonton residents would drop considerably. One of these colleges may even have a medical school which contributes to the high number of doctors in the city.

Assuming that all small towns exhibit the same characteristics of Leeville is risky. Small towns in rural or remote areas may not provide a healthy lifestyle for their residents. People of all ages in these towns are likely to find quality health care difficult to access. Certainly, the residents will have to travel some distance to see specialists of any sort. In the case of an emergency, a citizen may have to wait a significant amount of time for help to arrive and spend additional time being transported to a medical facility. Heart attacks and strokes, common among the elderly, are survivable if treated quickly, something not likely to occur in small, rural towns.

The longevity of Leeville residents may be a direct result of its proximity to the large city of Masonton. A healthy life requires balance. Leeville residents can relax in the comfort of their homes in the quiet, small town but be stimulated by the activities available in Masonton. Remaining active and interested and living close to adequate healthcare is as good a recipe for longevity as residing in a small town where little ever happens.

Argument Task 68

The following appeared in a memo from the business manager of a chain of cheese stores located throughout the United States.

"For many years all the stores in our chain have stocked a wide variety of both domestic and imported cheeses. Last year, however, all of the five best-selling cheeses at our newest store were domestic cheddar cheeses from Wisconsin. Furthermore, a recent survey by Cheeses of the World magazine indicates an increasing preference for domestic cheeses among its subscribers. Since our company can reduce expenses by limiting inventory, the best way to improve profits in all of our stores is to discontinue stocking many of our varieties of imported cheese and concentrate primarily on domestic cheeses."

Write a response in which you examine the stated and/or unstated assumptions of the argument. Be sure to explain how the argument depends on these assumptions and what the implications are for the argument if the assumptions prove unwarranted.

Strategies

A good place to start your analysis is by creating a statement that reveals the main idea of the argument. Although the writer is creating an argument, he may ultimately be stating a position, making a recommendation, or making a prediction. It may be helpful for you to determine which of these formats is most evident in the argument.

The manager of the cheese store uses the results from a survey conducted by the magazine, Cheeses of the World, to recommend that his business discontinue stocking imported cheeses and focus on domestic cheeses in an effort to increase profits.

Assumptions:

◆ Sales in the newest store predict what will be most popular in the chain's other stores.

◆ The survey in Cheeses of the World applies to stores in every country.

◆ The profit margin on imported and domestic cheeses is the same.

68

Alternative explanations:

◆ The newest store is located in Wisconsin.

◆ Best-selling cheeses are not necessarily the most profitable.

After completing these steps, you should have enough material to write your analysis. Remember that you are not creating a position of your own; you are evaluating the strengths and weaknesses of the existing argument. You do not have to include all of the points that you have created in your prewriting. In fact, during the process of drafting your analysis, other ideas may come to mind, and if they strengthen your analysis, you should include them.

 Sample Essay

It is the job of the business manager to take care of the bottom line. If he were able to increase profits, the owners of the business would be happy. In the case of this chain of cheese stores, the business manager may be putting the cart before the horse by suggesting that the stores focus on domestic cheeses only. While this argument seems logical on the surface, the stated and unstated assumptions in it deserve closer scrutiny before the company owners decide to jump on this wagon.

The readers of the memo may assume that the popularity of Wisconsin cheeses in the newest store predicts similar success with domestic cheeses in their other stores. This may or may not be significant. If the newest store is located in Wisconsin, all bets are off. Customers of the store would be inclined to support their local cheese makers. Wisconsin is, after all, the Dairy State, and fans of the Green Bay Packers are known as Cheeseheads and wear foam hats that look like wedges of cheese when attending a Packers' game. If the company has a store in Vermont, a state replete with dairy farms, it likely sells more Vermont cheeses than imported cheeses. Stores located in the country's largest cities like New York, Chicago, or Los Angeles are likely to sell more imported cheeses to satisfy the more demanding palates of their citizens or to supplement the ethnic diets of their diverse populations. Eliminating imported cheeses from the inventories in these stores could have a deleterious effect on profits.

The assumption that sales of domestic cheese will lead to increased profits may have holes in it. Profit can be expressed as a percentage or a dollar amount. It is derived from the amount of markup on the items sold in a store and is affected by general expenses of operation. Let's assume that the cheese stores have a 100% markup on their cheeses. In other words, they double the wholesale price to arrive at the retail price for each cheese. If a pound of Wisconsin cheese sells at a wholesale ratefor $5.00, its retail rate will be $10.00, and the store realizes a gross profit of $5.00. Now, if a pound of imported cheese costs $10.00, and the same 100% markup is applied, it will retail for $20.00 per pound and gross $10.00. It's easy to see that, in this case, the store must sell twice as much domestic cheese to make the same profit as on the imported cheese. The popularity of domestic cheeses guarantees neither higher total sales nor greater profits.

Using survey results to make important decisions requires careful consideration. A survey conducted by Cheeses of the World among its subscribers indicates a growing preference for domestic cheeses. It would be helpful to know how many subscribers there are and what percentage of them completed the survey. If this is an international publication, some respondents may have been referring to cheeses that Americans could only buy as imports. The business manager of the American cheese company in the argument needs this information before assuming that the survey results support his recommendation.

Most chain stores tailor their inventory to the location of each store. Macy's will not promote the same merchandise in Bangor, Maine that it does in Dallas, Texas. Bangor is a small city surrounded by even smaller towns and large rural areas. The population is largely working class. Dallas is home to millions, and the median income is far greater than that of Bangor residents. Macy's in Dallas is likely to have many more designer items than the Bangor store. This chain of cheese stores should probably adopt this same approach at each of its locations rather than assuming that the same items will sell well in each one. America is a country of great variety. Different ethnic, racial, and religious preferences exist side-by-side in communities across this great country. This cheese business should consider these variables before making decisions about the types of cheeses it stocks in each of its stores.

Argument Task 69

The following appeared in a magazine article about planning for retirement.

"Clearview should be a top choice for anyone seeking a place to retire, because it has spectacular natural beauty and a consistent climate. Another advantage is that housing costs in Clearview have fallen significantly during the past year, and taxes remain lower than those in neighboring towns. Moreover, Clearview's mayor promises many new programs to improve schools, streets, and public services. And best of all, retirees in Clearview can also expect excellent health care as they grow older, since the number of physicians in the area is far greater than the national average."

Write a response in which you discuss what specific evidence is needed to evaluate the argument and explain how the evidence would weaken or strengthen the argument.

 Strategies

The first step in performing your analysis consists of identifying the texts' key point, recommendation, prediction or hypothesis. All the other arguments and assumptions are designed to support this central claim. In this case, the author attempts to demonstrate that "Clearview should be a well sought-after retirement place".

The next step would involve creating a statement that summarizes the text by including the central claim and its supporting arguments.

The article writer claims that Clearview should be a well sought-after retirement place due to its many attractive features, chief among which are the areas' natural beauty and climate, quality healthcare, reduced housing costs and low taxes.

When considering the evidence that is necessary to support the arguments outlined in the text, it is important to keep in mind that arguments are based on assumptions – points that are taken to be true, without the need for proof. This is what you need to look for: explicit and implicit assumptions since they require evidence that is not already listed in the text.

Assumptions:

Explicit Assumptions	Implicit Assumptions
Retirees select living places based on nature and climate	• Consistent climate is important for people about to retire • Natural beauty is important for people about to retire
Low housing costs and taxes make Clearview desirable	• Lowering of housing costs makes them affordable • Lowering of housing costs makes Clearview desirable over other places • Housing costs are the main financial expenditure related to cost of living in Clearview • Taxes in Clearview are low • Taxes in Clearview are significantly lower than in neighboring towns
The number of healthcare providers is important for retirees	• Healthcare is overall important for older people when deciding to retire • The number of healthcare providers is significantly higher than the national average • Retirees rate healthcare quality based on the number of available physicians • The available medical practitioners have specializations in the fields that are important for retirees
Infrastructure improvement promises are a selling point	• Number of schools is an important selling point for retirees • Significant improvement of public services • The improvements will be completed in a time frame that makes them attractive to old people considering retiring in Clearview

After having established your assumptions, you can find the evidence that is needed to evaluate the argument by considering what proof is necessary to validate each implicit assumption.

Evidence:

◆ Survey containing a ranking of the reasons that old people consider to be important when choosing a retirement place

◆ Compare the income and mortgage allowance of the average retiree compared with Clearview housing prices

◆ Comparison between Clearview's housing costs and the area and national averages

◆ Percentage of monthly living costs assigned to housing

◆ Clearview's total living costs compared to the area and national averages

◆ Taxes in Clearview compared to national averages

◆ Taxes in Clearview compared to those of the neighboring towns

◆ The difference between the number of physicians in Clearview and the national average expressed in a percentage

◆ Comparison of the top medical specializations sought after by old people and the number of physicians having those specializations in Clearview

◆ Current state of public services reported to the expected improvements

◆ Expected terms of completion for the public service improvements

◆ Senior recreation places and volunteer opportunities

◆ Senior population percentage

Sample Essay

The article writer claims that Clearview should be an attractive location for retirement due to its many attractive amenities, including the areas' natural beauty and climate, quality healthcare, reduced housing costs, and low taxes. To evaluate the validity of this claim, additional information is needed about the town's affordability, number of existing senior activities, quality of life, public transportation, and health care facilities and personnel. One of the author's main arguments is that Clearview would be a great place to retire due to its affordability, especially in terms of reduced housing costs and low taxes. Affordability is not only determined by the cost of housing but also by the buying power of the future residents. By comparing the income and mortgage allowance of the average retiree with Clearview's housing prices, the article writer can determine whether the intended target audience has sufficient monetary resources to consider Clearview as a viable retirement option.

When proposing that Clearview is an ideal place to retire due to the low housing costs, the author needs to draw comparisons with the national and area specific averages to determine if the housing costs are low enough to encourage people to choose Clearview over other retirement locations. It is possible that housing costs in Clearview were previously high, so that the reduction in cost results in market prices that remain higher than the ones in neighboring towns. In this case, people would be more likely to choose an alternate retirement destination and the author's argument related to the affordability of Clearview would become invalid. The opposite is also possible, with the housing costs of Clearview being lower than national or area averages, in which case, for fiscal reasons alone, Clearview would become a more attractive retirement destination. In addition to housing costs, there are a host of other expenses that add up to the monthly costs of living, and people looking for financially attractive retirement destinations would be likely to also take this information into account.

By comparing Clearview's monthly living cost with that of the area and national averages, the article writer could make a much more compelling case about the financial attractiveness of the town. If not only housing costs but also daily expenses prove to be lower than other neighboring retirement destinations then that is likely to make Clearview into a well sought-after retirement choice, as the article advertises. Should the monthly living costs be higher than those of the neighboring regions, Clearview could still be a good retirement destination based on its other selling points; however, it is not likely that it would become a top candidate.

Another issue to consider when advertising the financial attractiveness of the area is the taxes. The author should provide additional information on how the taxes in Clearview compare to nationwide taxes. While the author mentions that Clearview has better taxes than the neighboring towns, it is not clear just how high the taxes are, which is where the nationwide comparison comes in handy. Using this information, the author can establish if the taxes are low for the area, but overall high when compared to national averages (in the case where Clearview would be situated in an overall expensive region) or if the taxes are genuinely low. Based on the outcome, he might choose whether it is prudent to advertise tax rankings as a key selling point.

When making a case for the desirability of Clearview as a retirement place, one also needs to take into consideration evidence related to the quality of life in the area, like the percentage of senior population in Clearview, the number of recreational places and volunteer opportunities, and the town's temperature and pressure statistics. While the author does mention that the climate is constant, he does not provide sufficient information to assess whether the areas' weather would be ideal for elderly people. A very constant but high temperature can prove to be a deterrent for elderly people, who, in general, seem to prefer milder climates. On the other hand, if the evidence were to reveal that Clearview has a consistently moderate climate, then that fact might prove to be a sufficient incentive to choose Clearview over a slightly cheaper alternative that has less than ideal weather.

Senior population percentages would also come in handy when assessing the quality of life in Clearview. According to Forbes, retirees prefer to settle in places where they can integrate more easily and share activities with other people belonging to the same age group. In this sense, Florida and Arizona are retirement favorites because they already have a large population of senior citizens and provide a support system for newcomers. In this sense, if Clearview has a low number of senior citizens, and subsequently fewer senior targeted activities, retirees might choose to live in a town with a bigger elderly community, regardless of whether it might be more expensive. However, should Clearview have a nicely developed senior citizen community, then people would be more likely to retire there instead of in a place that provides cheaper accommodations but no recreational opportunities. This data would come in handy when advertising the town as a top choice for retirement destinations.

69

Another claim made by the article writer is that healthcare is important for retirees and from this standpoint, Clearview would be an ideal place to retire as it has a great number of physicians. This argument rests on the assumption that the number of healthcare providers is indicative of the quality of the services. To assess the validity of that claim, the article writer would have to take into consideration Clearview's hospital rankings and report them to the number of physicians. In addition, given that there are certain afflictions that are more prevalent among the elderly, the writer should consider the top medical specializations sought after by old people and the number of physicians having those specializations in Clearview. This data would help evaluate whether Clearview's health prospects match the desires and requirements of the elderly.

All in all, the article writer makes a compelling case for Clearview being a top choice for retirement destinations by playing on the town's strengths that are most appealing to the elderly. However, the argument could do with improvements by placing financial data into national context to give perspective to the information, and by including information related to the quality of life.

Argument Task 70

The following appeared as a letter to the editor from a Central Plaza store owner.

"Over the past two years, the number of shoppers in Central Plaza has been steadily decreasing while the popularity of skateboarding has increased dramatically. Many Central Plaza store owners believe that the decrease in their business is due to the number of skateboard users in the plaza. There has also been a dramatic increase in the amount of litter and vandalism throughout the plaza. Thus, we recommend that the city prohibit skateboarding in Central Plaza. If skateboarding is prohibited here, we predict that business in Central Plaza will return to its previously high levels.

Write a response in which you discuss what questions would need to be answered in order to decide whether the recommendation is likely to have the predicted result. Be sure to explain how the answers to these questions would help to evaluate the recommendation.

 ## Strategies

The first step in performing your analysis consists of identifying the texts' key point, recommendation, prediction or hypothesis. All the other arguments and assumptions are designed to support this central claim. In this case, the author attempts to demonstrate that "a skateboarding prohibition will return Central Plaza to its previously high levels".

The next step would involve creating a statement that summarizes the text by including the central claim and its supporting arguments.

The Central Plaza store owner predicts that placing a skateboarding ban in the plaza will restore its economic profitability, given that the increase in the number of skateboarders is the likeliest cause of the increase of vandalism and decrease of business in the area.

When considering what questions are needed to evaluate the arguments outlined in the text, it is important to keep in mind that arguments are based on assumptions – points that are taken to be true, without the need for proof. This is what you need to look for: explicit and implicit assumptions since they lack the evidence required to prove their validity.

Society

70

Assumptions:

Explicit Assumptions	Implicit Assumptions
Skateboarders are responsible for the decrease of shoppers and business	• Shoppers are severely bothered by skateboarders • Skateboarders are the main reason why shopper traffic has decreased • Skateboarders are the main reason why business revenues have decreased • First the skateboarders appeared and then the number of shoppers decreased
Skateboarders are the cause of littering and vandalism in the area	• Vandalism and littering can be linked to the decrease in traffic and business • Only skateboarders could have committed the vandalism and littering acts • The vandalism can be directly linked to the skateboarders
A skateboarding ban will restore foot traffic and business revenues in the area	• Skateboarders will respect the ban • Vandalism and littering will diminish • Customers that left because of the increase in skateboarder numbers will return to the plaza once the ban is instated • Traffic will increase sufficiently to restore business revenues

Sample Essay

The Central Plaza store owner predicts that placing a skateboarding ban in the plaza will restore its economic profitability, given that the increase in the number of skateboarders is the likeliest cause of the increase of vandalism and decrease of business in the area. There are a number of questions that need to be taken into consideration in order to be able to evaluate how effective the store owner's proposal is.

The first thing that comes to mind when looking at the data presented in the letter is related to how much people are actually bothered by the increase in skateboarders. A possible answer to this question would be that shoppers experience only mild annoyance due to the number of skateboarders, and therefore skateboarding would not constitute the reasons for the decrease in shopper traffic. The alternative answer would entail that the people express being severely bothered by the presence of skateboarders in the plaza, to the point where they would not want to shop there anymore. In this case, the skateboarding ban would be effective in preventing more people from abandoning the plaza, and with sufficient time, the traffic in the area would be restored.

When making the recommendation to ban skateboarding in Central Plaza, the store owner assumes that skateboarders are the major cause for the area's decrease in shopper traffic and business revenue. In order to be able to make this claim, the shop owner should first try to figure out if there are any other reasons for the decrease in traffic and business. Should skateboarders prove to be the sole cause for the economic downturn of the plaza, then it is possible that the area would be restored once the ban is instated. The presence of other reasons like the appearance of a new shopping center, the start of the financial crisis or better competitor prices would suggest that the ban would be ineffective in restoring the economic health of the area, and the Central Plaza store owners should invest time and money into finding solutions for these causes, like redefining their pricing strategy or launching promotional campaigns.

The store owner's letter also begs the question of which process came first – the increase in skateboarders or the decrease in business. The increase of skateboarders before the reduction in shopper numbers would suggest that skateboarders could be a possible cause of the declining economic health of the area, but it does not necessarily imply that they are the main cause, as seen above with the other listed potential explanations. However, should the opposite become evident, namely that the number of shoppers coming to the plaza started declining before the skateboarders began frequenting the area, then this evidence would remove the blame from the skateboarders, since the problem existed beforehand. It is possible that skateboarders only started coming into the area because of the low foot traffic – a big open area with few numbers of people is more conducive to skateboarding than a bustling shopping center.

The store owner's letter seems to strongly suggest that there is a link between skateboarders and the vandalism and littering in the area. Before resting the blame squarely on the shoulders of a single group of people, the store owner should ask himself whether there are any other possible vandalism culprits aside from skateboarders. The existence of other groups that are capable of committing the crime in the area means that a skateboarding ban is less likely to put a stop to the vandalism in the area. If there are no other groups in the area that could commit the crime, then the possibility that the skateboarders are responsible for the vandalism increases tenfold. In this case a skateboarding ban will have a great impact on the number of vandalism acts committed during shopping times and depending on the customer's opinion on the deterrent effect of vandalism, it might even increase traffic in the area. This point raises another valid question that needs to be answered before the recommendations of the letter are implemented, namely: is vandalism related to the decrease in business and shopper traffic? If people consider it a major deterrent to shopping in Central Plaza then a skateboarding ban has a chance of invigorating the area's foot traffic, should skateboarders prove to be responsible for the acts. In this case a better use of resources would be to investigate and corroborate with the local police agents in order to discover the culprits, or organize patrols at night, when the crimes are most likely to occur. Should the vandalism prove to be unimportant to the people's decisions of shopping in the area it would not have much of a bearing on whether or not a skateboarding ban would be efficient.

70

The store owners' assumption that skateboarders might be responsible for the vandalism in the area needs to be supported by evidence, in order to validate the claim. The store owners of Central Plaza should first investigate whether there is any evidence directly linking the vandalism to the skateboarders before making their decision. Any kind of physical evidence like camera footage, or witness testimonies would be highly helpful in assessing the claim in the letter. The existence of such evidence would also make it easier to take action by involving the police in the proceedings.

Another question that comes to mind when analyzing the effects of the skateboarding ban on the plaza's economy is whether or not the skateboarders will actually respect the ban, once it is in place. If the answer to that question is no, then even if the skateboarders were to blame for the decrease in shoppers, the implementation of the measure would be useless since it would not be effective in deterring skateboarders from coming to the plaza. Should skateboarders be inclined to respect the ban, then its overall effectiveness would still depend on people's attitudes towards skateboarding.

All the issues discussed above represent just a small amount of the questions that need to be taken into consideration by the Central Plaza store owners so that they can have a better overview of the situation before making a decision. Much more evidence than what is presented in the letter needs to be brought to attention so that the shop owners can make an informed decision.

Argument Task 71

The following appeared in a memo from the vice president of marketing at Dura-Sock, Inc.

"A recent study of our customers suggests that our company is wasting the money it spends on its patented Endure manufacturing process, which ensures that our socks are strong enough to last for two years. We have always advertised our use of the Endure process, but the new study shows that despite our socks' durability, our average customer actually purchases new Dura-Socks every three months. Furthermore, our customers surveyed in our largest market, northeastern United States cities, say that they most value Dura-Socks' stylish appearance and availability in many colors. These findings suggest that we can increase our profits by discontinuing use of the Endure manufacturing process."

Write a response in which you examine the stated and/or unstated assumptions of the argument. Be sure to explain how the argument depends on these assumptions and what the implications are for the argument if the assumptions prove unwarranted.

 Strategies

Regardless of the approach you take, consider the following steps:

◆ Is there an alternative explanation for the events in question that can invalidate, either in whole or in part, the explanation given in the passage?

◆ How can I break the argument into its component parts to understand how they create the whole argument?

◆ Can I identify the line of reasoning used to create the argument?

◆ What does the author of the argument assume to be true for the argument to be true?

◆ Does the line of reasoning validate the conclusion?

◆ Can I imagine an example that refutes any or several of the statements in the argument?

◆ Am I able to evaluate the argument based on the quality of the facts and reasons presented in it?

Based on your responses to all or some of these questions, you must present a well-developed evaluation of the argument. You should take brief notes when you identify the argument's claims, assumptions, and conclusion. Jot down as many alternative explanations as you can along with additional evidence that might

71

support or refute the claims in the argument. Finally, list the changes in the argument that would make the reasoning more solid. It is more important to be specific than it is to have a long list of evidence and examples.

The argument cites a study about the company's sales of their Dura-Socks which seems to indicate that they are wasting money by continuing to use its patented and expensive Endure manufacturing process.

In developing your response, you are instructed to examine the stated and/or unstated assumptions of the argument, explain how the argument depends on these assumptions, and what the implications are for the argument if the assumptions prove unwarranted.

Assumptions:

◆ The assumption that the company is wasting money on the patented Endure manufacturing process underlies the claim that the company can save money by eliminating the process.

◆ The assumption that customers buy the socks for their stylish appearance and availability in many colors over any other feature of the socks. This underlies the argument that the Endure process is a wasted effort. The style and colors may simply enhance the desirability of the socks, not replace the appeal of the durability.

◆ The assumption that the survey results are valid and reliable. This underlies the company position that they are wasting money on the Endure process. The majority of the respondents to the survey may have been women for whom the fashionable aspects of the socks are more important than the durability. Too little demographic information about the respondents in the study makes the conclusion suspect.

◆ The assumption that profits will increase by discontinuing the use of the Endure manufacturing process. This underlies the claim that the study shows they are wasting their money on this process. Profits depend on several variables. It may be that the customers will expect the socks to have a lower price point if the durability is decreased. They may not continue to buy the socks at the current price point, thereby reducing revenues to the company both if they lose sales or they reduce price in response to customer complaints.

◆ The assumption that the survey of the northeastern US cities represents the buying habits of the majority of the company's customers. This underlies the argument that the survey in this region should influence the decision to eliminate the expensive manufacturing process. Other regional markets combined may equal or surpass the size of the market in the northeastern US cities. Eliminating the Endure manufacturing process may have a negative effect on sales in the remaining markets.

◆ The assumption that the advertising focus is ineffective. This supports the recommendation to eliminate the manufacturing process, as it appears that customers are buying the socks for reasons other than their durability.

◆ The assumption that this recent study should determine the future of the business. This underlies the argument that the process should be eliminated. How long has it been since the last study? If these studies are done on a regular, frequent basis, these findings may be a simple aberration. The results of several studies over time in several markets would better predict actions that the company should take.

Your notes do not have to be exhaustive. As you begin to write your essay, your brain will generate new ideas. Make certain that you keep the directions in mind as you develop your ideas. Use as many or as few paragraphs as you consider appropriate for your argument, but create a new paragraph when you move on to a new idea or example of support for your position. The GRE readers are not looking for a specific number of ideas or paragraphs. Instead, they are reading to determine the level of understanding of the topic and the complexity with which you respond.

You are free to organize and develop your response in any way you think will enable you to effectively communicate your evaluation of the argument. You may recall writing strategies that you learned in high school or a writing-intensive course that you took in college, but it is not necessary to employ any of those strategies. It is important that your ideas follow a logical progression and display strong critical thinking.

 ## Sample Essay

A company that has devoted considerable time and resources to patent a manufacturing process that uniquely positions itself in the marketplace is wise to consult its consumer base before making changes in its focus. It may be that Dura-Socks should eliminate the Endure process in order to increase company profits, but the argument cited has several weaknesses that should be addressed before permanently altering the features of the socks.

The company is relying on a survey of its largest market, the northeastern United States cities, to inform their decision to eliminate an expensive manufacturing process. One of the major flaws in this survey is the regional specificity. The other markets serviced by Dura-Socks in total may equal or surpass the size of the northeastern market. Eliminating the durability of the socks may have a negative impact on the purchases made in those other regions, offsetting any potential financial gain. The survey has too little demographic information to make it reliable. The age, gender, and lifestyles of those studied may influence their reasons for purchasing the socks.

Furthermore, this is a recent study. How regularly does the company conduct these studies? Studies are usually conducted to reveal trends. The company should compare the results of this study to those of previous efforts to determine the buying habits of its customers before making a decision about the future of its manufacturing process. The results of this recent study may simply be an aberration influenced by factors not considered in the study.

It is a leap from eliminating the Endure manufacturing process to increased profits. Company profits are dependent on many variables, and cost of manufacturing is only one of them. Consumers may balk at paying the same price for an item with fewer features which could lead to a drop in sales. In response, the company could decide to lower the price point. Both of these actions will result in decreased revenues and have a negative effect on the bottom line. Other factors that affect the company's profits might be increased utility expenses, higher

71

insurance costs, wages and benefits, and the cost of delivering the product. To assume that one manufacturing process is the greatest influence on profits is shortsighted.

Overall, the assumptions upon which this proposal is based do not stand up under scrutiny. Too many variables have been overlooked. Eliminating the Endure manufacturing process may benefit the company in the short term, but more studies and surveys across the company's market place should be conducted before making this weighty decision.

71

Society

Argument Task 72

The following memorandum is from the business manager of Happy Pancake House restaurants.

"Recently, butter has been replaced by margarine in Happy Pancake House restaurants throughout the southwestern United States. This change, however, has had little impact on our customers. In fact, only about 2 percent of customers have complained, indicating that an average of 98 people out of 100 are happy with the change. Furthermore, many servers have reported that a number of customers who ask for butter do not complain when they are given margarine instead. Clearly, either these customers do not distinguish butter from margarine or they use the term 'butter' to refer to either butter or margarine."

Write a response in which you discuss one or more alternative explanations that could rival the proposed explanation and explain how your explanation(s) can plausibly account for the facts presented in the argument.

 Strategies

Regardless of the approach you take, consider the following steps:

- ◆ Is there an alternative explanation for the events in question that can invalidate, either in whole or in part, the explanation given in the passage?

- ◆ How can I break the argument into its component parts to understand how they create the whole argument?

- ◆ Can I identify the line of reasoning used to create the argument?

- ◆ What does the author of the argument assume to be true for the argument to be true?

- ◆ Does the line of reasoning validate the conclusion?

- ◆ Can I imagine an example that refutes any or several of the statements in the argument?

- ◆ Am I able to evaluate the argument based on the quality of the facts and reasons presented in it?

Based on your responses to all or some of these questions, you must present a well-developed evaluation of the argument. You should take brief notes when you identify the argument's claims, assumptions, and conclusion. Jot down as many alternative explanations as you can along with additional evidence that might support or refute the claims in the argument. Finally, list the changes in the argument that would make the reasoning more solid. It is more important to be specific than it is to have a long list of evidence and examples.

In developing your response, you are asked to develop alternative explanations that could rival the explanation in the argument and explain how your explanation can account for the facts presented in the original explanation.

What conclusions and assumptions are either explicit or implied in the original explanation?

Assumptions:

◆ The writer assumes that all customers who do not complain are completely satisfied.

◆ The writer assumes that customers who do not complain when given margarine when they ask for butter cannot distinguish the difference.

◆ The writer assumes servers are accurately tracking customer reactions to the butter/margarine switch.

◆ The writer assumes customers use the terms butter and margarine interchangeably.

Evidence needed to evaluate the argument:

◆ Evidence on customer satisfaction surveys to indicate how customers were surveyed on their butter/margarine preferences

◆ Information on the number of servers who have interacted with customers requesting butter and given those customers margarine.

◆ Information on general preferences for butter and margarine.

◆ Information on sales trends for Happy Pancake restaurants during this transitional period.

After completing these steps, you should have enough material to write your analysis. Remember that you are not creating a position of your own; you are evaluating the strengths and weaknesses of the existing argument. You do not have to include all of the points that you have created in your prewriting. In fact, during the process of drafting your analysis, other ideas may come to mind, and, if they strengthen your analysis, you should include them.

Sample Essay

The business manager of Happy Pancake Restaurants reports that butter has been replaced with margarine at restaurants throughout the southwest. Customers have not been informed of the change, and, in fact, when customers of Happy Pancake request butter, they are given margarine instead. Based on what he concludes is a dearth of negative customer feedback, the business manager has determined that Happy Pancake customers either cannot distinguish butter from margarine, or that they use the two terms interchangeably. However, the manager's conclusion may not be the only explanation for the observations noted.

First, the manager notes that only 2% of customers complained, and concludes, based on this figure, that 98% of customers are happy. That is not necessarily the case. It may be that 98% of customers are less than satisfied, but not dissatisfied to the degree that they feel it necessary to lodge a complaint. If a customer has enjoyed his breakfast, found his pancakes fluffy, his coffee strong, and his fruit fresh, and the only disappointment was a pat of processed margarine where he expected sweet, creamy butter, he might not be motivated to fill out a complaint card or summon a restaurant manager to engage in a lengthy diatribe. He might, however, tell a friend or neighbor that the next time they are discussing where to have breakfast, Happy Pancake seems to be "going downhill" and doesn't even serve "real butter" anymore. The business manager will remain under the impression that this, and 98% of his customers are happy, but they are, in fact, growing slowly disillusioned with their once-favored breakfast spot.

Second, the manager points out that "a number of customers" who ask for butter do not complain when they receive margarine instead. That suggests that "a number of customers," in fact, do complain, when they receive margarine. What is the difference between these two numbers? Are servers tracking these complaints and reporting them to the business manager, or is he basing this on anecdotal observations? Without more concrete information on the number of people who reject margarine when they've requested butter, the business manager cannot use this information to support his claim.

Based on the vague notion of "a number of customers" who do not react negatively to being duped when requesting butter and receiving margarine, the business manager has drawn two possible conclusions. The first is that people cannot tell the difference between the two substances. That may well be the case. Or, it may be the case that people simply cannot be bothered to recall a server, who may also appear very busy in a breakfast rush at a busy restaurant, to correct her error. Customers may assume the server has made an error in bringing them margarine. In some cases, that error may result in customers tipping their servers less.

The business manager's second conclusion is that customers use the terms butter and margarine interchangeably to refer to either butter or margarine. This is perhaps the most far-fetched of his assumptions. He provides no evidence to suggest that Happy Pancake customers, in particular, are unable to distinguish between these two spreads, and since the colors and textures of the two foods are typically dissimilar, it seems unlikely that would be the case.

While the business manager may be trying to make a case to support discontinuing serving butter in Happy Pancake restaurants without impacting customers, he has not successfully shown that would be the case. What is more likely is that busy people are less likely to complain about a small part of their meal, such as butter or margarine, and that complaints made to servers are not being tracked accurately. The business manager would be better served to study this issue more closely before taking further action.

Argument Task 73

When Stanley Park first opened, it was the largest, most heavily used public park in town. It is still the largest park, but it is no longer heavily used. Video cameras mounted in the park's parking lots last month revealed the park's drop in popularity: the recordings showed an average of only 50 cars per day. In contrast, tiny Carlton Park in the heart of the business district is visited by more than 150 people on a typical weekday. An obvious difference is that Carlton Park, unlike Stanley Park, provides ample seating. Thus, if Stanley Park is ever to be as popular with our citizens as Carlton Park, the town will obviously need to provide more benches, thereby converting some of the unused open areas into spaces suitable for socializing.

Write a response in which you examine the stated and/or unstated assumptions of the argument. Be sure to explain how the argument depends on these assumptions and what the implications are for the argument if the assumptions prove unwarranted.

 Strategies

Regardless of the approach you take, consider the following steps:

◆ Is there an alternative explanation for the events in question that can invalidate, either in whole or in part, the explanation given in the passage?

◆ How can I break the argument into its component parts to understand how they create the whole argument?

◆ Can I identify the line of reasoning used to create the argument?

◆ What does the author of the argument assume to be true for the argument to be true?

◆ Does the line of reasoning validate the conclusion?

◆ Can I imagine an example that refutes any or several of the statements in the argument?

◆ Am I able to evaluate the argument based on the quality of the facts and reasons presented in it?

Based on your responses to all or some of these questions, you must present a well-developed evaluation of the argument. You should take brief notes when you identify the argument's claims, assumptions, and conclusion. Jot down as many alternative explanations as you can along with additional evidence that might support or refute the claims in the argument. Finally, list the changes in the argument that would make the reasoning more solid. It is more important to be specific than it is to have a long list of evidence and examples.

In developing your response, you are instructed to examine the stated and/or unstated assumptions of the argument, explain how the argument depends on these assumptions, and what the implications are for the argument if the assumptions prove unwarranted.

Assumptions:

- ◆ All users of Stanley Park arrive by car

- ◆ Each car parked at Stanley Park represents a single user of the park

- ◆ Stanley Park will draw the same population as Carlton Park

- ◆ Park users are attracted primarily by the number of benches available for seating

- ◆ The best measurement of Stanley Park's usage is measured by weekday usage.

Evidence needed to evaluate the argument:

- ◆ Location of Stanley Park relative to the business district.

- ◆ The number of cars parked in the lot for Carlton Park (or, does Carlton Park have a lot at all)

- ◆ The number of people who typically arrive in each car at Stanley Park

- ◆ Information that shows the current 50 cars per day in the lot represents a decline from a time in the past when there were more cars

- ◆ Information about weekend usage at Stanley Park

- ◆ Information from users of Stanley Park on the interest in additional seating.

- ◆ Information on how open spaces at Stanley Park are currently used.

After completing these steps, you should have enough material to write your analysis. Remember that you are not creating a position of your own; you are evaluating the strengths and weaknesses of the existing argument. You do not have to include all of the points that you have created in your prewriting. In fact, during the process of drafting your analysis, other ideas may come to mind, and if they strengthen your analysis, you should include them.

Sample Essay

Based on the number of cars observed parked in the parking lot of Stanley Park on weekdays, the writer makes the argument that usage of Stanley Park has declined, and that installing more seating in the open spaces of the park will lead to an increase in the number of users. Both the claim, that the number of users has declined, and the solution, that additional seating will increase usage, are flawed, and are based on unsupported assumptions.

Initially, the writer assumes, first, that all users of the park arrive by car, and that every car parked in the parking lot represents a single user of the park. If each car represents a group of users, for example, a family with six children, the estimated number based solely on the number of cars is significantly lower than the actual number of people in the park. If people travel to the park by means other than cars, for example, by walking or bicycling, there is additional attendance that is not accounted for by simply counting cars in the parking lots.

Furthermore, the writer is counting only the cars in the Stanley Park lot on weekdays in order to make a comparison to the usage of Carlton. Perhaps Carlton Park is a small park located near the business district and is frequented by workers on weekdays, while Stanley Park is a suburban park that sees most of its usership on weekends. It could be that Stanley Park's parking lots overflow on weekends with families attending little league games, picnicking, or hiking through the park, while Carlton Park is completely empty on Saturday and Sunday. Without information on both weekday and weekend parking lot usage for parking lots for both parks, there is no way to make an accurate comparison.

In suggesting additional seating will increase users in Stanley Park, the writer assumes that park visitors use the two parks for the same reasons. It may be that Carlton Park offers ample seating convenient to offices and businesses in the center of the city, and is popular with workers taking lunch breaks, who look for seating. Stanley Park, however, might be more popular with groups who want to play organized sports such as baseball or soccer, and therefore prefer large open spaces. In that case, putting seating in the open spaces would likely decrease the number of people who use the park as there would be less space for playing these types of games.

Finally, even if all of the writer's observations are accurate, he has not shown that there is a decline in attendance at Stanley Park, only that the attendance at Stanley Park is less than that at Carlton Park. In order to show a decline at Stanley Park the writer would need to include information about past observations of the Stanley Park parking lots, indicating the average number of cars observed in the past to compare to the average number of cars currently observed.

Before going forward with any plan to alter the seating or availability of open spaces in Stanley Park the writer should request additional information. For example, he should learn more about usage of Stanley Park throughout the week, how the open spaces are utilized, and find out how users of the park reach the park. There is currently not enough information to make an informed decision.